Housing Costs & Government Regulations:

Housing Costs & Government Regulations:

Confronting the Regulatory Maze

Stephen R. Seidel

THE CENTER FOR URBAN POLICY RESEARCH
P.O. BOX 38
NEW BRUNSWICK, NEW JERSEY 08903

About the author:

Stephen R. Seidel has an M.C.R.P. degree from Rutgers University and is currently completing a J.D. degree at Rutgers School of Law-Newark. He has been associated with McKinsey & Co., the U.S. Environmental Protection Agency, and the Center for Urban Policy Research. Mr. Seidel wrote this book while a Research Associate at the Center for Urban Policy Research.

Cover design by Francis G. Mullen
Published in the United States of America
by the Center for Urban Policy Research
New Brunswick, New Jersey 08903

Library of Congress Catalogue Number: 77-88474
ISBN: 0-88285-042-3

To my parents

Contents

SECTION III — CONCLUSIONS AND APPENDIXES

LIST OF EXHIBITS

Contents

CONTENTS

Contents

Preface

The private housing industry in the United States has delivered a product which is the wonder of the world: private one-family dwelling within the reach of the broad middle class. The sheer flow of such construction has permitted a vast, general upgrading of the nation's housing stock. Levels of overcrowding, for example, have been drastically reduced. A monument to this delivery system was the Census Bureau's decision, as of 1970, to sharply alter its measurement of defective dwellings. The old definitions of private toilet facilities and other physical parameters simply would not suffice — the proportion of Americans who were on the negative side of these historic registers had become relatively trivial. Even in the central cities, beset by the problems of an aging housing stock and lack of reinvestment complicated by multifamily units, the housing problem increasingly could be viewed not so much as one of physical structures but rather of neighborhood decline, and to that degree outside the conventional houser's capacity. The years since World War II had seen many striking and unusual events. Certainly not least among them was the shift from a majority of Americans renting their housing to their owning it. While the tract development was often the butt of intellectual's jokes — the new suburbanite bewildered by which of the several look-a-likes on the block really belonged to him — these were criticisms laughed at by the elite few at the same time that reality represented a tremendous increase in living standards.

At a time when the Soviet Union's seven-year housing plan called for ten square meters per person (approximately 100 square feet) and Sweden had multiyear waiting lists for apartments with seven hundred square feet, the average size of the newly built one-family American house had nearly doubled to nearly 1,500 square feet since the first wave of post-World War II construction.

Now barely a half dozen years later, the housing delivery system of the United States is an endangered species. New housing costs have soared well beyond the reach of many middle-class Americans. An entire host of

ix

reasons has been espoused for this increasing imbalance as newspaper reporters, congressional committees, and bewildered consumers alike attempt to define the dynamics of the current situation. The greed of developers, general inflation leading to very specific speculation in land, the new worldwide competition for building materials as exemplified by the Japanese impact on plywood prices, all these and a host of others have their adherents.

Part of the problem, as defined by this study, is the increasing role of government at several levels imposing a whole series of new cost structures on the development process. Stephen Seidel and his associates at the Center for Urban Policy Research at Rutgers University have attempted to bring this vast disorderly array into some comprehensive form. The arguments as to minimum required standards in an increasingly complex world versus delivery costs are never ending. However, it is our hope that the work in hand will provide some useful definitions. There are some broad public issues that must be kept in mind as one reviews the intricacies of building codes and of subdevelopment and land dedication requirements. It is perhaps worthwhile to overview them as a group before turning to the detail of the study.

Much of the flow of new construction in the last several decades was made possible by development on the installment plan. The standard criticism leveled at American tract development frequently focused on the failure to provide appropriate infrastructure. While the housing unit itself was by world standards uniquely finished (one only has to look for contrast at the closetless unfurnished kitchens of much of the housing being constructed in western Europe) the infrastructure surrounding the house was frequently relatively primitive. Sewerage facilities, sidewalk construction, school and recreational development were often inadequate — if not immediately, then certainly in prospect. And these deficiencies were thoroughly reported in the proper media. In recent years, steps have been taken·in many jurisdictions to insure that the full panoply of support elements is built into the original development. As detailed in this study, for example, the dedication of land for schools and parks has become a fairly standard requirement for the builder preceding the development process. Sidewalk and street development specifications have increasingly been enhanced. Not uncommonly, developers are charged not merely with the provision of appropriate sewerage inputs but also with substantial hook-up charges before their developments will secure certificates of occupancy. Indeed, these latter are advancing as rapidly or moreso than any other single charge and in some jurisdictions now exceed $2,000 per housing unit. Much of this has been applauded as an overdue acknowledgment of the real costs of housing and, further, as being much more rationally provided at the initiation of the housing unit life cycle rather than being added over a period of years as the increasing needs — and tastes — of the consumer and the community were felt.

What has not been appreciated nearly enough, however, is that the provision of housing infrastructure on the installment plan, while an economist's nightmare, tended to be consonant with the family income life cycle. It permitted our society to house relatively youthful households at an early stage of their income growth cycle. In the course of time, streets had to be paved and sidewalks installed; with the eventual increase in school-age population, educational facilities had to be built and parks provided. The process was very messy and frequently very expensive. The infrastructure expense cycle, however, tended to parallel the income growth cycle of the residents. Moreover, much of the added infrastructure was provided through relatively inexpensive financing through tax exempt funding. Expenditures therefore, were largely absorbed by the housing occupant through increased taxes. While certainly there was much grumbling about the latter, there was a substantial discount of their actual impact through the deductibility of such local tax payment against federal income tax requirements.

The supposed crudeness of the system and the impact on those whose income did not increase commensurate with the support of new infrastructure costs, as well as a new community consciousness fearful of increasing tax rates, produced a general response requiring all the infrastructure to be supplied in advance. This process is detailed in the several sections of this work. The results are far more "rational," provide a better living environment in many cases — but effectively *exclude* a substantial portion of the market.

Clearly, there are arguments for both sides of the ledger sheet in areas as controversial as this. But equally evident is the failure to cost out the fiscal impact of the combination of virtues that is now called for — and which must be paid *in advance*. Each and every requirement documented in this study has its defenders, whether it is a setback requirement for a housing unit which provides a much more impressive siting for the individual house (at the cost of additional development requirements; piping, sewerage lines, etc.), a no-burning provision in land clearance which insures the atmospheric purity (and may cost several thousand dollars per acre to be added to housing costs), or any of the other elements which are discussed herein.

Our problem is not that of virtue versus sin (though certainly many zoning requirements have been viewed as specifically exclusionary to the poor and to minority groups), it is rather in many cases much more difficult

— *the clash between rival virtues*. In this battle, housing delivery per se, as against many of the stipulations on priorities within the development process raised by both local and federal government, has taken a back seat. The results have been a very clear line of increments in housing costs as a result of governmental action.

There is a familiar process in biology, of organisms not only being acted on by their environment, but in turn conditioning that same environment so as to make it more hospitable for their continuance. The very increment in housing costs, in part a function of government action, brings on the demand for further government intervention to lower those costs. But this latter increase in government role has largely been one of subsidization rather than cost reduction.

There is much more attention turned to various forms of mortgage guarantees, interest subsidies, mortgage stretchouts, and tax abatements than to the underlying realities of basic costs. While, for example, in the area of hospital care we are now going through a period of very painful reevaluation of the impact of government requirements and subsidies in inflating costs — and the necessity of deflating them, this process has yet to reach the housing market.

Yet the sheer growth of the imbalance between America's housing costs and consumer incomes means that subsidy mechanisms which should be geared to those most in need are increasingly absorbed by the lower middle range of households. One of the very basic rules of economics is that a subsidy to everyone is a subsidy to no one. As one sees, for example, Section 8 income limitations moving to a point where they support the housing of people with incomes in excess of $15,000 a year, the danger becomes evident.

Americans of lower income have largely — and despite many criticisms, most successfully — been housed by the process of filtering down. The production rate of new housing in the United States has exceeded that of the growth of households and has permitted a vast upgrading of housing facilities for the less affluent. In order for this process to continue effectively, however, new housing has to be produced reasonably inexpensively. The price of failure is indicated by the enormous increments in the costs of used facilities. At this writing, for example, the median used house sold this past year had broken the $45,000 mark. There was much question whether the boom in one-family housing, not over the $50,000 median, can be continued or whether it is merely a temporary speculative flare of households desperate to secure facilities, no matter what the burden, before the price of housing soars completely out of sight.

xii

The one-family house in the United States has a unique function. It provides not merely shelter but a device for capital accumulation. It is the focal point for family activity, and more than anything else it is the goal of most Americans. Its continued provision therefore is of the utmost importance as a priority for our society. We are long past due for a complete reevaluation of the role of government at all levels in product delivery within this market. A substantial rethinking of government structures will not in and of itself insure a widening of the stream of new construction — but it is an essential input.

George Sternlieb, Director
Center for Urban Policy Research
Rutgers University
New Brunswick, New Jersey

Acknowledgments

This book represents the combined efforts of many individuals. The original notion was carefully nurtured during the crucial design stages by Dr. George Sternlieb, Director of the Center for Urban Policy Research. The financial support of the Smith-Richardson Foundation provided the necessary resources for the work, and Leslie Lenkowsky of that foundation deserves special thanks for his continued support and advice throughout the study period.

The primary credit for this final report goes to the individuals who spent the endless days, nights, and weekends engaged in the research supporting this book. Karen Peterson was primarily responsible for the zoning and subdivision chapters. Barbara Greer was responsible for smoothing out the complexities of surveying municipalities' zoning and subdivision ordinances, the analysis of those surveys, and final changes in those chapters. David Listokin offered his considerable expertise in the area of housing finance and is responsible for Chapter Eleven. Robert Hall successfully took on the assignment of tackling the still relatively unexplored area of energy conservation regulations. He also contributed greatly to the project with his field work in New Jersey.

Other members of the project, each of whom performed a vital function in this undertaking, were John Cannito (environmental regulations), Ken Hess (housing cost components and environmental regulations), Barry Kozyra (finance regulations), Dennis Barry (survey work), Ron Parker (survey work and analysis), Peter Poole (survey work and report production), George Schwartz (initial workplan and building codes), and Robert Burdick (survey processing).

Also involved in this project were subcontractors responsible for determining the costs of regulation through fieldwork undertaken throughout the country. Professors Fred Case at UCLA and Michael Stegman at the University of North Carolina at Chapel Hill performed this vital element of the project. Bill Meehan of Stanford University deserves mention for his excellent analysis of the effects of Petaluma's growth control ordinance on housing. He also rates special thanks for the excellent advice and insights he offered me throughout the project.

I would also like to acknowledge the countless practitioners both in government and the housing industry who so graciously accommodated the demands of our staff. My thanks go in particular to Don Priest of the Urban Land Institute; Bryan Patchan of the National Association of Home Builders; John Bukovinsky, formerly of the New Jersey Home Builders Association; Charles Johnston of the U.S. Homes Corporation; Colin Green of the University of Dundee; John McConnaughey of the National Bureau of Standards; and Larry Burrows of Gladstone Associates.

Thanks are also due to other members of the Center's staff, especially Professors Robert W. Lake and Monica Lett for their advice, encouragement, and support throughout the project. Warmest appreciation is also extended to the typists at the Center, Joan Frantz, Lydia Lombardi, and Anne Hummel, for their yeoman service; to the Center's librarian, Natalie Borisovets; and to Bill Dolphin, the Center's computer analyst. Finally, I would like to thank Joseph Zimmerman for editing the manuscript, Margaret Roeske and Cynthia Koch for their fine proofreading, and Barry Jones, the Center's publications director, for guiding the book through the publication process.

S.R.S.

Section I
Purpose and Scope

Government regulation of the residential development process has increased rapidly over the past several years both in the scope of its coverage and the magnitude of its impact. While many of these regulations are aimed at positive objectives—preserving the environment, making homes safer, reducing sprawl, etc.—all too frequently these regulations, as they are implemented, result in significantly increasing the price and reducing the number of new housing units. In many cases this result is intentional: a community manipulates its regulations to prevent the construction of moderately priced housing. But even where exclusion is not the intent, by requiring units which are more energy-efficient, which will stand forever, and which are environmentally unobtrusive, the final selling price of the house must necessarily be beyond the means of all but the wealthy.

This report analyzes the extent to which government regulations are responsible for the recent rapid inflation in the price of new housing. Seven areas of regulation which will be examined in detail are building codes, energy-conservation codes, subdivision requirements, zoning controls, growth controls, environmental controls and financing regulations. Within each of these areas attention will be paid to the types of requirements now in use and ways in which their cost impacts can be minimized.

1

Chapter One:
Introduction

Food, shelter and clothing are the normative fundamentals of a basically decent human life. Without those necessities, the Hobbesian description of life as "nasty, brutish and short" would be an accurate characterization. This book is about the relationship of government regulations to housing and the kinds of effects that those regulations have on the ability of the housing industry to adequately supply necessary shelter.

In the United States, owning a home has always been the sign of success. It is the single biggest step on the ladder of upward mobility; the most important and burdensome purchase made by most families. But housing has become too expensive. The pedestal upon which the "Great American Dream House" now rests is beyond the financial reach of the vast majority of Americans.

The number of housing starts has dropped far below what can, by any reasonable standards, be considered an acceptable level. From a peak of almost three million units constructed in 1972, the number of starts dropped to just over half that number in 1975. The evidence available for 1976–1977 suggests that the expected recovery will not gain enough momentum to return production to an acceptable level.

3

The availability of new housing must be considered an essential ingredient to both the economic and social vitality of the nation. In the past, the housing industry has borne many important economic functions. For example, during the Depression, it was used as a contercyclical force to stimulate the economy. For the post-World War II generation of home buyers, housing was the primary reason for savings and capital accumulation. But the ever-increasing costs of housing have effectively eliminated the ability of the industry to successfully perform these economic functions.

While many factors of the market have played their roles in pushing up the price of housing, this study focuses on one of the most important interventions contributing to cost increases — the impact of government regulations on new housing. Many of the other factors responsible for increasing costs, such as inflation and high interest rates, may be only a temporary function of current economic conditions. Even if those forces were mitigated, government regulations would remain, and would still be responsible for preventing the delivery of a moderately priced house.

The Need for Research

Surprisingly little has been written on the impact of governmental regulations on housing costs.[1] The most comprehensive studies on this subject date back to the Kaiser and Douglas Commissions' studies.[2] While their reports were excellent documents at the time, they are now nearly a decade old and therefore do not reflect the changes and new problems experienced by the housing industry since their publication. Just one example illustrates such change. The Kaiser Commission's study makes no mention at all of environmental controls, while the Douglas Report allocated only five of its hundred pages to this topic.

The more recent literature also has substantial shortcomings. While much has been written discussing related topics, such as the legality of zoning ordinances,[3] the confiscatory nature of environmental controls,[4] and the inhibitory effect on innovation by building codes,[5] these studies have not been designed to trace the direct links between government regulations and housing costs. They suffer from inadequately specifying exactly what the government regulations affecting housing costs are. We simply do not know the kinds, or the scope, of the regulations affecting the residential development process. The existing literature suffers also from inaccurate and incomplete treatment of the costs associated with these regulations. Nor are the reasons for government intervention, and the real benefits achieved by it, incorporated into existing analyses. Finally, there has been very little analysis of the actual mechanics of the enactment of these regulations — how one form of regulation is adopted instead of another, or if alternatives exist to re-direct government intervention.

The Scope of This Book

The purpose of this research effort is to document and analyze the several topics raised in the previous section of this chapter. For too long a time, public policy has been based on inadequate information; e.g. outdated reports, anecdotal material, and biased information. This report is intended to serve as a first step towards remedying that situation.

To accomplish this goal, extensive survey work was undertaken with the express purpose of obtaining the hard facts necessary for developing a better understanding of the regulatory forces involved in home building. Approximately 300 public agency officials at all levels of government throughout the nation were interviewed to gain insight into the regulatory functions which their offices perform. Two surveys were conducted. The first involved interviewing the staff of building departments concerning their building codes in 100 randomly selected municipalities. The second major survey of public officials was conducted to obtain information relating to zoning and subdivision ordinances and practices. The ordinance codes of eighty municipalities were ordered and analyzed, and then our staff contacted those responsible for the administration of those codes.

An extensive survey of the home builders' industry was included as another major aspect of our research efforts to gain the perspective of those who are directly affected by these regulations. Over 33,000 land developers and home builders were mailed a questionnaire and asked to participate in our study, of which approximately 2,500 responded. In addition, 400 of those who responded were directly contacted by telephone by members of our staff. This group of developers and builders were asked a very detailed series of questions covering all aspects of the regulatory process.[6]

Finally, to obtain a closer perspective on how the regulatory process actually operates, as well as to observe its impact on the housing industry, we initiated case studies of specific residential construction projects in New Jersey, North Carolina and California.[7] Our approach to this field work was to trace back a recently completed project to its inception and examine the effect of regulations on its development.

Thus, a combination of research strategies — examining the literature, surveying those involved, builders and regulators alike, and conducting case studies — were employed to provide the comprehensiveness necessary to approaching this subject.

Soon after beginning our research, we realized that the costs of regulations are indeed a good example of a whole which is greater than the sum of its parts. We have therefore included within the scope of this book those areas of regulations which significantly affect the cost of housing. The seven basic areas examined in detail are: building codes, energy codes, subdivision controls, zoning regulations, growth controls, environmental restrictions and financing regulations. This book therefore follows the natural links between regulatory requirements and their final costs and effects. Each of the links is worthy of more detailed study. But the purpose of this work is to see the chain as a whole, with particular attention to the connections between the links.

The Organizational Format

This report is divided into three major sections. The first provides an overview of the housing market, the housing industry, and government regulations. This section is concluded by a conceptual framework for defining and analyzing the impact of regulations. The second section deals with the research undertaken in each of the seven substantive areas of regulations. In each chapter of that section, the various regulations relevant to the particular category being examined are described. Their strengths and weaknesses are discussed, and their impacts assessed. Finally, the concluding section summarizes the findings, and proposes recommendations for ways in which government regulations can be made more effective while also being less burdensome to the housing industry.

NOTES

1. A very thorough search of the literature conducted by Edward Bergman under contract to the National Science Foundation produced only 12 reports containing any significant empirical work relating to this topic. See Edward M. Bergman, *Evaluation of Policy Related Research on Development Controls and Housing Costs,* 3 Vols., (Chapel Hill, North Carolina: The Center for Urban and Regional Studies, 1974).
2. See respectively, U.S. President's Committee on Urban Housing, (Edward Kaiser, Chairman), *A Decent Home,* (Washington, D.C.: Government Printing Office, 1968), and National Commission on Urban Problems, (Paul Douglas, Chairman), *Building the American City,* (New York: Praeger Publishers, 1969).
3. See, for example, Richard Babcock and Fred Bosselman, *Exclusionary Zoning: Land Use Regulation and Housing in the 1970's,* (New York: Praeger Publishers, 1973), and Lawrence Sager, "Tight Little Islands: Exclusionary Zoning, Equal Protection, and the Indigent," *Stanford Law Review,* Vol. 21 (1969), pp. 767-800.
4. See, for example, Mary Brooks, *The Needless Conflict: Housing Equity and Environmental Protection,* (Washington, D.C.: American Institute of Planners, 1976).

5. See, for example, Advisory Committee on Intergovernmental Relations, *Building Codes: A Program for Intergovernmental Reform,* (Washington, D.C.: U.S. Government Printing Office, 1966); and Charles Field and Steven Rivkin, *The Building Code Burden,* (Lexington, Mass.: Lexington Books, 1975).

6. When initially tested, the instrument written for use in these interviews was found to take nearly an hour. We soon discovered, however, that home builders would willingly give us that much of their time to discuss what they considered a very important issue.

7. Those supervising the fieldwork were, in North Carolina, at Chapel Hill; in California, Professor Frederick Case of the Dept. of Planning, UCLA, with the assistance of Dr. Harold Davidson of the real estate research and investment counseling firm bearing his name; and in New Jersey, Mr. Robert Hall, a member of the staff of the Center for Urban Policy Research.

Chapter Two:
The Housing Market
and Government
Regulations

This chapter presents the initial step in drawing the link between housing costs and government regulations, with particular attention to understanding the reasons behind the housing slump. The first section describes the supply and demand characteristics of the housing market. The next section delves more deeply into the supply side, breaking down and tracing the cost components of a typical single family house. The last section details the extent to which government regulations impact on these various cost components.

The Housing Market: Supply and Demand

Between 1971 and 1975 the number of housing starts plummeted from a high of nearly 3 million units to a low of approximately 1.38 million units. (See Exhibit 2.1) In 1976, some recovery, particularly in single-family construction, does appear to be occurring, but the multi-family and mobile home markets remain significantly below previous levels of production. Unless these products and reasonably priced single-family units can be rejuvenated, then the prospects of opening up the housing market to middle income families remain dim. The inability of the industry to provide moderately priced housing appears to be primarily responsible for the continuation of the depressed condition of the housing sector.

9

EXHIBIT 2.1

New Housing Units Starts 1967-76

(in Thousands)

Year	Structures with 1-4 Units	Structures with 5 Units or more	Mobiles*	Total
1967	929.7	392.2	240.4	1562.3
1968	995.7	549.7	318.0	1863.3
1969	909.4	590.1	412.7	1912.2
1970	911.0	558.0	401.2	1870.2
1971	1286.0	798.5	496.6	2581.1
1972	1461.5	917.0	575.9	2954.4
1973	1257.2	800.3	566.9	2624.4
1974	965.9	386.8	329.3	1682.0
1975	963.3	208.1	212.7	1384.1
1976*	1308.9**	270.9**	269.2**	1849.0**

*Figures are for the number of mobile homes shipped and may slightly over-state the actual number sold.

**Projection based on first seven months of the year.

Source: U.S. Bureau of the Census, "Housing Starts," *Construction Reports*, C-20, July, 1976.

The High Cost of Housing

The fact that the price of new single-family homes has increased significantly over the past few years comes as a surprise to no one. But the magnitude of the increase is shocking. The median sales price of single-family residential units has almost doubled from $23,400 in 1970 to over $50,000 in September, 1976. A more detailed breakdown of housing units further illustrates the disappearance of the moderately priced house. (See Exhibit 2.2) In 1970, over 73 percent of new single-family construction sold for under $30,000. By 1976 this price group had been reduced to 13 percent. At the other end of the spectrum, during this same six year period, the number of units selling for $40,000 or more increased from 12 percent to 60 percent. A more detailed breakdown of the units built in 1976 shows that 33.6 percent had sold for over $50,000, with nearly one-fifth priced over $60,000.[1]

Nor can this rapid increase in price be attributed to a better, higher quality product. For example, the average square foot of floor area of a new house has actually decreased slightly over the past few years going from 1,695 sq. ft. in 1974 to 1,588 sq. ft. in 1976.[2] In an attempt to hold down the

EXHIBIT 2.2

SALES PRICE OF NEW ONE FAMILY HOUSES: 1970-76

Price of Home	Year	Percent of New Homes*
Under $30,000	1970	73%
	1976	13%
$30,000 – $40,000	1970	17%
	1976	27%
Over $40,000	1970	12%
	1976	60%

*Percents will not add to 100 due to rounding.

SOURCE: U.S. Bureau of the Census, "Characteristics of New One-Family Homes," *Construction Reports*, C-25, 1970, 1976.

price of housing, an increasing number of home builders tried — with mixed results — to market a scaled-down version of their product by reducing lot size, the number of bedrooms, basements, and closet space.

THE EFFECTS OF INFLATION

If income were increasing at a rate commensurate with the price of housing, then the high cost of housing would not be a problem. And for most of the period since World War II that has been the case. But no longer. The reversal of this historic trend — housing prices now rising faster than income — must be considered a significant factor in the downturn of the housing market. (See Exhibit 2.3)

ABILITY TO PAY

This changing relationship of income to housing cost is further reflected in the proportion of families now able to afford new housing. (See Exhibit 2.4) Since 1963 the ability to own a new home, as measured by the relationship of price to income, has declined from 44.3 percent of all families to a level of 31.2 percent in 1975. This is a 30 percent decrease over the past in twelve years. Although the annual shift in the percentage of families able to afford a new home has been somewhat erratic, the basic trend is evident. Given this reduction in the number of families able to afford new housing, it is not surprising that construction starts have plummeted during the past several years.

EXHIBIT 2.3

CHANGES IN HOUSING COSTS AND INCOME: 1965–76

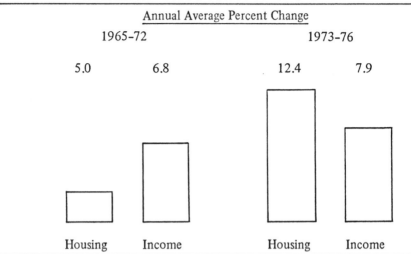

Annual Average Percent Change

1965–72		1973–76	
5.0	6.8	12.4	7.9
Housing	Income	Housing	Income

SOURCE: U.S. Bureau of the Census, "Characteristics of New One-Family Homes," *Construction Reports*, C-25; and "Consumer Income," *Current Population Reports*, P-60, 1976.

The ability to pay criterion is based on comparing annual housing expenditures to annual income. The generally applied rule-of-thumb is that one should not expend more than 25 percent of one's income for housing. This figure should pay the mortgage, property taxes, and insurance, all of which are in part dependent on the initial selling price of the house.

By holding all other factors constant (interest, property tax rates, etc.) except the price of the house, it is possible to estimate the impact of changes in housing costs on the availability of new housing. (See Exhibit 2.5) If new housing could still be built for $30,000 per unit, then families with incomes over $15,500 (42.4% of all families) would be able to enter the new housing market. Because of the flat distribution of income which exists above the median, even a small increase in housing price will significantly reduce the number of families able to afford new housing. Thus, the number of families able to purchase a $35,000 house would be reduced by 7200, or just 29.6% of all families would be able to afford new housing. The next jump, from a $35,000 to a $40,000 house, decreases the percentage of families from 29.6 to 21.7. Finally, for the case of a $55,000 house, an income of $26,000 would be required, which reduces the potential market to 10.5 percent of all families.

EXHIBIT 2.4

PROPORTION OF AMERICAN FAMILIES ABLE TO
AFFORD THE MEDIAN-PRICED NEW HOUSE*

Year	Median Price	Annual Housing Expense	Required Annual Income	% of All Families with Min. Income	% Annual Change
Construction Rpt. C25 Prices					
1963	$18,000	$1,704	$ 6,820	44.3%	-
1964	18,900	1,812	7,250	44.0	- 0.7
1965	20,000	1,908	7,630	40.4	- 8.2
1966	21,400	2,124	8,500	42.4	+ 5.0
1967	22,700	2,280	9,120	41.2	- 2.8
1968	24,700	2,580	10,320	37.6	- 8.7
1969	25,600	2,796	11,180	38.3	+ 1.9
1970	23,400	2,652	10,610	45.2	+18.0
1971	25,200	2,808	11,230	44.0	- 2.7
1972	27,600	3,109	12,430	42.8	- 2.7
1973	32,500	3,684	14,740	36.8	-14.0
1974	35,900	4,332	17,330	33.2	- 9.8
1975	39,300	4,812	19,250	31.2^e	- 6.0

e = estimate

*Annual housing expense not adjusted downward to reflect income tax savings due to deduction of mortgage interest and real estate taxes.

SOURCE: Bureau of National Affairs, "Current Developments," *Housing and Development Reporter*, Vol. 4 (June 14, 1976) p. 16.

PROJECTING FUTURE HOUSING NEED

While the ability to pay for housing suggests the actual *demand* for the product, another measure of the market potential may be calculated based on *need*. What must be realized is that projecting the future need for housing is an extremely tenuous proposition. By definition, the number of households at any point in time is approximately equal to the number of housing units occupied plus vacancies. Future need must therefore be examined both in terms of replacement (due to uninhabitability and natural destruction) and changes in the number of households. These are in turn somewhat dependent on the availability of alternative shelter. The most famous forecast of the future need for housing was issued by the Kaiser Commission, which in 1968 stated that 26 million new units would be

EXHIBIT 2.5

NUMBER OF FAMILIES ABLE TO AFFORD NEW
HOUSING BY PRICE OF UNIT

Price of Unit	Annual Expenditure Required[1]	Required Income[2]	Number of Families	Percent of Families
$30,000	$3,882	$15,528	23,848	42.4%
$35,000	4,414	17,656	16,648	29.6
$40,000	4,971	19,884	12,205	21.7
$45,000	5,477	21,908	9,618	17.1
$50,000	6,008	24,032	7,031	12.5
$55,000	6,539	26,156	5,906	10.5

NOTES: [1]Mortgage characteristics used were 20 percent down, 9 percent
interest, 30 year term. Other monthly housing expenditures were
derived from *FHA Trends of Home Mortgage Characteristics.*

[2]Calculated as four times annual housing expenditures.

SOURCE: U.S. Bureau of the Census, "Consumer Income," *Current Population
Reports*, p. 60, 1976.

required during the next decade. A more recent estimate of future housing
need was presented in hearings before the Senate Subcommittee on Housing
and Urban Affairs.[3] (See Exhibit 2.6) In this report, it was calculated that
somewhere between 1.9 and 2.3 million new units would be needed in each
of the next five years.

SUMMARY

The most obvious change in the housing market which has occurred over
the past few years is the rapid escalation of the cost of new housing. Despite
measures to cut back the amenities of the unit built, the rise in the cost of a
new home exceeded increases in income. The result has been that fewer and
fewer families can afford to enter the market for new housing. The next section attempts to pinpoint specifically why the price of housing has increased
so rapidly.

Examining the High Cost of Housing

To better explain the increases in the price of housing, it is necessary to
break down the unit into its components and to trace changes in the cost of
these components over time. The major components to be examined are

EXHIBIT 2.6

HUD'S ANNUAL AVERAGE CONSTRUCTION NEEDS: 1975-80
(Thousands of Units)

	Series A	Series K
Net Additional Household Formation[1]	1,637	1,226
Family Households	1,019	961
Primary Individuals Households	617	265
Vacancy Adjustments[2]	141	100
Replacement of Inventory Losses	593	590
	2,370	1,916

NOTES: [1]See "Population Estimates and Projections," Current Population Reports, No. 607, (August 1975), p. 25.

[2]Based on a vacancy rate of 6 percent for rental units and 1 percent for owner-occupied units.

SOURCE: U.S. Congress, Subcommittee on Housing and Urban Affairs, *Housing Goals and Mortgage Credit: 1975-80*, p. 79.

land development costs and house construction costs. In addition, within each of these two categories, the costs of financing will be examined separately.

Unfortunately, there is a distinct lack of the detailed cost information needed to undertake a *national* analysis. However, some recent state studies do exist, and two such case studies will be cited which examine the cost changes over time of a typical home built in Colorado and Maryland.[4] These two reports represent a wide spectrum of the housing market. At the low end of the selling price scale is the Colorado home which was priced at $30,000 in 1975. At the upper end of the scale is a home in Maryland listed at $74,500 in 1977.

THE COST OF HOUSING IN COLORADO

The Colorado example is a 1,050 square foot single-family house built on an 8,160 square foot lot. In 1970 it sold for a very reasonable price of $18,310. If the same unit were constructed today, it is estimated that it would cost $30,400. (See Exhibit 2.7) The most significant proportional price increase was the cost of the front-end money required by the home builder. Construction financing costs increased by 173 percent between

EXHIBIT 2.7

COST OF REPRESENTATIVE HOUSE IN COLORADO: 1970-75

Cost Component	1970	1975	Dollar Increase	Percent Increase
Site Development	$ 3,450	$ 6,350	$2,900	84%
Site Carrying Costs	660	1,540	880	133
House Construction	13,189	19,754	6,565	50
Construction Financing	1,011	2,756	1,745	173
	$18,310	$30,400	$12,090	66%

SOURCE: Beckert, Browne, Coddington & Associates, Inc., "An Analysis of the Impact of State and Local Government Intervention on the Home Building Process in Colorado 1970-75," Colorado Association for Housing and Building, 1976, p. 14.

1970 and 1975, both because the amount of money needed per unit increased by 50 percent and because interest rates had also climbed. Site carrying costs, based on the cost of raw land, the costs of improvements, the interest rates paid and the length of the development period was determined to have increased by 133 percent. (See Exhibit 2.8)

Some of these cost increases can be attributed to the 2.5 percent increase in the interest rate paid on loans. But the price of land had also increased sharply, from $1,143 to $1,714 per plot, while the costs of land improvements had actually more than doubled. Of the site development expenditures, the major cost increases had been a $900 jump in the sewer and water tap fees and a $150 expense to put in an underground storm sewer system.

The construction component, while making up over 50 percent of the total dollar increase, had the smallest percentage jump in costs. Though much of the increase can be attributed to inflation both in wages and materials, a closer look suggests approximately $1000 of it can be attributed to changes in the building code which made mandatory such items as smoke detectors, thicker insulation, flame retardant carpeting and other health and safety features.

THE COST OF HOUSING IN MARYLAND

Using the same methodology, the suburban Maryland Home Builders Association compared the costs of a 1,219 square foot single-family house built on a 10,000 square foot lot in 1972 to its expected costs in 1977. Because the price of the initial unit was already so expensive, costing over $50,000 in 1972, the overall five year price increase of 26 percent was con-

EXHIBIT 2.8

FINANCIAL CARRYING COSTS FOR THE TYPICAL HOME
IN COLORADO: 1970-1975

	1970		1975	
Land holding period (years)	2.5		2.8	
Development period (years)	1.2		1.2	
Total holding period (years)	3.7		4.0	
Land loan interest rate	8.0%		10.5%	
Land value per acre	$4,000		$6,000	
Land lot cost @ 3.5 DU/acre	$1,143		$1,714	
Land loan points (2)		$ 23		$ 34
Land loan interest		$345		$ 734
Development loan amount*	$2,450		$5,170	
Development loan points (2)		$ 49		$ 103
Development loan interest rate	8.0%		10.5%	
Development loan interest		$240		$ 664
Total Site Development Interest Cost & Loan Fees		$657		$1,535

*Excludes refundable deposits

SOURCE: Beckert, Browne, Coddington & Associates, Inc., "An Analysis of the Impact of State and Local Government Intervention. . .", p. 11.

siderably lower than that found in Colorado. The relative increases, however, were found to be quite similar. (See Exhibit 2.9)

As was the case in Colorado, within the land development and the construction stages of the residential construction process, financing and carrying costs had the highest percentage increase. The costs of subdivision improvements with its 40.7 percent increase was also found to be significant. Finally, the cost of materials and labor was once again responsible for the largest absolute increase in costs, but can not be considered a high percentage increase relative to other components.

SUMMARY

These two examples of changes in the cost components of new housing suggest that the major increase in costs can be attributed to the high front-end money now required to build a home. This increase in financing charges must be attributable to several factors: the increase in interest rates, the higher costs of the residential unit itself, and the increased length of the development process.

EXHIBIT 2.9

COST OF HOUSING IN MONTGOMERY COUNTY 1972-77

Component	1972	1977	Percent Increase
Land Development			
Raw Lot	$ 2,996	$ 3,964	24.4%
Carrying Cost	982	1,984	50.5
Bond & Permit Fees	1,526	2,252	32.2
Improvements	4,177	7,042	40.7
Total Finished Cost	$ 9,681	$15,242	36.5
House Construction			
Materials & Labor	$35,212	$46,053	23.5
Financing	2,027	3,900	48
Other Costs	3,486	3,000	-13.9
Total Construction	$40,725	$52,953	23
Total Cost, House & Lot	$50,406	$68,195	26%

SOURCE: "The High Cost of Housing in Montgomery County, Maryland," The Suburban Maryland Home Builders Association.

To some extent, these cost increases in housing are inevitable. Inflation, with its higher cost of materials and higher wages will necessarily boost the price of a unit. The question of government fiscal strategies which result in high interest rates generally is outside of our study. The focus of our report is rather on the non-inflationary cost increases which government regulations do influence. Included in this category would be the price of land, lot development (subdivision) requirements, the length of the development process, and certain questionable structural requirements.

The two case studies suggest that a significant part of the price increases do fall within these areas and that these costs are increasing most rapidly. The last section in this chapter extends the analysis to those regulations which impact on the construction process.

The Scope of Government Regulations

Regulations affecting the housing industry have dramatically increased in number over the past few years. Many of these regulations are intended to prevent the types of damage caused by past developments. Inadequate infrastructures in subdivisions and lack of environmental attention are just two examples of areas which in the past caused significant problems. But the new wave of regulations in addition to achieving valid objectives may also serve entirely different purposes — including the erection of economic barriers to keep out low- and moderate-income families.

THE LEVELS OF GOVERNMENT REGULATING HOUSING

The bulk of regulations impacting on residential construction are exercised by local governments under their police power. This situation is not surprising because central to our system of government is the principle that local concerns should be dealt with by local governments. Thus the many subdivision controls, land use restrictions (primarily zoning), building codes, and increasing environmental impact assessments are administered at the local level.

But as the problems of local control are beginning to surface, the state is playing a more prominent role in regulating the housing industry. While local control can be too parochial and administratively inefficient, state controls are improvised as an alternative to federal intervention. State regulatory activity has increased particularly in the area of building and energy codes and environmental protection. The latter group includes regulations of critical areas, the coastal zone and large-scale developments.

Finally, the federal government has increased its activity particularly in the areas of environmental protection and housing finance. The various federal anti-pollution laws, while not yet significantly affecting residential construction, do contain the underpinnings of such controls.[5] Finally federal laws, as we shall see, have a significant impact on the availability of — and conditions for — mortgages as well as the costs and procedures used at the time of settlement.

LINKING REGULATIONS AND HOUSING COSTS

Returning to the cost breakdown of the housing unit, it is strikingly evident that most regulations affect those components which have experienced the largest percentage increase over the past five years. (See Exhibit 2.10) The largest number of regulations are found in the subdivision approval process. They affect both the cost of land development and its financing. The second largest number of regulations influence the price of unimproved land. Included in this group are the numerous environmental regulations limiting the availability of land and zoning restrictions establishing minimum lot size and development densities.

Although the exact number of government regulations affecting a particular development will vary depending on its location and design, the following examples illustrate the task confronting the home builder.

EXHIBIT 2.10

GOVERNMENT REGULATIONS AFFECTING THE COST OF HOUSING

Level, Type of Regulation	HOUSING COST COMPONENT AFFECTED					
	Unimproved Lot	Land Development	Land Development Financing	Structural Materials and Labor	Construction Financing	Mortgage Financing and Settlement Costs
Federal Government						
Clean Air Act	X					
Coastal Zone Management Act	X	X	X			
Consumer Product Safety Act				X	X	
Federal Noise Control Act				X		
Federal Water Pollution Control Act	X	X	X			
FHA and VA Mortgage Programs						X
National Flood Insurance Programs	X	X	X	X	X	
Occupational Health and Safety Act				X	X	
Real Estate Settlement Procedures Act				X	X	X
State Government						
Building Codes				X	X	
Coastal Zone Management	X	X	X			
Critical Areas Restrictions	X	X	X			
Land Development Acts	X	X	X			
Sewer Moratoria	X	X	X			
Local Government						
Bonding Requirements			X			
Building Codes				X	X	
Energy Codes				X	X	
Engineering Inspection		X	X			
Environmental Impact Review	X	X	X			
Mechanical Codes				X		
Plat Review		X	X		X	
Sewer Connection Approval and Fee		X	X			
Shade Tree Permits		X	X			
Site Plan Review		X	X			
Soil Disturbance Testing		X	X			
Utility Connection Fees		X	X			
Water Connection Approval and Fee		X	X			
Zoning	X	X	X			

In the case of the suburban Maryland residential unit a total of eighteen permit fees and four bonds were required at various stages of the process. The majority of these requirements — thirteen of the fees and all four bonds — were related to land development. The remaining five permits involved aspects of the residential structure itself.

A recent development in southern New Jersey, an area which cannot by any means be considered particularly restrictive or regulated, nonetheless required during the land development process a total of fourteen reviews of various stages of water, sewer, and site plans; six agency fees; four permits; and the payment of one bond. In addition, before construction of the actual structure could begin, a building permit and plumbing inspection fee were also required and must be added to the list.

A final example of the multitude of government regulations encountered in building residential units draws upon a recent study conducted of the steps required in obtaining permission to develop in Los Angeles.[6] This study found that for a single typical project a total of thirty-six different offices had to be contacted, twelve different application forms filed, and eighty-seven supporting documents (though many were duplicates) produced.

The most lucid summary of what is detailed in this chapter was written to us by a homebuilder in his comments on our questionnaire. He stated:

> The subject of your research is a very painful one for me. I have built over 1,000 homes. These all have been below the average selling price for the time and area. Almost all of my customers were buying their first home. I believe that I have accomplished much by creating the opportunity for these customers to become homeowners and taxpayers. However, the recent trends in over-regulations have made it impossible to build and sell to this market. I realize that all of these minimum requirements and environmental reviews, consumer protections etc. supposedly have the customer's best interest at heart. But the total cost of this package is astronomical. The result is that decent housing is now denied to the people who need it most. The human cost is very great and the loss of opportunity has hit the same persons that the regulations were supposed to help. Basically the value received is much less than the cost.

The next chapter elaborates on this builder's ironic comment. Based on nearly 2,500 responses to our mail questionnaire, the impact of government regulations as experienced by home builders will be examined.

NOTES

1. U.S. Bureau of the Census, "Characteristics of New One-Family Homes," *Construction Reports* C-25, 1976.
2. Based on data compiled by the U.S. Bureau of the Census, "Characteristics of New One-Family Homes, *Construction Reports* C-25, 1974; and National Association of Homebuilders, *Construction Cost Data Components,* (Washington, D.C.: 1976).
3. U.S. Senate Committee on Banking, Housing and Urban Affairs, *Housing Goals and Mortgage Credit: 1975-80,* Ninety-Fourth Congress, First Session, (Washington, D.C.: U.S. Government Printing Office, September 1975).
4. The two reports are "An Analysis of the Impact of State and Local Government Intervention in the Home Building Process in Colorado 1970-75," prepared by Bickert, Coddington and Associates, Inc. for the Colorado Association for Housing and Building (Denver, Colorado, April 1976) and "The High Cost of Housing in Montgomery County, Maryland" prepared by the Suburban Maryland Home Builders Association (Silver Spring, Maryland: 1976).
5. See, in general, Fred P. Bosselman, et. al., *EPA Authority Affecting Land Use,* (Washington, D.C.: U.S. Environmental Protection Agency, 1974).
6. Alisa Belinkoff, "Consumer Pays for Government Delays," *Los Angeles Times,* June 6, 1975.

Chapter Three:
Surveying the
Housing Industry

Reliable, detailed information describing the housing industry's experiences with government regulations is an essential ingredient to a successful understanding of the problems affecting this vital sector of our economy. Without this type of information, any recommendations concerning changes in government regulations would be subject to the same criticisms leveled at existing government policies — that they are determined without any assessment of their impact on either the housing industry or ultimately on the housing consumer.

The specific objectives of our survey of the housing industry were threefold. (A copy of the survey instrument used is presented in Appendix A.) First, we wanted to determine the extent to which government regulations are problematical compared to other aspects of conducting business in this industry. Secondly, we wanted to learn the relative importance of each regulation: which specific regulations are considered more burdensome than others. Finally we attempted to delve into the actual relationship between regulations and cost increases. Each of these subjects was further examined to determine if such factors as the size of a firm, its primary activity or the geographical region of its operations influenced the impact of government regulations.

Survey Design

The Center for Urban Policy Research undertook an extensive survey of the home builder industry. The 26,000 builder membership of the National Association of Home Builders (NAHB) was mailed a questionnaire with a cover letter from their president, soliciting support of our undertaking. Our response rate was almost 10 percent, a remarkably high rate of return for a mail survey. The second phase of our home builder survey involved mailing a cover letter and postcard to the 7,000 members of the Urban Land Institute (ULI) asking for their assistance in our study. While the NAHB list contains primarily small builders, the ULI membership includes most of the major land developers throughout the country. From the returns of both the ULI and NAHB mailings, 400 firms were randomly selected for detailed interviews by telephone. The results of these interviews are reported throughout this book in the specific chapters where they are most applicable. The substance of this chapter is based primarily on the almost 2,500 questionnaires received from the mail survey of the NAHB membership.

The Universe of Home Builders

The home building industry can be divided into three classifications of firms based on their primary activity. A small number of firms are involved only in the land development process. (Henceforth this group will be referred to as *developers*.) The primary activity of this group is to acquire raw land, obtain the necessary approvals and permits and add the required infrastructure to produce finished lots. Because of the economies of scale involved in the development process, the size of their projects tend to be quite large. The second classification refers to home builders (henceforth referred to as *builders*) who construct residential units on these finished lots. The third category, and by far the dominant type of firm, refers to those whose activities include both land development and building. This group will be referred to as *home builders*. This breakdown by firms' activity is significant in that different regulations affect different stages of the construction process.

The responses received from our mail survey accurately represent the full spectrum of the residential construction industry. (See Exhibit 3.1) Over 60 percent of the responding firms were involved in both development and building, with the second largest group being builders (36.5 percent). Relatively few firms interviewed (2.5 percent) were active only in land development.

EXHIBIT 3.1

SCOPE OF BUILDING ACTIVITY

Firm's Activity	Number of Firms	Percent of Firms
Land development	58	2.5
Residential construction	850	36.5
Both	1,419	61.0
Total	2,327	100.0

SOURCE: Survey of the Home Builder Industry, Center for Urban Policy Research, Summer 1976.

It has become accepted doctrine that regulations are stricter in the Northeast than in the South or West, and this observation is increasingly cited as the reason for the decline of building activity in the Northeast. It becomes important therefore to examine the aspects of regulations in terms of possible regional variations. A comparison of 1972 Census data describing the residential construction industry confirms that our regional breakdown represents the distribution of the residential construction firms. (See Exhibit 3.2) In the North Central and the West, the percentages in each survey are almost identical. The slight shift in industry growth from the Northeast to the South since the Census of 1972 is to be expected because of the increased building activity in the Sunbelt.

The final important characteristic of those surveyed which could influence the effect of government regulations is a function of the size of the firm. The question of whether or not larger firms are likely to incur the same magnitude and type of problems as small firms must be addressed. (See Exhibit 3.3) Our survey adequately represents a wide range of both small and large builders and developers. As suspected, those who only engage in residential construction tend to operate on a smaller business scale than those involved exclusively in land development or in both land development and residential construction.

Comparing Government Regulations to Other Industry Problems

Certainly not all the ills of the housing industry can be directly attributed to government regulations. It is necessary to obtain some relative measure of the burden of regulations compared to other problems confronting home builders. Earlier surveys of the NAHB membership in 1964 and 1969 had not identified government regulations as significant problems.

EXHIBIT 3.2

REGIONAL DISTRIBUTION OF RESIDENTIAL CONSTRUCTION FIRMS

Region	Industry Census (1972) Percent	CUPR Survey (1976) Percent
Northeast	22.5%	18.3%
South	36.0	41.0
North Central	24.0	23.6
West	17.5	17.1
Total	100.0	100.0

SOURCE: CUPR Survey of the Home Builder Industry, Summer 1976, and U.S. Department of Commerce, *1972 Census of Construction Industries*, Series SIC-1521 and SIC-1531, "General Contractors-Single-Family Houses and Operative Builders" (Washington, D.C.: U.S. Government Printing Office, 1975).

EXHIBIT 3.3

NUMBER OF UNITS DEVELOPED BY TYPE OF ACTIVITY OF FIRM*

Activity of Firm	NUMBER OF UNITS				
	0-15 (n=664)	16-100 (n=1026)	101-500 (n=489)	501+ (n=122)	Total (n=2301)
Land Developer	55.4%	19.6%	17.9%	7.1%	100.0
Builder	41.9	46.4	10.6	1.2	100.0
Developer & Builder	19.5	46.5	26.9	7.1	100.0

*Average annual rate over the past five years

SOURCE: Survey of the Home Builder Industry, Center for Urban Policy Research, Summer 1976.

(See Exhibit 3.4) At those times, the industry's principal problems were related to the costs and availability of materials and labor. The table does, however, indicate that some changes in the relative weight of the problems of doing business occurred during those five years. Mortgage and construction financing, which had been listed most often as the "most significant problem" in 1964, five years later had fallen to only the third on the list of problems. Meanwhile, those problems directly related to government regulations, such as codes, zoning and FHA and VA appraisals, actually declined in importance over this same time span, moving down from a total of 15.4 percent in 1964 to 4.1 percent in 1969.

EXHIBIT 3.4

NAHB SURVEY OF SIGNIFICANT PROBLEMS ENCOUNTERED:
1964 AND 1969

| | Percent Distribution* | |
| | 1964 | 1969 |
Problems in Doing Business	Survey	Survey
Most Significant Problem Encountered		
Construction Costs and Material Costs	11.6%	26.7%
Labor Costs and Lack of Skilled Labor	12.8	13.0
Lack of Suitable Land and Land Costs	3.2	9.3
Construction Finance and Mortgage Finance	14.9	3.6
Merchandising & Selling	11.7	2.3
Codes	6.1	1.3
Business Management	5.5	2.0
Zoning	4.8	1.8
FHA & VA Appraisals	4.5	1.0
Lack of Materials	0.0	0.2
Other	2.6	1.4

*Totals will not add to 100 due to nonspecific responses.

SOURCE: Michael Sumichrast and Sara A. Frankel, *Profile of the Builder and His Industry* (Washington, D.C.: National Association of Home Builders, 1970), p. 95.

Our survey of the NAHB membership list showed a dramatic shift in the relative importance of the problems of doing business. (See Exhibit 3.5) The results show emphatically that government regulations and the attendant bureaucratic controls are now considered the most significant problem of doing business. While recognizing that the survey dealt specifically with government regulations, the magnitude of the industry's concern with this problem was astonishing. Government imposed regulations were cited by 38 percent of the respondents as their most significant problem in doing business in 1975, the last full business year before the survey. The unavailability of financing was the closest challenger, cited as most significant by 22.5 percent of the respondents.

The dominance of the problem of government regulations is further substantiated if a simple weighting scheme is used to aggregate what were considered by respondents to be the three most significant difficulties in doing business. Using a weighted response, the results show that government regulations had a total problem-score of 30.0, with inavailability of financing next in line with a score of 20.9.

EXHIBIT 3.5

Significant Problems In Doing Business
(n = 2176)

| Problems in Doing Business | Order of Significance* | | | |
	Most	Second	Third	Weighted Average**
Lack of Suitable Land	14.6%	18.0%	18.0%	16.3
Materials Shortages/Costs	10.7	17.9	27.9	16.0
Labor Shortages/Costs	6.2	14.5	20.4	11.3
Inavailability of Financing	22.5	20.8	16.4	20.9
Government Imposed Regulations	38.0	25.1	15.7	30.0
Other	7.9	3.7	1.6	5.5
Total	100.0	100.0	100.0	100.0

*May not add to 100.0 due to rounding.
**Based on a 3, 2, 1 weighted scale with totals divided by a factor of 6.

Source: Survey of the Home Builder Industry, Center for Urban Policy Research, Summer 1976.

A breakdown by region of what was considered to be the most significant problem illustrates that in all sections of the country government regulations was cited most frequently. (See Exhibit 3.6)

They were, however, considered a greater problem in the more densely developed regions of the Northeast and West than in the South and North Central states. The strong relationship between the problems of regulations and the availability of land is also specifically noteworthy. In both the Northeast and the West these two problems were considered far more significant than in the remaining two regions.

Since most regulations affect the land development process, it is not surprising that the firms which specialized in this area overwhelmingly indicated this factor as their most significant problem. (See Exhibit 3.7)

Yet builders, who are more concerned with such problems as the price of lumber and the availability of take-out financing also ranked government regulations nearly equal to those of financing. Even more telling is the response of those involved in both land development and building. This group, which is confronted by the full range of industry problems, overwhelmingly ranked regulations as its primary concern.

The extent to which government regulations were considered the primary problem was also found to increase with the size of the firm. (See Exhibit 3.8) Whereas only 30.6 percent of the small firms (annual con-

EXHIBIT 3.6

MOST SIGNIFICANT BUSINESS PROBLEM BY REGION

Problems in Doing Business	Northeast (n=394)	South (n=900)	North Central (n=511)	West (n=367)
	Region*			
Lack of Suitable Land	18.8%	11.6%	12.9%	18.5%
Material Shortages/Costs	11.4	12.3	8.8	8.2
Labor Shortages/Costs	1.8	7.6	8.8	4.1
Inavailability of Financing	15.0	26.1	25.2	17.4
Government Imposed Regulations	43.1	33.8	36.8	46.6
Other	10.0	8.7	7.4	5.2
Total	100.0	100.0	100.0	100.0

*May not add to 100.0 due to rounding.

SOURCE: Survey of the Home Builder Industry, Center for Urban Policy
Research, Summer 1976.

EXHIBIT 3.7

MOST SIGNIFICANT BUSINESS PROBLEM BY FIRM'S ACTIVITY

Problems in Doing Business	Land Developer* (n=53)	Builder* (n=808)	Both Builder and Developer* (n=1347)
	Type of Activity		
Lack of Suitable Land	3.8%	18.8%	13.1%
Material Shortages/Costs	1.9	15.6	7.6
Labor Shortages/Costs	3.8	8.3	5.0
Inavailability of Financing	22.6	25.2	20.7
Government Imposed Regulations	60.4	25.5	44.8
Other	7.6	6.5	8.8
Total	100.0	100.0	100.0

*May not add to 100.0 due to rounding.

SOURCE: Survey of Home Builder Industry, Center for Urban Policy
Research, Summer 1976

EXHIBIT 3.8

MOST SIGNIFICANT BUSINESS PROBLEM BY FIRM'S SIZE

	Size of Firm (units)*			
Problems in Doing Business	0-15 (n=676)	16-100 (n=1048)	101-500 (n=487)	more than 500 (n=122)
Lack of Suitable Land	17.2%	15.6%	10.3%	9.8%
Material Shortages/Costs	13.9	11.3	6.2	5.7
Labor Shortages/Costs	7.8	6.8	3.9	2.5
Inavailability of Financing	22.8	20.4	24.8	28.7
Government Imposed Regulations	30.6	38.7	45.4	43.4
Other	7.7	7.1	9.4	9.9
Total	100.0	100.0	100.0	100.0

*Calculated as the annual average over the past five years.

SOURCE: Survey of the Home Builder Industry, Center for Urban Policy
Research, Summer 1976.

struction of 0-15 units) chose regulations as their most significant problem,
45.4 percent of firms building 101-500 units and 43.4 percent of firms constructing over 500 units gave the most significance to the regulatory
problem.

Aspects of Government Regulations
Perceived as Problems

The second part of the survey attempted to specify which aspects of
government regulations caused the greatest difficulties. The choices covered
a wide range of possible problems. They included such potential difficulties
as delay, the arbitrariness of actions by local officials, the paperwork burden, lack of coordination among regulators, etc.

The two dominant aspects of regulations considered most burdensome
by the industry were local administrative discretion and unnecessary delays.
(See Exhibit 3.9) These were each cited by over 25 percent of the respondents. A commonly repeated theme found throughout was that home
builders strongly resented the lack of technical knowledge of local government officials. In many instances, the power of such officials exceeds their
knowledge and understanding of what the regulations require and what the
builders request. Delay, which is a universal by-product of the administration of regulations, can wreak havoc on this industry in which time
means money. In addition, rapidly changing market conditions also
require that the time from start to completion be minimized.

EXHIBIT 3.9

MOST BURDENSOME ASPECTS OF GOVERNMENT REGULATIONS
BY REGIONS (PERCENT*)

Aspects of Regulations	Northeast (n=386)	South (n=887)	North Central (n=502)	West (n=375)	National Average (n=2150)
Local administrative discretion	33.9%	22.0%	28.3%	24.5%	25.9%
Unnecessary delays	21.8	27.5	21.3	30.1	25.7
Costs of paperwork, filing permits, etc.	10.9	17.6	21.3	14.1	16.8
Limitations on what can be built	13.7	10.0	11.8	8.0	10.7
Lack of coordination among government agencies	14.5	17.6	14.3	19.5	16.3
Other	5.2	5.3	3.0	3.7	4.6
Total	100.0	100.0	100.0	100.0	100.0

*May not add to 100.0 due to rounding.

SOURCE: Survey of the Home Builder Industry, Center for Urban Policy
Research, Summer 1976.

A regional breakdown shows that the problems of administrative delay
are reasonably constant throughout the country. While local discretion was
considered most burdensome in the Northeast and North Central, delays
were cited most frequently in the South and West.

The primary activity of the respondent was related to the areas of government regulations which proved most burdensome. (See Exhibit 3.10) For
instance, those firms concerned only with building cited the costs of paperwork, fees, etc., most frequently as their most troublesome problem (23.7
percent). Only 8.0 percent of land developers ranked this problem first.
This group was far more concerned with the problems of local discretion
(34.0 percent) and delay (30.0 percent). Those firms active in both stages of
the residential construction process overwhelmingly sided with the land
developers and chose local discretion (28.6 percent) and delay (27.7 percent)
as the most burdensome aspect of their experience. This variation between
developers and builders can be attributed to the different regulations which
confront each. Builders are less likely to be confronted by delays because
they have to deal with fewer agencies than land developers. In addition, the
various structural codes confronting builders are far more specific in what

EXHIBIT 3.10

MOST BURDENSOME ASPECTS OF GOVERNMENT REGULATIONS
BY ACTIVITY OF FIRM

	FIRM'S PRIMARY ACTIVITY		
Aspects of Regulation	Land Development (n=50)	Home Building (n=786)	Both Development and Building (n=1337)
Local administrative discretion	34.0%	21.8%	28.6%
Unnecessary delays	30.0	22.5	27.7
Costs of paperwork, filing permits, etc.	8.0	23.7	12.6
Limitations on what can be built	8.0	12.0	9.7
Lack of coordination among government agencies	18.0	16.2	16.5
Other	2.0	3.8	4.9
Total	100.0	100.0	100.0

SOURCE: Survey of the Home Builders' Industry, Center for Urban Policy Research, Summer 1976.

they require than subdivision and environmental regulations and therefore do not leave as much room for administrative discretion.

 ### The Time Factor in the Development Process

As previously suggested, time is indeed money when it comes to delay in the development process. *Most homebuilders estimate that for every additional month added to the completion date, there is a 1-2 percent increase in the final selling price of the unit.* These costs which accrue can be attributed to the continuation of such overhead expenses as staff, property taxes and interest payments on monies already invested in the development. In addition, inflation may also take its toll.

As part of our analysis, we asked those surveyed to specify the approximate number of months which had elapsed from their decision to develop their particular residential project to the completion of their work on that project. The results point to a major problem in the housing industry. (See Exhibit 3.11) In 1970, 78.9 percent of the respondents stated that their projects were completed in less than a seven month span. By 1975, this figure dropped precipitously to only 27.3 percent. At the other extreme,

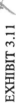

EXHIBIT 3.11

REGIONAL VARIATION OF THE TIME INVOLVED IN THE RESIDENTIAL DEVELOPMENT PROCESS: 1970-75
(PERCENT OF RESPONDENTS)*

Months	Northeast (n=326)		South (n=679)		North Central (n=398)		West (n=313)		Total (n=1716)	
	1970	1975	1970	1975	1970	1975	1970	1975	1970	1975
Less than 4	42.6%	5.8%	42.7%	12.4%	45.3%	16.1%	43.3%	8.6%	44.0%	11.7%
4–6	34.9	12.6	35.8	18.0	31.4	14.1	38.7	13.4	34.9	15.6
7–12	15.4	21.2	15.1	25.8	17.3	28.6	14.8	24.9	15.5	25.3
13–18	5.9	23.9	5.7	24.7	4.4	21.9	2.3	31.6	4.6	24.9
19–24	0.6	19.6	0.6	13.0	1.3	11.8	0.7	13.1	0.7	13.9
25–36	0.3	11.3	0.0	4.4	0.3	6.3	0.0	5.4	0.1	6.3
37 or more	0.3	5.5	0.0	1.8	0.0	1.3	0.3	2.9	0.3	2.4
Total	100.0	100.0	100.0	100.0	100.0	100.0	100.0	100.0	100.0	100.0

*May not add to 100.0 due to rounding.

SOURCE: Survey of the Home Builder Industry, Center for Urban Policy Research, Summer 1976.

only 0.3 percent of the respondents replied that in 1970 their projects typically required more than three years for completion compared to 8.7 percent in 1975.

A comparison of the average number of months required for project completion in 1970 and 1975 further illustrates the significance of this shift in the industry's production process. In 1970, the average number of months was 5.0 compared to 13.3 months in 1975. Based on these numbers, and a 1 percent cost increase for each month of delay, it is possible to approximate the cost impact of an extended development period. For a $40,000 home, a delay of 8.3 months may mean an increase of $3,320 in the price of the unit. No compensating benefits are received from such costs incurred simply because the regulatory approval process has been lengthened.

The data also suggest that while there was no significant regional variation in the length of the residential construction process in 1970, a regional differential now does exist. (See Exhibit 4.11) For example, in 1975 only 5.8 percent of the respondents in the Northeast and 8.6 in the West could select the category of less than four months as the time needed for them to complete a project. In the North Central region, this time frame was cited by 16.1 percent and in the South, 12.4 percent, of those responding. The greater delay caused by regulations in the West and Northeast is substantially in accord with our previous finding, that in these two regions government regulations were considered most burdensome relative to other problems of doing business.

Since the development process differs for each of our three categories of firms, it is also necessary to examine each category individually. (See Exhibit 3.12) This exhibit clearly illustrates the increased delay caused by the increase in the proliferation in number of regulations affecting land development. Those firms engaged exclusively in building were not hampered as seriously by such regulatory delays. In 1970, land development was a relatively expeditious activity, with 69.6 percent of firms responding that less than seven months was necessary for completion. That same year, 86.9 percent of the builders cited this period as the time typically required for a project. In 1975 the percentage of land developers capable of completing their work on a project in less than seven months fell to 10.2 percent compared to 52.6 percent of builders. *Thus, the five year period had affected the length of the land development phase significantly more than the building phase of construction.*

The Effect of Regulations on Locational Decisions

The adage ''once burned, twice shy'' is quite appropriate in the context of regulations. The number, the content and the administration of

EXHIBIT 3.12

TIME INVOLVED IN THE DEVELOPMENT PROCESS BY TYPE
OF FIRM'S ACTIVITY: 1970-75
(PERCENT OF RESPONDENTS*)

Months	Developers (n=46)		Builders (n=449)		Both Developers and Builders (n=1221)	
	1970	1975	1970	1975	1970	1975
Less than 4	28.3	2.0	61.7	28.6	38.4	5.8
4-6	41.3	8.2	25.2	24.0	37.9	12.4
7-12	17.4	30.6	8.5	20.1	18.2	27.4
13-18	10.9	34.7	3.6	14.8	4.8	28.6
19-24	2.2	10.2	0.9	8.3	0.5	16.0
25-36	0.0	12.2	0.0	3.3	0.2	7.0
37 or more	0.0	2.0	0.2	0.9	0.1	2.8
Total	100.0	100.0	100.0	100.0	100.0	100.0

*May not add to 100.0 due to rounding.

SOURCE: Survey of the Home Builder Industry, Center for Urban Policy
Research, Summer 1976.

regulations play an important part in deciding where to build. (See Exhibit
3.13) On the average, just over 10 percent of the firms replied that government regulations were not a consideration in where to build and approximately 22 percent said location should be slightly considered. This
means that nearly two out of three firms considered the relationship between location and local regulations an important factor. Once again it was
the Northeast (71.6 percent) and the West (76.6 percent) where regulations
had the greatest impact on the decision where to develop.

Regulations also were found to have the greatest impact on large
residential construction firms. Whereas regulations were not considered by
14.6 percent of firms which built 0-15 units per year, only 1.6 percent of the
largest firms (500+) were not at all concerned with the regulations in the
area in which they were considering developing. (See Exhibit 3.14) This
rather substantial variation may in part be based on the wider geographic
latitude available to the bigger firms. But what also must be kept in mind is
that larger developments often encounter greater resistance and are affected
by many regulations which only apply to developments in excess of a
specified number of units.

EXHIBIT 3.13

IMPORTANCE OF GOVERNMENT REGULATIONS IN
DECIDING WHERE TO DEVELOP (BY REGION)
(PERCENT)

Size of Firm* (units)	Number of Municipalities	Not Considered	Considered Somewhat	Important Consideration	Total
Northeast	(405)	9.6	18.8	71.6	100.0
South	(971)	11.8	22.9	65.3	100.0
North Central	(521)	10.6	24.2	65.2	100.0
West	(384)	6.3	17.2	76.6	100.0
Average	(2239)	10.2	21.7	68.2	100.0

*May not add to 100.0 due to rounding.

SOURCE: Survey of the Home Builder Industry, Center for Urban Policy
Research, Summer 1976.

EXHIBIT 3.14

IMPORTANCE OF GOVERNMENT REGULATIONS IN DECIDING
WHERE TO DEVELOP BY SIZE OF FIRM
(PERCENT)

Size of Firm** (units)	Number of Firms	IMPORTANCE IN DECISIONS WHERE TO DEVELOP*			
		Not Considered	Considered Somewhat	An Important Consideration	Total
0–15	694	14.6%	25.2%	60.2%	100.0%
16–100	1075	9.2	23.1	67.7	100.0
101–500	508	7.5	15.7	76.6	100.0
500+	127	1.6	17.3	81.1	100.0
Average Total	2404	10.0	21.8	68.1	100.0

*May not add to 100.0 due to rounding.
**Annual average over the last five years.

SOURCE: Survey of the Home Builder Industry, Center for Urban Policy
Research, Summer 1976.

The Burden of Specific Government Regulations

In an attempt to determine which specific government regulations were considered by the residential construction industry as most burdensome, we asked our respondents what percent of the final selling price of a unit could be attributed to unnecessary aspects of regulations. While by no means an exact definition, we defined "necessary costs" as those requirements essential to health, safety and general welfare. Not surprisingly, the responses tended to vary widely. Nonetheless the question does provide useful information concerning the relative burden of the various areas of regulation.

Far and away the area of regulation cited as containing the most unnecessary costs was subdivision controls. (See Exhibit 3.15) Over 72 percent of the respondents estimated that unnecessary aspects of this area of regulation were responsible for more than 5 percent of the total price of the unit. The second most burdensome area of regulation was zoning in which only half as many (36.3 percent) of the respondents believed that costs were unnecessarily increased by more than 5 percent.

At the other end of the spectrum, coastal zone regulations (76.0 percent), floodplain restrictions (54.5), and energy codes (50.2) were considered by the highest percentage of respondents not to cause any unnecessary increases. Because these regulations are the ones with the most limited geographic application and are relatively new, this finding is not at all surprising. Nonetheless, in places affected by these regulations they were considered to unnecessarily increase costs.

Building codes, long considered one of the principal agents for increased costs, showed a wide diversity in the responses. Almost as many respondents thought that they did not unnecessarily increase costs at all, as the number which attributed a greater than 5 percent increase to that particular set of regulations. This finding can be attributed to the wide variation in both code content and administration and will be examined in detail in the chapter dealing specifically with building codes.

The clamor over environmental controls, while not overwhelming, does surface in our results. This area of regulation ranked third behind subdivision and zoning as responsible for more than a 5 percent increase in costs. The fact that many jurisdictions still do not require impact statements is undoubtedly the reason why 38.3 percent reported that they did not cause any unnecessary increases.

EXHIBIT 3.15

UNNECESSARY COSTS OF REGULATIONS
(N=2471)

Type of Regulation	No Increase (less than 1%)	Significant Increase (1-5%)	Very Significant Increase (more than 5%)	Total
Building Codes	26.7%	39.8%	33.6%	100.0%
Coastal Zone Regulations	76.0	8.1	16.0	100.0
Energy Codes	50.2	31.0	18.9	100.0
Environmental Impact Statements	38.3	26.0	35.7	100.0
Floodplain Protection	54.5	20.5	25.0	100.0
Mortgage Finance Requirements	30.1	40.4	29.5	100.0
State Land Development Laws	44.2	23.2	32.6	100.0
Settlement Costs	36.8	34.3	28.8	100.0
Subdivision Requirements	7.6	20.3	72.1	100.0
Zoning	39.7	24.1	36.3	100.0

*May not add to 100.0 due to rounding.

SOURCE: Survey of the Home Builder Industry, Center for Urban Policy
Research, Summer 1976.

SUMMARY

This survey of the residential construction trade provided a broad overview of the industry's experiences with government regulations. Several
distinct factors were observed to significantly influence the impact of
regulations on housing costs.

The initial finding was that, contrary to previous surveys in past years,
government regulations were now considered to be the primary problem in
doing business. Regulations were found most burdensome by those
operating in the western and northeastern regions of the country, by those
involved specifically in the land development process, and by the larger
firms.

The two specific aspects of government regulations which were pin-
pointed as causing the most problems were local administrative discretion
and unnecessary delay. With regard to the latter, the average development

time was found to have increased over a five year span from 5.0 to 13.3 months. Based on a 1 percent cost increase for every month of delay, $3,320 may be added to the price of a $40,000 home. Not surprisingly, much of the increase in time was found to have accrued in the land development, as opposed to the building stage, of the construction process.

Subdivision controls were overwhelmingly cited as the regulation most responsible for unnecessarily increasing the costs of housing. Other specific regulations frequently mentioned as unnecessarily adding to the cost of housing were environmental impact statement requirements, building codes, and zoning restrictions.

Chapter Four:
Examining the Costs
of Regulations

Examining the costs of government regulations sounds as if it should be relatively easy to do. One could simply add up the cost-effects imposed by the regulations, come up with a total, and the cost to the home-builder, and therefore to the consumer, would be apparent.

It is exactly such a simple, arithmetical process which has caused many people to overlook the far-reaching cost effects of government regulations. Just as everything King Midas touched turned to gold, so it seems that everything touched by government regulations becomes complicated and difficult to trace. Often, housing regulations have effects which do not become clear until they are put into practice, and sometimes the regulations have effects that were not even intended. Compliance with some government regulations in housing imposes a cost so far removed from the apparent effect of the regulation that the cost is often not identified, or it is computed as coming from another source.

It is the purpose of this chapter to provide a clear framework for understanding *all* the costs of government regulations. Much of the existing literature on the impact of government regulations is deficient in its assessment of what should rightly be defined as a regulatory cost. Customarily, only the most directly immediate costs of regulation, such as filing fees, reports, and so forth, are considered as the total calculation of costs imposed by government. The less direct cost effects of requirements, such as changes in the densities of materials, are often ignored.

This chapter also presents a framework for evaluating the *cost-effectiveness* of regulations. It goes beyond the initial step of identifying costs and describes a format for determining which costs of regulations are acceptable and even necessary, and which costs add unnecessarily to the final price of the unit.

The first part of this chapter will provide a comprehensive context for identifying the resulting costs of regulations. An understanding of why and how government regulations do in fact impose costs on the developer is essential to any attempt to developing potential strategies to mitigate their impact. The second half of this chapter provides several case studies enumerating the costs of regulations. These examples are not offered as statistical prototypes of costs engendered by regulations; but rather as illustrations of the application of our holistic approach. In addition, by tracing a project from its inception to its completion, both the operational and monetary impact of regulations can be examined.

 ## What Are the Costs of Regulations?

To provide a simple but useful framework for identifying the costs of regulations, they will be divided into three categories: direct costs, the costs of delay and uncertainty, and the costs of unnecessary or excessive requirements.

 ### DIRECT COSTS

Direct costs are primarily those attributable to the administration of regulations. Regulations require enforcement and government agencies are most often established to ensure compliance. Fees are required to support these agencies. In addition, regulations also frequently require that applications be filed, public hearings attended, and documents presented. All of these steps result in expenses generally referred to as *transaction costs.* And almost all are paid directly by the developer.

This category of costs is the easiest to identify. They can be found directly as a budget item on a developer's expenditure sheets (usually included under overhead) and among the bills submitted by engineering, environmental and legal consultants.

THE COSTS OF DELAY AND UNCERTAINTY

A second type of transaction cost, and one which often is difficult to ascertain, relates to inefficiencies in the administrative process. Problems of delay caused by government intervention in the development process has become a major factor in driving up the price of housing. Most developers estimate that the final selling price of a unit must be inflated approximately 1%-2% for each month of delay during the latter stages of the development process.

The specific costs caused by delay vary significantly depending on the internal organization and financing of both the project and the firm involved. Most frequently the costs of delay relate to such overhead expenditures as staff, property taxes, inflation, and interest, which continue regardless of whether or not work on a project has been halted. As previously determined, the most debilitating of these costs involves front-end money — i.e., investments made at the very beginning of a project and therefore costly money, either as equity or as loans.

Land development and construction loans are often available only at high interest rates and must therefore be turned over as quickly as possible. If delays were limited to the very beginning of the development process, costs and risks would be minimized. Unfortunately as approvals are piggybacked on previous approvals, no step in the process is entirely free from the potential for delay. The uncertainty of when or if approvals will be granted also frequently confounds such time dependent arrangements as land purchase options and lines of credit for construction and take-out financing. Finally market studies showing a strong immediate demand for one type of housing are often meaningless when years of delay pass and cloud the picture.

The delay factor is extremely difficult to calculate. No standards exist which state how long an administrative review, such as a rezoning request or an environmental impact approval, should take. What is known, however, is that review limits written into law are generally ineffective. A practice which appears to be growing more customary is for public review agencies to automatically request that the home builder sign a waiver of any legislated time limit. Not wanting to alienate those whose permission to develop is essential, home builders are left with no choice but to sign.

Developers must also always remain conscious of the possibility that a project will be prohibited entirely because of government regulations. Although in most cases negotiated changes are made and permission to develop is granted, instances do occur in which such an agreement cannot be reached.

A project will usually be terminated when the developer believes that the changes requested by a government agency no longer leave him/her with an economically viable proposal. Our telephone survey of 400 home builders illustrates the extent to which this conclusion is reached. (For a discussion of the sample and the questionnaire itself, see Appendix B.) Nearly 20 percent of those polled reported that they had found it necessary to terminate a project because of government regulation. The expenditures made for this project are largely nonrecoverable costs and are usually calculated into future development plans, thus increasing prices in "successful" projects.

THE COSTS OF UNNECESSARY OR EXCESSIVE REQUIREMENTS

This third category concerns those costs associated with the substantive aspect of regulations. By setting minimum standards and requirements, regulations frequently have the effect of legislating what a home builder cannot build and what must be built. Any study of the costs of regulations must necessarily take these considerations into account. For example, subdivision regulations often specify that a particular storm drainage pipe must be twenty inches in diameter, whereas an experienced developer may know that only a twelve-inch pipe is warranted. The difference in costs must be directly attributed to regulations.

Also included in this area are costs associated with the disruption of the free market mechanism caused by regulations. A zoning ordinance which limits the number of multi-family lots available for development, thereby driving up their price, is an example of this cost impact.

Another type of cost which fits into this category concerns changes made in a project for approval to develop. These "costs of mitigation" frequently occur during both subdivision and environmental review and can be quite substantial. They would include the costs of design changes, added requirements, and the opportunity cost of foregone profits. The alternative to reaching some negotiated agreement would be to challenge the agencies' decisions in the courts. This is a lengthy and expensive process with an all too high probability of failure. If, however, a legal challenge to an unreasonable regulation should ensue, this too must be considered a cost of regulation.

To determine which items fall into this final cost category is a difficult problem. Sound judgement must be exercised to distinguish between necessary and unnecessary or excessive regulations. The only threshold criterion which exists is the vague mandate that a regulation must "promote the health, safety and general welfare of the public." In operation, this definition is of little utility. Almost any requirement can be phrased to fit within these parameters. A better defined approach is possible when well defined standards or model codes can be used to judge a specific regulation. But there are also limits to this approach. Widely accepted standards are few and far between, and while they cannot always be taken as the most reasonable representation of minimum requirements in some specific circumstances, they can and should be used as means for evaluating regulations.

An example will help clarify why the distinction between necessary and unnecessary regulations is essential to an understanding of this subject. Let us say that a developer owns land which rests on a shallow aquifer from which the surrounding community draws its water. The town does permit residential development on this property, but not surprisingly prohibits the use of septic tanks. The developer then challenges this restriction in court as being an illegal restriction on the use of his/her property. Both common sense and decades of past mistakes have taught us that the community's restriction — under these circumstances — is justified and reasonable. Government regulations cannot be blamed for the costs of that developer's law suit as well as the profits he/she lost by not being able to build using septic tanks.

Developers cannot and should not be allowed to develop whatever and whenever they may desire and then blame any interferences on government regulations. But on the other hand, truly unnecessary government regulations must be identified and labeled when they cause unnecessary costs.

In addition to the use of commonly accepted industry wide standards as a way of drawing distinctions between necessary and unnecessary regulations, our survey asked home builders their opinions of whether they considered specific regulations as reasonable. While this approach obviously has its limitations, and would seem to be begging for biased responses, the replies received were overwhelmingly on the conservative side. In fact, when asked what changes they would make in construction if certain regulations were not in effect, most answered, "I'd probably do things much the way I do them now. It's the only way I know how." A second commonly cited limiting consideration was that many of the regulatory requirements were necessary from a marketing perspective. Yet there is also industry consensus that a substantial body of superfluous and often haphazard requirements remains which unnecessarily add to the cost of housing.

SUMMARY

Estimating the costs of regulation is a task complicated both by problems of definition and a lack of reliable information. In addition, it is conceptually a very challenging endeavor. Our analysis has identified three categories of costs: direct or administrative costs, indirect administrative costs (delay and uncertainty), and the monetary costs of unnecessary or excessive regulations. The following section attempts to go one step further in developing our conceptual framework.

What Is Meant by the "Costs" of Regulations?

Government, at least in theory, will not interfere with the operations of an industry without due cause. Intervention has, however, become commonly accepted in two types of situations. Regulations are often instituted to overcome an inadequacy in that traditional allocator of resources, the operation of the free market. This type of deficiency often surfaces in cases of a monopoly when there is insufficient market information or when externalities predominate. An example of the latter is the upsurge of environmental regulations which require a developer to consider the effects of his/her actions on the surrounding properties, a consideration which would not otherwise be examined.

The second justification for government intervention is to promote a social policy. Maximum economic efficiency is willingly sacrificed in these situations. Most of these regulations necessarily involve some form of income redistribution or transfer payments. A clear example is the various low-income housing subsidy programs.

COST REALLOCATION

Both justifications for government intervention (market inadequacies and implementing a social goal) underscore an extremely important concept in defining the costs of regulation. In both of these circumstances, regulations are imposed because a problem, with its attendant costs, already exists. Proposed government regulations attempt to solve that problem. Most frequently, this is accomplished by reallocating the costs associated with the problem. For example, the preparation of an environmental impact statement before receiving development approval must be considered a cost incurred because of a regulation. But without the requirement, the potential environmental damage (and therefore costs) would not necessarily be considered as part of the development process. Thus, the environmental impact statement requirement does impose costs on the developer, but this is done to insure that potentially greater — and perhaps irreparable — injury is averted.

Energy codes offer another example. By requiring a certain minimum level of insulation, an expense is added to the initial cost of the unit. The justification is that more than this cost will be saved in reduced fuel bills over an appropriate time, and the national goal of energy independence will be furthered.

These examples illustrate the two primary cost allocative impacts of regulations. In the EIS example, a property owner was forced to consider and internalize the potential environmental impact which his/her project may have had on neighboring properties. In the case of energy codes the costs are reallocated over time — an initial expense is required to achieve future savings and to serve national policy.

The most common cost reallocation imposed by regulations is the shift from what was previously considered a public cost, paid out of general municipal funds, to the balance sheet of the private developer. As municipalities, through the use of cost-revenue analysis, become increasingly aware of the costs to the community of new residential development, they will attempt to shift more of this burden to the new residents. This is particularly true when the municipal fisc is already overburdened and in municipalities where a "last one in" mentality predominates, i.e., the present residents wish to limit and define the number and characteristics of newcomers.

The requirement of land dedication is a common example of this shift from a once public to a now private cost. In the past the provision of recreational space had been considered a municipal responsibility. But the demand for this resource has increased, while the cost of land also has soared. As a result, municipalities are increasingly requiring that new developments provide this service for their own residents. Several inequities are obvious in this policy. It is extremely difficult to determine if a specific public service benefits only one development or the entire community. In addition, the residences of the new development not only pay entirely for the development costs of such recreational land in their own neighborhood, but also contribute through their taxes to the support of the recreational services provided throughout the municipality.

SUMMARY

Two important questions underlie the cost allocative effect inherent in many of the regulations impacting on housing. First, in evaluating this aspect of the effect of a regulation, the issue of who should bear these cost burdens must be addressed. What exactly is the proper and desired distribution of costs among the consumer, the developer, and government? Secondly, limits must be placed on what quality and safety should be required in the initial construction phase. Can we afford to build houses which will last 200 years or which will have reduced occupancy costs if these units have very high initial costs which can be borne only by the few? If, in the long run, this course is adopted because it would be more efficient, then a decision must be reached as to how these units will be financed. The unfortunate trend has been to look at the benefits of the regulations in protecting the environment, improving the quality of a development, etc., without also recognizing that new housing is being priced out of the range of middle income families. Thus the issue of cost reallocations between private parties, from the municipality to the developer, and over time must be squarely addressed in any formulation of changes to reduce the cost impact of government regulations.

The imbalance inherent in the reallocative effect of government regulations is accentuated by the financing realities for individual families. Lenders are wary of approving mortgages for families whose annual housing expenditures are greater than 25 percent of their income at the time they apply for a loan. The high initial price of a house translates into higher monthly payments and results in fewer people qualifying for mortgage money. This occurs despite the fact that most young homeowners' incomes will increase substantially as they grow older. Thus low initial charges at the price of subsequent operating/tax realities have been much more complimentary to the American life/home buying cycle than the effort to smooth the future at the expense of the present.

The Costs of Regulations: Case Studies

Four case studies follow the broad framework constructed in this chapter. Taken as exemplary studies, they should help to make clear the real cost effects of government regulations as they have affected housing in the recent past. The broad context for understanding the effect of government regulations established in this chapter will pervade the remaining body of this book. Even as the separate cost effects are examined more closely in the detailed specifics of the chapters which follow, the cumulative effects of the regulations on the housing industry and the housing market should be kept in mind. The costs of unnecessary requirements and delay, coupled with the re-distributed costs imposed by many regulations, are present in every facet of the housing industry.

The four case studies of residential projects will illustrate the effects of regulatory costs on new housing. To present a fair and realistic national perspective, fieldwork was undertaken in New Jersey, North Carolina and California. The cases included here were not selected as indicative of the norm. No such "norm" exists in this widely diverse field. Instead, they should be read as histories of the effects of regulations on the social, temporal, and monetary costs hidden in the regulatory system. These studies cover the projects from their inception to their conclusion.

Case Study #1: New Jersey

Although housing starts throughout New Jersey have sharply slumped during the past several years, one type of development has been flourishing.

Adult communities, located in the southern portion of the state where the climate is relatively mild and land is inexpensive, have successfully located both a market and a setting. The particular development we examined was a 71 unit addition to an existing 1420 unit development which, having just received its last approval in the summer of 1976, was set for development to begin.

History of the Development This project was not in fact initially conceived of as an adult community. When the developer first purchased the land in 1958, his intention was to construct a "planned community" of 900 single-family detached homes, complete with a country club, lake, industrial areas, etc. It was then thought that the units would sell for the now paltry price of $10,000. The township however had other ideas. In 1960 it denied the necessary zoning change for the development on the grounds that it would have placed too great a burden on the local public services.

Concurrent with the developer's fight to obtain zoning approval, both he and other developers were successfully tapping the retirement community market in nearby townships. This type of development results in far less of a burden to the community because of the absence of school-aged children, thus faciliting municipal approval. The developer went to work between 1965 and 1967 to obtain a zoning amendment which would allow this adult community subdivision. It was obtained in 1967 when approval was granted for a 1420 unit development.

Not approved however was a nineteen acre tract of land upon which a shopping center had been proposed. It is this tract of land on which the additional 71 units are now being constructed. The units are single-family homes built on lot sizes of 5,000 square feet for detached units and 4,000 square feet for doubles and quadruples. All were limited to one-story, with wood frame and slab-on-grade construction. They are to sell for the currently reasonable price of approximately $38,000.

Direct Costs A total of fourteen plan reviews, six fees, four permits and one bond were required by the local, county, and state governments from the time the project was first initiated to the beginning of construction. Once that stage begins, then building, plumbing and electrical inspections and fees must also be added to this list. The costs incurred in complying with this aspect of government regulation totaled approximately $1,200, or 3.2 percent of the final selling price of the unit. (See Exhibit 4.1).

These costs can further be broken down to identify the amount paid in fees to government agencies and other expenses such as the preparation of reports and legal fees incurred in obtaining the necessary approvals. Fees amounted to 78 percent of the total direct costs of regulations. In-house and consulting costs amounted to $161 or the remaining 22 percent of the direct

EXHIBIT 4.1

REGULATORY COSTS AND PROCESSING TIME IN THE
LAND DEVELOPMENT PROCESS

| | Cost ($/Unit) | | | |
Regulation	Fees	Consulting Costs	In House Expenses	Time (Months)
TOWNSHIP				
Utilities				
Preliminary Sewer Approval	$ 5.00	$ .28	$ 1.41	1
Tentative Sewer Approval	6.34	.28	1.41	1
Final Sewer Approval	9.51	.28	2.82	2
Sewer Inspection Fee	41.20	–	–	–
Sewer Connection Fee	300.00	–	–	–
Preliminary Water Approval	5.00	.28	1.41	1
Tentative Water Approval	5.92	.28	1.41	1
Final Water Approval	5.92	.28	2.82	2
Water Inspection Fee	25.63	–	–	–
Water Connection Fee	100.00	–	–	–
Electricity Connection Fee	200.00	–	–	–
Total/Unit	$704.52	$ 1.68	$11.28	8
Plans Review				
Sketch Plat Approval	1.41	7.89	4.28	3
Preliminary Plat Approval	16.41	85.35	28.17	5
Final Plat Approval	11.41	29.58	7.04	3
Engineering Inspection Fee	84.34	–	–	–
Performance Bond	67.46	–	–	–
Total/Unit	$181.03	$122.82	$35.44	11
Supplemental				
Shade Tree Permit	5.00	–	–	1
Environmental Impact Statement	–	(a)	(a)	(a)
Building Permit and Certificate				
of Occupancy	125.00	–	–	–
Plumbing Inspection Fee	10.00	–	–	–
COUNTY				
Utilities				
Sewer System Approval	1.41	–	.71	1
Plans Review				
Sketch, Preliminary & Final	–	(b)	(b)	1
Supplemental				
Electrical Inspection Fee	20.00	–	–	–
STATE				
Utilities				
Sanitary Sewer Permit	2.21	.28	14.08	5
Environmental				
CAFRA Permit	–	32.39	21.13	14
Stream Encroachment Permit	–	4.23	1.41	3
Total	$894.17	$161.40	$88.05	25
Total Cost of Compliance:			$1,143.62	
Total Process Duration:			27 months	

(a) included in township preliminary plat approval
(b) included in township approval costs

costs of regulations. Since the units built were models frequently used by the developer, the latter amount was thought to underestimate the usual expenses incurred during this process.

The Costs of Delay   Tracing back the project to the time the land was first purchased vividly illustrates how the costs of delay will vary depending on the stage of the development process. (See Exhibit 4.2) Between the time of land acquisition and the submission of the sketch plat, carrying costs for the entire 19 acre tract were only about $83 per month, or $1.17 per unit per month. However during the approval process and the construction phase, carrying costs increased to about $2000 per month, or $28 per unit per month.

The zoning amendment took two years for approval and in addition another 5 years elapsed after the original application for rezoning was denied. This required a delay in the decision to build and added $100 per unit in carrying costs.

More serious delays were encountered in obtaining the Department of Environmental Protection's State Coastal Area Facilities Review Act (CAFRA) permit. This delay occurred well into the approval process: preliminary township approval, which consumes most of the developer's time and money, was a prerequisite to CAFRA application. A 10 month delay added nearly $300 to the price of each house.

The Costs of Unnecessary or Excessive Requirements   We have attempted to identify those impacts of government regulations which unnecessarily add to the cost of the house. To determine exactly what these costs were, we sought to isolate those changes which would have been made in the existing development had there been no government regulations. These unnecessary costs were estimated to be $1,700 per unit or 4.5 percent of its selling price.

Site Improvement Costs (Exhibit 4.3)   The most significant increase in site improvement cost is the state restriction on open burning of waste vegetation in site clearance. It is estimated that this regulation adds about $2,500 per acre or, in this case, $211.27 per unit.

The state also requires that all utilities be placed underground. The developer now incurs this cost of about $200 per unit. In the past the utility company had provided this service.

Local requirements, such as sidewalks on both sides of the street and a forty-foot pavement width on a local street, both of which the developer believed to be excessive, added $207.78 and $185.14 per unit respectively in redundant costs over modest but adequate equivalents.

The total unnecessary site improvement costs attributable to government regulations are $877.17 or about 2.3 percent of the selling price of the unit.

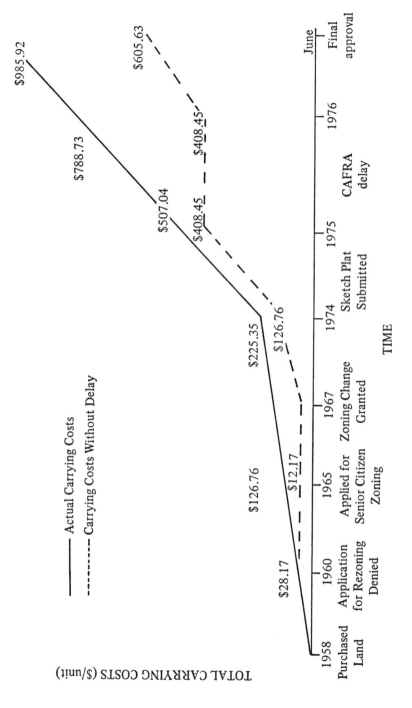

EXHIBIT 4.2

Effects Of Delay On Carrying Costs

EXHIBIT 4.3

UNNECESSARY SITE IMPROVEMENT COSTS
ATTRIBUTABLE TO GOVERNMENT REGULATIONS

Item Required	Cost/Unit With Regulation	Cost/Unit Without Regulation	Government Imposed Cost/Unit
Site Clearance			
— open burning of waste vegetation prohibited	$253.52	$ 42.25	$211.27
Sanitary			
— 8" & 10" pipe required where 6" is adequate	$182.86	$166.45	$ 16.41
Manholes			
— 17 required, only 15 are necessary	$125.70	$110.92	$ 14.78
Sidewalks			
— required on both sides of street, but not needed at all	$207.78	-0-	$207.78
Pavement Width			
— 40' required where 30' is adequate	$740.56	$555.42	$185.14
Trees			
— 80 required, none necessary	$ 45.07	-0-	$ 45.07
Surveying Monuments			
— 18 required, only nine are necessary	$ 13.44	$ 6.72	$ 6.72
Utility Lines			
— must be underground	$200.00	-0-	$200.00

Total Cost/Unit: $887.17

Construction Costs (Exhibit 4.4) Local building codes increase the cost per unit by $825.00 over what is believed to be structurally necessary. Reinforcing wire mesh used in the supporting slab ($175 per unit), cast iron and copper piping ($350 per unit) and copper electrical wiring ($200 per unit), were considered by the developer to be unnecessary expenses incurred without significantly increasing the quality or value of the home.

Summary This case study details the magnitude of the cost impact of government regulations. The direct costs of regulations were found to be $1,200 per unit, the costs of delay $400, and the costs of unnecessary requirements $1,700. Government regulations directly accounted for $3,300, or 8.7 percent, of the final selling price. If appropriate com-

EXHIBIT 4.4

UNNECESSARY CONSTRUCTION COSTS
ATTRIBUTABLE TO GOVERNMENT REGULATIONS

Item Required	Net Government Imposed Cost/Unit
Reinforcing wire mesh in supporting slab (normally not used)	$175.00
Underground cast iron and copper pipe (plastic normally used)	$350.00
Copper electrical wiring (aluminum normally used)	$200.00
Framing material quality (cheaper grade normally used)	$ 50.00
1/2″ plyscore siding (3/8″ normally used)	$ 50.00
Total Cost/Unit:	$825.00

missions, financing costs and markups were included the proportion would hover around 10 percent.

Any interpretation of these numbers must be undertaken with great care. They are not meant to suggest that if government regulations were eliminated the cost of a house would be reduced by 8 to 10 percent. Nor is it meant that no benefits are received for the government induced expenditures. What this example does provide, however, is a comprehensive analysis pinpointing the exact dimension and incidence of costs attributable to government regulations.

CASE STUDY #2: CHAPEL HILL, N.C.

Unlike the first example which was primarily concerned with identifying the costs of regulations, this case study examines the impact of regulations on the marketability of the product. It provides insight into how government regulations exacerbate other problems often confronted by home builders, causing a catastrophic boondoggle which results in both a reduction in the number of units constructed and an increase in the price of those built.

In early 1972, five principals, including the owner of the twenty-seven acre site, a development corporation, and an architectural firm formed a limited partnership for the express purpose of developing a condominium project in Chapel Hill, N.C., to contain 167 dwelling units which would be priced in the $25,000 to $30,000 range. Application for rezoning of the land and for a special use permit was filed with the city manager in the fall of 1972 and was heard at a jointly sponsored Planning Board/Board of Aldermen public hearing on November 27, 1972. Special use permits are required as an additional stage to the approval process in Chapel Hill for all unified housing developments which is defined to include condominiums. The rezoning was necessary because the parcel was then divided into two different use classes. The larger portion of the tract (20 acres) was zoned for R-15, low density single-family development, while a smaller portion (seven acres) was zoned R-3, which is the highest density residential use class permitted. The application requested the entire tract to be rezoned R-6, a medium use class which would increase the potential number of dwellings on the entire site by 12 percent over the number then permitted. Rather than be satisfied with the marginal number of additional dwellings the site could accommodate under the requested use class, the developers argued that with rezoning they would be better able to distribute the dwellings on the site in a manner which would reduce the necessity for extensive clearing.

For Chapel Hill, the rezoning application was handled with relative dispatch, with the mayor breaking a tie in favor of the request some two-and-one-half months after the public hearing. Despite the rezoning, it will be recalled that no development could proceed on the site without a special use permit. About one month after the rezoning and special use applications were filed, the Planning Board interrupted their consideration of the merits of the latter request because of their concern for the potential traffic the development might generate on an access road that runs through the town's primary recreation property. Then, at the request of the town's Recreation Commission, which was also concerned about traffic congestion and the safety of the children who use the recreation center, the Planning Board agreed to delay its consideration of the permit request until April so that the Commission could complete its study of current and anticipated use of the recreation center. Then, on April 9, 1973, the Planning Board again recommended to the Board of Aldermen that the special use request be given further study. This time, however, the Aldermen overruled the planners and, on that same date, some four-and-one-half months after the request was first made, the Board approved the special use permit by a split vote.

The special use permit contained 17 stipulations that became part of the project plans as approved. The special use permit included among its requirements that:

1. a 60 foot easement be provided to maintain access to adjoining properties;
2. the principal drive be a dedicated public right-of-way, constructed to town standards, be curbed and guttered and have a sidewalk paved to town standards;

3. prior to issuance of any building permits, any soil erosion and sedimentation control measures recommended by the County Soil and Water Conservation District be carried out;
4. access for handicapped persons be provided to the swimming pool and recreation areas;
5. detailed landscaping plans which would be reviewed by the Chapel Hill Appearance Commission and approved by the Board of Aldermen prior to the issuance of any building permits should include:
   a. building colors and materials
   b. design and location of exterior lighting and signs
   c. design and location of parking areas
6. a bridge over the creek at the project entrance be designed to the Corps of Engineers' standards, with final plans to be approved by the Corps, the town manager, and the Chapel Hill public works department;
7. water lines and fire hydrants be constructed and installed to utility company standards and located as approved by the Fire Department;
8. a bulk trash collection plan be submitted;
9. a plan for interior on-site circulation be submitted;
10. the developer petition for incorporation of site into town upon the town's approval of the special use permit;
11. construction begin within one year from April 9, 1973, and be completed within three years.

On November 7, 1973, one year after the rezoning and special use permit applications were filed, the developers took out a grading and clearing permit and two weeks later filed for a permit to construct the bridge over the creek that bordered the property. The developers were ˙able to secure development financing from a local commercial bank in the amount of $610,000 and an initial construction loan in the amount of $1.3 million, at a rate which floated four points above prime. Despite the timely receipt of a firm credit line, shortly after receiving special use approval, they petitioned the Board of Aldermen to modify the approved construction schedule, which they felt they could not meet. In their petition they requested permission to phase development over three years beginning in November, rather than in April as originally intended. Each phase would be completed within one year's time, with project completion now scheduled for November, 1976.

On November 26, 1973, the Board of Aldermen agreed to the proposed modification and then seized upon the opportunity to further modify the special use permit specifically to ensure that all promised site improvements would be made on time. The posting of a performance bond was required in an amount ($215,000) sufficient to cover the full cost of all project amenities, including club house, tennis courts and swimming pool, main drive and bridge. The bonding requirements were met by the developer, and grading and related site improvements commenced in December of 1973. In January, 1974, a plumbing application permit fee of $3,443 was paid to the town for making sewer connections, while in February, electric permit fees of $790 were paid to secure electrical service to the site. Also in February, the first building permits were secured at a fee of $1,161, while in May heating permits were secured for the first dwellings at a cost of $201. In September 1974, certificates of occupancy were obtained for the first eight attached dwellings. In the same month, five more units were completed.

Development activity continued rather slowly, with land improvements required under the modified special use permit being completed approximately on schedule. Progress on the completion of all phase I dwellings was poor, and in November 1974, the second of three requests was made for phasing construction activity over a longer period of time. First, the developer wanted an extension of the phase I development time from November of 1974 to April of 1975 and then requested a further extension to April of 1976. As things now stand, the project, which was initially required to be completed by April of 1976, is programmed for completion in April of 1978, some six years after initial planning was begun. Presently, the bridge, access road, required land improvements and all amenities have been completed, and 64 dwelling units have been constructed, most of which have been sold and are occupied. Work on phase II has not yet begun and may not be commenced, at least not by the same limited partnership which has suffered serious financial setbacks over the development period.

Discussions with the project principals shed interesting light on the broader issue of the effects of local regulations on development costs as well as on the narrower one of local discretion. Among the first causes of their many difficulties, the developers speak of untimely delays, red tape and overly restrictive requirements imposed on their project through the vehicle of the special use permit. Two specifically cited examples are the bridge over the creek, which cost $54,000 to build when in their judgement a box culvert at a fraction of the price would have sufficed, and the sidewalk along the full length of the main access road ($19,600), which they claim would not be used by residents of the project, who would enter the development through other pathways. From a marketing standpoint, moreover, they argue that the imposition of a performance bond requirement at the time the city first modified the special use permit forced what they viewed as the premature completion of road, utility, and amenity improvements. Because the local housing market, like its national counterpart, had weakened significantly by mid-1974, the developers, if given a choice, would have phased improvements somewhat differently and saved some portion of the $215,000 improvement cost for which bond was posted.

From the community's standpoint, however, imposition of bonding requirements made good sense in view of the developer's early request for modification of its previously approved construction schedule, the fact that the project was a condominium development with facilities to be deeded over to a homeowners' association, and because the limited partnership had little prior development experience. In the eyes of the city, the public interest would be served by as rapid a completion as possible of all land improvements which the developers had pledged to provide.

Reconstructing the major land development costs for Village West crystalizes some of these problems. Estimated development costs totaled almost $615,000, exclusive of land costs which the partnership did not have to bear directly. When prorated across the full complement of 167 dwellings to be built, the average improvement cost is a reasonable $3,680. (See Exhibit 4.5) But only forty-nine dwellings were completed as of April, 1976, with the remaining 18 houses in phase I still under construction. Sales have been so slow, averaging only 2.6 units per month between April, 1974, and November, 1975, that the developers postponed their plans for construction of the second and third phases. When prorated across the 49 completed and occupied dwellings in phase I, average improvement costs skyrocket to more than $12,500 per unit, while if they are amortized over the full 67 units comprising this phase, the unit cost still exceeds $9,000. These costs, it will be remembered, are exclusive of land costs or of an opportunity cost reflecting the alternative use of the capital tied up in the land.

EXHIBIT 4.5

LAND DEVELOPMENT COSTS FOR A CONDOMINIUM
SUBDIVISION: CHAPEL HILL, NORTH CAROLINA
1975

Cost Item	Total	Per Dwelling (49 units)
Engineering	$ 9,495	$ 194
Rough grading	52,553	1,073
Storm, sanitary sewers	57,076	1,165
Water	35,296	720
Curb, gutter paving	51,237	1,046
Electric service	1,516	31
Bridge	54,844	1,119
Amenities	98,804	2,016
Sidewalk	19,692	40
Real estate taxes	4,760	97
Other	32,104	655
Interest	197,588	4,032
Total development cost	$614,965	$12,550

Summary A soft housing market, a combined development and construction loan floating four points over prime and a city directive to complete planned improvements on a schedule which reflected a stronger sales climate than actually existed, combined with an inexperienced development entity, resulted in serious financial hardship to the partnership. As of January 1976, the developer had paid $197,500 in financing charges on its development and construction loan. Total estimated costs for completion of the sixty-seven dwellings and all land improvements exceeded $2.3 million. Average sales price hovered around $32,000, which will not be sufficient to pay all hard costs plus interest on the loan, let alone returning a profit to the landowner. Many of the problems encountered in this project can be attributed to the inflexibility built into the rather lengthy development process. Government regulations acted to accentuate this problem in two respects. First, they are responsible for increasing the length of the process. Secondly, through subdivision agreements and site plan review, they require that specific plans be devised at an early stage of the process.

CASE STUDY #3: CALIFORNIA

As the number of agencies and the levels of government involved in regulating the development process grow, its complexity increases. Each new path added to the maze must be met by equivalent and costly flexibility in development and financing plans. This case study explores the interrelationship between two regulators: the California Coastal Zone Conservation Commission and the Orange County Planning Board, with the developer caught squarely in between.

In 1972, the California Coastal Zone Conservation Commission (CZC) came into being to regulate all development activity along the entire California coastline. A permit approval process was implemented to cover the first 1,000 yards in from the mean high tide line. This was to be an interim policy while a comprehensive plan was created which would encompass an area five miles inland or to the peak of the nearest mountain range. The ramifications and complications which have derived from this legislation are far beyond the scope of this case study. However, the history of the Old Mill Pine project will yield some insight into the effect the CZC has on the development process.

At the end of March, 1973, escrow was opened for an 8.5 acre parcel of land. The sales price at this time was $385,000. For all practical purposes, the topography on this land was flat. The streets and utilities had all been installed. The property was zoned R-4 high density residential. Under this zoning ordinance the county would allow 128 units to be built on the parcel.

In May, 1973, plans were submitted to the county for conceptual approval. The plans were for 104 apartment units, within the 128 unit limit. There was no filing fee required with the submittal and within thirty days county approval had been received.

The next step would have been to apply for a building permit from the county. This would have taken approximately two months. Construction could have begun on the project as early as August of 1973 and now there would have been 104 more dwelling units available in Capistrano Beach. This did not happen.

Upon receiving county approval, the plans were then submitted to the CZC for approval. There was a $250 filing fee required. Prior to the public hearing with the actual commission, the CZC staff reviews the plans and makes comments to the developer and recommendations to the commissioners. The staff's initial response was negative. They felt that the density was simply too high and that other submittals were at densities of around 7.5 units per acre, not the 12 per acre proposed at Old Mill Pine. However, because CZC was brand new, there had been no previous projects reviewed by which to determine any precedent being set by the commissioners. The "other" projects being referred to were "plans in process" and lacked final determination. The most efficient recourse for the developer to take was to wait and see what densities the commission would approve. In October 1973, a public hearing was held regarding the "other" projects and densities of 7-8 units per acre were approved. It became clear that the 104 units (12 units per acre) approved by the county would never be allowed by this newly formed governmental agency.

The original plan was changed from 104 apartment units to 69 condominium units. The approval process had to begin all over again at the county level because of the plan revision. The revised plans were submitted to the county in January, 1974. The entire year of 1974 was spent making minor corrections and revisions for the county as well as preparing an Environmental Impact Review (EIR). The tentative tract map was not approved until December, 1974.

The EIR was originally completed for the apartment proposal at a cost of $4,000. For the condominium project, only an update was required. However, alternative uses became an important issue and thus a consultant was retained for $1,500 to carry out an alternative use study. The bulk of 1974 was spent submitting proposals to the county, having them sent back for corrections and then returned to the county. There were four submittals of this nature. The fee paid to the county was $481.50.

With county approval again in hand, the developer submitted his new proposal to the CZC on January 13, 1975. There was no second filing fee, the proposal was processed through the staff and a public hearing was set for March 10, 1975. The staff's recommendation to the commissioner was to deny approval. However, the staff had historically been more restrictive than the commissioner and thus the developer thought his proposal would nonetheless be approved by the commissioner. On March 10, 1975, the CZC saw this project for the first time. (Recall in October, 1973, the commissioner was approving density around 8 units per acre. The proposed at that time called for 12 units per acre and the developer decided to revise his plans without even going before the commission. This of course was done to save time, as denial was presupposed.) In what was a very close decision, the commission denied approval of the project.

The commission itself did not give a clear indication as to why the proposal was denied. The staff administrators reviewed the decision, and suggested to the developer that the total number of units be reduced by five and that the buildings be set back further on the lot. Architectural fees for this revision were $300.

In June, 1975, the new plans were submitted to the county. However, since the initial proposal in May, 1973, the county had approved and adopted a new General Plan. This plan set forth guidelines which reduced the density of allowed development in the vicinity of the subject site.

Although the zoning had not as yet been changed to be consistent with the General Plan, the county's policy was to require a conditional use permit for the subject property. Thus, the summer of 1975 was spent complying with county requirements to receive a conditional use permit. In addition to the $120 filing fee, there were $1,550 in consultant fees to revise the plans. As a result of this interaction with the county, the total number of units was again reduced to fifty-eight. In December of 1975 the conditional use permit was granted and the plans approved.

These plans were then submitted to the CZC and on April 1, 1976 received approval.

In May, 1976, the developer received a letter from the county indicating that a zone change was being considered for the subject property and surrounding land, a total of thirty acres. This was expected by the developer as it is general practice to bring the zoning ordinance into conformance with the General Plan. On June 22, 1976 a public hearing was held and this property was down-zoned from R-4 to R-1. It was the determination of the county to allow this project, as long as construction began prior to the expiration of the conditional use permit, which was December 15, 1976.

As would be expected, the actual market for this type of residential unit underwent some changes during this three year period. To meet the market demand, revisions in floor plans were required. These revisions were made and sent to the county along with a $25 fee. Approval was readily received and the revisions were presented to the CZC with another $25 fee. This case study is being prepared in mid-September 1976 and approval is expected to be received in the very near future.

Once acquired, the developer has the task of applying for and receiving a building permit. The developer estimates that two months should be ample time in which to acquire a building permit from the county. Assuming that this process begins by October 1, the permit should be received by the end of November, thus leaving fifteen days until the conditional use permit expires. If construction does not begin and the permit expires, it is possible that this entire permit approval process will have to begin again.

Summary   This example highlights the administrative inefficiencies which a lack of coordination among government entities may produce. While the planning virtues of the original proposal's twelve units per acre may be debated, it was initially presented in October 1973. CZC approval of the now twice restructured proposal was not received until April, 1976. A total of two and one-half years was involved in the process of reaching agreement between the developer, the CZC, and the county. Ultimately it is the consumer who must pay. And the burden of carrying costs and risk is not trivial. If a more streamlined negotiation process were used which clearly outlined the options available to a home builder in developing a specific plot of land, then the existing costly inefficiencies could be significantly reduced.

CASE STUDY #4: THE PROBLEMS OF PLANNING FOR DELAY

As suggested by the last case study, the possibility of government delay can wreck havoc on development plans. This is particularly true given the widely fluctuating availability and cost of front-end money, and the changing nature of market demand. One solution to this problem is to purchase only an option on land and to obtain development approvals before an outright commitment to buy is made. This technique was attempted in this case study, but as we shall see, the length of delay, nonetheless, undercut this strategy.

Between September and November, 1973, a Greensboro, North Carolina developer of midpriced subdivision housing obtained two options to acquire two contiguous tracts of land totaling about seventy acres for an average price of $4,500 an acre. The first option, for seven and one-half months, cost $3,000 and was subsequently renewed for four months at an additional price of $1,440, while the second was originally written for a five month period at a cost of $5,000 and subsequently extended for six months at no additional charge. Thus, for an initial out-of-pocket expense of $9,440, the developer acquired an opportunity to package a seventy acre residential subdivision. Ideally, the package would be put together in the six-month period dictated by the shorter of the two options so that the decision to exercise the option would be made with the certain knowledge that development would immediately follow. Optioning the land rather than purchasing it outright made sense on several grounds. First, as a matter of course, a great deal of money can be saved if all of the conceptual, planning and engineering work can be accomplished, and development, construction and permanent financing commitments made before any equity must be spent for the land purchase.

In this particular case, it made even more sense because a zoning change was necessary. The land was currently zoned for 40,000 square foot lots with a required minimum lot frontage of ninety feet. At less than one finished lot to the acre, raw land costs would total almost $6,000 per lot. With raw land accounting for around 50 percent of the finished lot cost, an improved lot would cost around $12,000 and the sale price of each house would have to approach $60,000 to be economically viable. This was substantially more expensive than the $40-45,000 homes the developer believed to be readily marketable. Thus, a rezoning would be necessary if the land was to be developed, and because of the uncertainties of this possibility, it made sense to option the land rather than purchase it outright. Finally, because the land was located in an environmentally sensitive watershed area, and there was growing public concern with problems of sedimentation caused by excessive surface water runoff, the developer realized that substantial advance work had to be done to design an acceptable subdivision if the rezoning effort were to be successful. By using options, the developer acquired lead-time to work out his problems at minimum cost. If all of his efforts failed, he would not exercise his options and would write off his $9,440 cash investment as one of the costs of doing business.

Theoretically, the developer could approach the County Commissioners with any number of rezoning options. Since the land was on the outskirts of Greensboro, he could have requested a rezoning from R40 to R20, with the 20,000 square foot lots tapping into the city's water and sewer systems. The R20 zoning would have permitted an average of one and one-half finished lots to the acre and a raw land cost of around $3,000 a unit. There were other alternatives; R12 zoning works out to around three lots to the acre and raw land costs of $1,500 a unit, while R12M can accommodate 12 units per acre, which works out to a raw land cost of only $375 a unit. In practical terms, however, the developer's options were not that wide. The Commissioners, concerned with increasing congestion in the inlying county areas, and with an inadequate road system, and sensitive to the limited growth movement, informally let it be known to developers that R12M and R12 zoning requests had little chance for approval.

Instead of making a straightforward request for an R20 rezoning with 20,000 square foot lots in standard subdivision form, the developer chose to request a rezoning to conditional use, which is a use class in which the applicant defines and then defends his own development parameters in terms of existing general public development policies. The heart of the development scheme embodied in the conditional use request was a combination of R12 and R12M use classes on small portions of the seventy acre parcel, with substantial portions of the tract to be left in open space. Where straight R12 zoning would permit around three lots to the acre, the developer planned to build at a density of just 2.1 dwellings; instead of the twelve units per acre permitted under the R12M use class, the higher density portions of the site were to be developed at just 4.2 units per acre. Overall, where the combination of the two use classes requested would have permitted 407 units to be built, the developer's plans called for just 219 dwellings.

The developer's intention was to organize the tract on a cluster basis, with one section containing ninety-three single-family lots, each having 12,000 square feet, and a higher density townhouse section containing 126 dwellings. More than 40 percent of the entire tract was to be left in permanent open space and deeded to the homeowners' association which was to be an integral element of the cluster development scheme. Tennis courts and a swimming pool, which were projected, were to be deeded to the association as well.

With the conceptual work largely accomplished, including master sketch plans and basic engineering studies, and with financing commitments in hand, the developer applied for a rezoning of the tract from R40 to conditional use in December of 1973. Importantly, this first request came some six months before the expiration of the first of the developer's two land options. After review by the County Planning Board, which recommended denial of the rezoning request for reasons of an inadequate road system to handle anticipated traffic that would be generated by the development, the County Commissioners unanimously rejected the application on January 22, 1974.

With only a few months still remaining on his options, the developer was faced with a statutory prohibition against requesting the same rezoning for a period of twelve months from the date of the previous rejection. Inasmuch as the county had recently enacted a planned unit development (PUD) amendment to its zoning ordinance, he decided to apply for a zoning change to R-PUD residential, a use class that was consistent with his original design concept of cluster development. Over the next few months he concentrated his efforts on obtaining the documentation required on the PUD ordinance. Essentially, the requirements involve the review of the proposed development by various county, city, and state agencies, each of which must certify that it can provide the development with necessary services or facilities or that the PUD is consistent with public development policies.

The multi-layered review process takes time and is not always sensitive to the inevitable winding down of the clock on time-limited land options. Nevertheless, by the time the shortest of the two options had expired on May 30, 1974, four agencies had approved the project. Given approvals in hand by the Greensboro Public Works Department, which certified the adequacy of the city's water and sewer systems to serve the PUD; guarantees as to the availability of private trash collection service; the State Department of Transportation's assurances that the proposed development would not seriously affect the regional traffic pattern; the County Fire Marshal's certification that the development would not overburden existing equipment and manpower; and a guarantee by the County Superintendent of Schools of available classroom space for the PUD's anticipated population of school-age children, the developer chose to exercise his option on the first of the tracts, which contained thirty-nine acres of land. The thirty-nine acres were acquired through execution of a land sales contract which called for the payment of $47,000 at closing and the payment of three subsequent annual installments. At closing and upon payment of each installment, approximately one-quarter of the thirty-nine acre tract would be released to the developer.

With the approval process grinding on, the developer was now committed to the project to the tune of almost $50,000 in hard cash. Subsequent city and state agency approvals were received, and despite the Planning Board's recommendation that the rezoning request again be denied for essentially the same reasons for which it rejected the initial conditional use request, on August 21, 1974, the County Commissioners approved the R-PUD rezoning application on a split vote. Thus, from the time that the developer optioned the land to the point at which rezoning was approved consumed eleven months.

Within thirty days of the rezoning, the option was exercised on the remaining thirty-one acre tract. Acquisition of this parcel involved a payment of 28 percent of the purchase price of $33,462, the immediate release of three acres, and a seven percent purchase money mortgage requiring three annual installments. Thus, before any development could take place at all, the developer had a total of some $80,000 of his own cash in the land and title to thirteen of the seventy acres in the parcel. Normally, the developer can recover some of his initial equity through his development loan proceeds if he can get a good land appraisal from his commercial lender. In this particular case, not only was this not possible, but the developer lost his original development loan commitment from his commercial bank. The nominal reason for cancellation of the committment was the lender's fear that market inexperience with the PUD concept could adversely affect sales. More likely, the reason for the turnabout was that between September, 1973, and August, 1974, the Greensboro housing market badly slumped, with the multifamily sector becoming particularly sluggish.

Indeed, it was not until June, 1976, some twenty-two months after the rezoning request was approved, that a combined development-construction loan commitment was again secured for the project. By this time, two additional installments had to be made on each of the parcels. As of June, 1976, the developer's own hard cash committed to the land totaled in excess of $206,000. Today he is in the unfortunate position of owning outright substantially more land than originally intended, with the result that this capital tie-up has increased his credit needs for the rest of his development operation. Nor is there much reason for optimism in the forseeable future, since he cannot begin to develop the multi-family portion of his land until the market regains its strength. In the meantime, another installment on each of his parcels comes due in just a few months.

For a combination of reasons, more than $206,000 was committed to the purchase of the PUD land before a spade of earth was turned. The capital base, as the developer refers to his equity, which he used to turn over one-and-one-half times per year, has been effectively tied up for three years. The opportunity costs of the sunk investment can be crudely estimated by applying the developer's average cost of credit over the holding period to the installment payments made on the land between mid-1973 and mid-1976. Using a 13.6 percent average interest rate, with three lump sum payments on each of the tracts, total interest costs would have amounted to $30,500 over the thirty-six month period assuming a 75 percent land purchase loan. When allocated over the planned 219 dwellings, the carrying charge averages $139 a house. This is the amount of interest that would be directly attributable to purchasing the land outright prior to development. It does not include interest on any development loan. While the $139 does not seem like much money, given the magnitude of the problems the developer confronted, it is probably a serious underestimation of the real holding cost. Additional installments on the land are due in January 1977 and the developer is just beginning to develop only the first section of the PUD containing forty-two dwellings. Charging the entire holding cost against section 1 results in a carrying charge of $726 per dwelling. (See Exhibit 4.6) Given the developer's average estimated land improvement cost per dwelling of $4,453, the addition of a pro rata share of holding or opportunity costs to each lot will increase this figure by between 3 and 16 percent, depending upon how the allocation is made.

Summary   It is clear that initial development plans did not work in this case, and the question is — why not? As with so many planning-development issues, there is no simple answer. Is eight months inordinately long to have to wait for a rezoning decision? Most developers we spoke with

EXHIBIT 4.6

LAND AND IMPROVEMENT COSTS FOR SECTION
OF PLANNED UNIT DEVELOPMENT
NORTH CAROLINA, 1976

Cost Item	Per Lot	%
Engineering	$ 310	7
Clearing	202	5
Grading streets	405	9
Soil erosion	107	2
Storm draingage	429	10
Sanitary sewers	631	14
Water mains	667	15
Water & sewer acreage fees	226	5
Curb, gutter, paving streets	1,167	26
Underground electricity	71	2
Misc. & contingency	238	5
Subtotal	4,453	100
Carrying costs*	726	
Total	$5,179	
Typical lot 80 x 125 Lots/acre 2.43		

*prorated over 42 dwellings

surely thought so and point to this kind of problem as the cause of much of their difficulties. When developers, however, are asked which steps in the process they would eliminate, or which approvals they would consider entirely frivolous, they have no ready answers. Surely the adequacy of the road system, the availability of water and sewer facilities, classrooms, trash collection, and related services and facilities are all important to the success and marketability of the development. Even the newly implemented measures to control surface runoff, the cost of which was estimated by the developer's engineer to add $107 to each lot's improvement cost, did not cause him much consternation. Rather, it was the collection of *all* the regulations, and *all* of the paperwork that continues to mount up while the option clock expires, that caused the most distress. The political nature of the rezoning process and the fact that the Planning Board or Commissioners can pick on traffic or any one of a dozen other reasons for denying a rezoning request — despite all the documentation and studies that claim otherwise — contribute to developer bitterness. Indeed, as part of his particular effort to secure a rezoning, the developer paid more than $8,000 in engineering and legal fees for detailed plans and for presentations made on his behalf at public hearings, Planning Board, and County Commission meetings. Thus only by looking at the sum total of these difficulties can one ascertain the true nature of the problem confronting the housing industry.

SUMMARY

As this chapter has suggested, there is no easy way to measure or even to conceptualize the costs of government regulations. Our analysis has suggested two related approaches: first, the identification of costs related both directly and indirectly to government regulations and, secondly, an examination of the origin of those costs.

Costs were defined to be direct or indirect administrative costs (transaction costs) and the costs of unnecessary of excessive regulation.

Our analysis of the origins of costs of regulations showed that most could be traced to cost reallocations. In particular, costs were being shifted both from public sector and from other private parties to the developer, and from the future to the present. The net result of these shifts has been to dramatically increase the initial price of housing and thereby severely limit the number of families able to afford these units. Regulations are supposed to have the effect of increasing the quality of new housing, and of reducing any burden on the municipality, but these same regulations also significantly increase the cost of housing to the consumer.

The case studies examined in this chapter further highlighted the effect of government regulations on housing. The first case study of a development in southern New Jersey showed that approximately 8-10 percent of the final selling price of each unit could be attributed to the costs of regulation. The other three case studies in North Carolina and California demonstrated the interaction between government regulations and the successful marketability of the units. They showed that unless all of the many pieces of the development puzzle come together at exactly the right time, the viability of the project will be in jeopardy. Particularly acute problems which were examined dealt with delay, multi-level review, and the inflexibility of the process.

The problems of the housing industry will further be explored in the next chapter, which presents the results of our nationwide survey of the home builders' industry.

Section II
Specific Areas
of Regulation

In an attempt to better understand and more clearly identify the cost increasing aspects of government intervention, a detailed study of seven primary areas of regulation was undertaken. Within each of these areas, several questions were confronted. First we asked if government intervention was at all necessary and if so why, and what should its objectives be? Assuming that a role for government was deemed necessary, we then examined the nature of the regulatory mechanism in use and asked what are the advantages of this form of regulation over others. Surveys were conducted to provide information relating to the specific types of regulations and administrative processes now in use. The results were analyzed in terms of the cost impact of these regulations attributable both to the disruption of the free market and to administrative inefficiencies.

The seven areas of regulation which follow are building codes, energy conservation regulations, subdivision controls, zoning regulations, growth controls, environmental protection regulations, and financing regulations.

Chapter Five:
The Effect of
Building Codes
on Housing Costs

Construction expenditures account for approximately 80 percent of the total costs of a residential unit. But unlike the land development process, which is subject to a multitude of government requirements, once construction of the unit itself has begun, the only significant public control is the building code.[1] Thus the magnitude of the impact and the relative simplicity of the regulation combine to make building codes a prime target for cost-reducing strategies.

This chapter identifies and analyzes two types of costs attributable to building codes: those associated with the disruption of the free market, and those related to administrative inefficiencies in implementing the code. Similar to any government regulation which changes the incentives and imposes constraints on the operation of the free market, building codes affect the production efficiency of the industry and inhibit innovation. The second cost category, administrative inefficiencies, concerns such unnecessary costs as those created by outdated codes, jurisdictional variation and inept enforcement.[2] Finally, underlying all building code requirements is the essential question of determining the cost-quality trade-off — how safe, how fireproof, and what longevity do we desire in our buildings and how much are we willing to pay for these quality features?

The first section in this chapter presents background information describing the goals of building codes, how they operate and the problems they create. The second section discusses the market disruptions caused by this system of regulating construction. The third section presents the operational aspects of the existing code machinery. Information on local implementation of codes, based on a survey conducted by the Center for Urban Policy Research of 100 municipalities' building departments, is discussed in the fourth section. The fifth section summarizes the previous analysis and attempts to estimate the actual cost savings possible through code reform. The final section presents cost reducing strategies and reforms.

The Building Code Regulatory System

THE GOALS OF BUILDING CODES

Government's role in regulating construction has long been an established facet of the building process. The earliest of these regulations had as their principal objective the punishment of negligent builders.[3] As society became more urbanized this regulatory goal was superseded by the importance of protecting property and lives from the ravages of fire. Finally, as the complexity of construction techniques increased, codes have also performed the role of ensuring both the homebuyer and the lender of some publically established minimum of safety and quality.

OPERATIONS AND PROBLEMS

Codes seek to achieve these goals by regulating both building techniques and materials, either directly through the use of *specification* requirements, or indirectly through the use of *performance* standards. The latter method is far more complex in that it establishes criteria based on standards of health and safety (e.g., a wall must retard the spread of fire for two hours) and permits the use of any material which is capable of achieving the required level of performance.

Once a code has been adopted by the appropriate jurisdiction, the next stage in the building control system is implementation. Enforcement is usually assigned to a local government's building department, which examines the plans of a proposed building to ensure compliance with code provisions.[4] On-site inspections are also conducted to verify that the actual construction is in accordance with the approved plans. At last count, there were over 8,000 jurisdictions in this country actively administering a building code.[5]

The most extensive evaluation of building codes dates back to the 1968 report prepared by the Douglas Commission. Unnecessary costs are inherent in building codes that:

1. delay construction,
2. prevent the use of modern materials,
3. inhibit creative design,
4. include antiquated and outdated provisions,
5. lack effective procedures for up-dating,
6. are controlled by a small group of special interests.
7. are enforced by inadequately trained and qualified officials,
8. lack a proper appeal procedure,
9. are often arbitrarily enforced by local officials,
10. inhibit the marketing of mobile homes and prefab units,
11. prevent large-scale building,
12. should be administered at the state level.[6]

Summing up these inefficiencies, two commentators writing for the Kaiser Commission estimated that building code reform could achieve savings ranging from 1.5 to 7 percent of the total cost of a unit.[7] The range of this estimate indicates the varying degrees of efficiency in the 8,000 local jurisdictions, yet they do provide the basic parameters of the unnecessary costs attributed to building codes.[8] The following sections examine these regulatory inadequacies more closely, with particular attention to the magnitude of the costs they create.

The Impact of Building Codes on the Housing Market

Are Building Codes Necessary?

The threshold issue which must be addressed in evaluating building codes is why government has deemed it essential to regulate the private construction market. In other words, if left to follow its own course, would the private market be capable of achieving the same objectives as those attained through building codes?[9]

Two specific areas of experience suggest that some form of government intervention in building construction may be necessary.

The complexity of today's construction methods renders it unlikely that the prospective home buyer will have sufficient technical knowledge to make an informed decision about the structural integrity of the unit. Building codes serve as a substitute for for complete knowledge on the part of the consumer by ensuring that at least a minimum level of quality is built into the unit.[10] Without codes there would be little incentive for builders to incorporate more than a minimal degree of structural integrity in their product because most consumers are not capable of distinguishing between varying degrees of structural soundness.

The second market imperfection which suggests the need for government intervention relates to externalities. For instance, home buyers would tend to underinvest in safety features, thinking only of the potential damage to their own properties, without considering the effect of fire or a collapsing building on surrounding properties. Building codes have the effect of readjusting this parochial investment decision by requiring that the potential external costs be considered in deciding how much safety will be built into the unit.

If experience dictates that some form of intervention in the building industry is necessary, it does not demand that those codes be legislated by the government. In France, there is no government promulgated building code. Instead, codes are written by the liability insurance companies, this being the result of a provision in the Napoleonic Code which places liability for major construction defects during a ten year period on architects and contractors. To protect themselves against possible liability, those in the construction field obtain insurance which is made contingent on their compliance with minimum construction standards as established by the insurance companies.[11]

MARKET DISTORTIONS CAUSED BY BUILDING CODES

While ensuring that certain public goals are met, building codes do create inefficiencies in the free market. Codes establish minimum levels of housing quality and require that all consumers, regardless of their individual consumption preferences, purchase at least a minimum package of quality and safety features. Such requirements prevent the market from reaching its own equilibrium point. Yet granting that government must establish the minimum level of standards, there is no feasible method for determining the optimum level of safety and stability to be required by building codes. For example, several additional safety features, such as smoke detectors and ground fault interruptors, have recently been added to the list of requirements in many jurisdictions, often without adequate consideration of either their cost-effectiveness or consumer preference.

The second market distortion caused by the minimum standards of building codes is that they require home buyers to invest present dollars to ensure future soundness. This is required despite the fact that most home buyers' incomes will increase rapidly over the years and they would therefore be better capable of affording these structural improvements at some later date. Nonetheless, building codes impose those costs on them at the time of the initial purchase of the unit, a time when they least can afford it. This problem is further compounded by traditional mortgage availability criteria which is based entirely on present earnings.

Summary

This analysis of the effects of building codes on the market structure reflects the trade-off between economic efficiency and the attainment of the social goal of protecting the general welfare. Whether or not an optimum solution is achieved can only be determined by examining the regulatory system in operation. The next section moves from this somewhat theoretical discussion of market impacts to an evaluation of the building code regulatory mechanism as it has been implemented.

Who Promulgates Codes?

There are two basic components to the building regulatory system. The initial step is agreement on the contents of the code, and its adoption. Once a code is adopted, the second component of the system is its implementation. This includes establishment of a code enforcement procedure, a building department and a mechanism for maintaining technical currency. Each of these will be detailed in the following sections with emphasis placed on potential weaknesses which may result in unnecessary costs.

The State/Local Realignment

The past five years have witnessed a major shift in jurisdictional decision-making authority in determining the contents of building codes. While enforcement for the most part has remained at the local level, many states have recently acted to accept the authority that has always been legally theirs to adopt statewide building codes.[12]

A 1970 survey of municipalities with populations over 10,000 undertaken by the International City Managers Association showed that 73.5 percent of the cities surveyed based their code on one of the four model codes[13], while state or county based codes were used by 13.5 percent and locally based codes by 10.8 percent of those cities sampled.[14] The results of a 1976 survey of 100 municipal building departments conducted by the Center for Urban Policy Research showed that a shift has occurred away from locally promulgated codes to increased reliance on both state and model codes. (See Exhibit 5.1) For a discussion of the sample and a copy of the questionnaire, see Appendix E.

Since most state codes simply reference one of the model codes, the dominance of the latter group has become significantly more pronounced.

EXHIBIT 5.1

Technical Basis For Building Code Adopted

(n=100)

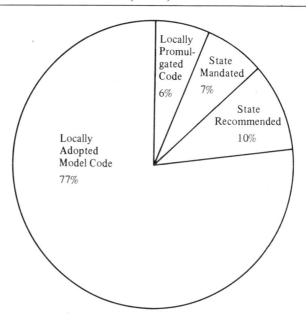

SOURCE: Survey of Building Departments, Center for Urban Policy Research, Winter, 1976.

This conclusion is further substantiated by a preliminary report recently published by the Office of Building Standards and Codes Services of the National Bureau of Standards which summarized state building code regulations.[15] This survey provides clear documentation of this realignment toward both increased state involvement and greater reliance on model codes. (See Exhibit 5.2) The results can be summarized as follows:

1. Fifteen states have statewide codes affecting one- and two-family construction (four additional states have building codes affecting only multi-family construction).
2. Of these fifteen states, nine had a mandatory state code, while four state codes were offered only as guidelines to local governments. (Two states did not respond.)
3. Of the nine mandatory code states, six utilized minimum codes, while the remaining three required the adoption of a specific code.

4. Thirteen of the statewide codes are based on existing model codes. Eight use the Uniform Building Code as their basis, four use the Basic Building Code and one uses the Southern Building Code.

This shift away from locally promulgated codes is further substantiated by the results of our building department survey. When asked if they had ever changed from one code to another, we found that over one-third of the municipalities responding had moved away from a local code. (See Exhibit 5.3)

THE PERVASIVENESS OF MODEL CODES

The spread of model codes on two fronts — both their adoption directly by local governments and indirectly through the increasing number of states referencing their use — suggests that their impact should be closely scrutinized. Before undertaking this aspect of our analysis, the question of why their influence has spread must first be addressed.

The popularity of model codes can be easily understood. They provide a relatively inexpensive mechanism for drafting and updating a code.[16] Moreover, once adopted, municipalities retain complete discretion over the contents and revisions of these model codes. They may accept what provisions they see fit, alter others to their own locality and discard what they find unacceptable.

There is little significant difference between the four model codes. In fact, these four groups now jointly issue the *One and Two Family Dwelling Code*.[17] Other activities aimed at eliminating unnecessary duplication and discrepancies between codes include the formation of the Model Codes Standardization Council, which was organized to develop uniform language and standards, and the formation of the National Research Board, whose purpose is to facilitate the testing and evaluation of new products seeking acceptance by the model code groups.

CONTENT: THE CODE CHANGE PROCESS

Model code groups accept suggestions from all interested parties concerning changes which should be made in their code's provisions. These suggestions are then submitted to a subcommittee, in the related construction field, and/or a code change committee, both of which are comprised of member building officials. These committees listen to arguments on both sides of the issue, which are usually presented by representatives of those special interest groups most affected by model code changes, e.g., trade associations, the manufacturers of competing goods, and the trade unions. After weighing the testimony, the committee makes its recommendations to the entire membership at an annual meeting where the matter

EXHIBIT 5.2

SURVEY OF STATE BUILDING CODE ACTIVITY
(As of June 1975)

State	State Building Code A[a]	B[b]	Date Adopted	Application[c]	Technical Basis[d]	Local Amendments
Alabama						
Alaska		X	1958	Man/Min	UBC	Yes[1]
Arizona						
Arkansas						
California	X	X	N.R.	N.R.	UBC	N.R.
Colorado	X	X	N.R.	N.R.	UBC	N.R.
Connecticut	X	X	1971	Man/Min	BBC	N.R.
Delaware						
Florida	X	X	1977	Man/Min	N.R.	Yes[2]
Georgia	X	X	1974	Vol.	SBC	N.R.
Hawaii						
Idaho	X	X	1975	Man/Min	UBC	Yes[2]
Illinois						
Indiana	X	X	1974	Man/Min	UBC	Yes[2]
Iowa	X	X	1973	Vol.	UBC	N.R.
Kansas						
Kentucky						
Louisiana						
Maine						
Maryland	X	X	1973	Vol.	BBC	N.R.
Massachusetts	X	X	1975	Man	BBC	N.R.
Michigan	X	X	1974	Man	BBC	Yes[2]
Minnesota	X	X	1971	Man	UBC	N.R.
Mississippi						
Missouri						
Montana	X	X	1975	Man/Min	UBC	Yes
Nebraska						
Nevada						
New Hampshire						
New Jersey						
New Mexico	X	X	1974	Man/Min	UBC	Yes
New York	X	X	1951	Vol.	State	N.R.
No. Carolina		X	1935	Man	SBC	Yes
No. Dakota						
Ohio		X	1959	Man/Min	N.R.	N.R.
Oklahoma						
Oregon		X	1975	Man/Min/Max	UBC	Yes
Pennsylvania						
Rhode Island						
So. Dakota						
Tennessee						
Texas						
Utah						
Vermont						
Virginia		X	1973	Man/Min/Max	BBC	N.R.
Washington		X	1974	Man/Min	UBC	N.R.
W. Virginia						
Wisconsin		X	1974	Man/Min	State	N.R.
Wyoming						

NOTES: a. As applied to 1- and 2-family residential construction
           b. As applied to multi-family residential construction
           c. Mandatory, Minimum; Maximum and Voluntary
           d. Uniform Building Code (UBC); Basic Building Code (BBC);
               Southern Building Code (SBC). All are model codes.
           1. Must be equal to state code provision
           2. Only with state approval
           N.R. Not reported

SOURCE: Office of Building Standards and Codes Services, "Status of Statewide
Building Code Regulatory Programs," Nov. 6, 1975.

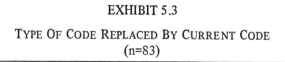

EXHIBIT 5.3

TYPE OF CODE REPLACED BY CURRENT CODE
(n=83)

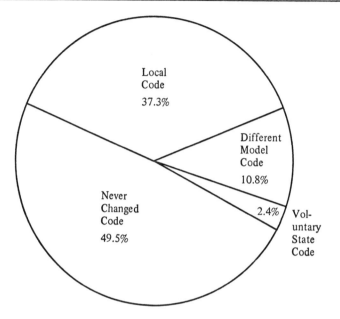

SOURCE: Survey of Building Departments; Center for Urban Policy Research, Winter 1976.

can once again be debated. A code provision's ultimate fate is determined by a vote taken by the member building officials.

With only minor variations, this code change process is used by all the model code groups. It is enthusiastically supported by them as being an open and democratic process in which all views are fully aired before the final determination is made by building officials — those most qualified to play this role.

There remains some question, however, as to the efficacy of this process. Most of the information presented before both the subcommittees and the entire membership is supplied by trade associations and manufacturers. In examining this step in the process Francis Ventre, a prominent student of the code system, has stated:

Model codes may provide the aura of the technological currency and the illusion of the removal of technical decisions from the arena of local politics, but more often than not the politics of national trade associations are played just as heavily at the model code meeting as at the local city hall.[18]

This conclusion is not surprising given the fact that product manufacturers and trade associations are playing for such high stakes.[19] Their costs incurred in the code approval process can be passed on to the consumer. Meanwhile public interest groups, often with little resources to draw on, must travel at their own expense and support their own research and documentation.[20] *Noticeably absent from these conferences are any strong voices speaking out in support of the consumer.*

The problem of biased information is particularly troublesome because of an underlying deficiency in the process. There are no firm, universal technical criteria upon which to base a code change decision.

CONTENT: THE DEVELOPMENT OF STANDARDS

For building officials to determine whether or not a particular provision is acceptable, it is essential that some criteria exist by which the proposed change can be evaluated. To fulfill this need, a rather complex system of testing laboratories and standard-writing organizations has developed. Standards may be of three types: engineering practice, materials and test.[21] In forming the basis upon which code provisions are to be evaluated, they are most often simply referenced in the text or the appendix of a building code.[22]

Over 150 different groups now develop standards. They represent such varied interests as trade associations, government testing laboratories, and associations whose primary purpose is to set standards.[23]

Theoretically, the formation of standards performs an essential role; yet in practice, the performance tests from which they are derived fall considerably short of providing a strong foundation upon which code provisions can be based. The simple fact is that many of the test processes upon which standards are based are clearly inadequate representations of actual building conditions. This point is a central theme of a recent paper on fire regulations which details the inadequacies of various tests, such as the commonly accepted "flame spread rating."[24] David Hemenway, in his exhaustive analysis of the standard setting process, supports this conclusion. He states: "In many areas good performance standards are impossible (or to use economists' jargon, too costly) to write."[25]

If the technical basis is inadequate to support a standard, then how are they developed? This question was squarely addressed by the National Commission on Fire Prevention and Control which reported:

As it is now, both specification requirements (such as ½ inch thickness for gypsum sheeting) and performance standards (such as 3 hours of fire-resistance in certain securing walls) are the product of judgements based on past experience or speculation, rather than firm knowledge of fire behavior.[26]

Perhaps even worse than relying on past experience and speculation is the fact that standards appear to be disproportionately influenced by trade interests, which is reminiscent of the model code change process. The American National Standards Institute (ANSI) claims that it requires a national consensus before it adopts a standard. Hemenway's analysis of its operations suggests otherwise. "It [ANSI] is largely financed by the large scale enterprise; most of the standards approved are written by organizations dominated by large scale enterprises."[27]

Congressional attention is currently focused on the problems inherent in the existing system — a system that is tantamount to industry self-regulation; standards are set by industry controlled forces and later rubber stamped when adopted by government bodies. Hearings were held during the past two years before the Anti-Trust and Monopoly Subcommittee which inspired the drafting of the "Voluntary Standards and Certification Act of 1976."

In introducing this bill, Senator Abourezk surveyed the problems of the existing standards system:

. . .voluntary standards and certifications, in their present form, must be challenged, because they are a basic component of industry attempts to restrain trade by price-fixing, boycotting, controlling supply, and foreclosing new technology from the market.[28]

This bill is an attempt to establish uniform procedures aimed at ensuring the fair and adequate representation of all interested parties in the standard setting process.

An example of the potential abuse of the existing system is vividly portrayed in an investigative report published by Ralph Nader's Center for Auto Safety detailing the recent history of the mobile home industry.[29] It should first be noted that mobile homes have traditionally not been regulated by local building codes; instead, most states had passed specific legislation controlling their construction.[30] Almost all of these state mobile home building codes were based on the standard (ANSI 119.1) developed by a sectional committee on mobile homes of the American National Standards Institute.

The Nader report, *Mobile Homes: The Low Cost Housing Hoax*, examined the process by which this standard was developed. It concluded that:

1. Industry representatives constituted 36 percent of the committee's membership, but an even greater percentage of those attending and voting at each working session.
2. The industry controlled virtually all the technical data and research upon which decisions were based.
3. The Committee lacked any mechanism for reviewing consumer complaints.[31]

The problems identified by this report have not gone unnoticed. In 1974, Congress passed the National Mobile Home Construction and Safety Standards Act which, when implemented, will centralize control over construction standards within the Department of Housing and Urban Development.[32]

Although federal controls may improve the standard setting process, it must be recognized that underlying any attempt to write a standard, or for that matter to adopt a specific building code provision, is an implicit decision concerning a cost-quality trade-off. For example, it must be decided at what point an extra ten minutes of fire resistance no longer justifies the concomitant increase in price. There is absolutely no justification for either building officials or standard writing groups as they exist today to be the sole parties to make this decision. A more democratic process, inviting a stronger voice for the ultimate consumer, along with more accurate knowledge about the causes and effects of damage, is required.

Local Implementation of Building Codes

Even with the increased reliance on state adopted codes, the actual administration of codes has remained at the local level. In all but the nine states with mandatory statewide building laws, the specific provisions of codes are determined by the officials of each municipality. Unnecessary costs may occur at this stage when codes require excessive safety features or exclude new materials with properties similar to those of existing, more expensive products. Even in those states with mandatory codes, implementation occurs at the local level. The unnecessary costs created during this stage of the control process may also occur when administrative inefficiencies create delays or when local discretion is abused.

LOCAL CONTROL OF CODE CONTENT

The extent to which code requirements will be obsolete or unnecessary is primarily a function of how often the code is amended. According to our survey of building departments, more than two-thirds amend their codes at least every four years. (See Exhibit 5.4) The remaining one-third, however, allow this period between revisions to extend for a significantly longer time. Given the changes in technology, this delay would appear to result in the exclusion of cost-reducing innovations.

Code currency was explored by the Douglas Commission in 1967 and again by Ventre in 1970.[33] Both surveyed municipal building departments

EXHIBIT 5.4

FREQUENCY OF CODE REVISIONS

(n=97)

Frequency of Revision	Number of Municipalities	Percent
Annually	25	25.8
Every 2 years	10	10.3
Every 3-4 years	33	34.0
Every 5-6 years	3	3.0
Infrequently (when thought necessary)	26	26.9
Total	97	100.0

SOURCE: Survey of Building Departments, Center for Urban Policy Research, Winter 1976.

to determine the degree to which commonly accepted provisions had been adopted by local governments. Using a list of fourteen items, of which all but plastic pipes had been accepted by model code groups both surveys clearly portrayed the degree of local resistance to change. (See Exhibit 5.5) The results also showed that while model code municipalities were less restrictive, they nonetheless frequently prevented the use of many commonly accepted provisions.

The same technique was incorporated in our survey of building departments using an updated list of possible code requirements. (See Exhibit 5.6) Several of these provisions, such as the requirement for smoke detectors, security features on doors and windows, ground fault interruptors and fire rating walls and doors between the garage and living areas, have been cited as either excessive or ineffective in protecting life and property. Other provisions, such as prohibitions against the use of plastic pipes, automatic plumbing vents, and aluminum wiring, have been cited as restricting the use of less expensive, equally effective materials.

The results of this survey indicate that requirements for smoke detectors and fire rating walls for garages have been incorporated in many state and model codes. The major exception to this is that no local codes had yet incorporated the smoke detector requirement. This may be a result of the tendency, reported by Ventre, for local codes to be updated less frequently than model or state codes.[34] Plastic pipes are still prohibited in 30 percent of the municipalities surveyed, a slight improvement since 1970. Neither automatic plumbing vents, an innovation safely used for years in mobile homes, nor aluminum wiring, which is still suffering a blemished reputation

EXHIBIT 5.5

Percent Of Communities Prohibiting Specific Construction Innovations

Code Changes	No. of Cities Reporting	All Governments Reporting (A)	By Type of Code			1967 Douglas Survey (E)	A–E
			Model (B)	State (C)	Local (D)		
Nonmetallic sheathed electrical cable	771	14.7	13.1	9.1	32.5	13.0	+ 1.7
Prefabricated metal chimneys	832	11.1	9.1	14.0	20.8	19.1	– 8.0
Off-site preassembled combination drain, waste, and vent plumbing system for bathroom installation	805	38.5	34.3	47.6	56.5	42.2	– 3.7
Off-site preassembled electrical wiring harness for installation of electrical service entrance to dwelling	751	51.7	36.6	59.6	67.1	45.7	+ 6.0
Wood roof trusses, placed 24″ on center	840	5.2	3.8	7.2	12.8	10.0	– 4.8
Copper pipe in drain, waste and vent plumbing systems	818	4.9	4.2	3.8	10.6	8.6	– 3.7
ABS (acrylonitrite butadeine-styrene) or PVC (polyvinyl-chloride) plastic pipe in drain, waste, and vent plumbing systems	826	47.0	42.9	49.5	71.3	62.6	–15.6
Bathroom or toilet facilities equipped with ducts for natural or mechanical ventilation in lieu of operable windows for skylights	836	2.6	2.5	2.8	3.1	6.0	– 3.4
Party walls without continuous air space	750	26.4	25.8	19.6	38.6	26.8	– 0.4
Use of single top and bottom plates in non-load bearing interior partitions	836	20.0	20.2	20.4	26.3	24.5	– 3.6
Use of 2″ x 3″ studs in non-load bearing interior partitions	833	32.3	29.7	33.3	48.4	35.8	– 3.5
Placement of 2″ x 4″ studs on center in non-load bearing interior partitions	841	42.6	39.7	38.2	66.7	47.3	– 4.7
In wood frame construction sheathing at least 1/2″ thick in lieu of corner bracing	834	14.9	13.7	14.7	23.2	20.4	– 5.5
Wood frame exterior walls in multi-family structures or three stories or less	819	25.0	19.7	39.0	44.7	24.1	+ 0.9

SOURCE: Ventre, *Urban Data Service Reports*, p. 5.

EXHIBIT 5.6

CURRENCY IN BUILDING CODES: 1976

Code Provision	TYPE OF CODE		
	State (n=17)	Model (n=77)	Local (n=6)
	(percent responding affirmatively)*		
Requires			
Smoke Detectors	70.6	50.0	0.0
Safety features on doors and windows	0.0	10.7	16.7
Ground fault interruptors	25.0	59.5	33.3
Fire rating wall between garage and living area	85.7	77.8	83.3
Prohibits			
Automatic plumbing vents	87.5	72.2	66.7
ABS or PVG plastic pipes in drain, waste and vent plumbing systems	29.4	25.3	33.3
Aluminum wiring	88.2	76.3	83.3

*Columns should not add to 100.

SOURCE: Survey of Building Departments, Center for Urban Policy Research, Winter 1976.

because of earlier installation problems, are innovations which show signs of gaining code approval.

JURISDICTIONAL VARIATION

Local control over code contents also creates interjurisdictional inefficiencies. This is reflected in increased costs to the developer, who must alter building plans to comply with the provisions of a specific municipality's ordinance in addition to limiting the use of mass-production economies. It also increases the costs to housing manufacturers, who must seek separate code approval in each municipality.

In an attempt to determine the scope of jurisdictional conflicts, our survey asked building officials to estimate the extent to which their code differed from those of the neighboring communities. (See Exhibit 5.7)

One-third of those communities with either state recommended or locally promulgated codes replied that "significant variation" existed between their codes and those used by neighboring communities. Not sur-

EXHIBIT 5.7

CODE VARIATION AMONG NEIGHBORING COMMUNITIES
(n=95)

Type of Code	Number of Municipalities	No Variation	Minor Variation	Significant Variation	Total
State-recommended code	(9)	11.1%	55.6%	33.3%	100%
State-mandated code	(7)	42.9	57.1	0.0	100.0
Model code	(73)	8.2	72.6	19.2	100.0
Locally promulgated code	(6)	0.0	66.7	33.3	100.0

SOURCE: Survey of Building Departments, Center for Urban Policy Research, Winter, 1976.

prisingly, the least variation was found among municipalities with state-mandated codes, although even in these municipalities administrative discretion appears to frequently result in minor variations. Results from model code jurisdictions were mixed. While 8.2 percent reported no variation, more than double that number stated that significant jurisdictional variation does exist.

The content of building codes plays a vital role in determining the efficiency of the regulatory system. While mandatory state codes have effected some improvement, particularly in eliminating jurisdictional discrepancies, significant problems remain.

IMPLEMENTATION OF CODES

Even an up-to-date code, if not properly administered by the building department, can result in unnecessary costs. Unnecessary delay and discretionary abuse by building officials are the two main problems encountered in implementing codes.

Lack of Administrative Coordination   A principal obstacle preventing an efficient building regulatory system is the myriad of municipal officials who must inspect and approve a structure before a certificate of occupancy can be issued. (See Exhibit 5.8)

More than half of the cities surveyed required approval by the plumbing inspector and the electrical inspector in addition to the building inspector. Not surprisingly, this lack of a coordinated evaluation procedure often results in unnecessary duplication and delay.

EXHIBIT 5.8

PARTICIPANTS IN THE BUILDING PERMIT APPROVAL PROCESS
(n=100)

Participant	Percent*
Building Inspector	100.0
Electrical Inspector	63.0
Plumbing Inspector	56.0
Plan Inspector	35.0
Mechanical Inspector	29.0
Zoning Inspector	12.0
Fire Inspector	11.0
State Officials	8.0
County Officials	5.0

*Will not add to 100 due to multiplicity of answers.

SOURCE: Survey of Building Departments, Center for Urban Policy Research, Winter 1976.

The Role of the Building Official   Building officials are predominantly recruited from the construction industry. The 1970 ICMA survey reported that over 75 percent of the Chief Building Officers were previously employed in construction related positions.[35] This fact suggests that building officials more readily accept construction products and techniques familiar to them from their own past experiences, and are reluctant to approve innovations.[36] This problem becomes accentuated the longer they have been away from the field, and the more technical the nature of newly introduced products. As performance standards replace specifications in code provisions, the technical expertise of the building official will become increasingly vital. For example, most model codes now include a *caveat* that gives local building officials the authority to "approve any such alternative provided he finds that the proposed design is satisfactory and complies with accepted design criteria."[37]

When confronted by novel design proposals, there are few reliable sources from which a building official may obtain the information necessary to pass judgement on the plan. While the model code groups do offer such a service to their members, our survey found that only 31.3 percent of the municipalities consulted this source. (See Exhibit 5.9) More frequently, officials tended to rely on their own experience, with its resultant status-quo orientation. Other important sources for judgement were tests conducted by independent laboratories, manufacturers' specifications and trade association reports. The extent to which these

EXHIBIT 5.9

BASIS FOR DETERMINING ACCEPTABILITY OF ITEMS
NOT SPECIFIED IN THE CODE
(n=99)

Source of Information	Percent*
Professional judgment of building officials	50.5
Tests conducted by independent labs	38.4
Recommendations from model code groups	31.3
Manufacturers' specifications	13.1
Tests conducted by trade associations	11.1
Government-promulgated standards	4.0

*Will not add to 100 due to multiplicity of responses.
SOURCE: Survey of Building Departments, Center for Urban Policy Research,
Winter 1976.

sources may be biased in their evaluation remains a question, as discussed
earlier. That they must be used by building officials clearly suggests a
weakness in the system.

Code Implementation in New York City   Two recent reports, one by the
New York Times and the other by New York's Department of Investigations have uncovered widespread corruption in the city's Building
Department. The Department of Investigation's undercover unit reported
that:

. . .we found virtually 100 percent of the City employees with whom we had con-
tact were directly involved in corrupt acts or had knowledge of their existence.[38]

The report estimated that the "average corrupt inspector or supervisor"
could at least double his salary through illicit cash payments.[39] The *New
York Times* report estimated that about 1 percent of total construction costs
or $25 million dollars annually was paid out as graft. Both these in-
vestigations noted that a considerable number of these bribes were not used
to get building officials to approve construction which falls below building
code standards. Rather developers simply wish to avoid harassment by
building officials and to avoid costly delays in obtaining the many approvals required during the construction process.

Estimating the Costs of Building Codes

Any attempt to put a dollar value on the cost impact of the building code
system is a matter of educated guesswork. Most commentators base their

estimates on interviews with builders and their general familiarity with the building code system. The previously mentioned estimates contained in the Kaiser Commission report of 1.5 to 7 percent of the price of a house are representative of this methodology. Other reports have incorporated various statistical manipulations in an attempt to isolate the costs of building codes. Muth and Wetzler's regression analysis produced a result of a 2 percent saving on the cost of construction if local codes were less restrictive.[40]

None of these attempts to estimate the unnecessary costs of building codes is particularly useful. They fail to pinpoint the specific aspects of the regulatory system by which these costs have been generated. Using a case study approach, the following section attempts to highlight the costs with each particular problem area. Excessive safety requirements, the product approval process, and the impact of codes on production efficiency will be detailed.

EXCESSIVE SAFETY REQUIREMENTS: FLORIDA AND COLORADO

The most straightforward method of estimating the costs of building codes is simply to add up the total dollars saved if unnecessary and excessive provisions were eliminated. While this underestimates the total costs of the regulatory system to the extent that administrative inefficiencies and the dampening effect on innovation are not included, it does provide a useful lower-range estimate. However, distinguishing code provisions that are necessary from those which exceed the scope of protecting the general welfare must be undertaken with great care.

The Florida Home Builders Association attempted this type of a cost analysis in their report, "Nice But Not Necessary."[41] They listed forty-two code provisions commonly found in local ordinances throughout the state. The suggested changes listed in Exhibit 5.10, along with thirty-seven others listed in the summary of their report, could result in a several thousand dollar reduction in the average price of a home — and according to the Florida Home Builders Association, little in the way of safety would be lost.

An analysis of changes in the last five years in building codes in Colorado shows a similar trend toward increased safety requirements.[42] (See Exhibit 5.11) Smoke detectors, flame retardant carpeting and increased insulation for appliances make for a safer living environment. But the price one pays for this added safety must necessarily result in a more expensive home. In this case, new code requirements amounted to $1,100 or 5 percent of the selling price of the typical house in Colorado.

EXHIBIT 5.10

"Nice But Not Necessary" Code Requirements

Item	Why Unnecessary	Saving/Unit
Ground fault interruptors	Only necessary on outside or near ground level outlets	$60-$135
Smoke detectors	Lack of efficiency; should be up to buyer	$35-$100
Fire rating wall and door between garage and living area	Should be up to buyer	$50
Placement of controls on rear of stove	May be outweighed by risk of reaching around stove top to use controls	$25-$35
Copper wiring	Aluminum wiring is adequate when properly installed	$100

Source: "Nice But Not Necessary," Florida Home Builders Association.

The Code Approval Process: The Story of Plastic Pipes

A new building product has little chance of gaining a foothold in the market unless it first is incorporated into building codes.[43] Nor is this a simple achievement; it can take many years and cost millions of dollars. While probably not typical of the approval process, the fate of plastic pipes serves as a warning of what may happen to those who seek to market a new building product.

Acrylonitrile-butadiene-styrene (ABS) pipe was invented by the U.S. Rubber Company in 1948.[44] Its first widespread use was in the mobile home industry, where it became an established feature as early as 1958. Two years later, the Federal Housing Authority (FHA) approved of its use for residential construction in drain, waste and vent (DWV) plumbing. It was not until 1966 that the first model code group, the Southern Building Code Congress, approved of its use for DWV plumbing. However, once model code approval is received, the war is still not won. It then becomes necessary for local governments, who are not obligated to adopt model code changes, to decide for themselves whether or not to accept this material. As shown by our code currency survey questions, roughly 30 percent of the municipalities sampled still prohibit the use of this material.

For many years, the Plastic Pipe Institute, in an attempt to gain regulatory acceptance of their product, has lobbied before such groups as

EXHIBIT 5.11

COLORADO CODE CHANGES: 1970-75

Requirement	Added Cost
An air intake duct from the outside to the furnace for heating combustion	$ 150
Increasing thickness of ceiling insulation from 4 inches to 8 3/4 inches and wall insulation from 1 1/2 inches to 4 inches	300
Storm or double glazed windows	250
Separate ground fault insulation circuit breakers for bathroom and outside circuits	50
Smoke detector	50
Flame retardant carpeting	50
New electrical and insulation requirements for installed appliances	50
Stricter compaction requirements around foundations and utility lines	50
Basement window large enough for fully equipped fireman to get through	50
Permits (building and installation)	100
Total	$1,100

SOURCE: Bickert, Browne, Coddington & Assoc., "The Impact of Government Intervention on the Home Building Process," p. 12.

model code meetings, state legislatures, Congress, and, most frequently, local building departments. They estimate that approximately $500,000 has been spent annually to support these lobbying efforts. Much of the resistance has been generated by the Cast Iron Soil Pipe Institute, the trade association for competitive pipes currently accepted by model codes.[45] Other dissenting voices were those of labor unions fearing that the ease of installing plastic pipe would eliminate their jobs. This illustration suggests that the administration of building codes has a significant dampening effect on innovation in the building materials industry.

The costs associated with product approval must ultimately be passed on to the consumer in the form of higher prices. But the risks and costs associated with new product approval are so great that only the most determined efforts by a competing industry can possibly be successful. An environment not conducive to attracting research and development funds has been created.

THE EFFECTS OF CODES ON PRODUCTION EFFICIENCY

It is extremely difficult to isolate the effect of building codes on production efficiency. While it is quite true that the housing industry has remained fragmented and labor intensive,[46] many factors other than codes contribute to this end. Also serving to inhibit any movement toward a more capital intensive industry are: weather conditions limiting the length of the production season; wide fluctuations in demand due to changes in economic conditions; and the high costs of transporting manufactured units.

Any specific estimate of the indirect costs associated with preventing increased production efficiency would be little more than guesswork. It is possible, however, to highlight the effects of building codes by comparing the past performance of the mobile home industry to that of the manufactured housing industry. A comparison aimed at isolating the effects of codes is potentially productive because until recently mobile home regulation had fallen outside the scope of local building code control, while manufactured housing had been included in the local code's jurisdiction.[47]

The past performances of the mobile home and manufactured housing industries have differed dramatically. Many mobile home companies have been highly profitable; have been able to produce a reasonably priced product; have achieved a high degree of automation; and have actively expanded their market. (See Exhibit 5.12) Meanwhile, the manufactured housing industry has failed to capture a significant part of the market. In several respects, local building codes have prevented these producers from taking advantage of the potential benefits of industrialized production. The existence of a multitude of local codes requires that a home manufacturer does one of two things: the firm can either set production to meet the strictest of requirements, and therefore achieve maximum savings from assembly line techniques, or it can alter production specifications as required to comply with local laws. Both alternatives necessarily involve increased costs.

The fragmented code system also acts to inhibit manufacturers from achieving the necessary market aggregation vital to large scale production and lower unit cost. Because they are forced to forego large capital investments, the production technique actually used by most home manufacturers is labor intensive and quite similar to that used for a conventionally built home, although it is carried out in a factory.[48] This method of manufacturing in part explains why these units have failed to achieve significant price economies over onsite construction.

Based on this analysis of the effects of codes on manufactured housing, it is not surprising that when surveyed both in 1955 and 1970, the home

EXHIBIT 5.12

A COMPARISON OF THE MOBILE HOME AND MANUFACTURED HOUSING
INDUSTRIES: 1974*

Characteristics	Mobiles	Manufactured Housing
Industry sales	330,000 units[1]	82,000 modular homes built[4]
Average price of unit	$7,770; this includes furnishings but excludes land or site rent[3]	Roughly comparable to conventionally built units[2]
Number of producers	350 companies[4]	200 companies[4]
Plant average production	500 units[4]	328 units[4]

*1974 data are used because it is the last year of production not influenced by the change to federal regulation of mobile homes.

NOTES: 1. *Construction Reports — Housing Starts,* Bureau of the Census. Since 1973 sales have suffered as part of the overall housing slump, but appear to be regaining their past strength.
2. The National Association of Home Manufacturers.
3. The Manufactured Housing Institute.
4. *Automation in Housing,* July/August 1975. Data for manufactured housing are limited only to those companies listed as modular producers.

manufacturers regarded building codes as their most significant problem.[49] Over half of the firms surveyed in 1970 responded that they believed codes added significantly to their costs of production.[50]

SUMMARY

The cost implications of building codes have been discussed in terms of requirements relating to excessive safety features, restrictions on the use of innovative materials and the prevention of the achievement of maximum production efficiencies. Since the recent slump in residential construction, government reform of building codes has surfaced in several areas. Innovative programs aimed at rectifying many of the past inadequacies shall now be examined.

Revamping the Building Code Systems

A principal deficiency in the existing code system is the inadequacy of the existing criteria upon which codes are based. Without a solid foundation of standards, the succeeding steps in the building code process cannot be effective. The federal government took what could be a major step forward in filling this void when, as part of the "Housing and Community Development Act of 1974," it created the National Institute of Building Sciences (NIBS). The primary function of NIBS is the:

> development, promulgation, and maintenance of nationally recognized performance criteria, standards and other technical provisions for maintenance of life, safety, health, and public welfare suitable for adoption by building regulating jurisdictions and agencies including test methods and other evaluative techniques relating to building systems, sub-systems, components products and materials with due regard for consumer problems.[51]

While NIBS's legislative mandate appears to be exactly what is needed to give building codes a more solid technical foundation, there remains some doubt as to whether this promise will ever be realized. Two years after its passage, some rumblings about appointing a Board of Directors have surfaced — only the first step in its development. President Ford's initial nominations have been criticized for being overrepresentative of industry and labor.[52] Nor has Congress appropriated the $5 million authorized for NIBS's first year's activities. Another potential problem is the emphasis within the Act to fully utilize the existing private and quasi-governmental institutions, such as testing laboratories and standard setting groups. Unless the rules of the game used by these groups are changed, the only result will be further government legitimization of self-regulation by private industry.

AN ECONOMIC IMPACT STATEMENT

Another step which would elucidate the essential cost-quality trade-off of building regulations is the requirement of the economic impact statement for code change decisions.[53] This methodology would weigh the costs of complying with a proposed requirement against the projected potential benefits in terms of property and lives saved. For example, before requiring the installation of ground fault interruptors, it would be necessary to estimate the total cost of installing these devices and compare this figure to the expected benefits from fewer injuries, deaths, and property loss due to electrocutions and fires.

THE NEW JERSEY UNIFORM STATE CONSTRUCTION ACT

Another major problem area involves local administration. An initial beneficial change should involve requiring a statewide mandatory code in which local amendments, if permitted, would be allowed only with state approval. New Jersey is among the several states which have moved in this direction.[54] By eliminating local control of code content, enforcement will become less arbitrary, while the problems of market aggregation caused by fractionated codes would also be significantly reduced.

Once a mandatory statewide code becomes law, the next administrative problem is the inadequacies of local officials. While this problem is not as significant because the control of code contents is no longer within local jurisdiction, other costs caused by administrative delay and inaccurate code interpretations still must be eliminated. The New Jersey Act tackles this problem by requiring minimum qualifications, certification and training of all building officials.

CONCLUSION

This analysis of building codes examined both the inherent inefficiencies in the use of this regulatory device and the problems encountered in implementation. The key weaknesses found to exist are the setting of standards (determining the cost-quality trade-off), the code change process, the local control of code contents, and insfficient administrative practices. These inadequacies impose on the housing consumer both direct costs, in terms of requiring excessive health and safety features, and indirect costs, in terms of preventing production efficiencies and innovation.

NOTES

1. In addition to the building code, which is principally concerned with the shell of the structure, local building departments also commonly administer plumbing and electrical codes. Since these operate in a similar fashion to the building code, for the purposes of this discussion, they will be grouped together and referred to as one building code.
2. For a thorough discussion of the problems created by building codes, see the National Commission on Urban Problems, (Paul Douglas, Chairman), *Building the American City,* (New York: Praeger Publishers, 1968), pp. 254-272.
3. S.W. Nunnally, *Reducing Florida's Housing Costs Through Building Code Reform,* 2 vols., Special Report #731, Engineering and Industrial Experiment Station (Gainesville, Florida: University of Florida 1973), Vol. 1, p. 4.
4. For a comprehensive description of the building code regulatory process, see Richard L. Sanderson, *Codes and Code Administration,* (Chicago: Building Officials Conference of America, Inc., 1969).
5. Alan D. Manvel, *Local Land and Building Regulation,* National Commission on Urban Problems, Research Report No. 6, (Washington, D.C.: U.S. Government Printing Office, 1968), p. 23.
6. Douglas Commission, *Building the American City,* p. 255.
7. Respectively, Ralph Johnson, "Housing Technology and Housing Costs," Technical Studies, Vol. II, p.57; and Leland Burns and Frank Mittlebach, "Efficiency in the Housing Industry," Vol. II, p. 133 in *The Report of the President's Committee on Urban Housing,* (Edgar Kaiser, Chairman), *A Decent Home,* 3 vols. (Washington, D.C.: U.S. Government Printing Office, 1968).

8. Allegations about the costs imposed by building codes abound. For example, a 1958 *House and Home* study estimated that code confusion costs consumers approximately $1 billion annually: "House and Home Roundtable Discussion ponders $1 billion-a-year cost of too many codes, proposes a simple 6 point program to speed reform," *House and Home,* July 1958, Vol. XIV, No. 1, p. 115. More recently, Charles Field and Steven Rivkin suggest a saving of greater than 8 percent if codes were reformed. *The Building Code Burden,* (Lexington, Massachusetts: Lexington Books, 1975), p. 11.

9. In the most general of terms, building codes fall within the police power and therefore seek to achieve the social goals of protecting the health, safety and general welfare of the public.

10. Similarly, building codes provide mortgage lenders with at least an implicit guarantee of the structural integrity of the unit they are financing. For an excellent discussion of the market impact of codes see Colin Green, "Context, Issues and Missions of Building Codes," Center for Advanced Study, (Urbana: University of Illinois, 1973).

11. Evelyn Cibula, *Product Approvals for Building: An International Review,* (Garston: Building Research Station, 1974).

12. For a thorough, although somewhat outdated, analysis of the legal issues surrounding building regulations see Charles Rhyne, *Survey of the Law of Building Codes,* (Washington, D.C.: American Institute of Architects and the National Association of Home Builders, 1960).

13. The four model codes are promulgated by the Building Officals' Conference of America (BOCA), the International Conference of Building Officials (ICBO), the Southern Standard Building Code Congress, and the American Insurance Association.

14. Only 2.2 percent of the municipalities were without some form of building code. Charles Field and Francis Ventre, "Local Regulation of Building: Agencies, Codes and Politics," *Municipal Year Book,* 1971, p. 143.

15. Office of Building Standards and Codes Service, "Status of Statewide Building Code Regulatory Programs," (Washington, D.C.: National Bureau of Standards, Nov. 1975).

16. For example, membership in one model group, the Building Officials' Conference of America, costs between $100-$200 annually depending on the size of the city. Additionally, BOCA's Basic Building Code itself sells for only $8.00. Few cities can afford the $1.5 million spent by New York City to update its own code. See Field and Ventre, "Local Regulation of Building," *Municipal Yearbook,* 1971, p. 146.

17. One and Two Family Dwelling Code, 2d. ed., (Danville, Illinois: Interstate Printers and Publishers, 1975).

18. Francis Ventre, "Maintaining Technological Currency in the Local Building Code: Patterns of Communication and Influence," *Urban Data Service Report* (Washington, D.C.: International City Managers Association, April, 1971), p. 3.

19. Only when a code change threatens the privileged position of another industry group will the sides be more evenly matched. The classic battle pitting the Plastic Pipe Institute against the Cast Iron Soil Pipe Institute is detailed in a later section of this report.

20. Letter on file at the Center for Urban Policy Research from Andrew Sabhlok, Executive Director of *Building Code Action,* a public interest group actively involved in building code reform, March 25, 1976.

21. David Falk, "Building Codes in a Nutshell," *Real Estate Review,* Vol. 5, No. 3, (Fall 1975), p. 83.
22. For example, the *One and Two Family Dwelling Code* provision governing the use of gypsum sheathing board refers to standard specification C79-67 promulgated by the American Society for Testing and Materials (ASTM), p. 173.
23. The government recognized clearinghouse for standards is the American National Standards Institute. Other leading standards setting groups are the American Society for Testing and Materials and such trade organizations as the American Plywood Association and the American Concrete Institute.
24. Schodek, Daniel, "Fire in Housing: Research on Building Regulations and Technology," Working Paper No. 38, (Cambridge, Mass.: Joint Center for Urban Studies, January 1976), p. 41.
25. David Hemenway, *Industrywide Voluntary Product Standards,* (Cambridge, Mass: Ballinger Publishing Company, 1975), p. 77.
26. National Commission on Fire Prevention and Control, *America's Burning* (Washington, D.C.: U.S. Government Printing Office, May 1973), p. 83. For a first attempt at more accurately understanding the causes of fire damage, see Frederic Clarke, III and John Ottoson, "Fire Death Scenarios and Fire Safety Planning," *Fire Journal,* (May 1976), p. 20.
27. Hemenway, *Industrywide Standards,* p. 88.
28. S.3555 introduced by Senators Hart and Abourezk,. See also *Congressional Record,* Vol. 122, No. 90, June 11, 1976, p. 3; and Hearings before the Subcommittee on Anti-Trust and Monopoly, 94th Congress, 2nd Session, *Voluntary Industrial Standards,* March 22, 23, 1976.
29. Lynda McDonnell, *Mobile Homes: The Low Cost Housing Hoax,* The Center for Auto Safety, (New York: Grossman Publishers, 1975).
30. Patrick W. Cooke, "State Building Regulatory Programs for Mobile Homes and Manufactured Buildings — A Summary," NBS Technical Note 853, (Washington, D.C.: National Bureau of Standards, 1974).
31. McDonnell, *Mobile Homes,* pp. 168-9.
32. See Title VI of the Housing and Community Development Act, Public Law 93-383; 42 U.S.C. 5301.
33. See respectively, National Commission on Urban Problems, *Building the American City,* p. 259, and Ventre, "Technological Currency," *Urban Data Service Reports,* p. 5.
34. Ventre, "Technological Currency," *Urban Data Service Reports,* p. 6.
35. Milton H. Grannatt and C. Thomas Sav, *Building Code Enforcement: Agencies and Officials,* Office of Building Standards and Codes Services, (unpublished report), (Washington, D.C.: National Bureau of Standards, 1973), p. 12. This report contains an updated analysis of the survey data gathered by Ventre.
36. Field and Ventre, "Local Regulation of Building," *Municipal Yearbook 1971,* p. 141.
37. *One and Two Family Dwelling Code,* p. 4.
38. A two year investigation was conducted by the Department of Investigation, City of New York, entitled "Preliminary Report to the Mayor on Findings of Corruption in the Construction Industry and in the Buildings Department" Nicholas Scoppetta, Commissioner, November 7, 1974. See also the reports on a six week investigation undertaken by the *New York Times*; David K. Shipler,

"Study Finds $25 Million Yearly in Bribes Is Paid by City's Construction Industry," June 26, 1976, col. 3, p. 1.

39. This poem was offered by one building department member during the course of a conversation about corrupt practices being held with other members of the department. It was recorded by one of the investigators.

"We stood eyeball to eyeball and toe to toe,
    Just for a moment it was almost touch and go.
    But he quickly changed his tactics,
    And with a filthy grin he said,
    Welcome Mister Inspector, won't you come in?
    He then went to his pocket,
    And a roll he then withdrew —
    Of brand new twenty dollar bills,
    And he offered me a few."

Department of Investigations, "Preliminary Report," p. 5.

40. Richard F. Muth and Elliot Wetzler, "The Effect of Constraints on House Costs," *Journal of Urban Economics,* Vol. 3, 1976, p. 64.

41. The Florida Home Builders Association, *Facts,* Vol. IV, No. 7, November, 1975, p. 1.

42. Bickert, Browne, Coddington & Assoc., Inc., "An Analysis of the Impact of State and Local Government Intervention on the Home Building Process in Colorado, 1970-75." Prepared for the Colorado Association for Housing and Building, (Denver, Colorado, 1976).

43. For an analysis of this aspect of Field and Ventre's data, see Sharon M. Oster and John M. Quickley, "Regulatory Barriers to the Diffusion of Innovation: Some Evidence from Building Codes," Institution for Social and Policy Studies, Working Paper 770, (New Haven: Yale University, 1976). They found that the educational level of the chief building officer and the degree of unionization in a municipality exert the strongest influence on the diffusion of innovative building code changes.

44. This and the following information was provided by Mr. A. B. Hunter, Southern Field Representative, Plastics Pipe Institute, Atlanta, Georgia. Letter from Mr. Hunter on file at the Center for Urban Policy Research, June 28, 1976.

45. See testimony by Mr. Jerome H. Heckman, Counsel to the Society of the Plastics Industry before the Subcommittee on Activities of Regulatory Agencies; *The Effect Upon Small Business of Voluntary Industrial Standards,* (Washington, D.C.: U.S. Government Printing Office, 1968), Vol. 2, pp. 670-714.

46. It is estimated that there are over 400,000 firms directly involved in construction. By relying heavily on subcontractors, capital investment can be minimized and entry and exit facilitated during fluctuations in demand. See, in general, Sumichrast and Frankel, *Profile of the Builder and his Industry,* (Washington, D.C.: National Association of Home Builders, 1970).

47. This situation has been radically altered over the past few years. Twenty-five states have just recently passed mandatory statewide manufactured-housing codes. See Cooke, et al., "State Building Regulatory Programs for Mobile Homes and Manufactured Buildings — A Summary," NBS Technical Note 853, National Bureau of Standards (Washington, D.C.: U.S. Government Prin-

ting Office, 1974). As previously stated, mobile home regulations, once controlled at the state level, now fall within the federal government's jurisdiction.

48. Field and Rivkin, *The Building Code Burden,* p. 30.
49. *Ibid.,* p. 5.
50. *Ibid.,* p. 98.
51. See Title VIII of the Housing and Community Development Act of 1974. Public Law 93-383; 42 U.S.C. 5301.
52. Bureau of National Affairs, "Current Developments," *Housing and Development Reporter,* Vol. 3, No. 26; May 17, 1976, p. 1188.
53. This methodology is currently being explored by Dr. John McConneghey, an economist at the National Bureau of Standards. A similar type of analysis is now being used as part of the review process adopted by the Consumer Product Safety Council in evaluating its decisions concerning changes in consumer goods.
54. The uniform State Construction Act was signed into law in October 1975 and took effect on January 1, 1977. For a summary of the history and contents of the Act, see Sidney Willis, *et al.,* "The Municipality's Role Under the New State Uniform Construction Code Act," *New Jersey Municipalities,* January, 1976, pp. 12-31.

Chapter Six:
The Effect of Energy Conservation Regulations on Housing Costs

In October of 1973, the Arab oil embargo brought to light the seriousness of this country's energy problems. Yet this crisis must be viewed only as the nudge which stirred the sleeping giant — for too long a time we had been wasteful in our use of energy and increasing our dependence on foreign oil supplies. The reduction in that supply and its increase in cost have forced us to recognize our past excesses. For housing, this recognition principally means the construction of units that use and conserve energy more efficiently. Since late 1973, considerable government activity has been focused on reducing the energy consumption by residential units. The cold of "the Winter of 1977" has emphasized the need for such activity.

This chapter discusses the potential effectiveness of government activity in the area of residential energy conservation. Particular attention is paid to the costs of energy saving measures and their impact on the housing market. The first section of this chapter presents baseline data on the costs of residential heating. The second section discusses the market reaction to these price increases. The third section describes specific government programs, both at the state and federal level, aimed at conserving energy. Finally the cost effectiveness of these policies will be examined.

High Energy Costs and the Housing Market

The historical price trends for fossil fuel and electricity (80 percent of which is produced from fossil fuels) suggest several significant occurrences. From 1953-1970, the price of fuel and utilities increased at the average of 1.7 percent each year. The prices of other consumer goods and services moved upward at an average rate of 2.7 percent per year. During 1971, this trend had reversed, and the prices of fossil fuels and electricity have been increasing more than twice as fast (11.2 percent compared to 4.0 percent) as prices of other consumer goods and services.[1] It was the relative inexpensiveness of energy compared to other inputs prior to 1971, which is responsible for our increasing dependence on this good. It should also be noted that the price had begun to increase prior to the Arab oil embargo and that this political crisis only quickened the rate of increase.

ENERGY AS A PERCENT OF OPERATING COSTS

The impact of the increase in the price of electricity and fossil fuels is illustrated by the change in the operating cost breakdown of a single-family unit. (See Exhibit 6.1) In the five year span from 1970 to 1975, heating and utility costs have increased from $26.51 to $42.52 per month. This 60 percent climb is greater than that of either debt service or taxes and insurance. Because these figures are for FHA insured homes, which have mandated minimum insulation requirements as part of its Minimum Property Standards, they no doubt tend to underestimate the total energy use increase for all conventional housing. Since they also represent a national average, the larger increases in costs for the northeast region are somewhat mitigated.

A similar increase has been experienced in the utility costs of operating a garden apartment. (See Exhibit 6.2) Between 1970 and 1974, fuel bills have increased by 14.5 percent annually, compared to only a 5.7 percent annual increase for the previous four year span. As a percentage of total operating costs, utilities have increased from 21 percent to 26 percent over the entire eight year study period.

The Market Response to Higher Prices

One would expect that even without government intervention higher utility costs would lead to the construction of more energy efficient units. In areas where builders are incorporating energy saving features in their construction plans, they have become a primary selling point.[2] But for the most part, because of significant market impediments, there has been little voluntary movement toward an energy efficient unit. The reasons for this failure,

EXHIBIT 6.1

TOTAL MONTHLY HOUSING EXPENSES FOR SINGLE FAMILY HOMES

	1970	1971	1972	1973	1974	1975	% Increase (1970–1975)
Debt Service	$136.34	$135.07	$133.85	$129.60	$164.19	$203.18	49%
	(65.6%)	(63.2%)	(60.5%)	(59.6%)	(63.6%)	(64.7%)	
Real Estate Taxes and Insurance	$ 34.22	$ 38.93	$ 41.30	$ 39.47	$ 41.38	$ 48.45	42%
	(16.4%)	(18.2%)	(18.7%)	(18.2%)	(16.0%)	(15.4%)	
Maintenance and Repairs	$ 10.91	$ 11.70	$ 13.57	$ 15.02	$ 16.36	$ 20.05	84%
	(5.2%)	(5.5%)	(6.1%)	(6.9%)	(6.3%)	(6.4%)	
Heating and Utilities	$ 26.51	$ 28.13	$ 32.56	$ 33.37	$ 36.38	$ 42.52	60%
	(12.8%)	(13.1%)	(14.7%)	(15.3%)	(14.1%)	(13.5%)	
Total	$207.98	$213.83	$221.28	$217.46	$258.31	$314.20	51%

SOURCE: U.S. Dept. of Housing and Urban Development, FHA Trends of Home Mortgage Characteristics 203(b), "Average Monthly Payment Characteristics," 1970, 1975.

EXHIBIT 6.2

THE CHANGING PICTURE OF
GARDEN APARTMENT OPERATING EXPENSES
1966-1974

Expense	1966* % of Total Operating Expenses	Annual Percent Change (Simple) 1966-1970	1970* % of Total Operating Expenses	Annual Percent Change (Simple) 1970-1974	1974* % of Total Operating Expenses
Operations	27.0	(4.2)	31.0	(9.3)	31.0
Utilities	21.0	(5.7)	23.0	(14.5)	26.0
Maintenance and Repairs	16.0	(3.9)	16.0	(15.3)	19.0
Taxes and Insurance	36.0	(-2.0)	30.0	(1.1)	24.0
Total	100.0	(2.9)	100.0	(8.9)	100.0

*n = 18,655 unit — National Sample (Garden, Unfurnished, Year Built 1961-1966)

SOURCE: Derived from Institute of Real Estate Management, *Income/Expense Analysis: Apartments, Condominiums and Cooperatives*, Chicago, 1975. As cited in George Sternlieb, et al, "The Private Sector's Role in the Provision of Reasonably Priced Housing" in *Resources for Housing*, Proceedings of the First Annual Conference, Federal Home Loan Bank Board of San Francisco, 1976, p. 219.

both from the builder's position (supply side of the market) and from the prospective buyer's standpoint (demand), will next be detailed.

THE DEMAND FOR ENERGY EFFICIENT UNITS

There are several ways to conserve energy in residences but, aside from simply turning down the thermostat, such changes as additional insulation, alterations in design and construction techniques, and the utilization of energy conservation devices all result in an increase in the purchase price of the home. Traditional design of residences, as well as of all construction, is aimed at the lowest initial cost, speed of construction and ease of marketability, and *not* for minimum occupancy or operating costs.[3] Above all, it is the low initial cost for which the housing consumer is shopping. Although savings can accrue over a period of years from the intallation of a more costly energy conservation system, the homebuyer is still attracted to the product with the lowest purchase price for a number of reasons.

The first and most important reason for this attraction is availability of a mortgage. As the price of a home increases, the mortgage, the down-payment required and the financing charges increase accordingly. The real difficulty of obtaining the necessary capital to purchase the house is now compounded with the need to raise additional capital to pay for the investments which promise future savings. Given the current "ability to pay" criterion of financing institutions, it is obvious that many homebuyers, particularly those of previously marginal credit risk, would be excluded altogether from the new home market.

A second reason a prospective homebuyer is less concerned with energy costs is the lack of familiarity with the concept of life-cycle costing. A study by Fraker and Schacker at Princeton University points out that many buyers did not consider energy operating costs of prime importance in the selection of a home, but were more concerned with low purchase price, low down payment and easy accessibility to place of work.[4] And this is consonant with lifetime earning patterns — if not lifetime operating costs. As Professor Robert Socolow adds, "Most home purchasers are young and have rising income, so that their operational discount rate is considerably higher than society's as a whole."[5] This suggests that as a group, young homebuyers are less willing to spend money at the present time to achieve possible savings in the future.

Finally, a more basic reason for the attractiveness of low initial low price tag is that the buyer knows what the purchase price is and what the mortgage terms are, while savings to be gained through lower fuel bills are in the future, and therefore uncertain.

THE SUPPLY OF ENERGY EFFICIENT UNITS

From the builder's viewpoint there is little reason to provide an energy saving unit, if consumer demand is weak. As was previously suggested, because of the higher initial cost, such construction would actually result in a competitive disadvantage with other, less energy efficient units.

But in addition to this lack of demand, other industry characteristics have also acted to limit the provision of a more energy efficient unit. These were summarized as follows in a Government Accounting Office report to Congress:

1. The fragmented character of the housing industry tends to slow any introduction of change in the construction process;
2. Builders are reluctant to experiment with new products and techniques because they are perceived as being risky under many market conditions, and financial institutions are reluctant to grant mortgages for these innovations;

3. Slow growth in housing technology because of the existence of a vast number of divergent and restrictive state and local building codes.[6]

In summary, the market mechanism cannot be relied upon to ensure the reduction of energy consumption in residential use. Purchasers are not particularly interested in the lifecycle cost savings obtainable through initial expenditures on energy survey measures. This reasoning can be attributable to the existing mortgage criteria whereby high initial costs will exclude the marginally qualified family from the housing market and because increased operating costs are less onerous over time as family income also increases.

Government's Role in Energy Conservation

To reduce the impact of increased energy prices on the consumer and to achieve the national goal of energy independence, government activity in energy conservation has increased significantly. Several different approaches have been used. Government informational programs are attempting to increase consumer awareness of the benefits of an energy efficient home. Financial incentives (tax credits) for the installation of energy saving devices are written into tax laws, and, in some instances, regulations require the installation of these devices. Most of these activities have taken the form of the federal government providing financial incentives to the states to take action. The various programs affecting housing both at the federal and state level, and the costs associated with them, shall now be detailed.

FEDERAL ACTIVITY

Educational Programs   The Federal Energy Administration has instituted various consumer education programs directed toward voluntary energy conservation. "Operation Button-Up" provides information to individuals on the benefits of remodeling homes for energy efficiency. This program also involves the mobilization of local organizations to help achieve energy conservation. "Project Conserve" aids individuals in identifying specific actions that should be taken in their homes. Homeowners complete a questionnaire for computer analysis and receive specific recommendations for saving energy, from lowering thermostats to installing added insulation.

The National Bureau of Standards (NBS) published two pamphlets for consumers: "7 Ways to Reduce Fuel Consumption in Household Heating Through Energy Conservation" and "11 Ways to Reduce Energy Consumption and Increase Comfort in Household Cooling." NBS also periodically distributes leaflets entitled "Home Energy Saving Tips from NBS."

Providing Financial Incentives A number of bills have been introduced in Congress proposing tax credit incentives to homeowners for incorporating energy conservation improvements. Of the bills which have progressed the furthest, one is the "Energy Conservation and Conversion Act of 1975" (H.R. 6860) which passed the House on June 17,1975, and is presently in the Senate Finance Committee. Included within its provisions is a tax credit for home insulation and solar energy equipment.[7]

A second bill, the "Energy Conservation in Buildings Act of 1975" (HR8650), would establish a program of grants to assist low-income persons in insulating their homes.[8] Low interest loans for the installation of solar equipment were also proposed, but did not appear in the bill approved by the House.

After months of debate Congress passed the "Energy Conservation and Production Act" which was signed into law on August 14, 1976.[9] This act provides funding for several housing-related programs:

1. A three-year, $200 million grant program to be administered by the Federal Energy Administration to help low-income persons weatherize their homes,
2. A $200 million energy conservation demonstration program, to be administered by HUD, to encourage other homeowners to insulate their homes or install energy-conserving equipment,
3. A three-year, $105 million program to be administered at the state level through FEA to provide owners of homes and other buildings with information on the costs and benefits of energy conservation.

In addition, Title III of the Act requires HUD to promulgate energy conservation performance standards for new residential buildings. To facilitate their implementation, grants will be made to state and local governments adopting these programs.

On December 22, 1975, President Ford signed the "Energy Policy and Conservation Act."[10] This act authorizes the expenditure of $150 million over the next three years to assist states in voluntarily developing and implementing energy conservation plans. Each state plan must include certain elements, one of which is mandatory thermal efficiency standards and insulation requirements for new and renovated buildings.[11] Each state is to consider all energy conservation measures with a goal of reducing the projected 1980 energy consumption level by 5 percent.

Minimum Property Standards (MPS) and Energy Conservation The MPS, mandatory in all FHA insured homes, are not intended to serve as a substitute for building codes; they were originally "intended to describe those characteristics in a property which will assure present and continuing utility, durability, and desirability as well as compliance with basic safety and health requirements."[12] Energy conservation was not an objective until 1971, when additional insulation was required for that purpose.

Although federally insured new housing only made up 23 percent of all new housing in 1975,[13] the MPS actually have a broader application. In 1975, in a survey of builders throughout the country, the General Accounting Office found that "even though the MPS are required for the federally insured new housing, builders are generally building all their housing to HUD standards to qualify their housing for any type of financing (federal or private) that a homebuyer chooses,"[14] A summary chart of the results of that survey is presented here. (See Exhibit 6.3) The MPS require new housing to have storm doors and windows in areas where the annual heating degree days total 4,500 or more. A heating degree day is defined as the amount by which the average temperature falls below 65°F during the heating season. In general, many builders included storm doors and windows in those areas, while others made them optional. It would appear that these regulations, although only mandatory for a quarter of the new housing, have a much broader impact on the housing industry.

State Activity

Born in the era of "the new federalism," energy conservation has been deemed by the federal government to be within the domain of state control. In an analysis of Congressional legislation, it seems clear that federal activity will concentrate on increasing the supply of domestic energy through

EXHIBIT 6.3

Survey Of Builders' Compliance With MPS
(percentages)

Insulation Areas	Exceeding HUD Standards	Same as HUD Standards	Total Exceeding or Equaling HUD Standards
Ceiling	25.6	58.9	84.5
Outside Wall	7.7	76.9	84.6
Between Floors & Unheated Areas	46.2	15.4	61.5
Crawl Spaces	5.1	20.5	25.6
Duct Work in Unheated Areas	10.3	30.8	41.1

Source: Report to Congress from Comptroller General of the U.S., *Energy Conservation Standards*, June 1975, Appendix I, pp. 29–30.

research and development incentives, while the reduction of demand through energy conservation will be carried out only in a limited and voluntary manner and primarily at the state level.

States have the authority to enforce conservation policies through the police power. Thus, the relationship between the federal and state governments in the area of energy conservation assumes a form similar to that of air and water pollution control. Congress might require a minimum level of conservation efforts (e.g., a 5 percent reduction by 1980) and leave to the states the decision of implementation strategies more sensitive to local conditions and values.

While the Federal government must maintain the dominant role in the determination of overall energy policy, many of the states have taken the initiative in the advancement of energy conservation programs. New Jersey is typical in that it sees itself as having an educational and regulatory function in reducing the demand for energy.[15] A task force report recognized that buildings vary greatly in their energy efficiency and that most of the building codes applicable in the state contained little about energy conservation. The report recommended the adoption of a statewide building code and the addition of an energy conservation component which would include performance and design standards to be applied to all new residential, commercial and some industrial structures. The report also recommended the creation of a state department of energy, which, among other functions, would prepare an energy conservation amendment and a monitoring system to appraise the state's energy situation, with the underlying objective being to make the public aware that there is a genuine need to conserve energy.[16]

Although there has been a considerable amount of state legislation proposed for energy conservation in buildings, only a few states have actually adopted regulations that require energy saving devices or techniques. A 1976 survey of building energy authority and regulations by the National Bureau of Standards showed that only seven states have energy regulations, and in only five are they applicable to single-family residences.[17]

States having passed such legislation are California, Minnesota, North Carolina, Oregon and Virginia. (See Exhibits 6.4 and 6.5) Of these five only California has a separate energy authority responsible for administering the regulations; the other states rely on a statewide building code authority as the vehicle for energy conservation regulation. Fourteen states are considering adoption of a model energy regulation, or are using it for developing guidelines with modification and deletions. Among these are North Carolina, Oregon and Virginia which already have their own regulations, but are considering the broader standard.

EXHIBIT 6.4

SUMMARY OF STATE ENERGY CONSERVATION REGULATIONS

State	Enacted	Proposed	STATUS Considering ASHRAE 90-75	No Activity	COVERAGE Single Family	Multi- Family
Alabama				X		
Alaska		X				
Arizona		X				
Arkansas				X		
California	X^a	X			X	X
Colorado						X
Connecticut		X	X			
Delaware		X				
Florida		X	X			
Georgia		X				
Hawaii		X				
Idaho		X				
Illinois		X				
Indiana		X	X			
Iowa		X				
Kansas		X	X			
Kentucky				X		
Louisiana		X				
Maine		X				
Maryland		X	X			
Massachusetts		X	X^b			
Michigan		X	X			
Minnesota	X				X	X
Mississippi				X		
Missouri				X		
Montana			X			
Nebraska				X		
Nevada		X			X	X
New Hampshire		X				
New Jersey		X	X			
New Mexico		X				
New York		X			X	X
No. Carolina	X		X		X	X
No. Dakota		X				
Ohio	X					X
Oklahoma				X		
Oregon	X		X		X	X
Pennsylvania		X				
Rhode Island		X	X			
So. Carolina		X	X			
So. Dakota		X				
Tennessee		X				
Texas		X				
Utah		X				
Vermont		X				
Virginia	X		X		X	X
Washington		X			X^c	X
W. Virginia		X				
Wisconsin		X			X^d	X
Wyoming		X				

NOTES: (a) Non-residential regulation under development in the Energy Resources Conservation and Development Commission

          (b) Adopted ASHRAE 90-75 effective January 1, 1976, but State Building Code Commission placed an indefinite moratorium on that action

          (c) Thermal insulation standards in statewide code vetoed by Governor; waiting for Uniform Building Code to adopt thermal standards

          (d) Regulations suspended by Legislative Joint Committee for Review of Administration Roles

SOURCE: *Building Energy Authority and Regulation Survey: State Activity*, National Bureau of Standards, March 1976.

EXHIBIT 6.5

SUMMARY OF PROMULGATED STATE REGULATIONS

State	Date Effective	Coverage	Authority	Type	Nature
California	Feb. 22, 1975	All Buildings	State Energy Resources Conservation and Development Commission	Prescriptive	• Maximum U-value for Components • Glazing Limitations • Weatherstripping
Minnesota	Jan. 30, 1975	All Buildings	Statewide Building Code	Performance	• Maximum U-value for entire building • Maximum Energy Consumption Level
North Carolina	Jan. 1, 1975	Residential Bldgs. of 3 or less stories	Statewide Building Code	Prescriptive	• Maximum U-value for Components • Weatherstripping
Ohio	June 1, 1976	All buildings except 1, 2, 3 family residential	Statewide Building Code	Performance	• Maximum Allowable Energy Load (Btuh)
Oregon	July 1, 1974	Residential Bldgs. of 3 or less stories	Statewide Building Code	Prescriptive	• Maximum U-value for Components
Virginia	Jan. 15, 1976	All Residential Buildings	Statewide Building Code	Prescriptive	• FHA Minimum Property Standards

SOURCE: *Building Energy Authority and Regulations Survey: State Activity*, National Bureau of Standards, March 1976.

In addition to individual states, the model building code organizations are considering adopting standard 90-75 promulgated by the American Society of Heating, Refrigeration and Air Conditioning Engineers (ASHRAE) either in its entirety or in a revised form. Since many of the states rely on these model codes for direction, their adoption of this standard could facilitate the addition of energy conservation regulations to the state codes. For example, Virginia has adopted the FHA Minimum Property Standards as an interim measure while waiting for BOCA, in its model code, to adopt a revised form of ASHRAE 90-75. In June, 1976 BOCA approved the revision and Virginia now plans to discuss its adoption in its next legislative session. The International Congress of Building Officials, another of the model codes, has also endorsed the ASHRAE standard.

In California, the State Energy Resources Conservation and Development Commission has been given the power to regulate and adopt energy conservation standards in all new buildings. Concerning residential construction, energy insulation standards have been included in Title 25 of the California Administrative Code, and became effective on February 22, 1975. These standards are prescriptive in nature and require minimum insulation standards and maximum U-values for individual components of various types of residential construction. A change in the standard, effective April 18, 1975, permits an increase in the U-value of certain components in exchange for a decrease in others, so that the "overall heat gain or heat loss of the building does not exceed the total resulting from conformance to the stated U-values."[18] This gives the developer, architect or engineer the flexibility and opportunity to choose a less costly method of construction.

Two other states, Oregon and North Carolina, also have very similar prescriptive standards with almost identical U-values for each component. In Oregon, the Energy Conservation Board was created in September of 1975 to adopt rules to provide for maximum energy conservation in design, construction and repair of buildings. The standards in Oregon have been effective since July 1, 1974 and are implemented and enforced through a statewide building code. North Carolina also uses a statewide code but relies on a joint committee of representatives from both the state and private industry to recommend energy conservation regulations to be adopted by the State Building Code Commission. The current standards were effective as of January 1, 1975.

Nevada has mandatory minimum insulation standards established by the Public Service Commission, applicable to all public and private buildings, effective since May 17, 1975.

Virginia has a mandatory statewide code and has adopted the Minimum Property Standards of the Federal Housing Administration effective from January 15, 1976.

Minnesota is unique in that, effective January 30, 1976, it has adopted the only performance-oriented energy conservation code which is applicable to all new residential buildings as well as additions, alterations, and repairs to existing buildings. In this case, each building is given an overall maximum U-value which is the sum total of U-values for various components. This allows for flexibility in design because the insulation can vary in each component (e.g., an increase in opaque wall insulation can offset a decrease in door thickness).

The Costs of Energy Conservation

There is no simple, clear-cut method for evaluating the costs of energy conservation requirements. While it is possible to calculate the expenditures made on extra insulation and double glazed windows and to compare these costs to the savings from reduced utility bills, this only tells part of the story. It fails to include the cost to those families excluded from the housing market because of higher initial costs due to energy saving changes. A second shortcoming of such calculation is its failure to consider the changes in a homeowner's income over the life cycle of his/her tenure in that residence.

As our survey of the states suggested the primary mechanism for implementing energy conservation requirements has been through a building code type regulation. The National Conference of States on Building Codes and Standards requested the National Bureau of Standards to develop technical criteria to serve as a foundation for such a standard. The American Society of Heating, Refrigeration, and Air Conditioning Engineers (ASHRAE) was then requested to prepare a regulatory standard (based on the NBS report) that would eventually be accepted as a national standard. This standard addresses single- and multi-family residences and commercial buildings, and pertains specifically to energy conservation aspects of the building. ASHRAE 90-75 is basically a specification standard and covers the components of the building shell, the heating, cooling, and ventilation equipment, lighting and systems control equipment. The standard is not mandatory, but it is expected to provide a starting point for states and communities to make their codes more energy efficient.

According to an NBS survey, fourteen states are actively considering adopting 90-75, most with only slight modifications.[19] Much of the opposition to the adoption of this as a national code is focused on the fact that it is a specification, and therefore of a restrictive nature, rather than being performance-oriented.

THE COST OF ASHRAE 90-75

In a study sponsored by the Federal Energy Administration in 1975, Arthur D. Little, Inc. of Boston issued a report on the impact of implementation of ASHRAE 90-75.[20] This study shows that there are savings possible with the use of energy conservation standards. The results of the study show that single-family units would increase in price by $384, but the energy saved would offset this price hike in 3.4 years. (See Exhibit 6.6)

EVALUATING THE COSTS OF ENERGY CONSERVATION REQUIREMENTS

In 1971, John C. Moyers conducted a study of the value of thermal insulation in residential construction and calculated the net savings to the consumer realizable through the addition of storm windows and various levels of insulation. In the study, Moyers concluded that the economically optimum amount of insulation is greater than the regulations prescribed.[21] The optimum point is one at which additional construction costs are minimized and annual savings are maximized so as to get the shortest possible payback period. He also showed that a requirement for the inclusion of storm windows and foil insulation is economically justifiable for most areas of the county.

EXHIBIT 6.6

COST IMPACT OF ASHRAE 90-75

Type of Construction	Additional Design Cost	Annual Energy Savings	Straight Payback
Single family detached (1500 ft^2)	$ 384	$ 112	3.4 years
Low Rise Apt. (18,000 ft^2)	1,620	5,580	3.5 months
Office Bldg. (40,000 ft^2)	6,400	16,000	4.8 months
Retail Store (32,400 ft^2)	2,916	22,032	1.6 months
School (40,000 ft^2)	6,000	28,000	2.6 months

SOURCE: A. D. Little, Inc., *An Impact Assessment of ASHRAE 90-75*, pp. 5-7.

In evaluating this finding, it is important to consider the changes that have taken place since 1971. The optimal point is extremely sensitive to the price of energy, as well as other factors, such as morgage rate and installation costs. An increase in the price of energy, especially electricity, would tend to make the optimal design one with greater levels of insulation and control of fenestration than indicated by Moyers.[22] Also, if the mortgage rate and/or installation and material costs have increased to a greater extent than the price of energy, the savings due to energy conservtion would be reduced. Moyers's study was based on the 1965 MPS, but since then the requirements have been altered several times, the latest change occurring in 1974. To determine the effect of the new standards on construction costs and energy savings, Moyers's methodology was employed in a recent report presented to the Committee on Banking, Housing and Urban Affairs. (See Exhibit 6.7) This analysis showed various payback periods both for region of the country and for different energy sources. The longest payback periods, extending to over thirteen years, were found in the warmer climates where gas heat was in use. The shortest payback periods, and therefore those areas best suited for energy code requirements, were the northern cities where electric and oil heat predominated.

In addtion to Moyers's study, the federal government has sponsored a number of studies on the costs and benefits of energy saving techniques and devices. Hittman Associates of Columbia, Maryland, was contracted by HUD to assess the impact of certain energy saving components. This report concluded that energy consumption in existing single-family residences can be reduced as much as 36 percent with the incorporation of such devices as storm windows and doors, extra insulation, and weatherstripping.[23] The cost of these components was $965 but the annual operating savings was $150. So in 6.4 years the consumer's initial investment would have been paid back.

SUMMARY

While it is difficult to ascertain the specific costs associated with each state regulation, the various studies showing the effect of energy conservation measures do conclude that savings in fuel costs are possible; and that these savings will be recouped over a period of several years. Trends in energy supply and demand would seem to indicate that prices will continue to increase and certainly energy conservation is a logical response to reduce the impact of higher prices. The issue remains, however, as to what is the most efficient means of achieving energy conservation. A mandatory policy without some tax benefits or other method for reducing the initial cost impact of conservation measures would prove quite burdensome to consumers

EXHIBIT 6.7

COMPARISON OF THE CURRENT FHA THERMAL STANDARDS
WITH THOSE PREVIOUSLY IN EFFECT:
CONSTRUCTION COST AND ENERGY SAVINGS

	Increased Construction Cost	Increase in Annual Payments	Annual Fuel Cost Savings	Net Annual Savings	Straight Payback
Atlanta					
Gas Heat Electric Cool	$ 193.33	$ 19.64	$ 14.97	$ -4.67	12.9 years
Oil Heat Electric Cool	$ 193.33	$ 19.64	$ 23.93	$ 4.29	8.1 years
Electric Heat Electric Cool	$ 160.43	$ 16.29	$ 29.07	$ 12.78	5.5 years
New York					
Gas Heat Electric Cool	$ 943.43	$ 94.91	$108.09	$ 13.18	8.7 years
Oil Heat Electric Cool	$ 943.43	$ 94.91	$164.71	$ 69.80	5.7 years
Electric Heat Electric Cool	$ 768.71	$ 78.08	$312.83	$234.75	2.5 years
Minneapolis					
Gas Heat Electric Cool	$ 296.03	$ 30.07	$ 31.76	$ 1.69	9.3 years
Oil Heat Electric Cool	$ 296.03	$ 30.07	$ 54.96	$ 24.89	5.4 years
Electric Heat Electric Cool	$ 232.42	$ 23.61	$ 66.03	$ 42.42	3.5 years
Seattle					
Gas Heat Electric Cool	$1129.74	$114.75	$177.73	$ 62.98	6.4 years
Oil Heat Electric Cool	$1129.74	$114.75	$289.28	$174.53	3.9 years
Electric Heat Electric Cool	$ 893.93	$ 90.80	$127.03	$ 36.23	7.0 years
Los Angeles					
Gas Heat Electric Cool	$ 105.99	$ 10.76	$ 7.86	$ -2.90	13.5 years
Oil Heat Electric Cool	$ 105.99	$ 10.76	$ 15.25	$ 4.49	7.0 years
Electric Heat Electric Cool	$ 88.51	$ 8.99	$ 18.27	$ 9.28	4.8 years

NOTE: Basis of calculation:
30-year, 9 percent mortgage   1,800 ft.^{2} floor area
2.5 percent property tax rate   260 ft.^{2} window area
0.4 percent insurance cost   1974 average utility prices
2.5 percent income tax rate

SOURCE: Hearings on Emergency Housing & Housing Energy before Senate
Committee on Banking, Housing and Urban Affairs, February
13, 1975.

and result in further dampening new housing activity. The continued use of a voluntary conservation program, however, for the several reasons discussed in this chapter, is doomed to failure. Thus it appears that some mandatory steps must be taken. It is hoped, however, that this additional area of government intrusion will consider its potential impact on the housing market and on housing consumers.

NOTES

1. U.S. Department of Labor, Bureau of Labor Statistics, *Handbook of Labor Statistics, 1975* (Washington, D.C.: Government Printing Office, 1975), pp. 313-342.
2. June R. Vollman, "Saving Energy: How Builders are Doing It . . . and Selling It," *House and Home,* (April 1976), p. 62.
3. Harrison Fraker and Elizabeth Schacker, *Energy Husbandry in Housing: An Analysis of the Development Process in a Residential Community, Twin Rivers, New Jersey,* Princeton University, Center for Environmental Studies Report No. 5 (Princeton: 1973), p. 45.
4. *Ibid.,* pp. 71-7.
5. Robert Socolow, "Energy Conservation in Housing: Concepts and Opinions," in *Future Land Use,* ed. Robert W. Burchell and David Listokin, (New Brunswick: Center for Urban Policy Research, Rutgers University, 1975), p. 314.
6. Comptroller General of the United States, *Report to Congress on National Standards Needed for Residential Energy Conservation,* (Washington, D.C.: General Accounting Office, 1975), p. 5.
7. U.S. Congress, House, *A Bill to Provide a Comprehensive National Energy Conservation Program,* H.R. 6860, 94th Cong., 1st sess., 1975.
8. U.S. Congress, House, *A Bill to Assist Low Income Persons in Insulating Their Homes, to Facilitate State and Local Adoption of Energy Conservation Standards for New Buildings, and to Direct the Secretary of Housing and Urban Development to Undertake Research and to Develop Energy Conservation Performance Standards,* H.R. 8650, 94th Cong., 1st sess., 1975.
9. For a summary of the provisions of the Act see Bureau of National Affairs, "Current Developments," *Housing and Development Reporter,* Vol. 4, No. 6, (August 6, 1976), p. 231.
10. "Energy Policy and Conservation Act," (1975).
11. *Ibid.,* Sec. 362 (c)(4).
12. "Minimum Property Standards for One and Two Family Living Units," FHA No. 300, Rev. January 1965.
13. U.S. Department of Commerce, Bureau of the Census, *Construction Reports, New One Family Houses Sold and For Sale,* March, 1976.
14. *Report to Congress on Standards for Energy Conservation,* p. 14.
15. "Energy," New Jersey Task Force Report, (Trenton, N.J.: May 1974), p. 59.
16. *Ibid.,* p. 117.
17. Robert M. Eisenhard, *Building Energy Authority and Regulations Survey: State Activity,* Office of Building Standards and Code Services, National Bureau of Standards, (Washington, D.C.: U.S. Government Printing Office), (March, 1976), pp. 8-44.

18. California, *Administrative Code*, Title 25, Chapter 1, Subchapter 1, Article 5, Section 1094, as reported in Department of Housing and Community Development Information Bulletin, SHL 75-3, April 11 1975.

19. U.S. Department of Commerce, National Bureau of Standards, *Building Energy Authority and Regulation Survey: State Activity*, by Robert M. Eisenhard (Washington, D.C.: U.S. Government Printing Office, 1976), p. 3.

20. Arthur D. Little, Inc., *An Impact Assessment of ASHRAE Standard 90-75, Energy Conservation in New Building Design*, (December, 1975), pp. 5-7.

21. John C. Moyers, *Value of Thermal Insulation in Residential Construction: Economics and the Conservation of Energy*, Oak Ridge National Laboratory Report, ORNL-NSF-EP-9, (Oak Ridge: 1971).

22. Charles A. Berg, "Conservation via Effective Use of Energy at the Point of Consumption," in *Energy: Demand Conservation and Institutional Problems*, ed. Michael S. Macrakis, (Cambridge, Mass.: MIT Press, 1974).

23. U.S., Dept. of Housing and Urban Development, *Residential Energy Conservation*, Hittman Associates, Report 76, HUD-HAI-1, (Washington, D.C.: U.S. Government Printing Office, 1975).

Chapter Seven: The Effect of Subdivision Regulations on Housing Costs

Subdivision Regulations and Housing Costs

Subdivision regulations set out the conditions under which a plat of land may be divided into smaller parcels for development. Early subdivision regulations required only the disclosure of certain engineering and surveying data as a prerequisite to plat approval. By contrast, present-day ordinances contain lengthy litanies of mandatory on-site and off-site improvements and complex approval procedures. Sewer, drainage and water lines, streets, curbs, gutters, shade trees and fire hydrants are among the many public improvements which have become the responsibility of the private developer.

It has long been recognized that subdivision exactions add appreciably to the cost of housing. One author, writing in 1934, asserted that "compliance with minimum standards with respect to street grading and the installation of water mains and sanitary sewers often may increase the total home cost as much as 20 percent."[1]

The absolute level of improvement costs has increased dramatically in the last decade. For example, the following cost breakdown for the Northern Virginia area shows a 74 percent increase in lot development costs in the period between 1969 and 1975 with particular cost categories increasing by as much as 490 percent (sewer and water tap fees).(See Exhibit 7.1)

119

EXHIBIT 7.1

Cost Breakdown Of Land Development
For A Typical New House Built In Northern Virginia:
1969-75

Lot Development Items	1969	1975	Total Percent Change
Engineering & site planning	$ 500	$ 1,000[1]	100.0%
Sanitary sewer	736	1,281[2]	74.1
Street	560	1,262[2]	115.4
Sewer & water tap fee	275	1,625[3]	490.9
Water system	492	1,020[2]	107.3
Clearing	177	410[4]	131.6
All others	3,353	4,015	19.7
Total lot development cost	$6,093	$10,613	74.1%

NOTES: All items include labor and materials
House measurements: 2,340 sq. ft., which includes 396 sq. ft. of
unfinished basement.

1. 50% of increase due to higher standards and longer processing time.
2. Higher standards responsible for significant portion of increase.
3. Entire increase represents higher fees.
4. Entire increase due to stricter burning regulations.

SOURCE: Edward R. Carr & Associates, Annandale, Va. cited in National
Association of Home Builders, *Economic News Notes*, May 1975, p. 4.

Similarly a recent analysis of changes in land improvement costs in
North Carolina from 1974 to 1976 shows that in just two years, costs have
risen 23 percent. (See Exhibit 7.2) A portion of this increase is the effect
of inflation, but government regulations have also played a significant
role. For example, a prohibition against the burning of vegetative waste and
debris from the land clearing, thereby requiring it to be hauled away, has increased clearing costs by 94 percent.

More useful than the absolute cost of subdivision regulations, however,
is an estimate of the cost impact of excessive or unnecessary requirements.
In a 1968 study prepared for the President's Committee on Urban
Housing (The "Kaiser Commission"), Leland Burns and Frank Mittelbach
estimated the cost of excessive requirements in both subdivision and zoning
ordinances to be between 2 and 4 percent of the final housing price.[2] The
authors acknowledged the difficulties involved in computing the costs of
such ordinances:

EXHIBIT 7.2

COMPARATIVE UNIT COSTS OF LAND IMPROVEMENTS
IN NORTH CAROLINA: 1974-76

Cost Item	1974	1976	Total Percent Change
Land clearing (acre)	$800.00	$1,550.00	94%
Land grading (cubic yd.)	.65	.70	8
15" storm sewer (linear ft.)	6.75	7.50	11
30" storm sewer (linear ft.)	15.00	17.00	13
8" sanitary sewer (linear ft.)	5.50	5.75	5
6" water line (linear ft.)	6.20	6.50	5
30" curb & gutter (linear ft.)	3.50	4.25	21
6" stone, 2 1/4" asphalt street (square yd.)	3.23	3.97	23

SOURCE: Field interviews with major developers in North Carolina, Center for Urban Policy Research, Summer 1976.

Not the least of these [difficulties] is the lack of comprehensive, up-to-date surveys on the provisions or ordinances throughout the nation....The details of subdivision and zoning ordinances will have important consequences that require in-depth study before firm conclusions can be reached.[3]

It is clear that more information is needed about subdivision regulations and housing costs before sense can be made out of the puzzling array of costs and benefits exhibited by this form of land use control.

Some form of control of subdivision development is necessary to ensure the adequacy of public services and to avoid completely unguided development. The history of the early part of this century, in which unrestrained development resulted in shoddy subdivisions and near-bankrupt municipalities, dramatized the need for control over the development process.

There is little agreement, however, about the degree of restriction and the kinds of requirements which are appropriate to subdivision control. Many subdivision residents and developers claim that present-day requirements are excessive and place unfair burden on owners of subdivided land in favor of other sectors of the population. Advocates of low-cost housing claim that such regulations are used to exclude moderate-income people by making the cost of site improvement, and therefore the ultimate cost of housing, prohibitive for this group.

This chapter attempts to put such criticisms into perspective by bringing together more detailed information on the exact nature of subdivision requirements throughout the country. The first section of this chapter outlines the historical context of municipal control over the division of land. The second section examines the various objectives of subdivision controls. The third section extends the discussion to the costs of achieving these goals. It provides an economic framework for discussing the cost impact of subdivision controls. Two surveys, one of municipal ordinances and practices, and one of home builders, are the primary sources of information for the fourth section, which details exactly what requirements are currently imposed during the subdivision approval process and suggests ways in which the costs associated with these requirements can be reduced. For a discussion of the judicially established parameters of what can and cannot be required under the subdivision ordinance, see Appendix C, "Legal Limitations on the Use of the Subdivision Control Power."

A Historical Perspective of Subdivision Controls

The history of subdivision regulations in the United States can be divided into four separate periods.[4] The earliest regulations, appearing in the late 1800's and early 1900's, were concerned mainly with facilitating plat recordation and transfer of title. With the publication of the Standard City Planning Enabling Act in 1928,[5] the concept of subdivision controls shifted to the encouragement of comprehensive land use planning, and the developer became responsible for many subdivision public improvements. Since World War II, regulations have placed an increasing emphasis on land for recreational areas, schools, open space, and the provision of off-site public improvements. A fourth phase, which is emerging in the 1970's, has begun to emphasize controlling growth and protecting environmentally sensitive areas.[6]

The earliest subdivision regulations in the United States appeared in the late 1800's.[7] Requirements for recordation of subdivision plats were instituted to ease transfer of title and minimize fraud by ensuring accurate records of ownership. Minimal preconditions attached to the recordation of plats included disclosure of engineering and surveying data. Plat maps were substituted for the traditional metes-and-bounds method of delineating property boundaries, thus reducing the likelihood of errors.

Speculative land practices in the early part of this century led to a second phase of subdivision regulations in which sound land-use planning, in addition to ease of land transfer, was emphasized. Excessive subdivision by land speculators, which artificially inflated the price of developed land, led to widespread tax delinquencies and foreclosures when real estate prices plunged in the late 1920's. Municipalities, which had bonded to make public improvements for these subdivisions in expectation of future development, were left with the double burden of heavy indebtedness and properties that provided little or no revenue. Such bleak financial situations led to local ordinances which required the developer to install streets, water, sewer and drainage lines, and other public improvements as a condition to plat approval.[8] These exactions represented an attempt by municipalities to shift the risk of future demand for residential land to the private investor.

By 1934 there were at least 269 municipal planning commissions in 29 states with power to regulate land subdivision, as well as 156 commissions with advisory powers concerning such regulations.[9] This activity on the local level was spurred somewhat by the Standard City Planning Enabling Act. The Act, which included subdivision regulations as one of several comprehensive planning tools, was used by some states to fashion enabling legislation, but unlike the Standard Zoning Enabling Act, it made little immediate progress toward standardization of subdivision controls.

In the period after World War II, the trend was toward increasingly restrictive regulations. The rapid development of the suburbs in the postwar period placed severe fiscal stress on many municipalities. Ordinances requiring dedication of land for recreational areas and schools, or fees in lieu of dedication, became increasingly common. Ordinances requiring that the developer contribute to the cost of off-site improvements for sewers, water, and drainage facilities also proliferated. .

The primary challenge in the emerging fourth phase of subdivision control lies in greater control of the timing and location of development. In a 1968 study, the National Commission on Urban Problems (the Douglas Commission) emphasized the inadequacies of the present battery of land use controls for controlling the location and timing of growth.[10] Traditional subdivision regulations have been unable to eliminate, and have in fact exacerbated, the scattered development patterns known as "leapfrogging."[11] Because subdivision requirements are generally more restrictive in municipalities closer to the urban core, developers tend to "leapfrog" over prime developable land in favor of outlying areas where regulations are less severe. The costs of this manifestation of urban sprawl are substantial, in transportation, sewer and water lines, and the destruction of natural space for recreational and other purposes.[12]

The Goals of Subdivision Regulations

PREVENTING PREMATURE AND PARTIAL SUBDIVISIONS

The experience of the 1920's and 30's demonstrated the necessity for urban growth strategies which minimize the premature and excessive subdivision of land and the development of partial subdivisions. It also demonstrated that government regulations were needed to ensure the attainment of these goals.

Premature or excessive subdivision of land creates an oversupply of lots relative to the demand, leading to the instability, and ultimate deflation, of property values. The lack of economic value of properties leads to tax delinquencies, widespread foreclosure and confused property titles. Partial development of tracts, or excessive dispersal of subdivisions, greatly increases the per-unit cost of providing public facilities by increasing distances and by necessitating under-utilization of facilities.

The costs created by premature, excessive and partial subdivisions inflict a burden upon the entire community. Government controls provide the mechanism for shifting the incidence of these costs. By requiring the developer to supply public infrastructure prior to marketing, the municipality ensures that it will be in the developer's interest to complete the project and provide acceptable housing to recoup his/her investment.

PREVENTING LOW-GRADE SUBDIVISIONS

Poor quality subdivisions, with inadequate public facilities and poor design, often lead to blight and instability of property values. The decline associated with poor quality design and an inadequate infrastructure exacts a tremendous cost in terms of decreased longevity of housing, increased costs of maintenance and repair, and deflated property values, and has a similar, though less pronounced, effect on adjacent neighborhoods.

Many of these costs are eliminated when the developer is required to conform to broader community standards. Thus, government regulations ensure that any municipal costs generated by substandard subdivisions will be minimized.

AN INVESTMENT PERSPECTIVE: REDUCING UNCERTAINTY AND RISK

As a corollary to the prevention of inferior developments, subdivision controls may also be viewed in part as a response to the uncertainty involved in making a residential investment. Both the developer and the home buyer, in calculating the value of future benefits from an investment, hope that such benefits will actually occur.[13] Subdivision regulations should also serve to reduce the investor's risk by ensuring an adequate infrastructure and by reducing uncertainty as to future property values. Where land dedication for parks or schools is required, this further stabilizes property values by ensuring the proximity of educational and recreational facilities, but this insurance is achieved only at the price of substantial "front end" costs.

Yet subdivision regulations may also increase risk. Since degree of risk is also a function of the time span of development, any additional delay creates costs, usually in terms of financing and carrying charges. Presumably, this increased risk ultimately is reduced to the extent that an area is economically stabilized by the presence of subdivision regulations.

It is important to realize that for the home buyer, the risk factor extends over the full period of ownership, whereas the developer's risk lasts only during the development, construction and marketing period.[14] This partially explains why developers may be less than enthusiastic about subdivision exactions. Minimizing short-term costs may be the best way for the developer to maximize his/her return.

THE EXCLUSIONARY IMPLICATIONS OF SUBDIVISION REGULATIONS

In addition to the aforementioned legitimate goals of subdivision controls, a more subtle and sometimes unintentional effect is to prevent the provision of moderately priced housing. The Douglas Commission articulated the problem in this way:

> The central problem of land-use regulation today is how to achieve the ambitious objectives of these regulations without, in the process, sacrificing other essential public objectives. Of greatest concern to the Commission is how to achieve the legitimate objectives without misuse of the rules to raise housing costs and exclude the poor.[15]

The desire to ensure high-quality subdivisions is sometimes synonymous, in effect if not always in intent, with the exclusion of those people who can afford only low-cost housing. Thus any rationale for extensive subdivision requirements justified on the basis of avoiding "blight" demands more than superficial inspection. The level of public improvements required must be scrutinized to determine whether or not the regulations are actually designed to erect an economic barrier to keep out the poor and, increasingly, those with a moderate income as well.

There are two basic methods by which the burden of subdivision improvements to the customer could be reduced while still achieving the various goals sought by these regulations. First, costs could be reallocated either to other parties (e.g. publicly financed) or to a later time; or second, through the elimination of excessive requirements and administrative inefficiencies, costs could be lowered. In both cases, the housing consumer's fiscal burden would be lightened. The following section details these cost reducing strategies.

The Cost Implications of Subdivision Controls

THE ALLOCATION OF COSTS

As previously discussed, reducing the unnecessary costs created by unplanned development is a primary rationale for subdivision regulations. The adverse effects of unplanned development — including premature or excessive subdivisions, low-quality subdivisions, and a high level of investment risk — can be minimized by requiring subdividers to bear the costs of public improvements.

The concept of "externalities" provides a useful framework for discussing the allocative goals of subdivision requirements.[16] "Negative externalities," or diseconomies, as they are termed, occur when not all the costs of an activity are borne by those persons benefiting from the activity. In the absence of subdivision exactions, external diseconomies are created: a municipality — and through its tax structure, existing residents — subsidize new subdivision residents by bearing the costs of services and facilities which the new residents require. On the other hand, if exactions require subdivision residents to bear the full cost of facilities from which other members of the community also benefit, external or positive economies accrue to the general community.[17]

The presence of externalities provides another justification for governmental intervention. Where costs are not fully absorbed by the parties generating those costs, government regulation has traditionally been used to minimize the breakdown of the free market system. Those amenities which are unmarketable, or only partially marketable, may be charged to the actors through government regulations. Many public improvements such as parkland, drainage and sewer systems, quality street design, and a host of other public facilities are only partially marketable; that is, the beneficiaries of these services will not voluntarily pay for their full cost in the free market. Subdivision regulations ensure the internalization of such negative externalities as: the increased demand on municipal sewage, utility, and drainage facilities; congestion of municipal recreational facilities and schools; and the increased traffic congestion.

By requiring that the developer assume these costs, the market once again becomes an efficient allocator of resources. But the internalization of these costs will necessarily result in higher prices. An alternative is to pursue a public policy which shifts these costs from the developer. Possible reallocative measures include redistribution by sector of the community, by budget item, and over a period of time.

Allocation by Sector A central allocation problem is the distribution of costs between subdivision residents and the rest of the community. This is a particularly crucial choice which must be faced and, of late, fiscally burdened municipalities have chosen to charge developers for improvements previously considered to be the local government's responsibility.

A closer analysis reveals discrepancies in the manner in which subdivision residents, residents of homes on nonsubdivided land, and apartment dwellers are treated with respect to the cost burden for improvements. A method is needed for equitable allocation of costs by sector of the population.

Allocation by Budget Item Often housing costs are reduced, only to appear in another item of the consumer's budget. This may occur, for example, when developers avoid land with highly restrictive subdivision regulations in favor of fringe areas which have less restrictive regulations. Any cost saving from lowered improvement costs may be partially offset by increased transportation costs to the central city or place of employment.

Allocation Over Time Many subdivision requirements are imposed with the intent of minimizing future costs. Where the discounted value of future cost savings is greater than the present expenditure required to produce that savings, it is economically efficient to incur the present cost. For example, more expensive pavement material generally requires less maintenance and repair. If the savings on maintenance costs outweighs the extra cost for pavement materials, it is unwise to attempt to cut costs by using a less expensive material. Unfortunately, future expenditures, which are dependent upon the volume and nature of use, cannot be predicted with precision. Nor does simply estimating life-cycle costs take into account changes in consumer income over time.

The decision as to whether or not to defer costs may be affected by the sector of the population which will incur the cost burden. Since maintenance and repair costs are generally borne by the municipality, a subdivision resident subjected to stricter construction specifications is in effect subsidizing the future taxpayers of the entire community.[18]

COST-REDUCING STRATEGIES

Those areas of subdivision controls which aggravate exclusionary tendencies, without making a concomitant and equal contribution to market stability and quality developments, raise housing costs. The following areas have been identified as potential means of reducing those costs:

1. elimination of totally unnecessary requirements;
2. reduction of excessive improvement standards; and
3. reduction of administrative costs and unnecessary delays.

In pursuing cost-reducing policies, the guiding principle is that only those improvements whose benefits outweigh their cost should be required. Applying this simple principle, however, is a researcher's nightmare. There is no practical method, for example, of quantifying the benefits of shade trees to the homeowner and the general community. Similarly, the added value provided by an extra two feet of street pavement is generally not susceptible to precise evaluation. The changing value of various improvements, depending on topological and subsoil conditions, as well as future population and usage patterns, compounds the difficulties of exact evaluation.

Unfortunately as the situation now stands the decision of what requirements and administrative steps are involved in the subdivision is made by the local governing body. A built-in incentive exists for them to require expensive, high-quality developments. Not only will these minimize the burden on the municipality, but they will also tend to increase property values in the surrounding neighborhood, i.e. the property of those who promulgate and administer the regulations.

THE COST IMPLICATIONS OF SUBDIVISION CONTROLS

Two possible strategies can be used to reduce the burden created by subdivision controls. A more equitable and socially desirable allocation of costs, both among parties and over time, could significantly lower costs to the housing consumer. The recent history of government controls has been to require the developer to bear an increased amount of this burden. The results of this policy have been that the quality of subdivisions has increased enormously, and their burden on the municipality has been reduced, but now few consumers can afford new housing. Nonetheless, the problem of allocating these costs remains.

The second strategy reduces costs through the elimination of excessive and unnecessary requirements and inefficient administration. The major difficulty in this area has been to define what requirements are necessary and what requirements do not justify their cost.

Survey of Subdivision Ordinances

As suggested by the earlier quotation from the Kaiser Commission report, surprisingly little factual information is available which details specific subdivision requirements and practices. Without such information, it is impossible to estimate the costs of controls or to make suggestio reduce these costs. To remedy this situation, we undertook a comprehensive survey of municipalities' subdivision requirements. (For a discussion of the sample, the survey technique and questionnaire itself, see Appendix F.) In analyzing the results, three aspects of the subdivision regulatory process will be highlighted — the administration of the ordinance, the standards and requirements, and the relationship between subdivision and zoning regulations.

THE ADMINISTRATIVE PROCESS

The complexity of the subdivision review process has increased dramatically in recent years. There are more requirements, stricter specifications, and a proliferation of governmental review boards. This has inevitably led to lengthier review periods, more extensive paper work and higher fees for engineering and architectural services. After providing a brief overview of the subdivision approval procedure, we will examine the various aspects of it which increase costs and discuss possible approaches to streamlining the administrative process.

The Subdivision Approval Process The power to approve plat applications generally rests with the local planning body, but in a few states the local legislative body gives final approval on advisement from the planning commission.[19] Applications must conform to the municipal zoning regulations, the local master plan, and the official map.

Most ordinances require at least two, and often three, approval stages. Fifty-three percent of the municipalities in the subdivision survey require a three stage process. The purpose of periodic review as plans are developed is to avoid unnecessary time and expense which would occur were a complete application required before review. In the first phase, the developer may be required to submit a sketch plat which shows the characteristics of the land, approximate location of proposed structures, and ownership of adjacent tracts.[20]

The second phase, the preliminary plat application, involves a more detailed plan of the subdivision. Specific improvement and dedication requirements are established at this stage, and a public hearing is generally held to solicit the views of affected parties.[21] The various agencies which review the application — such as the health board, fire commission, environmental commission, school board, and various regional and state agencies[22] — submit their recommendations during this phase. The survey of municipalities revealed that an average of four to five agency approvals are sought. Those approvals most frequently are required from the fire department (48.7 percent), the health department (42.5 percent), the County Planning Board (32.5 percent) and both local (25.0 percent) and state (25.0 percent) environmental agencies.

Final approval, a ministerial act, is granted when all conditions under which preliminary approval was granted have been met. This stage also often includes the posting of a performance guarantee. Final approval authorizes the plat to be recorded with the county clerk or registry of deeds.

Municipal Fees The vast array of filing fees and fees for permits, inspections, and review contribute substantially to development costs. Filing fees often must be paid prior to each review phase.[23] Municipal inspection and review fees may include fees for review of water systems, sanitary sewer plans, storm drainage plans, and periodic on-site inspections of construction as it progresses.[24] Frequently fees are also imposed to tap-in to existing sanitary sewage and water systems. Exhibit 7.3 summarizes the fees charged by the surveyed municipalities.

The rationale behind the imposition of fees on developers is to avoid burdening already hard-pressed minicipalities with the costs of the review of subdivision applications. A 1965 Report by the American Society of Planning Officials suggests that in many municipalities fees are substantially lower than the costs of review.[25] This is corroborated by our municipal survey which indicates that only 20.5 percent of the municipalities considered their administrative costs to be covered by fees.

EXHIBIT 7.3

SUBDIVISION FEES CHARGED BY MUNICIPALITIES

Type of Fees Charged Developers	Number of Municipalities	Percent of Total*
Filing Fees		
Sketch Plat	13	16.7
Preliminary Plat	62	77.5
Final Plat	32	40.5
Review Fees	23	29.1
Inspection Fees	30	38.0
Permit Fees	31	38.2**
Tap-in Fees		
Sanitary Sewer	49	61.0
Water	58	72.2

*Does not add to 100.0 percent due to multiplicity of responses.
**Exclusive of building permits.

SOURCE: Survey of Municipalities, Center for Urban Policy Research, Summer 1976.

A report by the New Jersey Home Builders Association, however, indicates that municipal engineering review fees, which are often calculated as a percentage of the overall cost of design work, may often be excessive.[26] Nevertheless, most municipalities surveyed reported basing their review fee schedule on a percentage of the cost of public improvements to be constructed.

In the case of fees for tap-ins to preexisting sewerage and water systems, a very wide variation suggests that in some instances these fees exceed the costs involved. A recent study of two similar homes in the Washington, D.C. area revealed that the cost of obtaining water and sewer service in two Virginia counties differed by $1,000. The Northern Virginia Builders Association has this to say about Fairfax County fees:

> Fees charged for county supplied services to new development (are) designed to offset the cost of supplying this service; but in fact are used to generate revenue and finance services to existing residents. (In the case of Fairfax County, per unit cost to access sewer system is $1,000. An excess of $24.2 million was derived from this revenue source in the fiscal year 1975, which was subsequently used to satisfy the service demand of existing residents...).[27]

The survey of municipalities by the Center for Urban Policy Research also found a wide range in fees charged, from $3 to $1,750 for sanitary sewer tap-ins and from $15 to $500 for water tap-ins. Similarly a study in Howard County, Maryland found that water and sewer connection fees totaled $2,000/dwelling unit in the City of Columbia, as opposed to $625 in other parts of the county.[28] While it is difficult to establish an accurate cost in each case, it is significant that 64.5 percent of the 400 home builders surveyed by our staff considered sewer access fees to be excessive and 65.0 percent considered water access fees excessive. (For a discussion of the telephone survey of home builders, see Appendix B.)

The Costs of Delay　　Costs of delay can be prohibitive for a developer. Interest costs on interim financing increase steadily with the postponement of the construction phase. The opportunity cost of the money that remains tied up in a lengthy and uncertain subdivision review procedure may be considerable. In addition, the greater the development time, the greater the uncertainty about the profitability of an investment, because the investment climate becomes subject to greater fluctuations.

The respondents to the Survey of Municipalities were asked to estimate the amount of time it would take to go through typical procedures which might be necessary in the course of subdividing a typical plot. (See Exhibit 7.4)

As can be seen from the exhibit, 88.5 percent of the municipalities surveyed report less than five months was required for preliminary approval of a typical subdivision. Developers, on the other hand, reported very dif-

EXHIBIT 7.4

Estimate Of Time For Each Step During The
Land Development Approval Process

Procedure	Time Required	Percent of Municipalities
Preliminary approval	less than 2 months	50.0
(n=78)	2–4 months	38.3
	5–7 months	6.4
	more than 7 months	5.3
	Total	100.0
Final approval	less than one month	44.9
(n=78)	1–2 months	38.5
	3–4 months	10.3
	more than 4 months	6.3
	Total	100.0
Variance or special exception	less than one month	32.9
(n=74)	1–2 months	57.0
	3–4 months	7.6
	more than 4 months	2.5
	Total	100.0
Rezoning	less than on month	10.0
(n=74)	1–2 months	36.7
	3–4 months	40.0
	more than 4 months	13.3
	Total	100.0

Source: Survey of Municipalities, Center for Urban Policy Research,
Summer 1976.

ferent estimates of the time currently required to obtain the approval to
build. Only 14.5 percent reported being able to obtain necessary approvals
in less than seven months. (See Exhibit 7.5) The normally short time
required to obtain a building permit, once final subdivision is granted,
could not account for this discrepancy. However, as was noted in Exhibit
7.4, if a variance, special exception, or rezoning were required, approval
time would be lengthened considerably, even by the municipal officials'
estimates. Thirty-five percent of the developers report that they have found
it necessary to seek a zoning change in over 50 percent of their recent projects. This may account for much of the discrepancy in the two sets of responses. Additionally, it would seem that one's position on either side of the approval process tends to affect his/her perception of delay.

Perhaps of equal interest to the actual amount of time required is the developers' estimation of the increase in delay time that has taken place over the last five years. Exhibit 7.5 details this marked increase.

The sample is small, but as displayed in Exhibit 7.6, 100 percent of the category of low median-income municipalities estimate that preliminary approval — the most significant step in the subdivision process — is obtainable in less than five months. In contrast to this, only 75 percent of the high median-income municipalities estimate granting approval in this period of time. This variance suggests the need for more research in this area. Is delay being used as one of the tactics of exclusionary practice?

EXHIBIT 7.5

DEVELOPERS' ESTIMATES OF THE TIME
REQUIRED TO OBTAIN APPROVAL TO DEVELOP

| | Percent Developers | |
Time Required	1970 (n=346)	1975 (n=350)
Less than 7 months	72.2	14.5
7–12 months	25.0	27.5
13–24 months	2.4	47.0
More than 24 months	.4	11.0
Total	100.0	100.0

SOURCE: Telephone survey of the Home Builders' Industry, Center for Urban Policy Research, Summer 1976.

EXHIBIT 7.6

TIME REQUIRED FOR PRELIMINARY SUBDIVISON
APPROVAL BY MEDIAN INCOME OF MUNICIPALITY

| | TIME REQUIRED — PERCENT MUNICIPALITIES | | | |
Median Income*	Less than 5 Months	5 to 10 Months	More than 10 Months	Total
Low (n=11)	100%	0%	0%	100%
Moderate (n=28)	89	11	0	100
Middle (n=31)	87	10	3	100
High (n=8)	75	13	12	100

*For an explanation of income groupings, see Appendix F.

SOURCE: Survey of Municipalities, Center for Urban Policy Research, Summer 1976.

The New Jersey Municipal Land Use Law A recent example of a state legislature's attempt to streamline the approval process on the local level is found in the New Jersey Municipal Land Use Law, which took effect on August 1, 1976. The Act is significant for its attempts to simplify local procedures and to provide more specific review standards for local governments to follow.

The approval process in the New Jersey Act is pared down in several respects, thus creating the potential for substantial cost savings. The most potentially powerful cost saving provision is the establishment of maximum time periods for review.[29]

Of the eighty municipalities in our subdivision survey, twenty-seven had automatic approval provisions incorporated into their ordinances. The efficacy of these provisions may be questioned, however, since virtually all also provided for extension of the deadline by mutual agreement. Unfortunately, the use of this extension clause by municipalities is more often the rule than the exception.

Another streamlining technique found in the New Jersey Municipal Land Use Law, is that both the Board of Adjustment and the Planning Board are permitted to exercise powers traditionally relegated to another body. Planning boards may grant certain non-use variances and certain other permits, and the Board of Adjustment may approve site plans, subdivisions and conditional uses as part of use variance approval. This avoids the expense and delay of multiple approvals. Delay is further reduced by the elimination of "weak" planning bodies, that is, boards that act in an advisory capacity only. Finally, there is a section which provides that referral of an application to another municipal body will not serve to extend the maximum time period allowed for the approval process.

Negotiation v. Specification With the proliferation of requirements for off-site facilities and dedication of open space, the aspect of negotiation has taken a more prominent role in the subdivision approval process. The increased use of flexible zoning procedures such as planned unit development, cluster zoning and floating zones will also lead to an increased emphasis on negotiation of terms and conditions. Heavy reliance on negotiation of standards may be misused as an exclusionary device by leading to excessive improvement specifications. On the other hand, it may provide the flexibility needed to attain quality improvements at lower costs. Many of the local officials contacted in our survey saw the negotiation process as one means by which regulations might be relaxed to suit special circumstances. Guidelines and objectives for negotiated aspects of the approval process must be carefully delineated. Given the financial disincentive for the developer to litigate over conditions he/she considers excessive,[30] this cost-increasing tendency of the negotiation process is particularly important.

The overwhelming majority (72.4 percent) of municipal officials contacted in our subdivision survey reported that either none, or less than 10 percent, of their requirements were negotiated. Only 5.3 percent of the 80 municipalities reported negotiating more than half of their specifications, while 19.9 percent of the developers estimated that at least half are negotiated and half written into ordinance. Those aspects of the regulations most frequently mentioned as the object of negotiations were streetscape, sanitary and storm sewers and the provision of water facilities.

Performance Bonding The use of bonding or other performance guarantees to ensure the construction of required subdivision improvements is a widely-used alternative to the previous practice of requiring completion of construction before final plat approval. Types of guarantees include: surety performance bonds, in which a surety company guarantees, upon developer's payment of a premium, that all improvements will be made; escrow accounts in which cash, a note or other easily convertible instrument is deposited in a bank payable to the municipality; property escrow accounts, in which land, stock, or bonds are held in escrow; and sequential approval of segments of the subdivision without a guarantee. While each type of guarantee has limitations, each has value for particular developers, so it is important that municipalities provide several options for insuring construction of improvements.[31]

Perhaps the weakest feature of the surety performance bond method is that it discriminates against the small developer, who is more likely to be considered a bad risk by surety companies. Often small, "high-risk" developers are denied bonding outright, charged excessive premiums, or forced to provide extra collateral. Where collateral required by surety institutions is equal to the amount of the bond, the question arises as to why the collateral can't be provided directly to the municipality, thus eliminating the premium exacted. This is without a doubt an area of potential cost-savings in performance bonding.

The escrow account techniques eliminate the surety as a third party, but suffer from other deficiencies. Municipalities often require that a note in the full amount of improvements be deposited, thus tying up the developer's money as completely as if he/she had been required to construct improvements. If a portion of the note can be released as improvements are completed, this burden is reduced. In our survey, we found that roughly half (47.2 percent) of the municipalities contacted do allow for a reduction of the bond in this manner. Property escrow accounts such as stock and bonds often fluctuate in value, rendering them too unstable as collateral. Escrow techniques generally put a greater burden on small developers who have limited assests than on large builders.

Sequential approval of segments of the subdivision as improvements are completed, with no guarantee required, is ideal for the small developer, but may pose risks too great for many municipalities. The community has no remedy if the subdivider fails to complete any improvements.

The failure of municipalities to release bonds or other guarantees immediately upon completion of improvements is commonly cited as unnecessarily increasing developers' costs. While municipal officials must inspect the site to be certain that specifications were met, this process need not consume an inordinate amount of time if periodic inspections have been made on site as the work progressed.[32]

In sum, municipalities can take steps which will encourage the small scale developer, and reduce costs of securing guarantees without seriously increasing the community's risk. A wide choice of guarantees should be permitted and they should be released as soon as practicable.

Our survey results show that many municipalities do offer the developer a choice of performance guarantees. (See Exhibit 7.7). The most commonly used bonding methods were surety bonds and escrow accounts.

Thus, the administrative procedures of the subdivision approval process appear unnecessarily complex and time consuming. The process requires several stages of approval and a number of different agencies passing judgement on the proposal. Other factors contribute unnecessarily to the cost of the subdivision process. Either the improvements required in the ordinance are too inflexible, or if the ordinance does not mandate specifications, there are no proper guidelines and standards upon which a negotiated agreement can be equitably reached. The following section examines the specific improvements required by municipalities.

EXHIBIT 7.7

PERFORMANCE GUARANTEE OPTIONS OFFERED
BY MUNICIPALITIES

Method	Number of Municipalities	Percent of Total*
Surety bond	77	96.2
Escrow account	57	71.4
Property escrow	7	9.0
Sequential approval (no bond)	9	11.7
Letter of credit	5	6.4

*Total does not add to 100 percent due to multiplicity of replies.

SOURCE: Survey of Municipalities, Center for Urban Policy Research, Summer 1976.

Improvement Standards

Perhaps the greatest deficiency of many subdivision ordinances is their failure to establish flexible standards which will permit cost-reducing practices when local topographical, soil, drainage, traffic and other conditions permit. While the implementation of flexible construction design standards requires considerable expertise and experience on the part of municipal engineers and planning officials, the cost savings are potentially substantial.

The lack of uniformity among local subdivision ordinances has been well documented. A comparison of subdivision regulations derived from a 1973 study of the Baltimore region[33] shows the wide variation between the costs of complying with improvement requirements in different municipalities. (See Exhibit 7.8) This wide variation in the costs of complying with subdivision regulations suggests the presence of excessive requirements — and excessive costs — in some areas. The lack of uniformity encourages uneven development, or "leapfrogging."[34]

A significant part of the differences in subdivision costs can be attributed to the variation in the specifications for improvements. In particular, overdesign of improvements is often used as a means to ensure the high quality and high cost of a new development. Oversizing of water and sewer pipes is often required without regard to potential usage patterns. Similarly, residential street pavements are often designed to bear increased traffic that could be more rationally routed to collectors and subcollectors. Overdesign should not be an automatic response of municipal engineers, but rather a response to reasonably foreseeable population increases. Where overdesigning is necessary, an equitable method of cost apportionment must be found. One method is to reimburse the developer for the cost incurred in excess of the needs of his/her subdivision — 52.1 percent of the surveyed municipalities have such a provision in their ordinances.

It is interesting to note, however, the distribution of reimbursal provisions by median income level of the municipalities. Exhibit 7.9 reveals that 73 percent of the low-income group provide for reinbursement, whereas only 29 percent of the high-income group include this provision. Overdesign requirements are thus borne by the developer, and ultimately the homebuyer, in most high-income municipalities.

These general recommendations concerning overdesign can be applied to particular subdivision requirements. Potential cost reduction policies for streets, storm drainage, sewage, land dedication, and lot frontage are explored below.

EXHIBIT 7.8

MEASURABLE VARIATION IN SUBDIVISION DEVELOPMENT COSTS OF
SINGLE-FAMILY LOTS AMONG FIVE COUNTIES
IN METROPOLITAN BALTIMORE, 1973

Requirements	Density (D.U./Acre)			
	1	4	8*	16**
Per unit maximum	$5,000	$ 4,640	$ 2,530	$ 1,100
Per unit minimum	4,000	3,360	1,870	660
Difference	$1,000	$ 1,280	$ 660	$ 540
Per acre maximum	$5,000	$18,500	$20,100	$17,800
Per acre minimum	4,000	13,400	15,000	10,900
Difference	$1,000	$ 5,100	$ 5,100	$ 6,900
Percent open space required:				
Maximum	1%	9%	13%	17%
Minimum	0%	0%	0%	0%
Difference	1%	9%	13%	17%

*Represents a comparison among four counties only; one county prohibits
development at greater than 4.5 units per acre.
**Represents a comparison among three counties only; another county prohibits
development at greater than 10 units per acre.

SOURCE: Edward M. Bergman, *External Validity of Policy Related Research on
Development Controls and Housing Costs*, 1974, n. 77. Adapted from
Ming-Shyong Wu, "Public Improvement Costs for Residential Land
Development," 1973. The term "measurable" refers to street, storm
drain, water, sewer, and landscape requirements; the cost of open
space requirements is not included.

EXHIBIT 7.9

USE OF REIMBURSEMENT PROVISIONS BY
MEDIAN INCOME OF MUNICIPALITIES

Median Income of Municipality	PERCENT MUNICIPALITIES	
	Reimbursement Provided	Reimbursement Not Provided
Low (n=11)	73%	27%
Moderate (n=27)	59	41
Middle (n=28)	43	57
High (n=7)	29	71

SOURCE: Survey of Municipalities, Center for Urban Policy Research,
Summer 1976.

Pavement Width   A joint study by the Urban Land Institute, the National Association of Home Builders and the American Society of Civil Engineers on residential street design has recommended the following minimum pavement widths for various street types:[35]

Places, Lanes (local streets)	20 feet
Collectors	28 feet

These widths may be reduced only where enforceable regulations limiting on-street parking are in effect or where overall drainage plans to limit impervious surfaces have been implemented with due consideration to traffic and safety problems. In no case should street widths be less than eighteen feet, which is sufficient to permit one parking lane and one moving lane. Compared to the above standards, it can be seen that requirements for pavement widths for both local and collector streets as reported in the subdivision survey, are generally far higher than recommended. (See Exhibit 7.10) This indicates the presence of excessive overdesign in most municipalities. This point is reinforced when viewed in conjunction with the finding that 97 percent of the municipalities require off-street parking.

Developers were also asked about the specifications they encounter for local streets. Exhibit 7.10 illustrates the striking similarity of responses from municipal officials and developers. While municipalities were found to require a 30 foot or more pavement width in 62 percent of the cases, 51 percent of the developers reported similar requirements for their current projects. Moreover, 54.6 percent of the developers expressed the opinion that local street pavement widths are excessive. Their opinion falls squarely in line with the standard of twenty feet as an adequate width, and suggests that municipalities' requirements are indeed excessive. The cost to the developer for these extra feet in width can be enormous; it would include both construction costs and the foregone profits from the land dedicated to the municipality for use as a street.

Right-of-Way Widths   In present subdivision ordinances minimum rights-of-way are often rigidly fixed for various street types. A preferable approach is to permit a range of rights-of-way, depending upon such factors as projected future traffic patterns, the need for sidewalks, the feasibility of swales as a substitute for curbs and gutters, and other design decisions. A fifty foot right-of-way is the width most often mentioned as representing the upper limit of requirements for interior residential streets.[36] The right-of-way width is particularly important where land costs are high, because streets generally constitute 15-25 percent of the total subdivision land area. Cost savings to the developer in the form of more land for development can be considerable. Compared with the recommended maximum fifty foot

EXHIBIT 7.10

REQUIREMENTS OF PAVEMENT WIDTH FOR STREETS

Pavement Width	Percent Municipalities	Percent Developers
Local Streets	(n=77)	(n=327)
Less than 25 feet	12%	22%
25–29 feet	27	27
30 feet	17	18
31–39 feet	32	24
40 feet or more	12	9
Total	100	100
Collector Streets	(n=73)	
Less than 30 feet	12%	
30–35 feet	28	
36 feet	28	
37–40 feet	17	
More than 40 feet	15	
Total	100	

SOURCE: Survey of Municipalities, and Telephone Survey of the Survey of the Home Builders' Industry, Center for Urban Policy Research, Summer 1976.

right-of-way for a local street, the practices found in our survey of municipalities (41.8 percent over 50 ft.) again suggest excessive amounts of overdesign.(See Exhibit 7.11) The right-of-way for collector streets most often (56.2 percent) mentioned by respondents was sixty feet.

As with local street pavement widths, the developers surveyed reported very similar figures to those of the municipalities. Thirty-nine percent of the developers suggested that the local street right-of-way requirement was excessive. This would roughly correspond to any specification of over fifty feet.

The requirements for local street right-of-way widths were found to vary significantly with the median income level of the municipality.(See Exhibit 7.12) While only 25 percent of the low-income municipalities required more than the suggested maximum of a fifty-foot right-of-way, 47 percent of the high-income group fell into this category. The cost-increasing factor of requiring excessive right-of-way widths would seem to be another device to raise the cost of development in exclusive municipalities.

EXHIBIT 7.11

REQUIREMENTS OF RIGHT-OF-WAY WIDTH

Right-Of-Way Width	Percent Municipalities	Percent Developers
Local Streets	(n=79)	(n=332)
Less than 50 feet	6.3%	9.0%
50 feet	51.9	47.3
51–59 feet	6.3	7.6
60 feet	30.4	29.8
More than 60 feet	5.1	6.3
Total	100.0	100.0
Collector Streets	(n=73)	
Less than 50 feet	1.4%	
50–59 feet	19.1	
60 feet	56.2	
61–69 feet	9.6	
70 feet or more	13.7	
Total	100.0	

SOURCE: Survey of Municipalities and Telephone Survey of the Home Builders' Industry, Center for Urban Policy Research, Summer 1976.

EXHIBIT 7.12

LOCAL STREET RIGHT-OF-WAY WIDTH
BY MEDIAN INCOME OF MUNICIPALITY

Median Income	Number of Municipalities	50 Feet or Less (percent)	50 Feet or More (percent)	Total
Low	12	75%	25%	100%
Moderate	29	52	48	100
Middle	31	61	39	100
High	7	43	57	100

SOURCE: Survey of Municipalities, Center for Urban Policy Research, Summer 1976.

Collector street rights-of-way, as reported in the survey of municipalities, showed no correlation with the income level variable. They did appear, however, to be influenced by the population of the municipality. Exhibit 7.13 shows that of the least populous municipalities, 64 percent required a sixty-foot or more right-of-way for collector streets while 95 percent of the most populous required this greater width. This may be explained by the observation that subdividers are rarely required to construct and dedicate collector streets for the average subdivision. Collectors will usually be in place, having been constructed by the municipality or the county, and therefore are more responsive to the population of the entire municipality and its expected traffic load.

Sidewalks, Curbs and Gutters Some commentators have suggested that street appurtenances such as curbs, gutters and sidewalks should not be viewed as necessities in all cases. In fact, some drainage design concepts suggest that alternatives may be superior. The elimination of sidewalks, on one or both sides of the street, would be a major cost-reducing practice and may be advisable even where not dictated by run-off considerations. An impressive 87.4 percent of surveyed developers suggested sidewalks are being required where they are not necessary. It should be noted that cost savings from elimination of one or both sidewalks include not only the cost of construction, but also the decreased land dedication for rights-of-way, and lower maintenance and repair costs.[37]

Exhibit 7.14 details the responses obtained in the survey of municipalities on the questions concerning sidewalk, curb and gutter requirements. It is interesting to note that very few municipalities require sidewalks on one side only. This option could substantially reduce costs in

EXHIBIT 7.13

COLLECTOR STREET RIGHT-OF-WAY WIDTH BY
POPULATION OF MUNICIPALITY

		RIGHT-OF-WAY WIDTH REQUIREMENT Percent Municipalities		
		Less Than	60 Feet	
	Number of	Less Than	60 Feet	
Population	Municipalities	60 Feet	or More	Total
10,000–17,999	14	36%	64%	100%
18,000–24,999	17	38	62	100
25,000–49,999	23	13	87	100
50,000 and more	19	5	95	100

SOURCE: Survey of Municipalities, Center for Urban Policy Research, Summer 1976.

EXHIBIT 7.14

SIDEWALK, CURB AND GUTTER REQUIREMENTS

Requirements	Percent Municipalities*
Sidewalks (n=78)	
Always required — both sides	50.0
Generally required — both sides	17.9
Always required — one side	5.1
Generally required — one side	2.6
Generally not required	20.5
Never required	3.8
Total	100.0
Curbs & Gutters (n=77)	
Always required	72.7
More than 75 percent of time	11.7
51–75 percent of time	7.8
25–50 percent of time	3.9
Less than 25 percent of time	2.6
Never required	1.3
Total	100.0

*May not add to 100.0 due to rounding.

SOURCE: Survey of Municipalities, Center for Urban Policy Research, Summer 1976.

those municipalities that are currently requiring sidewalks on both sides and may be found to provide substantially as great a benefit, particularly in low-density residential areas.

As Exhibit 7.14 shows, there appears to be very little flexibility in curb and gutter requirements, with the overwhelming majority of municipalities considering them always to be mandatory. Indeed, of the developers surveyed, 66.3 percent felt that curbs and gutters were not always needed where specified and 64.2 percent stated that they felt that other drainage techniques were preferable to gutters. This would seem to be a fruitful area for investigation leading to significantly lowered costs in many subdivisions. On the subject of sidewalk width, again the findings from the two surveys provided substantially the same distribution as to frequency of occurrence.(See Exhibit 7.15) In cases in which expected pedestrian use and safety considerations warrant sidewalks, their width generally need not be

EXHIBIT 7.15

SIDEWALK WIDTH REQUIREMENTS

Width	Percent Municipalities* (n=69)	Percent Developers* (n=216)
3 feet	4.3%	12.5%
4 feet	59.4	57.9
5 feet or more	36.2	29.7
Total	100.0	100.0

*Does not add to 100.0 percent due to rounding.

SOURCE: Survey of Municipalities, and Telephone Survey of Home Builder Industry, Center for Urban Policy Research, Summer 1976.

greater than four feet, which permits one pedestrian and one bicycle lane. It was found in the survey of municipalities that, although only three of the eight high median-income communities in our sample required sidewalks, those three required a five foot width while none of the low median-income municipalities required more than a four foot width. Here again, excessive overdesign may be used to increase costs of improvements.

Streetscaping The cost of street signs, lighting and trees is generally imposed on the developer. The results of our survey of municipalities show that 71.8 percent require developers to provide street signs, 62.2 percent require developers to provide street lights and 57.5 percent require the provision of street trees. The necessity for street signs and lighting is indisputable, although illumination requirements are frequently excessive for the protection of nocturnal pedestrians. The requirements of street trees, however, is commonly decried by developers as an unnecessary luxury, and an amenity which should be at the option of the homebuyer. The costs for a single tree may vary from $50 to $150, depending on the caliber desired. The New Jersey Home Builders Association has estimated the costs of installing trees at $300 for a one-acre lot, based on the commonly-required spacing of one tree per 50 feet of curb. One might venture the comment that verdant foliage is perhaps less directly related to the health and safety of the community than are most other required improvements. If the desire to encourage the construction of low-cost housing is sincere, this is one cost area which more municipalities should consider making optional.

Block Length The length of blocks within a subdivision can have a major cost impact. As block length decreases, greater land area is consumed in cross streets, thus decreasing housing yield,[38] while increasing improvement costs.(See Exhibit 7.16) The following exhibit shows the improvement costs

EXHIBIT 7.16

EFFECT OF BLOCK LENGTH ON IMPROVEMENT COSTS

	Length of Block				
	1200'	1000'	800'	700'	600'
Linear Ft. Street/Lot	$ 39.00	$ 41.25	$ 43.85	$ 46.36	$ 48.00
Improvement Cost	$1,092.00	$1,155.00	$1,228.00	$1,298.00	$1,344.00
Added Cost	–	$ 63.00	$ 136.00	$ 206.00	$ 252.00

SOURCE: Jack Newville, *New Engineering Concepts in Community Development*, p. 47.

for a series of hypothetical blocks of 60' × 125' lots with varying block lengths. A 22 percent savings can be achieved in land and improvement costs by increasing the block length from 600 to 1200 feet.

In designing block length a balance must be struck between the added cost of decreased block length and considerations of safety and accessibility. Shorter block lengths increase the accessibility of a neighborhood to emergency and other vehicles, and reduce speeding by increasing the number of conflict points. In the American Society of Planning Officials' *Model Subdivision Regulations,* Freilich and Levi have recommended the very wide parameters of not less than 400 feet and not more than twelve times minimum lot width or 2,200 feet. The determination will, of course, depend upon local traffic conditions.[39] The trend to designing subdivisions with curvilinear streets made it difficult for municipal officials responding to our survey questions to estimate average block length. However, the average lengths of 400 feet and 500 feet were mentioned most often, with answers that ranged from 300 to 1200 feet. Thus costs are being increased in many cases by requiring blocks to be platted either at or below the minimum suggested length.

Drainage Systems Rather than immediately channeling water into underground pipes, drainage systems should use the full potential of soil absorption and surface evaporation.[40] This reduces the risk of downstream flooding and avoids a common municipal practice of "exporting" drainage problems to lower areas of the watershed. Since 59 percent of the surveyed developers expressed the opinion that underground piping requirements are excessive, one might assume that natural drainage is an underutilized alternative.

The implications of natural drainage systems for street design are several. First, grass swales may be preferable to curbs and gutters in many areas for prevention of downstream flooding. Second, elimination of sidewalks on local residential streets and *cul-de-sacs,* where low traffic volumes minimize safety hazards, will provide greater permeable surface area. Finally, with proper grading, streets themselves can be used to temporarily catch some storm water, subject to minimum access requirements. In sum, natural drainage can serve the double function of improving drainage design and reducing street costs.

The usefulness of above-ground drainage techniques depends upon the necessity for curbing, the soil's absorption capacity, possible adverse effects on ground water conditions, and the likelihood of downstream flooding.[41] Where traditional curbing, which composes about 95 percent of most urban drainage systems,[42] is necessary to reduce run-off and to protect street pavement from raveling and water penetration, street grading and layout can be used to channel water discharge directly to major drainageways rather than into small underground pipes. The avoidance of smaller diameter pipes is also cost-efficient because the cost per unit of hydraulic capacity diminishes with increased pipe size.[43]

Sanitary Sewerage   Overdesign is perhaps the most blatant cause of excess expenditures on sewerage systems. Newville's analysis of sewerage systems found that many municipalities design their systems for the greatest feasible density permitted by the zoning regulations. Approximately 10 percent of the municipalities surveyed admitted to basing their specifications on this criterion. This is unnecessary where projected future population may be estimated with accuracy, as in planned communities and other present-day residential patterns which are carefully detailed. Often municipalities design their sanitary sewerage systems to carry peak loads at only half capacity, thus requiring excessive pipe sizes. Minimum pipe size of 8 inches is often required where 6 inch pipes perform satisfactorily. The results of our subdivision survey showed that 24.6 percent of municipalities require pipes of 6 inches or less, while 75.4 percent require pipes of 8 inches or more.

Of the developers surveyed, 23.1 percent cited excessive pipe diameter as a significant factor in sanitary sewer construction costs. The minimum diameter of sewer mains required, as might be expected, seems to be influenced by residential density. Exhibit 7.17 reveals that the highest density group of municipalities almost universally require an 8" or larger main, whereas the two lower density groups require 8" or larger mains 78 percent and 65 percent of the time.

Even though the sample showed very little correlation between density and income level, the minimum diameter of sewer mains seems to be influenced by income level to an even greater extent than density. As can be seen in Exhibit 7.18, only 50 percent of the low-income group require 8"

EXHIBIT 7.17

MINIMUM DIAMETER OF SEWER MAIN
BY DENSITY OF MUNICIPALITIES

Density*	Number of Municipalities	4"	6"	PERCENT OF MUNICIPALITIES Size of Main 8" or More	Total
Lower	13	0%	22%	78%	100%
Lower middle	25	4	30	66	100
Upper middle	18	0	15	85	100
High	18	0	7	93	100

*For a description of the density number of groupings, see Appendix F.

SOURCE: Survey of Municipalities, Center for Urban Policy Research, Summer 1976.

EXHIBIT 7.18

MINIMUM DIAMETER OF SEWER MAIN BY
MEDIAN INCOME OF MUNICIPALITY

Median Income	Number of Municipalities	4"	6"	PERCENT OF MUNICIPALITIES Size of Main 8" or More	Total
Low	12	0%	50%	50%	100%
Moderate	22	0	23	77	100
Middle	25	4	16	80	100
High	6	0	0	100	100

SOURCE: Survey of Municipalities, Center for Urban Policy Research, Summer 1976.

or larger mains, while 100 percent of the high-income group require this size. Since not all of the high-income group are also the high-density group, it is logical to assume that the larger size main requirement is being used as another cost increasing device.

Intelligent placement of service laterals can often produce economies. For instance, where small lot size or cluster developments necessitate laterals at short distances, two sewer mains on a street, rather than the traditional single main down the center of the street, may produce real savings on lateral pipe footage.

Traditional Approach: One Main   Alternative Design: Two Mains

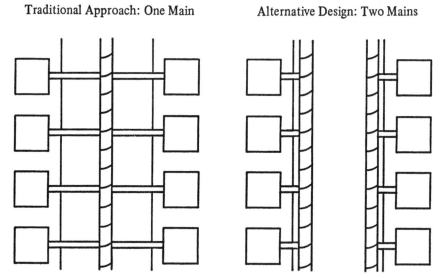

SOURCE: Derived from Newville, *New Engineering Concepts*, p. 29.

Manholes   Maintenance costs can be greatly reduced by wider placement
of manholes, which may constitute as much as 60 percent of the cost of a
collection system exclusive of laterals.[44] Eighty-five percent of the surveyed
municipal officials stated that the average manhole interval was 200-400
feet, with 300 feet mentioned most often. Only 12 percent of the respondents gave an average interval of 400-600 feet as their requirement. The
placement of manholes, however, is also dependent on the number of angles
in the sewer system, so that these figures realistically apply only to a straight
line main. Modern maintenance techniques reduce the need for frequent
manholes, as does proper grading of mains to minimize sedimentation of
solids. Eliminating over-design of pipes will also reduce sedimentation by
increasing the speed of water flow.

Water Facilities   The major purpose of a water system is to provide
potable water to residents of the community. However, the secondary function, that of providing water for fire protection, often determines the size of
the system and its flow characteristics, and hence its cost. If water mains
were designed only to transport domestic water, they would cost about 40
percent less than they do under today's fire protection standards.[45] Respondents to the survey of municipalities frequently stated that because of standards set by the local fire department, larger minimum pipe sizes were
required to provide sufficient flow to hydrants. Only 15 percent of the

municipalities surveyed permitted 4 inch minimum pipe sizes, while 59 percent required 6 inch mains and 26 percent required 8 inch mains. Pipe diameter was mentioned by 34.7 percent of the surveyed developers as being excessive.

Land Dedication and In-Lieu Fees for Parks and Schools Developers are often required to dedicate or reserve a portion of subdivision land for recreational facilities or schools. Alternatively, a cash contribution in lieu of dedication may be imposed. Confirming the rapidity with which this fairly recent technique of land use control has spread across the country, our survey revealed that 63 percent of the municipalities have either a mandatory or permissive provision for land dedication for parks and open space in their ordinances. Of these, 32 percent stated that they have actually required dedication in more than one-half of their new subdivisions. Twenty-five percent of the respondents reported requiring fees in lieu of dedication. Most based their fees on the cash equivalent of the value of the land that would have been dedicated.

The extent to which dedication is required for parks, recreation and open space was found to be strongly related to the income level of the municipality.(See Exhibit 7.19) Eighty-six percent of the high median-income municipalities either mandate or permit land dedication while only 50 percent of the low income group does. Again, maintenance of the exclusive nature of the municipality is being accomplished by what 56.9 percent of the developers surveyed considered to be an excessive requirement.

The next section discusses one additional method for significantly reducing costs without lowering the quality of subdivisions. This entails the relationship between lot size and subdivision costs.

EXHIBIT 7.19

LAND DEDICATION FOR PARKS, RECREATION
AND OPEN SPACE BY MEDIAN INCOME OF MUNICIPALITY

Median Income	Number of Municipalities	PERCENT MUNICIPALITIES Mandatory or Permissive	None Required	Total
Low	12	50%	50%	100%
Moderate	29	62	38	100
Middle	31	65	35	100
High	7	86	14	100

SOURCE: Survey of Municipalities, Center for Urban Policy Research, Summer 1976.

ZONING RESTRICTIONS AND SUBDIVISION COSTS

Lot Size and Frontage   A reduction in minimum lot size and frontage requirements is perhaps the best single technique for reducing subdivision improvement costs. Many per-unit improvement costs are directly related to the number of linear feet of street per lot, which determines costs of pavement, curbing, sidewalks, sewers and utilities. Linear feet of street is in turn largely governed by lot width, or frontage.

Exhibit 7.20 reveals that the impact of depth on linear feet of street per lot is minimal and that the focus should properly be on lot width. Whereas a 25-foot decrease in depth reduces street footage by about one foot, a corresponding decrease in lot width achieves a 16-foot reduction per lot.

The cost impact of lot width reduction can be estimated by first computing an average improvement cost per linear foot of street based on the various street-related improvements.(See Exhibit 7.21)

Using the average cost of improvements per linear foot, the added costs of increased lot width can be demonstrated, holding total lot size constant.(See Exhibit 7.22)

The $690 saving effected by reducing lot width, even in the comparatively narrow range from 70 to 50 feet, dramatically illustrates the possible effects of this cost reduction strategy.

In addition to lot width reduction, lot size reduction is another fruitful area for effecting savings. Clearing, grading, and engineering, in addition to raw land costs, vary directly with lot size. The New Jersey Builders Association has estimated improvement costs for varying typical lot dimensions for single-family detached homes. Exhibit 7.23 shows that a $10,658 saving can be realized by reducing lot size from one acre to 7,500 square feet. If housing of adequate quality is to be provided in the face of rising costs, something has to give. Reducing improvement costs through lot width and size reductions has the obvious advantage of creating no adverse effect on the quality of the improvements themselves. Whereas other cost-reducing policies discussed herein achieve savings through relaxation of specifications or elimination of certain improvements, decreased lot width and size only affect the *amount,* not the quality, of improvements required for each dwelling unit. This technique has the further merit of reducing expenditures for raw land costs, which are an increasingly significant component of total housing costs.[46]

EXHIBIT 7.20

LINEAR FEET OF STREET PER LOT DEPTH OF LOT* (IN FEET)

Lot Width in Feet	100	105	110	115	120	125
			(depth of lot in feet)			
50	31.46	31.67	31.88	32.08	32.29	32.50
52	32.74	32.96	33.17	33.39	33.61	33.83
54	34.05	34.27	34.50	34.73	34.95	35.18
56	35.38	35.62	35.86	36.10	36.33	36.57
58	36.75	37.00	37.25	37.50	37.75	38.00
60	37.75	38.00	38.25	38.50	38.75	39.00
62	39.16	39.42	39.68	39.95	40.21	40.27
64	40.61	40.89	41.17	41.44	41.72	42.00
66	41.61	41.89	42.17	42.44	42.72	43.00
68	43.12	43.41	43.71	44.00	44.29	44.59
70	44.12	44.41	44.71	45.00	45.29	45.59
72	45.69	46.00	46.31	46.63	46.94	47.25
74	46.69	47.00	47.31	47.63	47.94	48.25
75	47.19	47.50	47.81	48.13	48.44	48.75
80	50.33	50.67	51.00	51.33	51.67	52.00
85	53.57	53.93	54.29	54.64	55.00	55.36
90	56.92	57.31	57.69	58.08	58.46	58.85
95	60.42	50.83	61.25	61.27	62.08	62.50
100	62.92	63.33	63.75	64.17	64.58	65.00

*Full width street.

SOURCE: Jack Newville, *New Engineering Concepts in Community Development*, p. 46.

EXHIBIT 7.21

AVERAGE COST OF STREET RELATED IMPROVEMENTS*

Improvement	Cost Per Linear Foot
30′ pavement	$25.20
30″ curb and gutter	
(24″ apron, 6″ curb)	3.50
4′ sidewalk, 4″ thick	2.75
Sanitary sewer	
(8″ main)	10.60
Water Distribution	
(6″ main)	10.80
Storm Drainage	
(average of various sizes)	10.00

*These figures represent average cost per linear foot incurred on a large scale single-family subdivision in New Jersey in 1975.

SOURCE: Leonard Sendelsky, New Jersey Builders' Association, Testimony before the N.J. Senate County and Municipal Government Committee, July 11, 1975.

EXHIBIT 7.22

STREET RELATED IMPROVEMENT COSTS
BY WIDTH OF LOT

	WIDTH OF 7,500 SQ. FT. LOT		
	50 Feet	60 Feet	70 Feet
Depth	150 feet	125 feet	107.2 feet
Width-Depth Ratio	.30	.48	.68
Linear Feet of			
Street per Lot	34.6	39.0	44.5
Total Cost	$2,391	$2,695	$3,081
Added Cost	–	$ 304	$ 690

SOURCE: Derived from Jack Newville, New Engineering Concepts in Community Development, p. 47, and Leonard Sendelsky, New Jersey Builders Association, Testimony before the N.J. Senate County and Municipal Government Committee, July 11, 1975.

EXHIBIT 7.23

COMPARATIVE LOT IMPROVEMENT COSTS

Item	75' X 100' Lot Standard Requirements	100' X 200' (1/2 Acre) Lot Standard Requirements	200' X 200' (1 Acre) Lot Standard Requirements
1. Clearing	$ 625	$ 1,250	$ 2,500
2. Earth Balance	450	660	900
3. Sanitary Sewers	593	795	1,590
4. Sewer Laterals	135	135	135
5. Storm Drainage	560	750	1,500
6. Ditch Excavation	25	25	25
7. Water Distribution	604	810	1,620
8. Water Service	150	150	150
9. Curb & Gutter	392	525	1,050
10. Sidewalk	308	412	825
11. Pavement	1,948	2,610	5,220
12. Street Trees	100	150	300
13. Engineering	325	435	870
14. Municipal Fees	300	300	300
15. Utility Charge	900	900	900
16. Bond Premium	112	150	300
Total	$7,527	$10,057	$18,185

SOURCE: Leonard Sendelsky, New Jersey Builders Association: Testimony before the N.J. Senate County and Municipal Government Committee, July 11, 1975.

Summary of Findings

Over the years, subdivision ordinances have undergone a transformation from simple tools of plat recordation to sophisticated legal mechanisms which predetermine for years to come the physical, and to a great extent, the social character of large areas of the community. Subdivision ordinances can serve a useful purpose in facilitating orderly development and controlling the quality of that development. But the power to provide these controls may also be abused by individual municipalities, to the extent that growth becomes sprawl and quality design becomes synonymous with exclusion.

In the interest of protecting the value of their property, residents, through their elected and appointed municipal officials, promulgate regulations to ensure that those who move into the municipality will bear their burden of the cost of services the municipality provides. In recent years, many municipalities have increased their exactions on new subdivisions to cover not only the costs the new residents generate, but also to finance amenities which will be used to some extent by all residents. Over-designing of improvements and requirements of dedication of land for recreation, parks and open space are examples of this practice.

While the absolute cost of land improvement has escalated dramatically in the last decade, municipalities have generally failed to take these increases into consideration when revising their subdivision ordinances. Rather than modify requirements to reduce the impact of increased costs, many municipalities have maintained or increased the extent and stringency of their requirements. Our survey findings reveal that to a significant degree, the income level of a municipality, more than any other factor, determines the exaction placed on developers.

The combination of increased allocation of costs to developers, and thus to new residents, and the absolute increase in those costs serves to drive up the cost of new residential subdivisions so that those who are most in need of decent housing at a modest price are being excluded from the greatest part of the market. In order to reduce subdivision costs to new residents, it is suggested that the administrative process be streamlined, that the allocation of the cost burden be made more equitable and that requirements for public improvements be reduced wherever possible without substantially reducing the quality of development.

NOTES

1. Albert Farwell Bemis, *The Evolving House*. (Cambridge: The Technology Press, 1934) quoted in The Report of the President's Committee on Urban Housing, *A Decent Home,* 3 vols. (Washington D.C.: U.S. Government Printing Office, 1968), Vol. II; p.109.
2. Leland S. Burns and Frank G. Mittelbach, "Efficiency in The Housing Industry" in Report of the President's Committee on Urban Housing, *A Decent Home,* Vol. II., 1968, p.133.
3. *Ibid.*
4. Robert H. Freilich and Peter S. Levi, *Model Subdivision Regulations—Text and Commentary,* (Chicago: American Society of Planning Officials, 1975), pp.1-3.
5. "A Standard City Planning Enabling Act," U.S. Dept. of Commerce, § 14 (1928).
6. Growth controls and environmental concerns are discussed separately in chapters 9 and 10 of this report.
7. Wisconsin and Michigan were among the first states to require the surveying, registration and public approval of subdivision plats. Edward M. Bergman, et

al., *External Validity of Policy Related Research on Development Controls and Housing Costs,* (Chapel Hill: The Center for Urban and Regional Sciences, 1974), p.67.

8. Since plat recordation is generally a prerequisite to obtaining a building permit, subdivision regulations can in this way control the quality of residential development.

9. John Peps, "Control of Land Subdivision by Municipal Planning Boards," *Cornell Law Review,* 40 (1955), p.258.

10. National Commission on Urban Problems, (Douglas Commission), *Building the American City,* (New York: Praeger Publishers, 1968), p.245.

11. J. Noble, *A Proposed System for Regulating Land Use in Urbanizing Counties,* (Chicago: American Society of Planning Officials, 1967), p.16.

12. Advisory Commission on Intergovernmental Relations, *Urban and Rural America, Policies for Future Growth,* (Washington, D.C.: U.S. Government Printing Office, 1968), p.12.

13. A rigorous formula would involve a weighting, based on probability of occurrence of various levels of future benefits to reflect uncertainty as to future property value, use of adjacent property, proximity of public facilities and improvements, etc. The value of an investment is the weighted sum of the present value of all future levels of benefits minus the present value of occupancy costs.

14. This is not entirely accurate, because the risk factor may reduce the price a consumer is willing to pay for a home, and the developer's investment calculus is affected. This will ultimately depend upon market conditions and the consumer's knowledge and foresight.

15. *Building the American City,* Report of the National Commission on Urban Problems, p.208.

16. An externality may be viewed as a cost generated by, or an amenity accruing to, an actor for which he/she does not pay. Burns and Mittelbach provide an excellent framework for the treatment of externalities. They employ the concept of "Pareto Optimality" in concluding that optimization of the social product — not the elimination of externalities — is the desired goal in subdivision control. In brief, Pareto's theory is that the ends of maximum justice and efficiency will be attained by those policies which improve the welfare of society, while placing no member in a worse position. Alternatively, the presence of externalities is permitted when the gainers are able to compensate the losers and still be better off than previously. Thus, policies creating external diseconomies will be permitted only to the extent that such policies generate sufficient surplus "social goods" to permit compensation to the victims of the diseconomies. Unfortunately the difficulties inherent in any attempt to calculate social product and the extent of externalities minimize its usefulness here. Burns and Mittelbach, "Efficiency in the Housing Industry" in President's Committee on Urban Housing, *A Decent Home,* Vol. II, pp.92-3.

17. Burns and Mittelbach suggest: "The high ratio of externalities to direct returns, somewhat unique to housing, discourages investment in all but those items which generate returns directly to the investor. They quote economist Paul Samuelson on this point:
Urban land use and city planning is just shot through with external economies and diseconomies. It is there that you need programs and precisely there that the oldest theories of government have always said that free play of market forces will not work too well." Paul A. Samuelson, "The Dilemma of Housing," in Burnham Kelly (ed.), *Housing and Economic Development,* (Cambridge: Massachusetts Institute of Technology, 1953).

ile the subdivision resident eventually becomes one of the taxpayers, this ɡɪʋup is so large, and the maintenance and improvement costs are dispersed to such an extent, that each individual's contribution is minimal.

19. See, for example, Missouri Rev. Stat.§89.420, 88.444 (1969).

20. This initial step is not required by most state enabling statutes, but is often authorized by local ordinances. Freilich and Levi, *Model Subdivision Regulations*, p.51.

21. Although Section 15 of the Standard Planning Enabling Act provides for a mandatory public hearing on all subdivision applications, by 1975 only 16 states had included such a provision in their enabling legislation. Freilich and Levi, *Model Subdivision Regulations*, p.52.

22. Submission of plat applications to regional and state agencies is now required for all housing developments which are subsidized or insured by the federal government. See Office of Management and Budget Circular A-95, Title IV of the Inter-governmental Cooperation Act of 1968, Freilich and Levi, *Model Subdivision Regulations*, p.45.

23. The fee schedule may involve either a lump sum or an initial fee plus a small per-lot or per-acre charge. For a typical 15 lot subdivision, charges ranging from $5 to $825 were reported in the Survey of Municipalities. However, 57 percent of the municipalities charging fees charged less than $100.

24. Fairfax County, for example, requires between seven and twelve inspections at various phases of construction. Interview with Sidney O. Dewberry, of Dewberry, Nealon and Davis, a Fairfax County architectural and engineering firm, April 7, 1976.

25. American Society of Planning Officials, *Subdivision Fees Revisited* (Information Report No. 202, September, 1965), p.4.

26. Leonard Sendelsky, New Jersey Builders Association, Testimony before the N.J. Senate County and Municipal Government Committee, July 11, 1975.

27. Northern Virginia Builders Association, "Had It Not Been For the Courts...", Northern Virginia Housing Study Commission, May 15, 1975, p.20.

28. Ming Shyong Wu, "Public Improvement Costs for Residential Land Development: A Comparison of Five Counties in the Baltimore Region" (Baltimore, Maryland: Regional Planning Council, 1973), p.7.

29. For preliminary approval, these maximum review periods are: 95 days for a subdivision of more than 10 lots or a site plan of more than 10 acres; 45 days for a subdivision of 10 or fewer lots or a site plan of 10 or fewer acres. For final approval, the 45-day limit found in earlier legislation remains in effect.

30. The New Jersey Builders Association points up this problem on page 4 in its *Legislative Program and Policy Statement: 1976-77:* "Litigation, of course, is the last resort on the part of the builder, the more common result being the building of these extra and unnecessary costs into the purchase price of the product ultimately delivered to the individual consumer."

31. Brian Rogal, "Subdivision Improvement Guarantees," *ASPO Planning Advisory Service,* Report No. 298, January 1974.

32. The recently enacted New Jersey Municipal Land Use Law establishes a maximum period of 65 days within which the municipality must act upon the developer's assertion that improvements have been completed. The majority of our surveyed municipalities estimated that their bond release time fell within this limit.

33. Ming-Shyong Wu, "Public Improvement Costs in the Baltimore Region," p.7.

34. In the Baltimore Study Ming-Shyong Wu concludes: "The diversified public policies on land development suggests that there is a need for a more unified norm for all local jurisdictions. More unified land development regulations and standards will optimize the land development costs and environmental character throughout the region," *Ibid.*, p.21.

35. *Residential Streets: Objectives, Principles and Design Considerations,* (ULI, NAHB, and ASCE, 1974).

36. The recently-enacted New Jersey Municipal Land Use Law prohibits rights-of-way of greater than 50 feet for interior subdivision streets, unless it constitutes an extension of an existing street of greater width, or has already been shown on the master plan or official map at a greater width. It is important to note that 50 feet is the upper limit, and that where conditions allow, this figure can be pared considerably.

37. A graphic illustration of the pervasiveness and costliness of sidewalks is found on page 22 in *Residential Streets:* "One square mile of residential property often contains as much as 44 miles of sidewalk paralleling roadway pavements — currently about a $500,000 investment."

38. One author has estimated that a reduction in block length from 1200 feet to 600 feet will result in a 5 percent decrease in lot yield. Jack Newville, *New Engineering Concepts in Community Development,* Technical Bulletin 59, (Washington D.C.: The Urban Land Institute, 1967), p.42.

39. Freilich and Levi, *Model Subdivision Regulations,* p.83.

40. See, generally, *Residential Storm Water Management: Objectives, Principles and Design Considerations,* (ULI, NAHB, ASCE, 1975).

41. *Residential Streets,* p.37.

42. *Ibid.*

43. Newville, *New Engineering Concepts,* p.19.

44. *Ibid.,* p.29.

45. *Ibid.,* p.34.

Chapter Eight:
The Effect of Zoning Regulations on Housing Costs

Zoning regulations — once hailed as a primary tool of land use planning — are presently under attack as a major obstacle to equitable housing policy in the United States. Critics maintain that not only is zoning an improper instrument for achieving its ostensible purpose — that of separating incompatible land uses — but it also leads to wasteful land use patterns, unimaginative site design, and an ever-increasing degree of racial and economic segregation.

The comprehensive battery of restrictions that characterize local zoning ordinances often serve to exclude from the mushrooming suburbs all but the most affluent of prospective homebuyers. These regulations, which include minimum lot size, minimum lot width, minimum house size, maximum structure coverage, architectural standards, restrictions on permissible housing types, and a variety of other standards regulating the lot and structure, have severely damaged attempts to encourage low- and moderate-cost housing in the suburbs. The no-frills single-family house is "zoned out" of many of the suburbs in which development is occurring most rapidly. Further, multi-family dwellings and mobile homes, two important sources of low-cost shelter, are either severely undermapped or prohibited outright in many suburban communities. As grim consequences of these exclusionary devices, many low- and moderate-income families are left only with substandard and overcrowded housing in the nation's cities and older suburbs.

Many middle-income young and elderly families are forced to find homes outside the communities in which they have spent most of their lives. A primary goal of planning — to provide a variety of housing to suit different choices of lifestyles — is frustrated.

This chapter will first briefly explore the historical origins of zoning and the purposes which originally motivated its widespread adoption as a land-use control. Section two will discuss the rationales advanced to support zoning regulations today and the goals sought to be achieved by zoning. In the third section we discuss the incidence of specific zoning regulations and their impact on the various components of housing costs. Two surveys, one of municipal ordinances and practices and one of home builders are the sources used to detail the requirements which are being imposed.[1] The fourth section lists suggested cost reducing strategies. A summary of major points concludes the chapter.

Historical Development of Zoning

The traditional sanctity of private property rights, a dominant force in the settling of early America, began to erode in the late 1800's, when several cities enacted urban tenement laws restricting lot coverage.[2] In 1889, height restrictions were imposed on buildings in Washington, D.C., and a few years later in Boston.[3] These requirements in tandem with the burgeoning "city beautiful" movement, which pressed for more urban parkland, provided the backdrop for zoning regulations.

The first city-wide zoning ordinance evolved in 1916 from the efforts of a Fifth Avenue merchants group in New York City to protect their customers' sensibilities. The merchants, whose retail sales were being threatened by the encroachment of garment industry factories, persuaded the City of New York to establish zoning restrictions as a means of separating the manufacturing from the retail districts. These initial efforts were soon followed by the enactment of a comprehensive zoning ordinance in New York City.

The 1920's witnessed the rapid proliferation of state enabling legislation and zoning ordinances.[4] Although the state courts were divided on the issue of the constitutionality of zoning, the matter was finally resolved in 1926 by the U.S. Supreme Court in the case of *Euclid v. Ambler Realty,*[5] which held that the separation of incompatible uses was a legitimate means of promoting health, safety and the general welfare.

Since *Euclid,* the scope of zoning has broadened considerably. Today's ordinances, which regulate everything from off-street parking to the number of bedrooms, bear little resemblance to the first cautiously-drawn bulk and height limitations. Armed with the presumption of validity accorded them in the *Euclid* decision, municipal ordinances have withstood legal challenges on restrictions regulating minimum lot size, minimum house size, minimum lot width, prohibition of apartments and mobile homes, and a host of other restrictions.[6]

As detailed so well in the Douglas Commission Report, zoning has undergone radical changes in the past few decades.[7] Early zoning regulations were extremely permissive by today's standards. The role of the regulatory mechanism was substantially negative in that it sought merely to prohibit inappropriate development, to keep out less desirable uses. The early zoning process was conceived, not so much as a method to shape future growth, but as a tool to preserve established neighborhoods. Consequently, most zoning maps merely reflected the established pattern of existing development and provided for substantial districts of unrestricted development in underdeveloped areas.

With the increased scale and pace of development following World War II, the need arose for broader regulations designed to achieve planning objectives. For example, instead of listing prohibited uses in each district, as was formerly the practice, the newer ordinances listed permitted uses. Thus the old hierarchy of zoning uses was inverted and a more positive method of guiding development became the rule. Greater restrictions were employed to realize the newly acceptable aims of land use controls. The late 1940's and 1950's witnessed a widespread reduction in permitted residential density. A 1958 study of the Boston metropolitan area reported that, in the eleven communities that comprised the sample, the shift to larger lot sizes between 1946 and 1956 "reduced capacity for residential development in the area from 95,000 to 58,000 single-family dwellings, or a reduction of 39 percent from the 1946 figure."[8] Similarly, in 1960, 75 percent of Westchester County's vacant residentially-zoned land was zoned for one acre or more, in contrast to the lot sizes of one-eight of an acre which were common for single-family homes in the area a few decades earlier.[9] This increased restrictiveness was to be a harbinger of events to come.

The administration of zoning has also undergone substantial changes in recent years. Rather than the self-executing process envisioned for zoning when it was first established, administrative discretion has increasingly shaped the course of development. Variances, conditional uses, special exceptions and floating zones are devices through which zoning and planning boards *negotiate* with developers to achieve their objectives. While these techniques allow for more finely tuned planning approaches, they are also open to abuse by local officials, whose goals may be questionable.

To summarize the recent historical trend, zoning regulations have become more affirmative in nature, more detailed and more refined in order to further planning objectives. They have also become increasingly restrictive. Finally, their administration has become more sophisticated and discretionary.

The Current Uses and Abuses of Zoning

From simply keeping out noxious uses to positively directing growth orientation, prohibitions remain the dominant force underlying today's use of zoning ordinances. In the past, such uses as animal rendering plants and tall buildings were restricted. The modern equivalent is to prohibit the entrance of mobile homes or multi-family dwellings. The zoning ordinance is being used to protect the fiscal and/or social sanctity of the community. It is being used to protect the moral values of the community, as for example, to restrict pornography.

Whether or not each of the expanded objectives of zoning is valid depends in part on individual perspective. For the residents of a community, an ordinance which protects, and in some cases even enhances, the value of their property is most desirable. Moreover this coincides with our nation's historical reverence paid to the individual's private control of property rights. But for those people seeking entrance into this community, barriers erected through the use of zoning restrictions are considered an invidious discrimination. This section examines in detail several of the more prominent goals of zoning — externality zoning, the protection of property values, preserving the character of the neighborhood, and fiscal zoning. Finally, the situation in Houston, an example of a municipality without zoning, will be discussed.

EXTERNALITY ZONING

The earliest zoning regulations recognized the need for government intervention in the free market to avoid the expensive time-consuming and possibly volatile situation when someone used his/her property in such a way as to adversely affect neighboring properties. Nuisance law is typically backward-looking, i.e., a property owner could not litigate to protect his/her undiminished right to enjoy the property free from a nuisance created on another's property until that nuisance were actually in effect. Zoning restrictions, by limiting the negative impacts of private property owners on their neighbors, were viewed as a means of *protecting* property owners from the noxious effects of other users.[10] In economic parlance, this is translated into the elimination, or minimization, of negative externalities imposed by certain residents onto others. Thus "externality zoning" attempts to separate incompatible uses, and reduce negative effects below the level which would have occurred in an unregulated market.[11]

In an ideal world, the array of zoning districts in a community would isolate those uses which create negative externalities, thus minimizing external costs and maximizing total productive use of the land. It is necessary to determine whether zoning as it is practiced today efficiently achieves the goal of substantially reducing externalities. At least two empirical studies questioned the efficacy of presently constituted zoning regulations in reducing externalities in the residential property market.

A 1973 study of Pittsburgh's zoning ordinance concluded that the ordinance was much too detailed for the purpose of reducing externalities, and that external effects are much less subtle than the zoning ordinance implied.[12] The author concluded that greater reliance on the primary mechanism of the free market could better produce an efficient allocation of land resources.

An earlier study of the same ordinance suggested that a process of self-selection among purchasers may be operating to reduce externalities. Although the "character of the neighborhood" is a prominent factor in a homebuyer's purchase, if individual preferences differ amoung prospective purchasers, the adverse external effects will be minimized in the market.[13]

PROTECTION OR ENHANCEMENT OF PROPERTY VALUES

Closely allied to the goal of reducing the impact of negative externalities, but going beyond that limited goal, is the more general aim of zoning to protect property values.

The protection of property values is often advanced as a rationale for many highly restrictive zoning techniques. Because any neighborhood attribute which is objectionable to at least some residents will tend to reduce property values, this rationale has been used to mask concerns, both legitimate and illegitimate.

The point has been forcefully made that the concern with property values in zoning cases is merely a surrogate for a general antipathy to a wide variety of factors which influence neighborhoods.[14] For example, the concern with property values may be a surrogate for the desire to retain homogeneity of class, ethnic or racial composition, a highly prestigious neighborhood, or merely the amenities of space and privacy that low-density residential living offers. To claim that property values will fall as a result of a zoning action is merely to express a belief that there will be fewer or less desirable prospective purchasers in that neighborhood.[15]

Judicial response to the claim that property values must be protected against the intrusion of lower-quality residential developments has been inconclusive. While the protection of property values has been cited in numerous cases as one of the purposes of zoning, there is no agreement as to whether it will stand as the primary motive for excluding undesired land uses.[16]

PRESERVING THE CHARACTER OF THE NEIGHBORHOOD

A frequently stated alternative to "protection of property values" is "preserving the character of the neighborhood." Where there is a genuine architectural or historical character to be preserved, this goal of zoning may be a valid reason for government regulation. All too often, however, the argument that zoning is necessary to preserve the "character of the neighborhood" has become a catch-all for the avoidance of many changes which residents don't want. Basically, two under-currents of motivations can be found under this heading.

Amenities   Where low-density single-family development predominates, residents may seek to preserve the "rural" atmosphere, the low levels of traffic and noise, the open spaces, and the privacy created by wide spacing of residential lots.[17] In areas that are removed by some distance from the path of development, and therefore from market pressures, preserving a rural landscape for those who choose this life style is a commendable goal.

Homogeneity   A more sinister interpretation of the "character of the neighborhood" rationale is that it is a code for the desire to preserve economic, ethnic and racial homogeneity within a community. Many suburban residents, particularly in the more prestigious communities, wish to surround themselves with members of the same socioeconomic class, and they accomplish this by means of highly restrictive zoning regulations. Economic segregation is often synonymous with racial segregation, because blacks and other minorities dominate the lower income levels.[18] Thus, highly restrictive zoning is also a convenient method of achieving racial homogeneity and preserving ethnic purity.

FISCAL ZONING

Zoning regulations have increasingly been seen by local officials as a means by which to protect not only individual property values but also as a method to deal with the fiscal concerns of the municipality as a whole. Spurred largely by their heavy reliance on the local property tax as a means of obtaining revenue, many municipalities engage in "fiscal zoning." In their desire to protect the municipal tax base, communities attempt to exclude uses which require more in services than they contribute in taxes, and to encourage uses which provide revenues in excess of costs to the community. The search for "good ratables" has become a highly refined art in many areas of the country.[19] On the assumption that large houses contribute more to the tax base than they cost the community in services, municipalities frequently impose large minimum floor area restrictions and large lot requirements. This type of zoning rules out less expensive small houses which are perceived as resulting in greater burden on the municipal fisc relative to the amount of their contribution in taxes. This reasoning ignores the reality that large homes with many bedrooms attract large families with many school age children, requiring greater outlays for educational costs which typically make up 70 percent of most local budgets.[20]

Another widely held belief is that multi-family housing attracts low-income families and that low-income families have more children, who will put an extra burden on the public school system. On the strength of this belief, many communities limit multi-family dwellings, restrict the number of bedrooms in multi-family dwellings, or require amenities which will ensure that only luxury apartments will be built.[21] Overzoning for industrial uses is another tactic for increasing the tax base, which has the effect of decreasing the relative availability of residential land, thus increasing the cost of residential land.

One observer has provided a graphic analogy for fiscally motivated local zoning techniques, commenting that:

[L]and use planning in any comprehensive sense really does not exist in our larger urban areas. What does exist is a complex game of chess among localities, each attempting to palm off the undesired applicants for space upon their neighboring communities. This is warfare, not planning.[22]

So-called "fiscal zoning" is, in many cases, merely a response to myths, or inapplicable generalizations, about the revenue-producing characteristics of various housing types. A recent study of the fiscal impact of new housing on New Jersey communities concludes that different communities will have different trade-offs to make between costs and revenues, based more on the wealth and location of the community than on the type of housing that is built. Additionally it was found that there is little relationship between most communities' real fiscal interests and the actual zoning patterns in the communities. The authors wrote that the latter finding might be explained by a community's ignorance about its real fiscal interests or by the recognition that zoning patterns are actually determined by other than fiscal considerations.[23] As was mentioned in the discussion on protection of property values and preserving the character of the neighborhood, the stated goal of fiscal zoning may simply be window dressing for social exclusionary purposes.

Fiscal zoning as a valid exercise of the police power has not received undiluted blessings from the courts. While earlier cases, particularly in New Jersey, generally held that "pursuit of tax revenue" was a legitimate function of local officials, the changing trend of courts' attitudes towards exclusionary zoning has led to a more careful scrutiny of motives causing exclusionary effects.[24]

RELYING ON THE FREE MARKET: NON-ZONING IN HOUSTON

Although the use of zoning is so heavily institutionalized as to appear to be an immutable fact of life, many municipalities — including the thriving sunbelt metropolis of Houston, Texas — have managed quite well without it. Bernard Siegan undertook a detailed study of Houston,[25] a city which relies entirely on restrictive covenants (contracts between private property owners) to control land use. Siegan maintains that this private method of allocating land uses, combined with a heavy reliance on the free market, can be substituted for traditional zoning without loss of amenities, and with a substantial reduction in wasteful administrative costs. The case of Houston shows that economic forces tend to create a separation of uses even without zoning.[26] Where strong market pressures threaten to destroy a neighborhood with incompatible uses, strictly-enforced restrictive covenants are a sufficient means of guaranteeing separation of uses. However, the knowledge and financial resources necessary to legally enforce the covenants may be lacking in poorer neighborhoods which face the greatest market pressure. While zoning regulations also operate less effectively in transitional neighborhoods, they are at least less of a relative burden on the poor than private enforcement.

A striking difference between Houston and comparable zoned cities, is Houston's larger supply of apartments, a housing type typically used by low- and moderate-income people. This observtion lends support to the view that many zoning ordinances greatly under-map for multi-family use, relative to the market demand for that type of housing.

Although issue may be taken with Siegan's favorable assessment of Houston as a model of land use, his analysis is nonetheless intriguing for its attack on zoning by means of an actual case study. For those who caution that land use without zoning would be chaos, Siegan has a compelling rebuttal. Whether the private covenant system in Houston will continue to be effective remains to be seen. The Douglas Commission concluded that the real test will be met after large numbers of deed restrictions expire in the near future.[27]

THE JUSTIFICATION UNDERLYING ZONING REGULATIONS

Zoning regulations imposed by local government bodies serve, more or less effectively, to reduce the negative externalities that incompatible uses may cause. To the extent that zoning regulations may be relied upon, property values will be protected. While a municipality's motives are difficult to assess, it would appear that such stated objectives as the protection of property values, preserving the character of the neighborhood and fiscal zoning are frequently used to mask the unstated goals of economic and racial segregation. In at least one large city, Houston, a tentative conclusion is that market forces combined with private covenants have effectively taken the place of zoning.

These then are the intentions and effects of zoning; it is now necessary to examine in greater detail the specific techniques used to attain these goals. The next section of this chapter will attempt to do just that.

Zoning Techniques and Practices: Their Goals, Incidences, and Cost Impacts

Municipalities have assembled a diversified arsenal of zoning techniques. It is widely believed that the most commonly used "exclusionary" zoning devices are restrictions against multi-family units and against mobile homes, and requirements for excessive minimum lot sizes, lot frontages, and floor areas.[28]

The extent to which each of these techniques is employed by local governments was the subject of a survey of zoning practices conducted by the Center for Urban Policy Research. The survey of home builders will also be used to illustrate problems encountered in complying with zoning ordinances. These findings provide the substance of this section.

In addition, within the context of each of these potentially exclusionary techniques, an attempt will be made to draw the link, if in fact one does exist, between these regulations and housing costs. While recognizing that many of the cost impacts remain mere assertions, not yet having been subjected to rigorous empirical analyses, the existing state of the art — warts and all — is presented and discussed. Finally, a potentially significant cost factor relates to the administrative processes used to enforce the zoning ordinance. Such issues as the increasing use of the zoning variance and the trend towards more flexible controls will be assessed.

HOME BUILDERS' REACTIONS TO ZONING

To gauge the impact zoning regulations and practices have on the housing industry, home builders were asked how zoning regulations have affected or changed their development plans. (See Exhibit 8.1)

The major impacts of zoning as viewed by the home builders surveyed, were to increase the cost of the homes they built and to decrease the density of their development patterns. To a lesser degree, developers changed the location of development to less populated areas in order to build in conformance with less restrictive zoning which allowed a more economical product.

EXHIBIT 8.1

EFFECT OF ZONING REGULATIONS ON DEVELOPMENT PLANS
(n=378)

Change in Development Plans	Percent of Home Builders*
Build more expensive structure	60.6
Build less dense development	62.5
Build in less populated areas	40.9

*Will not add to 100.0 due to multiplicity of responses

SOURCE: Telephone Survey of Home Builders, Center for Urban Policy
              Research, Summer 1976.

MULTI-FAMILY ZONING REGULATIONS

A commonly used practice, particularly in suburban areas, is a restriction on multi-family development. Typically, this practice takes the form of a municipality either excluding entirely or under-mapping for multi-family homes. The justification for such a practice is often couched in either fiscal or aesthetic terms.

First, the fiscal motive may hold sway where there is a likelihood of large families who will increase the burden on school facilities. In most cases, fiscal motives for exclusion of multi-family housing have no sound basis in fact. Many apartment buildings provide a positive fiscal impact on the community.[29] Many suburban residents, whether justifiably or not, equate multi-family living with low-income people.[30] Their wish to maintain the suburbs as a preserve for the wealthy outweighs any fiscal benefits which may be gained from apartments.

A second motivation for exclusion of apartments may be a desire on the part of residents to preserve a low-rise, low-density environment. However, through the use of improved design and site planning techniques, multi-family homes may be built which are equally or more aesthetically pleasing than single-family developments. The stated aesthetic motive then may merely be a facade to mask the less socially acceptable motive of excluding those people who are likely to occupy apartment buildings.

Incidence of Multi-family Restrictions   New Jersey provides a striking example of the extent of the restrictions on multi-family uses. In 1972, only 6 percent of net residential land area in New Jersey was zoned for multi-family use.[31] Of this 6 percent, almost two-thirds of the land was zoned to permit only efficiency and one-bedroom apartments. Further investigation of this data revealed that only the six most rural municipalities contained 82 percent of the net residential land zoned for multi-family use. The report concludes: "If these (six municipalities) are excluded, the residential land zoned multi-family drops from 6.2 percent to just over one percent for the entire study area."[32] In a state experiencing powerful development pressures from the two metropolitan centers of New York and Philadelphia, the implications of this unbroken low-density mapping are particularly acute.

Our own survey of 80 municipalities across the nation shows a similar, though slightly less pronounced, aversion to multi-family uses.(See Exhibit 8.2)

While multi-family zoning amounts to 34.5 percent of residential land, the low-rise category, which includes two-family homes, townhouses and garden apartments, accounts for 71.6 percent of this total. This category is, of course, the least dense and therefore causes the least amount of opposition from single-family homeowners. Only 7.2 percent of the residential land is zoned for mid-rise which, for the purpose of our survey, we specified as being between three and eight stories. High-rise, which is specified as eight stories or higher, accounted for 2.6 percent of residential land in the municipalities surveyed.

The Impact of Multi-family Restrictions on Housing Costs Restrictions against multi-family homes have been dealt with in a number of recent court cases which have recognized the cost-increasing impact these restrictions have on housing. Since under-mapping or exclusion of higher density multi-family use creates a major obstacle to the construction of low- and moderate-income housing, recent cases have ruled against ordinances which

EXHIBIT 8.2

RESIDENTIAL ZONING BY TYPE OF USE**

Housing Type	Percent Residential Land
Single-family Detached	64.1
Low-rise Multi-family	24.7
Mid-rise Multi-family	7.2
High-rise Multi-family	2.6
Other*	1.4
Total	100.0

*Includes Mobile Home, PUD and other mixed height or use zones.
**Total residentially zoned land for 80 municipalities

SOURCE: Survey of Municipalities, Center for Urban Policy Research, Summer 1976.

exclude multi-family uses.[33] Even where multi-family dwellings are permitted, the design, height and bedroom restrictions contained in many ordinances are too restrictive to permit any real cost savings.[34]

In 1975, the national average rent for a typical unfurnished four room garden apartment of approximately nine hundred square feet was $215 per month.[35] This may be compared with an approximate $500 per month cost[36] of the average new single-family home priced at $50,500 and containing 1638 square feet.[37]

REGULATION OF MOBILE HOMES

Mobile homes, even more than multi-family houses, are systematically excluded from many municipalities. Most arguments against zoning for mobile homes cite the fact that they are aesthetically objectionable. However, they are the least expensive owner-occupied form of housing on the market today. As Norman Williams and Thomas Norman noted in their analysis of exclusionary practices, mobile homes are "efficient, readily available, and unnecessarily ugly."[38] Since that time, strides have been made both in the design of mobile homes themselves and in their site planning.

Incidence of Mobile Home Restrictions   As can be calculated from Exhibit 8.3, of the surveyed municipalities, 61.3 percent allowed mobile homes, though most attached conditions to their approval.

EXHIBIT 8.3

MOBILE HOME ZONING

Mobile Home Zoning	Number of Municipalities	Percent
Mobile Home Zone	16	20.0
Permitted by Right in Residential Zone	7	8.7
Permitted by Right in Commercial or Industrial Zone	2	2.5
Special Exception Use in Residential Zone	24	30.0
Special Exception Use in Commercial or Industrial Zone	19	23.7
Floating Zone	1	1.2
Prohibited in all Zones	31	38.7

NOTE: Will not add to 100.0 due to multiplicity of responses.

SOURCE: Survey of Municipalities, Center for Urban Policy Research, Summer, 1976.

The greatest number of municipalities permitted mobile homes only by special exception, a procedure that requires time, expense and diligence on the part of the applicant and is, at best, uncertain.

Cost Impact of Mobile Home Restrictions By prohibiting outright, as 38.7 percent of the surveyed municipalities do, and by under-mapping for mobile homes, communities prevent the extensive use of a cost-reducing form of housing. The average retail price for a typical fourteen by sixty-eight, nine hundred and fifty-two square foot mobile home was $11,440 in 1975.[39]

Recent judicial decisions have tended to agree with Justice Hall's famous dissent in *Vickers v. Township Committee of Gloucester Twp.*,[40] which argued that a developing community in the path of growth must make some provision for mobile homes.[41] For example, a proposed Statewide Housing Plan promulgated by the California Department of Housing and Community Development, recognizing the part that mobile homes play in lowering housing costs, recommends changes in local regulations to encourage the use of mobile homes and modular housing.[42] As the price of conventional housing soars, one can expect that pressure both judicial and legislative aimed at relaxing restrictions on mobile homes will increase.

We turn now from those restrictions which limit the amount or type of housing to those which specifically affect the density of housing.

MINIMUM LOT SIZE

The zoning technique used most often to establish the density of development in residential areas is regulation of minimum lot size. Typically, a community will establish several different single-family minimum lot size zones in addition to one or two minimum lot size zones for each multi-family use. Since there are other techniques which control density in multi-family zones with greater sophistication,[43] the minimum lot size will be discussed here in relation to single-family homes only.

The primary justifications for large lot zoning include:

1. The need for open space to promote the amenities of a rural atmosphere and to avoid overcrowding and congestion;
2. The need to regulate the timing and location of growth;
3. The need for large lots to overcome the problem of environmental damage, usually the lack of sewer facilities or unfavorable soil conditions;
4. The need to preserve the tax base.[44]

However, in assessing these goals, one must also consider the exclusionary effects of large lot zoning on the municipality and the region. Some factors to be investigated are:

1. Whether the regulations seem intended primarily to maintain the municipality as a preserve for the wealthy. Where the legitimate justifications seem weak or appear to be used as a cover-up for true motives, this conclusion may be warranted.[45]
2. Whether the regulations serve to ward off strong developmental pressures imposed by the suburbanization of the population. Where suburbanization pressures do not exist, a town's desire to preserve a rural atmosphere may be given more weight.
3. Whether the zoning is consistent with the character of the surrounding land.
4. The extent to which the municipality has provided zoning districts for higher density uses.

Given the widespread presumption of validity granted to zoning restrictions, as well as the large arsenal of justifications municipalities have stockpiled to justify their use of large-lot zoning, it is not surprising that many early cases failed to resolve definitively the exclusionary issues involved in large minimum lot size requirements. Recent cases, however, have examined the arguments for large-lot zoning with more sensitivity to the factors noted above and invalidation of large-lot requirements is now more common.[46]

Incidence of Excessive Minimum Lot Sizes Lot size requirements are much more restrictive today than thirty years ago. Whereas densities of five units to an acre were once standard in suburban areas,[47] lot minimums of one acre or more are becoming increasingly common. Multi-acre lot size requirements have often been established to slow the pace of suburban growth. Large-lot zoning is also used as an indirect method of ensuring the construction of only expensive, high-quality dwellings,[48] which will enhance both the prestige of the community and the municipal coffers. The move to very large lot requirements most often occurs in the high growth areas surrounding metropolitan centers, thus exacerbating an already tight real estate market. A case in point is New Jersey, for which a 1970 survey by the New Jersey Department of Community Affairs yields the following minimum lot sizes by county. An extraordinary 67 percent of single-family zoned residential land in New Jersey was in "acreage" zoning (40,000 squre feet or more). Only 5.1 percent of the single-family zoned land was in lot sizes of less than 10,000 square feet, the lowest measured category.(See Exhibit 8.4)

EXHIBIT 8.4

MINIMUM LOT SIZE REQUIREMENTS FOR SINGLE-FAMILY ZONED RESIDENTIAL LAND BY COUNTY IN NEW JERSEY

County	LAND WITH LOT SIZE RESTRICTIONS IN SINGLE-FAMILY ZONED RESIDENTIAL LAND					
	Less than 10,000 square feet (%)	10,000-19,999 square feet (%)	20,000-39,999 square feet (%)	40,000-119,999 square feet (%)	3 acres or more (%)	Total (%)
Bergen	4.3	19.1	21.5	55.1	0.0	100.0
Burlington	10.2	19.6	18.8	27.5	23.8	100.0
Camden	24.5	28.9	8.1	38.0	0.5	100.0
Essex	4.8	41.5	38.6	15.1	0.0	100.0
Gloucester	4.8	21.2	39.3	39.4	5.2	100.0
Hunterdon	0.1	0.7	2.1	66.6	30.5	100.0
Mercer	0.7	7.9	49.5	39.9	2.1	100.0
Middlesex	4.9	9.2	47.2	38.7	0.0	100.0
Monmouth	1.0	3.9	10.4	83.7	0.9	100.0
Morris	0.3	4.2	12.6	61.0	21.9	100.0
Ocean	16.9	10.0	4.3	68.8	0.0	100.0
Passaic	9.2	24.4	22.3	23.0	21.1	100.0
Somerset	0.2	0.4	13.9	60.8	24.6	100.0
Sussex	1.2	5.3	26.0	61.9	5.7	100.0
Union	31.4	37.2	7.4	24.1	0.0	100.0
Warren	1.8	2.0	33.6	56.7	5.8	100.0
Total Average	(5.1)	(9.0)	(18.8)	(54.7)	(12.3)	100.0

SOURCE: *Land Use Regulation: The Residential Land Supply*, Department of Community Affairs, Division of State and Regional Planning, Trenton, April 1972.

Only the first lot size, for which 34.4 percent of the single family land is zoned, would yield densities of 5 units or more per acre, which was formerly the norm. "Acreage" zoning, while much less prevalent nationally than in New Jersey, was found to comprise 9.1 percent of the single-family land in our surveyed municipalities in this category.(See Exhibit 8.5)

The regional breakdown for single-family minimum lot sizes also proved interesting.(See Exhibit 8.6)

It would appear that the Eastern region, with 84.2 percent of its single-family land in lot sizes 7,000 square feet or more, requires considerably larger lot sizes than any other region. This may be indicative of the desire to maintain private open space that is more prevalent in this region where the density of population is most keenly felt and public open space is often less available. It was also found that the Western region, which zones the highest proportion of its land for single-family homes (71.4 percent), requires the smallest lot sizes. Cities in the East zone 48.4 percent for multi-family housing, which would take some of the pressure off demand for single-family homes on small lots.

Cost Impact of Excessive Minimum Lot Size It is generally agreed that large lots tend to cost more than small lots, although empirical evidence shows that the cost increase is far from proportional to the increase in size.[49] A report prepared for the State of Connecticut in 1967 quoted prices for lots of various sizes in one Connecticut community: "$6,000 to $7,000 for a half-acre lot, $5,000 to $8,000 for a one-acre lot, and $7,000 to $9,000

EXHIBIT 8.5

SINGLE-FAMILY MINIMUM LOT SIZE*

Lot Size in Square Feet	Percent Land
0 - 6,999	34.4
7,000–9,999	28.5
10,000–19,999	19.2
20,000–39,999	8.8
40,000–79,999	6.0
80,000 or more	2.9
Unrestricted	0.2
Total	100.0

*Total single-family zoned land for 75 municipalities.

SOURCE: Survey of Municipalities, Center for Urban Policy Research, Summer 1976.

EXHIBIT 8.6

SINGLE-FAMILY MINIMUM LOT SIZE BY REGION

Lot Size in Square Feet	PERCENT SINGLE-FAMILY ZONED LAND Region			
	East N=18	North Central N=16	South N=18	West N=23
0-6,999	15.8	18.7	47.1	50.0
7,000-9,999	24.0	40.0	14.0	35.4
10,000-19,999	26.9	38.6	11.8	5.5
20,000-39,999	10.0	2.0	18.0	5.5
40,000-79,999	15.6	0.0	4.6	3.7
80,000 or more	7.8	0.0	4.5	0.0
Unrestricted	0.0	0.7	0.0	0.0
Total[1]	100.0	100.0	100.0	100.0

NOTE: [1]Total may not add to 100.0 due to rounding.

SOURCE: Survey of Municipalities, Center for Urban Policy Research, Summer, 1976.

for a two-acre lot."[50] At least one commentator has noted, however, that the cost curve rises most sharply in the smaller lot-size ranges — between 6,000 and 8,000 square feet[51] — which is the range within which exclusionary impact is most likely to be felt.

One reason for the decline in per-unit land prices as lot size increases is the imbalance that zoning regulations create between supply and demand. Zoning creates sub-markets for the various residential lot sizes, and because of the municipal propensity for large-lot zoning, the result is an oversupply of large lots and a shortage of small lots. The surfeit of large lots relative to the demand causes a reduction in the price which large lots command. Further, the shortage of small lots places the few available lots at a premium, thus greatly increasing their per-unit cost. Thus the effect is to facilitate large lot single-family development, while at the same time impeding or at least increasing the cost of development of small lots.

A more subtle impact of large lot zoning is the developer's frequently employed ratio between house size and lot size. The ratio results from the fact that lenders and appraisers are reluctant to value, for lending purposes, the improved land component at more than twenty percent of the total residential package. Where this ratio of 5:1 is being used, regulations requiring greater lot size and width and a high level of improvement will lead to the construction of a larger, more expensive house.[52]

One author attributes the lower per-unit cost of large lots to the operation of the law of "diminishing marginal returns."[53] After lots reach a certain (undetermined) size, each additional unit of land has less value to the owner. Beyond a certain size, the disamenities of large lots hold sway in the form of excessive isolation, increased transportation costs, and so forth. More specifically, the value of each added increment will decline sharply after the minimum lot size is surpassed, because the goals — whether exclusionary or more benign — of the large-lot zoning have already been achieved by this minimum. As Norman Williams has noted, the fact that enclosed space is more valuable than open space also explains the reduced cost impact of large lot requirements.[54]

In contrast to the preceding analysis, some authors have concluded that in many suburban communities, zoning restrictions may not be "binding": that is, that large-lot zoning may not force net density below that which would be obtained under the operation of the free market.[55] Using multiple regression analysis, Larry Orr concludes that zoning creates only a marginal interference with the free market, because lot sizes are generally set just above the free market level thus minimizing the cost impact.[56] The author advances the theory that suburban communities, where lot sizes are usually largest, are generally best suited to high-income development. This analysis was probably valid at the time; however, it is based on the assumption that the center city provides the employment for the region. The average worker earning a low or moderate wage was found to prefer staying in the city near his/her place of employment rather than budget for commuting costs. The major trend of this decade has been the movement of industry and office complexes to the suburbs. Assuming the average worker would still prefer to live near his/her place of employment, this puts added market demand pressure on the suburban land which is currently severely limited in supply by large lot zoning. Given the change in employment patterns, the correlation between highly restricted zoning regulations and high income residents becomes more significant.

As Exhibit 8.7 indicates, municipalities with high median family incomes zone less than 66 percent of their single-family land in lot sizes of less than 20,000 square feet (roughly equivalent to one-half acre), whereas 95.3 percent of single-family land is zoned for these minimum lot sizes in low median income municipalities. This pattern of economic segregation is increasingly inappropriate in view of the shifting pattern of employment.

The impact of zoning restrictions on the price of raw land is perhaps the most elusive aspect of zoning's cost effects due to the wide variation in real estate market conditions across the country and the myriad of factors influencing land prices. The following comparisons of raw land costs in two locales indicates that while the raw land costs have risen, total housing

EXHIBIT 8.7

SINGLE-FAMILY MINIMUM LOT SIZE BY MEDIAN FAMILY INCOME OF
MUNICIPALITY[1]

Lot Size in Square Feet	PERCENT LAND INCOME GROUP			
	Low N=9	Moderate N=28	Middle N=33	High N=10
0-6,999	24.9	49.1	27.5	27.9
7,000-9,999	36.9	28.0	30.4	16.2
10,000-19,999	33.5	14.9	18.4	19.8
20,000-39,999	3.6	1.5	10.2	27.4
40,000-79,999	0.0	6.5	7.1	6.5
80,000 or more	0.0	0.0	6.4	2.2
Unrestricted	1.1	0.0	0.0	0.0
Total	100.0	100.0	100.0	100.0

NOTE: [1] For income groupings, see Appendix F.

SOURCE: Survey of Municipalities, Center for Urban Policy Research,
Summer 1976.

costs have risen even more steeply. In fact, the cost of raw land as a component of the total package has actually decreased. (See Exhibit 8.8)

These findings suggest that improvement costs have risen so sharply in this period that their increased cost, capitalized into the raw land component, has exerted a downward pressure on the price of raw land itself. But counteracting this downward pressure is the upward pressure exerted on raw land price created by the use of the various exclusionary devices. It is extremely difficult to determine the extent of the effect of these two pressures on any one parcel. However, it is safe to assume that without the exclusionary practice, the cost of raw land as a percentage of total housing price would be considerably lower.

To date, the most attention has been placed on large lot zoning as an exclusionary device in both the literature and the courts.[57] However, many commentators have emphasized that lot *width,* more than lot size, is responsible for increasing housing costs.[58] The cost of many improvements required by local subdivision ordinances — streets, sidewalks, water and sewer facilities, etc. — is directly related to the number of linear feet of lot fronting on the street.[59] Thus, as lot width increases, these subdivision improvement costs increase proportionately. Although lot size itself is not the culprit here, lot size and lot width requirements are closely correlated.[60]

EXHIBIT 8.8

COST OF RAW LAND FOR TYPICAL HOMES IN TWO LOCATIONS

MONTGOMERY COUNTY, MD.		
		Percent
1972	1977	Change
10,000 square foot lot $ 2,996	$ 3,964	+24.4%
Total cost of home 50,406	68,195	+35.3
Land as a percent of		
total cost 5.94%	5.81%	- .13%

COLORADO		
		Percent
1970	1975	Change
Approx. 10,000 square		
foot lot $ 1,143	$ 1,714	+50.0%
Total cost of home 18,310	30,400	+66.0
Land as a percent of		
total cost 6.24%	5.64%	- .60%

SOURCE: The Suburban Maryland Home Builders Association, "The High Cost of Housing in Montgomery County, Maryland" (Silver Spring, Md., 1976); Colorado Association for Housing and Building, "An Analysis of the Impact of State and Local Government Intervention on the Home Building Process in Colorado 1970-75," (prepared by Beckert, Browne, Coddington and Associates, Inc., Denver, 1976), p. 14.

Furthermore, where minimum lot widths are not specified, width-to-depth ratios and minimum side lot requirements may create a *de facto* minimum frontage requirement.

Incidence of Minimum Lot Width Restrictions As with minimum lot size, minimum lot widths that were found to predominate in suburban New Jersey counties were considerably more restrictive than those in our national survey.(See Exhibit 8.9) Only 13.5 percent of the single-family zoned land in New Jersey permits less than 100 foot frontage. At the other extreme, more than 30 percent of the single-family zoned land required at least a 200 foot minimum lot width.

Our national municipal survey shows in Exhibit 8.10, 45.8 percent of residential land in these communities was zoned for lot widths of less than seventy feet, slightly more than the 34.4 percent zoned for minimum lot sizes under 7,000 square feet.[61] That 54.2 percent of lot widths exceed sixty-nine feet indicates that reductions in frontage requirements across the country could provide a substantial cost saving.[62]

EXHIBIT 8.9

MINIMUM LOT WIDTH FOR SINGLE-FAMILY ZONED LAND IN NEW JERSEY
COUNTIES

County	MINIMUM FRONTAGE RESTRICTIONS ON LAND PERMITTING SINGLE-FAMILY USE				
	0-99 Feet (%)	100-149 Feet (%)	150-199 Feet (%)	200 Feet Or More (%)	Total
Bergen	7.4	32.9	29.9	29.8	100.0
Burlington	20.1	41.5	4.0	34.4	100.0
Camden	47.8	30.9	11.5	9.8	100.0
Essex	13.4	50.3	7.7	28.6	100.0
Gloucester	10.3	53.6	29.2	6.9	100.0
Hunterdon	3.6	0.9	16.9	78.6	100.0
Mercer	9.6	28.2	34.8	27.2	100.0
Middlesex	8.0	67.3	14.5	10.2	100.0
Monmouth	3.6	8.8	8.9	78.7	100.0
Morris	2.3	45.7	28.6	23.4	100.0
Ocean	22.4	30.6	37.8	9.2	100.0
Passaic	32.2	53.7	8.3	5.8	100.0
Somerset	13.4	7.8	34.0	44.8	100.0
Sussex	1.7	18.4	51.1	28.8	100.0
Union	43.4	32.6	24.0	0.0	100.0
Warren	11.2	14.8	52.6	21.4	100.0
Total Average Percent	(13.5)	(32.2)	(23.3)	(31.0)	100.0

SOURCE: *Land Use Regulation: The Residential Land Supply*, State of New
Jersey - Department of Community Affairs, Division of State and
Regional Planning, April 1972.

EXHIBIT 8.10

MINIMUM LOT WIDTH FOR SINGLE FAMILY ZONED LAND*

Lot Width in Feet	Percent Land
0-69	45.8
70-99	22.8
100-149	13.7
150-199	5.0
200 +	6.5
Unrestricted	6.2
Total	100.0

*Total single-family zoned land for 75 municipalities

SOURCE: Survey of Municipalities, Center for Urban Policy Research,
          Summer 1976.

Cost Impact of Minimum Lot Width Requirements   The record is unclear as to whether, on balance, wide spacing of lots increase total public facilities installation costs. Since subdivision improvement requirements are generally less restrictive in fringe areas where large lot zoning predominates, the cost of extra linear footage of public improvements may be outweighed by the lower specifications required.[63] But since evidence points to increasing tightening of subdivision requirements in urban growth areas,[64] this benefit of widely-spaced lot zoning may be illusory.

MINIMUM FLOOR AREA RESTRICTIONS

Foremost among regulations which directly increase construction costs are minimum house size restrictions, which are commonly phrased in terms of a specified minimum of square feet of livable floor area.

Arguments used to support minimum building sizes include the protection of property values and the safeguarding of the public health by decreasing the emotional tensions resulting from crowded living conditions. The property value argument, when used alone, has been given short shrift by many courts, who view the rationale as an insufficient ground for upholding a zoning regulation. The public health rationale, on the other hand, has been given considerable credence.[65] Norman Williams notes, however, that as framed, the rationale is merely makeweight because the standard bears no relation to occupancy. Were the goal truly to avoid overcrowding, occupancy standards would have to be set for each home. This goal, of providing a healthful housing environment, might better be accomplished through the use of housing codes.

Incidence of Minimum Floor Area Restrictions Various standards have been derived based on minimum square feet per person necessary to maintain mental health.[66] These standards have been translated into minimum livable floor area requirements based on the number of people expected to reside in a unit. While these standards are necessarily highly subjective, as well as reflective of the middle class bias one might expect of most standard-setting groups, the gap between minimum standards (Exhibit 8.11) and currently required minimums (Exhibit 8.12) is significant. Of the eighty municipalities surveyed, it was found that 29.6 percent of the single-family and 27.1 percent of the multi-family zoned land was covered by minimum floor area restrictions.[67]

EXHIBIT 8.11

MINIMUM FLOOR AREAS PER DWELLING UNIT[1]

Dwelling Type Structures	Number of Bedrooms				
	0-BR	1-BR	2-BR	3-BR	4-BR
	Square Feet				
Detached, semi-detached and rows	445	580	815	1,040	1,245
Apartments	410	535	685	875	1,070

[1] Net areas in square feet.

SOURCE: Housing and Home Finance Agency, *Design Standards for Federal Personnel* (Washington, D.C., Bureau of the Budget, 1953).

EXHIBIT 8.12

MINIMUM FLOOR AREA RESTRICTIONS[1]

Dwelling Type	Square Feet					
	0-599	600-799	800-999	1000-1199	1200 Or More	Total
Single Family	13.8	18.6	14.5	31.1	22.0	100.0
Multi-Family	34.7	31.4	8.5	12.5	12.9	100.0

1. Percent of total land which is restricted by a Minimum Floor Area provision.

SOURCE: Survey of Municipalities, Center for Urban Policy Research, Summer 1976.

Comparing Exhibits 8.11 and 8.12, more than 50 percent of the single-family zoned land that is covered by a minimum floor area restriction requires at least 1000 square feet in livable floor space. This requirement would equate roughly with the standard for a three bedroom home. In the multi-family category, the requirement of over 1000 square feet (25.4 percent) is obviously excessive since this amount of livable floor area is normally associated with four bedroom apartments, a unit that is rarely built.

Cost Impact of Minimum Floor Area Requirements Our research supports the theory that motives other than the maintenance of public health are operating, and suggests that this is an area in which restrictions could be greatly lowered or removed without sacrificing the general welfare. The frequently used minimum first floor livable area is even more obviously unrelated to public health motives. Because the greatest cost of the house is incurred in constructing the foundation and first floors, this minimum requirement is directly related to house cost. The need to reduce these standards is heightened by the trend toward smaller family size. Large house size minimums also discriminate against small family units and single persons who may wish to purchase homes.

Because of the realities of housing construction costs, minimum floor area requirements are, in effect, minimum cost provisions.[68] Although some portions of a house are more costly than others, a general rule of thumb of $15 per square foot can be applied to obtain an estimate of the minimum cost of construction of a house.[69] For example, a typical minimum floor area restriction for a single family home of 1,200 square feet would militate a cost of at least $18,000 for basic house construction. This is exclusive of all other costs that make up the total figure. It is difficult to understand why the courts have traditionally been unwilling to equate floor area requirements with the universally disfavored minimum cost provisions. Although minimum floor area provisions accomplish an identical purpose, courts have been more receptive to the various rationales advanced to support a lower limit on house size.[70]

SUMMARY OF COST IMPACTS

Before discussing the administrative practices associated with zoning regulations, it may be useful to summarize and elaborate on the cost impacts which result from the cumulative effect of the various zoning techniques described. Zoning restrictions impact on every phase of housing costs. From the initial purchase of a residential site to the actual costs of occupying the structure, zoning regulations are reflected in increased costs.

Development Costs Both the price of raw land and the costs of improvements are increased in several ways by restrictive zoning practices.

There is much evidence to suggest that large-lot zoning increases unimproved lot costs, both by requiring the purchase of larger lots and by causing an "artificial" — that is, deviating from the free market — shortage of smaller residential lots. The cost of public improvements on residential lots is also pushed up by large frontage, or lot width, requirements.

Construction Costs   Construction costs are directly increased by the high minimum house size, or floor area, requirements in many communities. Applying a rule-of-thumb standard cost per square foot, it can be seen that minimum floor area requirements — as applied to both single-family and multi-family dwellings — are, in effect, minimum cost provisions for housing. Another blatant cost-enhancing technique is the prohibition, or under-mapping, of certain dwelling types, such as multi-family dwellings and mobile homes, whose designs permit cost savings. Finally, there is evidence that developers build more expensive homes on larger lots in order to keep a rough ratio between the value of the structure and the value of the land.

Occupancy Costs   Although development and construction costs tend to receive greatest importance in assessments of the cost impact of zoning, the increased costs of occupancy in low-density residential units must also be included in the calculus. These costs, briefly, may include: increased costs of landscaping and maintaining a large lot; the higher costs of maintenance for public improvements associated with wide lots; higher property taxes on residences with higher assessed values; and extra maintenance and utility charges necessitated by large homes.

Non-Housing Budget Items   The sprawl pattern created by low-density zoning restrictions has had an inflationary effect on the transportation network and infrastructure in suburban metropolitan areas. Low-density zoning has eliminated the feasibility of all modes of transportation except the private automobile, which presently dominates the suburban landscape. The much larger commuting distances necessitated by the wide dispersal of the population around employment centers takes its toll in terms of: the higher per-unit costs of the automobile as opposed to mass transit; the resources lost and pollution caused by legions of gas-guzzling cars; and the person-hours lost in travel time. It has been estimated that 2.77 hours per day per dwelling unit are spent in travel time by those who live in a low-density sprawl pattern, as opposed to 1.44 hours per day for those who live in a high-density planned community.[71] From a transportation strategist's point of view, large-lot, low-density single-family zoning makes no sense whatsoever. The cost of extending an expensive infrastructure in a low-density residential area also serves to drive up the cost of housing in a community. As environmental concerns limit the number of sites on which individual systems are allowed, expensive sewer and water systems must be extended to meet the needs of widely dispersed residents.

With low-density zoning, environmental costs are increased considerably through air pollution, noise pollution, soil erosion and paving over of permeable surfaces, and wasteful use of open space which results in degradation of wildlife and vegetation habitats.[72] These costs impact on both the private and public sectors, not just economically, but aesthetically.

ADMINISTRATIVE COSTS

Administrative delay can be tremendously harmful to a residential construction project. This is particularly true in recent years, as front-end financing costs have become more onerous. Many developers are forced to run the gamut of local boards of adjustment, planning commissions, and city councils in order to gain the necessary zoning approvals. Rezoning, variances, and special exceptions all may cause critical delay.

Zoning Change Procedures   The survey of home builders and developers shows that while over 40 percent rarely experience the delay caused by zoning change procedures, a striking 31.6 percent have encountered such delay in over 75 percent of the developments they have built.(See Exhibit 8.13)

Rezoning, a procedure commonly encountered, normally takes an average of three to four months, but may take twelve months or more. Variances and special exception uses require fewer steps, and thus may take only one or two months.[73] Each day absorbed in negotiations, hearings and preparation of plans increases the expense and risk of undertaking the project.

EXHIBIT 8.13

NECESSITY FOR ZONE CHANGE BEFORE CONSTRUCTION

Required	Number of Respondents	Percent
Almost never	155	42.9
5–10%	19	5.3
11–25%	22	6.1
26–50%	37	10.2
51–75%	14	3.9
More than 75%	114	31.6
Total	361	100.0

SOURCE: Telephone Survey of Home Builders, Center for Urban Policy Research, Summer 1976.

Interestingly, the zoning relief requested is granted more often than not (See Exhibit 8.14), indicating the possibility of excessive *pro forma* proceedings which could be pared without sacrificing the ultimate outcome. It appears that municipalities increasingly designate areas for large lots (holding zones) in expectation of zoning changes being made — but only after negotiations with the developer. Needless to say, this substantially increases the power of the municipality to demand concessions from the developer.

Planned Unit Developments (PUD) Particularly time-consuming are approval procedures for innovative zoning techniques such as cluster, planned unit, or planned residential, developments. Of the forty-eight respondents to the Survey of Municipalities who have some form of PUD ordinance, 47.9 percent stated that it took somewhat longer to gain PUD approval compared to approval time for a subdivision of equal size, and 8.3 percent said the approval time was significantly longer. This increased time for approval may be attributed to the heavy reliance on negotiations in setting development and improvement standards. While the emphasis on innovative design has been held out as a potential area of cost reduction (by allowing greater density without loss of open space and by permitting reduction in public improvement costs), it is doubtful that this cost savings has been realized in most instances, because of the exactions required and the delay caused by municipalities.

Although 79.2 percent of the municipalities' PUD ordinances do encourage clustering, which if implemented, could reduce improvement costs, the fact that the same or higher levels of improvements are actually required in 67.3 percent of the municipalities mitigates this cost-saving device. Gross density is held to the same standard that traditional zoning would allow in 58.3 percent of the cases.(See Exhibit 8.15)

EXHIBIT 8.14

ZONING RELIEF GRANTED

Requests Granted Relief	Number of Municipalities	Percent
Less than 25%	13	17.1
25–50%	12	15.8
51–75%	12	15.8
More than 75%	39	51.3
Total	76	100.0

SOURCE: Survey of Municipalities, Center for Urban Policy Research, Summer 1976.

EXHIBIT 8.15

DEVELOPMENT REQUIREMENTS UNDER PLANNED UNIT DEVELOPMENT
COMPARED WITH STANDARD ZONING AND SUBDIVISION

Characteristic of PUD Ordinance	Number of Municipalities	Percent[1]
Encourages clustering	38	79.2
Does not allow greater gross density	28	58.3
Requires same or higher level of public improvements	33	67.3
Requires longer approval time	27	56.3

1. Will not add to 100.0 percent due to multiplicity of responses.

SOURCE: Survey of Municipalities, Center for Urban Policy Research, Summer 1976.

The administration of PUD and similar ordinances has seemed to diminish their usefulness as a cost-reducing technique because of the excessive amount of negotiations involved in the process. Perhaps because of this procedure, very few projects have actually been built under many of the ordinances. Of the forty-eight municipalities with PUD ordinances, 25 percent have had none built and 43.8 percent have had only one or two built.

SUMMARY OF ADMINISTRATIVE COSTS

The use of discretionary municipal zoning powers as a device for excluding low-cost housing has been well documented in court cases charging abuse of this discretion.[74] While few would argue that zoning change procedures should be eliminated, several observations can be made about the ramifications of this cost-increasing process. First, the extent to which zoning relief is requested provides a good indicatiom of the extent to which the mapping of residential zones diverges from market forces. Where zoning changes are requested frequently, this indicates that developers perceive an untapped demand, and an imbalance in the supply of certain residential housing types.

Second, where wide discretion is given to local decision-making bodies — as in rezoning, variances, and particularly in PUD applications — there is latitude for using such discretion as bargaining leverage for requiring density changes, on-site improvements, and costly amenities, which may make a project financially unfeasible, or at least beyond the means of middle-income families.

Reducing the Costs of Zoning

Zoning has become an established facet of local gevernment's control over the use of the land within its borders. As the above analysis has suggested, when properly administrated, this power can achieve many positive planning objectives; but when abused it becomes a potent weapon to exclude moderately priced housing. This section presents several suggestions for the reform of the existing zoning mechanism.[75]

THE NEED FOR BETTER MIMINUM STANDARDS

To further the legitimate goals of zoning discussed in the second section of this chapter, some general observations may be made concerning cost-reducing strategies. It is essential that those who establish the various residential zones recognize the cost impact of the minimum standards that are to be adopted. Standards which are set unreasonably high so that they no longer bear any relation to the primary goal of protecting health, safety and welfare, must be assessed in terms of the impact they have on increasing the cost and reducing the quantity of housing. Minimum standards need to be set in such a manner that will allow for diversity of choice to suit individual tastes. In other words, standards must be scrutinized to achieve a level of compromise between quality and quantity. Quality goals must not be set so unreasonably high that costs are driven up to the point where quantity and diversity of housing are significantly reduced.

Finally, without the existance of adequate standards, the increased use of flexible zoning techniques may be (and frequently are) undermined by local officials demanding extortionary requirements in return for permission to build.

REFORM OF ZONING TECHNIQUES

There is considerable room for increasing the mapping for multi-family uses, which in comparison with single-family detached housing can produce cost savings both to the individual and the municipality.(See Exhibit 8.2) A reduction in the various amenity requirements such as bedroom restrictions, minimum floor area requirements and floor area ratios in conjunction with increased mapping for multi-family use would provide even greater cost savings.

Reducing the extent of mapping for large single-family lots could have multiple advantages in the direct reduction of sprawl and of raw land costs and the indirect reduction of improvement requirements and house size. It is difficult to empirically estimate the extent of the total savings, since reducing lot size may have multiple effects. Only where changes in zoning practices are accomplished by reductions in house size and amenities of the housing offered will there be significant cost savings.[76] Perhaps the greatest savings to be realized are in the level of lot improvements required and the extent of those improvements as measured by lot width requirements.[77]

Reductions in single-family minimum floor area requirements to more closely approximate genuine health standards would allow direct cost reductions in housing construction.(See Exhibit 8.16) This strategy would also facilitate the provision of smaller units to serve the growing market of singles, both young and elderly, and of small families.

The least expensive form of housing on the market today — the mobile home — needs to be reassessed in any planning of strategies to reduce housing costs. The establishment of mobile home zones with appropriate site planning requirements could provide significant savings while furnishing a viable alternative to the more expensive forms of single-family home ownership.

ZONING ADMINISTRATION

Both the Survey of Municipalities and the Home Builders Survey revealed the increasing use of negotiation in the zoning process. While some administrative flexibility is necessary and could be utilized to allow for innovative cost-reducing techniques, all too often negotiation results in more stringent requirements that increase costs. Even when a home builder is finally granted the zoning change desired, the costs may be increased through unnecessary delay.[78]

EXHIBIT 8.16

SINGLE FAMILY HOUSING REQUIREMENTS AS THEY AFFECT PRICE

Lot Size (sq. feet)	Lot Frontage (front feet)	Livable Floor Area (sq. ft)	Predicted Selling Price
43,500	200	1,600	$57,618
15,000	100	1,600	42,044
12,000	100	1,200	38,053
12,000	80	800	33,843

SOURCE: Sternlieb and Sagalyn, *Zoning and Housing Costs* (Rutgers University, Center for Urban Policy Research, 1972).

A reduction of administrative discretion exercised by an appointed body at the local level seems to be called for. In line with the proposals of the Douglas Commission, the administrative duties of local planning boards and zoning boards of adjustment could better be handled by a single agency which would be charged with administering a unified development code.[79] In this manner, the day-to-day problems of zoning would be handled by professionals under general guidelines set up by elected officials. The unification of procedures would cut down on the red tape that causes delay. Provision of maximum time periods for review of zoning changes, with requests to be considered granted if the time is exceeded, would serve, at least, to set guidelines for the administrative agency. Professional staffs would be more inclined to view proposals objectively and pass on their merits accourding to accepted planning criteria. The self-interest of an entrenched group, which is so often characteristic of planning boards as they are now constituted, would no longer dominate.

Local administration of zoning would also benefit from closer ties to other localities through regional planning bodies. Coordination of transportation systems and other public utility installations is vital since these impact so heavily on the pattern and cost of residential development. Often this coordination cannot be achieved locally.

The Costs of Zoning

The scope of zoning regulations has broadened over the years and the techniques have become more sophisticated so as to achieve positive planning objectives. At the same time, zoning regulations have become increasimgly restrictive and, in many instances, have been used as exclusionary tools.

Modern goals of zoning include reducing the external costs created by one property owner which impact on another, protecting and enhancing property values, preserving the character of the neighborhood and protecting the fiscal base of the municipality. It has been found that these legitimate goals of zoning regulations often have been subverted to accomplish economic and social exclusion.

Various techniques of zoning practice have been discussed in relation to their incidence as determined through a Survey of Municipalities and a Home Builders Survey. It was found that there is a general under-mapping for small lots. This was particularly true for the eastern region of the country. Minimum floor area restrictions were found to be established with little relation to public health requirements. The impact of lot size and the closely related lot frontage and minimum floor area requirements were found to be the most significant in increasing the cost of housing.

Administrative practices were found to increase costs through the excessive number of zoning changes required prior to development and through delay in processing zoning change requests. Discretionary powers of municipal zoning authorities were found to be increasingly used to negotiate with home builders to increase the degree of restrictiveness — especially in relation to density of development allowed.

It is suggested that municipalities, in furthering their legitimate goals of zoning, examine their techniques in relation to their impact on the cost of housing. Minimizing the use of standards to provide an increased quantity of housing at various size and quality levels is needed at this time. To provide efficient and equitable administration, it is suggested that a unified development code be adopted and administered by a professional staff under guidelines established by elected officials.

NOTES

1. For descriptions of these surveys, see respectively, Appendices B and F.
2. The first legislation restricting lot coverage was enacted in New York in 1867, and was soon followed by similar legislation in New Jersey, Pennsylvania, and Connecticut. National Commission on Urban Problems, *Building the American City* (New York: Praeger Publishers, 1971), p. 200.
3. The U.S. Supreme Court held the Boston height restrictions valid in *Welch v. Swasey*, 214 U.S. 91 (1909).
4. The Standard Zoning Enabling Act, issued by the Department of Commerce in 1924, provided the model for much of the enabling legislation.
5. *Euclid v. Ambler Realty*, 242 U.S. 364 (1926).
6. For a discussion of judicially imposed constraints to the use of zoning, see "Legal Limitations," Appendix D.
7. See generally, *Building the American City*, pp. 203-206.
8. Urban Land Institute, "The Effects of Large Lot Size on Residential Development," Technical Bulletin No. 32 (Washington, D.C.: ULI, 1958), p.7.
9. The Report of the President's Committee on Urban Housing:*A Decent Home* (Kaiser Commission); (Washington, D.C.: U.S. Government Printing Office: 1968), p.140.
10. This view of the zoning power is espoused by Alison Dunham, *Columbia Law Review*, 58 (1958), p. 670, who maintains that the elimination of negative effects, rather than the promotion of positive benefits, is the proper role of zoning regulations.
11. James Ohls, Richard Weisberg, and Michelle White, "The Effect of Zoning on Land Value," *Journal of Law and Economics*, 17 (1974), p.429.
12. Frederick H. Rueter, "Externalities in Urban Property Markets: An Empirical Test of the Zoning Ordinance of Pittsburgh," *Journal of Law and Economics* 16 (1973), p.336.
13. John Crecine, Otto Davis and John Jackson, "Urban Property Markets: Some Empirical Results and their Implications for Municipal Zoning," *Journal of Law and Economics,* 10 (1967), p.79. The authors are careful to point out that

the absence of indicators of interdependence in the model employed may simply mean that there are no externalities of the kind with which the model was concerned.

14. See, for example, Norman B. Williams, Jr. *American Land Planning Law,* (Chicago, Illinois: Callaghan and Co., 1974-1975), Vol. I, § 15.03.

15. Where there is lower demand for homes in a neighborhood, prices of existing homes will tend to fall.

16. See, Protection of Property Values in "Legal Limitations," Appendix D.

17. The 1958 Urban Land Institute study of Boston — "The Effects of Large Lot Size on Residential Development" — attempts to debunk the myth that large-lot zoning creates a "rural atmosphere." The authors suggest that only lots of 5 to 10 acres would successfully create a rural ambience.

18. See Williams, *American Land Planning Law,* Vol. II, § 62.01, p.609.

19. Notable among these is New Jersey, one of the last states to pass an income tax, and thus one of the most heavily dependent upon local property tax revenues.

20. James W. Hughes, "The Fiscal and Social Impact of Alternative Forms of Housing," in James W. Hughes, ed., *Growth Controls: New Dimensions in Urban Planning,* (New Brunswick, N.J.: Center for Urban Policy Research, Rutgers University, 1974), p.92.

21. See Hughes, "The Fiscal and Social Impact of Housing," for a detailed analysis of the fiscal impact of alternative housing types by the number of bedrooms they contain and the size of the household and the number of school children each generates.

22. Raymond Vernon, *The Myth and Reality of our Urban Problems* (Cambridge, Mass.: Joint Center for Urban Studies of the Massachusetts Institute of Technology and Harvard University, 1962), p.64.

23. Franklin James, Jr. and Oliver D. Windsor, "Fiscal Zoning, Fiscal Reform, and Exclusionary Land Use Controls," *Journal of the American Institute of Planners,* (April, 1976), pp.130-141.

24. In *Oakwood at Madison, Inc. v. Twp. of Madison,* 320 A. 2d 223 (1974) the court stated that "fiscal zoning is *per se* irrelevant." For a further discussion on this point, see "Legal Limitations," Appendix D.

25. Bernard Siegan, *Land Use Without Zoning,* (Lexington, Mass.: D.C. Heath and Co., 1972).

26. Bernard Siegan, "Non-Zoning in Houston," *Journal of Law and Economics,* 13 (1970), p.71.

27. *Building the American City,* p.220, n. 23.

28. Although overzoning for industry was found to be a technique of fiscal zoning used extensively in New Jersey, the Survey of Municipalities unearthed little evidence that this practice is prevalent nationwide. See, State of New Jersey, Department of Community Affairs, *Land Use Regulation: The Residential Land Supply* (Trenton: Division of State and Regional Planning, April 1972).

29. See in general, James and Windsor, "Fiscal Zoning, Fiscal Reform, and Exclusionary Land Use Controls," *Journal of the American Institute of Planners,* April, 1976.

30. Richard F. Babcock, *The Zoning Game: Municipal Practices and Policies,* (Madison: University of Wisconsin Press, 1966), pp.30-38.

31. *Land Use Regulation: The Residential Land Supply,* p.10A. The sample excluded one county which was almost entirely developed and four counties which were basically rural and were experiencing few development pressures.

32. *Ibid.,* p.10.
33. See, Restrictions Against Multi-Family Homes in "Legal Limitations," Appendix D.
34. The common practice of requiring a high ratio of one-bedroom to two- and three-bedroom apartments has also been dealt with in the courts. See, "Legal Limitations," Appendix D.
35. This figure was extrapolated from Institute of Real Estate Management of the National Association of Realtors, *Income/Expense Analysis,* (Chicago: 1976).
36. Includes principal, interest, taxes, insurance and operating and maintenance costs.
37. Robert Lindsey, "Housing Dream Is Fading at $50,000," *New York Times,* October 23, 1976, pp.39, 40.
38. Norman Williams and Thomas Norman, "Exclusionary Land Use Control," *Syracuse Law Review,* 22 (1971), p.484.
39. Telephone conversation with Mr. Mitchell of the Manufactured Housing Institute, Washington, D.C., November, 1976.
40. 181 A. 2d. 129 (1962).
41. See Section on Mobile Homes in "Legal Limitations," Appendix D.
42. Department of Housing and Community Development, Sacramento, California, *California Statewide Housing Plan,* October 5, 1976.
43. Height and bulk limits, minimum floor area requirements and floor-area ratios are commonly used to control density in multi-family zones.
44. See in general, *The Effects of Large Lot Size on Residential Development,* (The Urban Land Institute, Washington, D.C.: 1958).
45. See Williams, *American Land Planning Law,* Vol. II, § 38.23, p.42.
46. See Minimum Lot Size, in "Legal Limitations," Appendix D.
47. David Schoenbrod, "Large-Lot Zoning," *Yale Law Journal,* 78 (1970), p.1418.
48. Whether large-lot zoning will actually have this effect depends on the degree of correlation between lot size and house size.
49. Schoenbrod, "Large-Lot Zoning," *Yale Law Journal,* pp. 1423-24; an interesting ramification of this phenomenon is that, as large-lot zoning provisions are struck down by the courts and lot costs fail to plummet, the only party who stands to gain is the developer, who may reap windfall profits from small high-priced lots which he/she purchased under the former zoning regulations.
50. *New Directions in Connecticut Planning Legislation; A Study of Connecticut Planning, Zoning and Related Statutes,* (Chicago, Ill., ASPO, February, 1967), p.207. An earlier study, "The Effects of Large Lot Size on Residential Development," (Urban Land Institute, 1958), reported that a four-fold increase (from half an acre to two acres) could be achieved at less than a 50 percent increase in price.
51. Urban Land Institute, "The Effects of Large Lot Size on Residential Development," p.38.
52. Field interviews conducted with home builders in North Carolina.
53. Schoenbrod, "Large-Lot Zoning," *Yale Law Journal,* pp.1423-24.
54. Williams, *American Land Planning Law,* Chapter 65.
55. William Alonso, in *Location and Land Use,* (Cambridge, Harvard University Press, 1964), p.117, comments that zoning "will not always be a modification [of the free market situation] since usually zoning regulations and the free market result coincide." Whether Alonso still maintains this position, in the

face of the increasing restrictiveness of municipal zoning ordinances, is unknown to this author.

56. Orr maintains that his regression results show that if low-density zoning has any effect on occupancy, it operates only to the advantage of very high-income households (more than $25,000/year) at the expense of all other income groups, but that the real share of land devoted to each of these lower income brackets is largely unaffected by zoning. *Urban Land Value as it Relates to Policy* (Lexington, Mass.: Urban Land Research Analysts Corp., 1969), p.118.

57. See Minimum Lot Width in "Legal Limitations," Appendix D.

58. See, for example, *Building the American City*, p.214.

59. See Chapter 7 on subdivision improvements and housing costs.

60. Williams and Norman, "Exclusionary Land Use Controls," *Syracuse Law Review*, 22 (1971), p.475.

61. See Single-Family Minimum Lot Size, Exhibit 8.4.

62. See Subdivision Regulations, Exhibit 7.23.

63. Such improvements as sidewalks and street lighting systems are often optional in fringe areas. Also, individual septic systems are often permitted as an alternative to public sanitary sewer systems, thus paring costs substantially. One may question, however, the long-term planning wisdom of an approach which establishes the "sprawl" pattern of widely-spaced lots and which risks possible water table contamination from individual sewer systems.

64. See, Chapter 7 on Subdivisions.

65. See, Minimum Floor Area Restrictions in "Legal Limitations," Appendix D.

66. See, for example, American Public Health Association, Committee on the Hygiene of Housing, "Planning a Home for Occupancy," Public Administration Service, 1950; Housing Assistance Administration, Department of Housing and Urban Development, "Low-Rent Housing Manual," September, 1967.

67. The fact that less than one-third of the residentially zoned land was restricted by minimum floor area requirements is an indication of the questionable need for, and current legality of, these limitations.

68. Sternlieb and Sagalyn in their use of a linear regression model found minimum livable floor area to be the most important variable explaining variation in the selling price of single-family houses. Lynne Sagalyn and George Sternlieb, *Zoning and Housing Costs,* (New Brunswick: Center for Urban Policy Research, Rutgers University, 1974).

69. National average "hard cost" for construction of single-family detached homes, in subdivision, third quarter, 1976. Telephone conversation with Dr. Michael Sumichrast, National Association of Home Builders, Washington, D.C., November, 1976.

70. See Minimum Floor Area Requirements in "Legal Limitations," Appendix D.

71. Real Estate Research Corporation, *The Costs of Sprawl,* Department of Housing and Urban Development (Washington, D.C.: U.S., Government Printing Office, 1974), p.150.

72. *Ibid.,* pp.131-148.

73. See Subdivision Regulations, Chapter 7, Exhibit 7.5.

74. See "Legal Limitations," Appendix D.

75. Since our primary concern in this section is to discuss strategies which will reduce the absolute cost of housing, it is not our intention here to examine the many techniques which have recently surfaced whose purpose is simply to shift

the costs of zoning. For an in-depth discussion of cost-reallocative measures, see Donald G. Hagman, *Windfalls and Wipeouts: The Quiet Undoing of Land-Use Controls* (Los Angeles, University of California, 1973); John J. Costonis, "The Chicago Plan: Incentive Zoning and the Preservation of Urban Landmarks," *Harvard Law Review*, Vol. 85 (1972) 574-631; and Jerome G. Rose, ed., *Transfer of Development Rights*, (New Brunswick: Center for Urban Policy Research, Rutgers University, 1975).
Research, Rutgers University, 1975).

76. Sagalyn and Sternlieb, *Zoning and Housing Costs*, p.69.
77. See generally, "Subdivision Controls," Chapter 7.
78. See Exhibits 8.13 and 8.14 and text accompanying.
79. *Building the American City*, p.238.

Chapter Nine: The Effect of Growth Controls on Residential Development

Growth management by local governments can mean many things to many people. To the conservationist it is a device to preserve environmentally sensitive land; to the developer, it is a plot to deprive him of his livelihood; to the local resident, it is a way to maintain the present character of the community as well as a way to halt the soaring tax rate; but to those desiring to move into that community, it is just one more obstacle which must be overcome.

Municipalities justify increasing their control over private development decisions in terms of the benefits attainable from tighter public constraints on private land use decisions. Typically these benefits are seen in terms of holding down municipal costs and preserving a community's physical and social environment.[1] Many growth control ordinances do achieve these desirable goals with minimum adverse side-effects. Nonetheless, growth controls may have been used primarily as an exclusionary device. While it is extremely difficult to identify a municipality's motives for adopting a growth control ordinance, when the effect is to exclude moderately priced residential development, the controls must be closely scrutinized.

The advantages of greater control of growth were first highlighted in 1955 by Henry Fagin. He suggested that regulating the timing of development allows a municipality to:

1. economize on the costs of public facilities and services;
2. increase control over the eventual character of development;
3. maintain a desirable degree of balance among various uses of land;
4. achieve greater detail and specificity in development regulations; and
5. maintain a high quality of community services and facilities.[2]

The major focus of this chapter will be to evaluate whether growth control techniques actually do control the timing and sequence of development, and what effect these control devices have on residential development.

The first section of this chapter examines the reasons underlying the increased use of growth control ordinances. The second section describes the actual mechanics of each of these kinds of ordinances. The implications of these control mechanisms on future residential development costs and patterns will be discussed in the third section. The final section presents case studies of the impact of ordinances in use in Ramapo, New York and Petaluma, California.

The Rise of Growth Controls

To fully comprehend the intricacies of the "no-growth" movement, it is first necessary to describe the changes in development conditions which gave rise to these regulatory controls. Only when these new realities have been examined does it then become possible to identify the actors and their reactions which ultimately result in adoption of a growth control ordinance.

THE NEW REALITIES

In the past, economic growth has always been equated with increased opportunity and an improved standard of living. The doctrine of "more is better," though not written into our nation's constitution, has certainly always served as a guiding light — that is, until the beginning of this decade. Our recent confrontation with the energy crisis, a growing concern over preserving the environment, and a fear of continuing inflation have suggested a new perception to our society — that more may in fact not be better.

In its 1973 report, *The Use of Land,* the Task Force on Land Use and Urban Growth accurately pinpoints this recent phenomenon:

a new mood in America has emerged that questions traditional assumptions about the desirability of urban development. The motivation is not exclusively economic. It appears to be a part of a rising emphasis on human values, on the preservation of natural and cultural characteristics that make for a humanly satisfying living environment.[3]

Despite the desire to move away from the nation's past trend of increasing urbanization, the problems of growth still prevail — albeit on a more selective basis. While some regions are indeed facing both decreasing population and econc.nic decline, others are booming. The current dominant shifts in growth — from cities to suburbs and exurbia and from the Northeast to the "Sunbelt," — will provide the stage where future growth control battles will be fought.

Leaving the Cities Behind The path of residential development has dramatically shifted, first from the central cities to the suburbs and more recently extending beyond the suburbs to encompass non-metropolitan areas. In 1960 the residential mix was almost evenly divided between central cities, suburbs, and non-metropolitan areas. (See Exhibit 9.1) In the following decade, housing starts shifted rapidly toward the burgeoning suburbs. Growth rates in the urban fringe soared to three times that experienced in either rural or urban areas.

The second stage of the shift in residential location — that of increased development in the non-metropolitan areas — is evident from an examination of new housing units constructed from 1970-1974. (See Exhibit 9.2) Of the nearly 10 million new residences, only 21 percent were located in central cities, while 45.5 percent were built in suburbs, and 33.6 percent in the non-metropolitan areas.

EXHIBIT 9.1

CHANGES IN THE HOUSING INVENTORY BY LOCATION:
1960-1970
(in thousands of units)

Location	1960	1970
Non-Metro	33.8%	32.3%
Central City	35.0%	32.9%
Suburban	31.2%	34.8%

SOURCE: U. S. Bureau of the Census: Cited in Vincent Barabba, "The National Setting: Regional Shifts, Metropolitan Decline and Urban Decay," in Sternlieb and Hughes (eds.), *Post-Industrial America: Metropolitan Decline and Interregional Job Shifts,* New Brunswick, Center for Urban Policy Research, 1975, p. 36.

EXHIBIT 9.2

NEW RESIDENTIAL UNITS CONSTRUCTED BY LOCATION:
1970-1974
(in thousands)

Location of Construction	Units constructed since 1970	% of 1970-1974 Growth
United States	9,877	100.0
Central City	2,070	20.9
Suburban Ring	4,491	45.5
Non-metropolitan Areas	3,316	33.6

SOURCE: Based on the 1974 Annual Housing Survey as cited in *The Changing Issues for National Growth: 1976 Report on National Growth and Development,* (Washington, D.C.: Domestic Council, 1976), p.40.

A Nation of Sun Worshippers A major population shift from the Northeast to the West and the South, the area of the country frequently referred to as the "Sunbelt," is occurring.[4] (See Exhibit 9.3) From 1970-1975, the country's population increased by 4.8 percent; the growth rate of the Northeast and North Central regions fell significantly below that level, increasing at the rate of only 0.8 and 1.0 percent respectively. Meanwhile the South and West have been attracting more and more new residents, with 8.4 and 8.7 percent increases during this five year period.

What Do These Shifts Mean? The most obvious conclusion which can be drawn from these intra- and inter-regional shifts in growth is that selective growth will occur regardless of general economic conditions. Thus the real issue is not "growth or no-growth," more specifically it is the question of the future distribution of resources. Are we willing to abandon our cities, while concentrating our resources in the suburbs, in the South and in the West? Are opportunities to be available only to those who can afford to pursue them? Are we going to permit municipalities to erect economic barriers which demand, as a pre-condition of residence, an identifiable place on the socioeconomic ladder? These questions address the issues underlying the use of growth controls.

A second conclusion which can be drawn from our examination of demographic patterns is that the battles over limiting growth in the future will be fought primarily in suburban and rural areas, and in the South and the West. While no comprehensive survey of communities with growth controls has been undertaken, some specific areas which have received attention may be taken as representative of this phenomenon. The once rural counties surrounding Washington, D.C., the farm land and valleys outside

EXHIBIT 9.3

ESTIMATES OF THE RESIDENT POPULATION
OF REGIONS: 1970-1975
(numbers in thousands)

Region	July 1, 1975 (provisional)	April 1, 1970 (Census)	Change 1970-1975 Number	Percent
United States	213,121	207,304	9,817	4.8
Northeast	49,416	49,061	401	0.8
North Central	57,669	56,593	1,076	1.9
South	68,113	62,812	5,301	8.4
West	37,878	34,838	3,039	8.7

SOURCE: Bureau of the Census, as cited in *1976 Report on National Growth and Development*, p. 23.

of San Francisco, and the foothills of the Rockies near Denver have all witnessed rapid population increases followed by attempts to control growth.

The nationwide survey conducted by the Center for Urban Policy Research of 400 builders and land developers further substantiates the widespread use of growth control mechanisms. Respondents were asked whether they had encountered in their development activity any of a variety of growth control ordinances. The results are shown in Exhibit 9.4.

The most frequently used growth control ordinance was found to be sewer moratoriums. Almost half of the builders and developers had encountered this particular restriction. Ordinances relating to the availability of public services — either phased development controls or adequate public facilities ordinances — have been encountered by nearly one-third of the respondents. The use of absolute growth limitations, such as building or population capacities (CAPS) was encountered by only 5.8 percent of the respondents. This type of limitation has only recently been accepted by the courts, and this would account for this small percentage. Before the U.S. Circuit Court's acceptance of the Petaluma Plan, previous court decisions had struck down this type of ordinance.[5]

Every type of growth control method was found in use throughout the country but some are more regionally favored than others. (See Exhibit 9.5) In general, developers in the Northeast and the West were more likely to encounter growth restrictions. It is in these regions of the country that the existing high density development has the effect of making new growth most burdensome. But if growth in the South continues at its existing rapid pace, an increased reliance on tighter controls can be anticipated.

EXHIBIT 9.4

DEVELOPERS' EXPERIENCE WITH GROWTH
CONTROL ORDINANCES

Type of Ordinance	Number of Developers	Percent*
Sewer Moratorium	196	49.0
Phased Development/Adequate Public Facilities	128	32.1
Population and Building Permit Limitations/CAP Rates	23	5.8

*Several respondents reported experiences with more than one type of control mechanism.

SOURCE: Survey of the Home Builders' Industry, Center for Urban Policy Research, Summer 1976.

EXHIBIT 9.5

REGIONAL DISTRIBUTION OF BUILDERS ENCOUNTERING
GROWTH CONTROL ORDINANCES
(percent of builders)

	REGIONS*			
Type of Mechanism	Northeast (118)	South (117)	Northcentral (61)	West (75)
Sewer Moratorium	52.2%	45.8%	44.4%	50.0%
Phased Development/ Adequate Public Facilities	38.1	22.3	28.6	35.5
Population and Permit Limits/Cap Rates	6.8	1.5	4.6	13.2

*Numbers will not add to 100.0 due to multiplicity of responses.

SOURCE: Survey of the Home Builders Industry, Center for Urban Policy Research, Summer 1976.

A description of the process by which a community sheds its rural characteristics makes it possible to isolate the conditions which give rise to the adoption of growth control ordinances.

THE DECISION TO DEVELOP

The developer's decision where to build can be most clearly stated first in terms of demand — he/she asks, "Where do people with enough money to afford my product want to live?"; and second, in terms of supply — "At what location can I minimize my production costs?" It is the combination (the equilibrium point) of these two sets of conditions that determines the location of future development.

It should be emphasized that developers in selecting a location to build are simply responding to the market conditions in the same manner that any businessperson does. They choose suburban and rural locations because such a decision makes good business sense. It is here that the market is strongest. Consumer demand arises in these areas in part because of the growth of employment opportunities as industries continue to select nonurban locations. The strength of the market demand in these areas is further substantiated by data showing the incomes of those moving into and out of the central cities between 1970 and 1974. (See Exhibit 9.6) Assuming that housing expenditures account for 25 percent of the net $29.6 billion

EXHIBIT 9.6

INCOME IN 1973 OF FAMILIES AND UNRELATED INDIVIDUALS
14 YEARS OLD AND OVER WHO MIGRATED TO AND FROM
CENTRAL CITIES BETWEEN 1970 AND 1974

Subject	Living in Cities in 1970	Moved Out of Cities Between 1970 - 1974	Moved To Cities Between 1970 - 1974	Net Change Between 1970 & 1974
Families (thousands)	16,823	3,363	1,563	- 1,800
Mean income (dollars)	13,349	14,169	12,864	- 1,305
Aggregate income (billion dollars)	$224.6	$47.7	$20.1	- $27.6
Unrelated Individuals (thousands)	6,975	1,066	926	- 140
Mean income (dollars)	6,134	7,099	6,092	- 1,007
Aggregate Income (billion dollars)	$42.8	$7.6	$5.6	-$2.0

SOURCE: U.S. Bureau of the Census. Cited in Vincent Barabba, "The National Setting: Regional Shifts, Metropolitan Decline and Urban Decay," in Sternlieb and Hughes (eds.), *Post-Industrial America: Metropolitan Decline and Inter-regional Job Shifts*, (New Brunswick: Center for Urban Policy Research, 1975), p. 55.

aggregate personal income leaving the cities, then it is possible to conclude that an additional $6.8 billion was available for the support of new residential construction in non-urban locations.

The Supply of Desirable Land   It is also in these suburban and rural areas that developers are able to minimize their production costs. While the actual structural costs (nails, wood, etc.) vary little within a specific region, other inputs, particularly land and government-imposed regulations, may differ considerably in their cost impacts.

The price of land is determined by such considerations as its location; its proximity to employment, shopping, and highways; the condition of the surrounding communities; the state of the existing physical infrastructure; its present and future potential for a specific zoning use; and its topographical and environmental conditions. When each of these considerations is taken into account, the land on the suburban fringe is determined to be best suited for development.[6]

Much of the land being developed on the fringe was previously used for agricultural purposes. The U.S. Department of Agriculture estimates that of the 1.25 million acres of rural land lost each year, about 740,000 acres fall prey to urbanization.[7] Concern about this situation has prompted 28 state governments to adopt some form of farmland preservation legislation.[8] Even though the current rate of loss does not appear that significant,[9] if housing starts return to past levels, the problem could rapidly increase. For example, it is estimated that nearly 50 percent of all farms in New Jersey are now owned by speculators.[10]

Developers also gravitate to the urban fringe because of the characteristics of the land available there, compared to that available in already developed areas. In developed areas, the prime (least expensive and best suited) land for residential use has often been taken off the market, requiring a developer to look elsewhere. Not surprisingly, this leads directly to the phenomenon of "leapfrogging" and its resultant sprawled development pattern. Nonetheless, for the developer such a decision is the economically rational one.

Running from Regulations   The second principal area in which developers can limit costs involves government imposed requirements. Specifically, major savings can be achieved by choosing an area which demands less stringent development requirements. One study in Virginia, for example, showed that such subdivision requirements as sewer and water hookups, streets, and sidewalks could create cost differentials in two neighboring counties of as much as $2,800 per unit.[11] The less developed of the two counties in Virginia was the one in which it was less expensive to build. The problems of disappearing open space, an overburdened sewage system and inadequate school facilities are less likely to surface in a rural setting.

Therefore, these communities are not yet forced to impose on the developer the added burdens created by growth.

Nor is it accurate to assume that since a developer simply passes on any costs to the housing consumer, such expenses are not a consideration in deciding where to build. The more costly the regulations, the more expensive the houses which must be built, which results in a more limited potential market for the unit.

From the community's standpoint the results of a developer selecting a site where many costs can be transferred to the public can be disastrous. Robert Freilich, one of the leading proponents of phased growth controls, enumerates the following consequences:

1. increased land speculation
2. destruction of environmental reources
3. imbalance of growth beteeen types of uses
4. increase in the costs of public services
5. inefficient use of energy resources
6. poor quality in those services that are provided
7. development of negative policies concerning social, racial, and economic solutions.[12]

These problems combine to increase political pressure to limit future growth. Contrary to the early stage of a municipality's development, in which developers and landowners hold the balance of power, as time passes the number of new residents becomes large enough to dominate the political process.[13] And dominate it they do!

THE ENACTMENT OF GROWTH CONTROL

Throughout the country, people are harnessing the democratic process in order to demand the limiting of growth. In Boca Raton, Florida, citizens passed a charter referendum to set a limit on the total number of housing units.[14] In Dade County, after their requests for a building moratorium were twice rejected by the county commissioners, citizens gathered the required number of signatures and successfully passed a referendum putting a temporary halt on future development.[15] In Livermore, California, an organization called SAVE (Save All Valley Environment) also used the initiative process to ensure that anti-growth policies were adopted.[16] In Colorado the rallying cry of a movement to keep the 1976 Olympics out of Denver was "Don't Californicate Colorado,"[17]

Whether it is directly through passage of an initiative or indirectly by electing officials committed to a no-growth platform, citizens' demands are being heard. The resultant growth management system, aimed specifically at ameliorating the fears of the community, frequently is more a response to frustration than a positive, effective planning scheme. Based on his analysis of growth management activities in thirteen communities, Michael Gleeson noted that most growth control management focused on specific problems and gave little consideration to side-effects.[18]

Growth Control Techniques

Any discussion which seeks to categorize growth control ordinances must beware of oversimplification. Few communities use only one growth management technique. The usual case is a combination of programs to preserve farmland, to plan for capital budgeting, to zone out high municipal cost development, and to prevent an overburdening of facilities. These objectives are pursued using variants of such existing devices as tax rebates, subdivision controls, special residential permits, holding zones, and the power of eminent domain. The five techniques to be discussed here are: adequate public facilities ordinances, phased development controls, population and building permit limitations, urban service areas, and sewer moratoria. They were selected as the primary examples of the manipulations of the more traditional land use devices aimed specifically at controlling growth.

ADEQUATE PUBLIC FACILITIES ORDINANCES

In an attempt to relieve the pressure on the municipal fisc, several communities have adopted ordinances which establish the availability of public facilities as a condition for approval to develop. While this limitation on private development — that building will be restricted unless public facilities are available to absorb the added demand — appears to be quite rational, it is in fact a reversal of the historic pattern where municipal services would follow as of right in the path of private construction activity.[19] *Clarkstown, New York* The first instance of a municipality adopting an adequate public facilities ordinance was in 1955 in Clarkstown, New York.[20] Faced with the prospects of rapid growth because of the recent completion of the Tappan Zee Bridge and the resulting proximity to New York City, Clarkstown redesigned its zoning ordinance to minimize the expected problems accompanying the anticipated growth. It designated the area surrounding New City, at that time the most settled section of the township, for suburban type development on 15,000 square-foot lots. An outer ring was also drawn in which only one acre development was to be permitted. In the intermediate ring, development could occur as of right on one-acre lots, with the exception that, based primarily on the adequacy of the schools, a special permit could be issued to permit development on 15,000 square foot lots.

That this scheme successfully channeled growth into the more developed areas surrounding both New City and the major roadways was confirmed by a report analyzing that area's development pattern from 1955-65.[21]

When challenged in court, the scheme was held to be a valid exercise of the police power.[22] In its opinion, the court expressed its concern for the problems of rapid growth:

> Not incidental to the evils of overcrowding and undue concentration of population are generally the lack of proper schools and educational facilities. The extent of future needs on account of such facilities and plans therefore are matters relative to and of important consideration in connection with zoning.[23]

The Clarkstown growth control system came to an end in 1963 when major revisions were made in the zoning ordinance which eliminated the special permit provision of the intermediate ring.

San Jose, California   An overcrowded school system was also the motive behind an adequate public facilities ordinance passed in the city of San Jose, California.[24] Fearing that increased growth would exacerbate an already overburdened system, one in which nine of the twenty-three districts were either uncomfortably crowded or on double sessions, the citizens of San Jose passed an initiative in 1973 which established the availability of school-space as a condition for approval to develop.[25] The initiative also called for a study to be conducted of the problems accompanying residential growth and allowed developers to provide school facilities in order to obtain permission to develop.

Led by such civic organizations as the League of Women Voters and Citizens for Rational Planning, the ordinance was passed over the objection and without the support of the local elected officials. In fact, one advertisement in the campaign for its passage stated:

> For too long the City Council has approved subdivisions with hundreds of new homes without concern for already overcrowded schools. Rampant growth has been encouraged without giving sufficient attention to the economic and environmental effects on residents. Now you, the voter, can take direct action to insure orderly growth policies for San Jose.[26]

Livermore, California   The experience of Livermore, California presents a third example of a community attempting to cope with the problems accompanying a rapid increase in population. In the mid-1960's an interstate highway was extended through the hills which previously had isolated this valley from the San Francisco-Oakland metropolitan area. As a result of being within commuting distance from these urban centers, the population of Livermore jumped from 16,058 in 1960 to over 37,000 in 1970.[27] By the early 1970's the problems of growth had surfaced. The air quality had become a serious hazard to health, double sessions would soon be necessary for the schools, sewage facilities were overburdened and a water shortage was an imminent peril.[28]

In December 1971, faced with the dual crises of community opposition to growth and a severe water shortage, the City Council passed an ordinance establishing a maximum of 1,500 building permits to be granted within the city limits.[29] This measure was apparently believed to be inadequate, for an initiative calling for stronger action was organized by community groups and passed by a wide margin in April, 1972.[30]

Though vague and poorly drafted the ordinance essentially required that the issuance of residential building permits be based on a showing of adequate eductional facilities, sewage treatment facilities, and water supply. The standards upon which adequacy of services was to be measured was not specified, nor was it clear whether compensatory measures would be permitted.

New York City   The final example of a municipality seeking to protect itself from the financial pressures created by new development differs considerably from our previous case studies. This municipality is not in the throes of new development, nor has it recently undergone a rapid increase in population. What it does have in common with Clarkstown, Livermore, and San Jose is that all suffer from a severely overburdened municipal fisc. New York City has recently designated the still predominately undeveloped southern portion of Staten Island as a special zoning district — with the purpose of ensuring that future increases in density are compatible with the availability of public facilities.[31]

As the cost of public improvements soars as standards for water quality and sewage treatment increase, and as sensitivities to the environment are further awakened, it can be expected that more communities will turn toward adequate public facility ordinances. These factors combined with a new generalized fear of the future — of change and of newcomers — suggest that local political pressure will increasingly seek out this type of ordinance to control growth.

PHASED DEVELOPMENT CONTROLS

The logical extension of the adequate public facilities approach to land use control is the phase development ordinance. While the former deals only with what facilities are available at the moment, the latter, through its use of a capital improvements plan, also provides a timetable for future development decisions. Thus an owner of land can examine the municipality's plan for future capital expenditures, and determine when the necessary facilities will be available to permit development on a specific parcel of land.

Like the adequate public facilities technique, this type of land use ordinance also demonstrates the benefits of municipal control over the timing and sequence of development. An enlightened policy guiding future municipal expenditures would be aimed at encouraging development where facilities already exist and thereby would achieve economies for the municipality, while preserving open space. Only when insufficient steps are taken to insure that facilities are provided at a pace commensurate with demand is this type of control a tool to limit, rather than to guide, future development.

Ramapo, New York Not far from Clarkstown in Rockland County is the township of Ramapo. With the completion of the Tappan Zee Bridge, it too became a prime commuter location. Population had more than doubled in the decade from 1960-70, growing from 35,000 to 77,000. Ramapo recognized the problems which would accompany this rapid expansion if it were not properly directed; the township's first major step to control its future was to adopt a new master plan in 1969. This study produced the frightening conclusion that if growth were allowed to continue at its current pace, by 1979 a population of 100,000 people would fully occupy all the developable land within the township's boundaries.[32]

The response to this projection was to adopt its now well-known phased development ordinance.[33] As described in the ordinance, the purpose of this plan was:

1. to economize on the costs of municipal facilities and services to carefully phase residential development with efficient provisions of public improvements;
2. to establish and maintain municipal control over the eventual character of development;
3. to establish and maintain a desirable degree of balance among the various uses of the land; and
4. to establish and maintain essential quality of community services and facilities.[34]

The essential ingredients of the plan are detailed studies projecting over eighteen years the future location of public improvements for parks, schools, sewage facilities, drainage, recreation and roads. Based on these projections, the town adopted a capital improvements budget covering six years and a list of capital public works projects to be undertaken for twelve additional years. A system of points relating the adequacy of facilities to the development site was drafted to serve as the measuring stick for determining whether approval for development would be granted immediately or for some date in the future when the necessary infrastructure would be available. A total of fifteen points was required for the special residential permit, with zero to five points awarded for sewers, drainage, improved public park or recreational facilities and improved roads, and a maximum of three points based on the proximity of a firehouse.[35]

The plan also includes several devices to insure both its fairness and legality. Developers whose projects fall short of fifteen points are given a vested right to build at a specific date in the future, when, according to the capital improvements plan, adequate facilities are to be available, regardless of whether that public works project was actually undertaken. To circumvent any potential attack on the issue of an uncompensated taking, those properties that cannot be developed until some future date can apply to the Development Easement Acqusition Commission for property tax relief.

The Ramapo plan was upheld at the trial court level as a valid exercise of the enabling legislation governing zoning;[36] was reversed by a three to two vote by the Appellate Division, which ruled that control over the timing of development was outside the permissible scope of zoning;[37] and finally upheld by the Court of Appeals[38] (New York's highest court). In what is described by Norman Williams as "the most confusing major zoning opinion of recent times,"[39] the majority opinion, while acknowledging the problems inherent in the plan,[40] nonetheless considered it within the legislative authority of the town. In several instances, its decision suggests a wait-and-see approach:

> The answer which Ramapo has posed can by no means be termed definitive; it is, however, a first practical step forward toward controlled growth.[41]

Additionally, the Court recognized the limits of judicial scrutiny in an area of land use legislation and the need for such controls to evolve without judicial interruption.[42]

In evaluating Ramapo's phased development ordinance, one must be impressed by the substantial planning effort supporting its adoption. In fact, it is this particular aspect of the plan which has prevented the use of this technique by other communities. But Ramapo may have relied on a planning tool beyond the skills of the profession. The danger of basing a rather inflexible land use control system on capital expenditure projections for an eighteen year period is quite obvious. This and other problems of the Ramapo Plan will be discussed in detail in a later section, exploring the impact of the plan on the area's housing growth.[43]

POPULATION AND BUILDING PERMIT LIMITATIONS

Several communities have found a far less complex growth control system which in many respects must be considered the antithesis of the planning process. By setting an annual maximum number of building permits which can be issued, communities are not so much managing their growth as they are simply restricting it. A common variation of this technique, which has a similar effect, is placing an overall limit on the number of dwelling units or total population to be permitted in a community.

The reasons underlying the use of this type of control mechanism are essentially the same as those for the use of a phased development ordinance. The rapid increase in population creating a burden on the existing public facilities and the destruction of the so-called small town character of the community, still underly the justifications, though the latter motive may dominate in this form of control.[44] As was the case with the other kinds of controls, the impetus for action most often was generated by community citizens and not the elected officials. In this instance, however, the result is a particularly short-sighted, narrowly drawn, highly parochial growth restricting ordinance.

St. Petersburg, Florida The absurdity of this type of ordinance is best seen in the attempt by the City Council in St. Petersburg, Florida to establish as its population maximum 235,000 residents. In March 1974, it actually went so far as to pass this measure on its initial public reading. The flaw was that the population had already reached the 260,000 level and residential construction for 7,000 more people had been initiated.[45] According to the plan, the last 25,000 entrants to the community would be required to register and be designated as "temporary residents." They would be allowed to become permanent residents either when someone died or moved from the city. A six-month interim period was to be permitted before any temporary residents would be asked to leave. According to the newspaper accounts, included among the potential refugees were two bank presidents, the concert master of the Gulf Coast Symphony and several university professors.[46]Fortunately for these residents and the court, which necessarily would have had to declare such an ordinance invalid, the City Council had a change of mind and defeated the measure before it became law.[47]

Boca Raton, Florida On the eastern coast of Florida, the city of Boca Raton, while not quite exhibiting the hubris of St. Petersburg, nonetheless attempted to set an absolute limit on its growth. Backed by a group of local residents — the Citizens for Reasonable Growth — a charter amendment referendum was passed in November 1972, which established a housing unit limit at 40,000. While this was considerably below the current number of units, the limit was more a reflection of the sentiments of the population, than a sound planning recommendation.[48] This ordinance was successfully challenged in the Florida Courts.[49]

Petaluma, California   The city whose cap rate scheme has received the most notoriety is Petaluma, California. Less than ten years ago Petaluma was a small town located in a fertile farming valley. Petaluma grew in population from 14,000 in 1960 to more than 30,000 in 1975. Much of this increase and the soaring projections for future growth are based on the city's easy access to San Francisco over Route 101, a major highway extended into the valley in the early 1960's. After much public debate, the City Council adopted the Residential Development Control system which limited the future residential growth to 500 units in each of the next five years.[50] Those developers seeking to build in Petaluma present their plans to a Residential Development Evaluation Board which bases its allocation decisions on two sets of criteria relating: first, the projected impact of the proposed development upon public facilities, second, the quality of design and contribution to the public welfare and amenity.

In addition to limiting the absolute number of permits to be issued, this allocation process pits developer against developer, with the city having the final decision about which project, if any, is approved. This additional layer of control provides municipalities with enormous power over future development, a point well understood by other communities. According to the officials in Petaluma, they received at least one inquiry per week from other governments interested in adopting similar control ordinances.[51] When challenged in the courts, Petaluma received considerable financial assistance from other California communities to help pay legal fees.[52]

The District Court's strongly worded opinion invalidated the ordinance on the grounds that it was an unconstitutional infringement upon the right to travel.[53] Judge Burke's decision stated squarely that:

> The expressed purpose and the intended and actual effects of the "Petaluma Plan" have been to exclude substantial numbers of people who would otherwise have elected to immigrate into the city.[54]

The "compelling state interests" offered by the city as justification (inadequate water supply and sewage facilities, etc.) for this infringement of a constitutionally protected right was determined to be contrived and therefore insufficient to overcome the strict scrutiny test applied by the Court.[55] Though many commentators believed that this decision marked the launching of a potent argument to be used to attack growth control ordinances — a prohibition against infringement of the right to travel — this hope was soon dashed by the 9th Circuit's reversal.[56] Applying the doctrine of standing recently established by the Supreme Court with regard to land-use controls in its decision in *Warth v. Seldin*,[57] the Court of Appeals found that there was insufficient *injury in fact* to any of the plaintiffs on which to grant them standing.

The cry of Petaluma (as of now still acceptable to the Courts),[58] which allows a community to enact a growth restricting ordinance aimed at "preserving its small town character," has since been heard in other court cases and can be expected to reverberate throughout the country.[59] The potential influence that a widely publicized court decision can have on future policies is exemplified by the reaction to the *Belle Terre* decision validating anti-grouper laws.[60] Following that decision, twelve of the thirteen towns on Long Island enacted their own versions of this type of rental restriction.[61]

As these examples demonstrate, permit and population maximums should be considered the rotten apple in the barrel of growth control techniques. Typically devoid of any planning sense and not directed toward achieving any positive economies, they result only in enabling communities to turn their backs on the difficulties accompanying growth.

URBAN SERVICE AREAS

Development on the suburban fringe often has two disadvantages. It destroys prime agricultural land or aesthetically pleasing landscape; and, because of its distance from existing facilities, it is extremely expensive for the municipality to service. Like the adequate public facilities technique, the creation of "urban service areas" attacks both of these problems by influencing the timing and sequence of future developments. Unlike the cap rate technique, however, this type of ordinance attempts only to guide growth without establishing any absolute limits.

The main advantage of an urban service areas ordinance over an adequate public facilities ordinance is that it provides a more direct method of bridging the gap between municipal services and land use. A zone designated by a municipality as an "urban service area" has, or soon will have, adequate public services to support urban development. The boundaries for these zones are based on the existing pattern of development, natural physical barriers, the costs of extending services to an area and, to some extent, the carrying capacity of the land itself. The remaining territory, often termed a "rural service area" or an "agricultural reserve," is intended to remain sparsely developed.

Sacramento County, California Sacramento County is a major agricultural center located northeast of San Francisco. In 1973, to protect the farmland from sprawled development, the County government adopted the "County General Plan 1990," which established as its primary objective the channeling of future development into existing areas with high dwelling densities.[62] The location and amount of land designated an urban service area were based primarily on population and land use projections. Also incorporated into the plan were two measures to ensure that sufficient land was available to prevent a price increase due to inadequate supply. First 27 percent more land than the projected requirement was allocated for the urban services area and secondly, an annual review evaluating the accuracy and applicability of past projections was instituted.[63] Once an area has been designated an urban service area, several mechanisms are used to ensure that development occurs in the proper place:

1. capital improvement programs to coordinate future public expenditures with development;
2. assessment practices which recognize the significance of the planning function; and
3. community plans which serve as tie-ins to local, parcel by parcel planning.[64]

The county-wide coverage of the plan helps to ensure coordination of public works projects with local land use plans.

The Twin Cities, Minnesota   The Metropolitan Council, in preparing a comprehensive growth strategy for the Twin Cities region, has relied heavily on the urban and rural service areas mechanism to reduce the economic and social costs of unplanned development.[65] By limiting future major public expenditures for roads, parks, and sewers to those areas with an existing urban infrastructure, and incorporating this policy into local land use regulations, the Twin Cities region is trying to direct the future path of growth away from existing rural areas. As in the Sacramento plan, enough land is designated for urbanization to absorb the forecasted demand for development, plus a five year cushion for expected growth to encure that land prices do not become artificially inflated.[66]

Eugene-Springfield, Oregon   In an attempt to eliminate the existing development pattern characterized as "scatteration," the Lane Council of Governments developed the "Eugene-Springfield Metropolitan Area 1990 General Plan." By limiting future urban growth to designated urban service areas, several objectives may be realized:

1. preservation of prime agricultural land,
2. elimination of urban development in the flood plain,
3. reduction of scatteration,
4. more efficient use of existing public facilities,
5. preservation of the special character of the area, and
6. protection of open space.[67]

The potential problems with the urban service area technique of controlling growth are primarily rooted in our land use system, where power is maintained at the local level. This creates a balkanized state lacking any mechanism for coordination. Without a higher authority both coordinating and reviewing decisions by school boards, sewer districts and local governments, the designation of an urban service area may be little more than an exercise in wishful thinking. In addition, unless allowance is made for an adequate supply of land, this type of ordinance may lead directly to an artificially inflated increase in the price of residential lots.

SEWER MORATORIUM

While differing in several important respects from the previous techniques for controlling growth, the use of sewer moratoria is included in this section because its ultimate impact — restricting growth — is similar to these other control mechanisms. Whereas other growth control measures affect the whole range of problems accompanying growth, a sewer moratorium is aimed specifically at arresting the burden on the waste treatment system and cannot be justified under any other circumstances. The specific problems which usually result in the imposition of a sewer moratorium are:

1. insufficient capacity of transmission lines, interceptors, or treatment facilities;
2. inadequate standards of treatment which result in unacceptable levels of pollution; and
3. use of the same transmission system for both sanitary and storm drainage flows resulting in backups.[68]

Depending on the severity of the problem, the jurisdiction with authority (the state, county, special district or local government) may either place a ban on the issuance of new building permits or sewer hookups, or develop a rationing system aimed at slowing down the rate of additional demand. The amount of new construction and therefore the volume of sewage are severely limited until additional facilities become available. One possible side-effect of this limitation may be to redirect new development to those areas where facilities can support additional growth. A more likely occurrence, however, is that construction will be pushed into less developed areas, perpetuating a sprawled settlement pattern.

The increasing use of this type of growth control device can be attributed to a combination of recent events. The increased citizen concern for protecting the environment, the filling-in of older suburbs, and the more frequent use of cluster development have all played a part in necessitating the use of sewer moratoria.[69]

A dominant role is now played by the federal government. In 1922, the Federal Water Pollution Control Act set high standards for sewage treatment, while President Nixon's impoundment of funds cut the supply of money necessary to build adequate facilities. As a result, many communities were forced to impose a ban on new hook-ups. A 1973 survey conducted by the International City Managers Association reported that 19 percent of the responding cities had instituted some form of environmentally related moratoria.[70]

An example of the predicament created by this type of growth control is clearly illustrated by the situation in Prince George's and Montgomery Counties in the suburban Washington, D.C. area. The initial sewer moratorium was issued by the Maryland State Department of Health and Mental Hygiene on May 20, 1970 to ease the burden on existing treatment and trunk-line facilities. A 1973 evaluation of the effectiveness of the ban (still in effect at that time) reported that:

> the results [of the moratorium] have been disappointing. The increase in sewage flows has not tapered off. The residential construction rate has actually increased. . .
> Despite the fact that authorizations for sewer extensions have virtually ceased, there is no evidence that the moratorium is having the desired effect of either limiting or staging flows. . .[71]

Though sewer moratoria are initiated as only interim measures, Maryland's moratorium is now in its sixth year and was recently upheld as still valid by the U.S. District Court.[72] In this case, the court reasoned that the length of the infringement must be viewed in light of the scope of the problem.[73] Moreover there is evidence in a number of cases that sewer moratoria have been used by municipalities as "stop growth" devices — with little effort being made to rectify the infrastructure limitations which necessitated them.

Even short-term moratoria disrupt the housing market in several important respects. In his evaluation of this growth control device, Malcolm Rivkin lists as its inequities that they:

1. create short-term development spurts followed by a drastic decline in production;
2. result in particular hardships for small builders often temporarily forced out of business;
3. discriminate against apartments and other cost efficient high density housing;
4. act as a roadblock to low and moderate income housing by escalating the price of land available for construction;
5. act as a positive encouragement to urban sprawl, septic tanks, interim package treatment facilities; and
6. serve as a stimulus to complicated bureaucratic processes.[74]

This analysis of sewer moratoria has emphasized its disruptive effect on residential development; yet no one approves of allowing construction to continue unabated at the expense of increasing the level of pollution in nearby waters. But all too frequently, sewer moratoria have been abused by municipalities and used as a way to avoid increased growth without any meaningful commitment to remedying the situation. This has most seriously affected high-density, moderately priced housing.

The Economic Implications
of Growth Controls

The ostensible aim of a growth control ordinance is to reduce the economic, social, and environmental costs of growth to a community. The best of these plans attempt to both minimize and distribute these costs internally in a creative way by instituting a more rational land use design and limiting sprawled development. But other plans have a very different impact. Communities simply seek to avoid the costs of growth by shifting them to other communities or to the balance sheets of developers and ultimately to home seekers. A further look at the means and affects of such cost-shifts is warranted.

An example of the savings made possible by directing growth into those areas previously developed compares projections of the costs of public facilities under the existing growth pattern in the Minneapolis-St. Paul region to that of the same amount of growth channeled into currently under-developed areas. (See Exhibit 9.7) The Metro Council found that by relegating the projected 340,000 new residential units to one-fifth the proposed land area, a 75 percent reduction in the costs of public facilities could be achieved.

TRANSFERRING COSTS TO THE DEVELOPER

Restricting Development   As previously stated, private land development in this country has traditionally preceded public improvements, with the latter following as of right. Such growth control ordinances as adequate public facilities and phased development controls have reversed this pattern — no longer can a developer, as a matter of course, expect a municipality to extend the sewer lines or roads to his/her property. These restrictions may severely restrict what can be built on that land. This increased control over development patterns will undoubtedly result in a more efficient use of land, but an initial corollary effect will be an economic loss to those property owners who have purchased land with the expectation of developing it under the old rules, and an inflation in housing costs as land becomes a rarer commodity.

EXHIBIT 9.7

COST OF SELECTED PUBLIC FACILITIES UNDER TWO
GROWTH PATTERNS: 1970-1990

Assumptions	Continuing Trends	Guided Growth
Net new housing units to be built as:		
Contiguous Development	240,000	340,000
Scattered development	100,000	0**
Total	340,000	340,000
Land area preempted by urbanization	1,000 sq. mi.*	200 sq. mi.
Costs (Millions)		
Roadway Improvements, (freeways, principal arterials, minor arterials, collector roadways)	1,343	$368
Storm drainage (ditches and trunk lines)	115	53
Sanitary sewer (interceptor)	363	73
Sanitary sewer (trunks)	474	95
Water arterials	410	82
Total	$2,705	$671

*There would be pockets of urban development throughout a large portion of
the region, generally near lakes and along roads, with large amounts of vacant
land in between. Urban service demands are often generated by these clusters
of urban development.
**For study purposes only, it was assumed that no scattered housing would be
built in the Metropolitan Area. All forecasted growth was assigned to the
Urban Service Area to assure that sufficient land and urban services would be
available. However, it should be understood that *Development Framework*
Policies do recognize new housing in the Rural Service Area where services and
facilities are adequate. *Development Framework* forecasts 24,000 new households in the Rural Service Area between 1970 and 1990. Dispersal of these
houses is encouraged in order to prevent extensions of major public facilities.

SOURCE: Metropolitan Council memorandum, "Cost of Providing Services
to Alternative Regional Development Patterns," June 19, 1974. As
cited in Metropolitan Council, *Development Framework*, p. 10.

Some communities have recognized the inequity of restricting development because of their inability to immediately service these areas. Several
methods of compensation have been adopted to minimize the economic
hardship suffered by the property owner. The Ramapo plan, for example,
incorporated a development easement acquisition program which reduced
the property tax burden on land not yet ripe for development. Other com-

munities have adopted various forms of a less-than-fee acquisition program, particularly to protect existing farmlands, and when necessary have even resorted to purchasing full title to environmentally sensitive land.

An analysis of the growth potential of the mountain area surrounding Palo Alto, California produced an interesting result.[75] After estimating the projected costs to the municipality if this foothills area was developed, the report concluded that the city could actually save money in the long run by purchasing the properties.[76] While this may benefit those already living in Palo Alto, it also closes the door on those desiring to move into this community

Requiring a Development to "Pay Its Own Way" Inherent in many of the growth control ordinances is the notion that a development will be approved only if it does not create any additional burdens on the existing public facilities. Two jurisdictions, Loudon County, Virginia[77] and Boulder, Colorado,[78] have explicitly adopted this policy through their "pay your own way" ordinances. These ordinances require that the developer pay for any costs incurred by the municipality which are attributable to that development and which exceed the revenues the project will generate.

A less direct method of implementing the policy can be found in most adequate public facilities and phased development ordinances. This clause allows a developer to provide those facilities which are currently lacking in return for permission to build.

The adequate public facilities ordinance in San Jose, California clearly illustrates this transfer of costs to the developer. Since implementation of the ordinance in 1973, several agreements have been reached between school districts and developers requiring the latter to either provide additional facilities, make direct payment or delay construction to prevent overburdening the existing schools.[79]

In the case of Ramapo, where developers are also permitted to provide what usually are municipal services to achieve the required fifteen points for permission to develop, from 1969 through 1973 the "buy out" provision was used in twenty-one instances.[80]

Present vs. Future Costs Finally, a third aspect of transferring costs from the public to the developer involves communities attempting to reduce municipal costs which ultimately may result from new development. For example, by restricting the use of septic tanks at the time of development, a community can insure that later, when density increases, it will not have to bear the costly change to a municipal treatment facility.

While this type of requirement may produce higher quality developments, it does so at the cost of a more expensive product. Such requirements as open space and over-designed streets and sidewalks also have the effect of imposing a present cost on the developer so that the municipality can avoid either a maintenance or capital expense at some time in the future.

TRANSFERRING COSTS OUTSIDE THE COMMUNITY

Growth control ordinances aimed primarily at restricting the number of new residential units permitted (usually building permit limitations, population cap rates, and sewer moratoria) quite naturally result in shifting the costs of new development to neighboring communities. This phenomenon is succinctly described by William Alonso, who correctly suggests that whether or not an area grows is determined by regional, national and international forces and that local policies only define the intrametropolitan "form and distribution of that development."[81] He concluded that:

> A suburb may be able to keep population or industry out, but it can do so only by directing it to other suburbs or by keeping it cooped up in the central city.[82]

The *Development Framework* outlining the Minneapolis-St. Paul growth strategy includes within its policy recommendations the following warning to its neighboring jurisdictions: "Guiding metropolitan growth will probably increase growth pressures on counties adjacent to the Metropolitan Area."[83] It then calls on the State Legislature to require that all adjacent counties develop similar growth management systems.[84]

Most growth control plans discriminate against high density developments while permitting single-family homes built on large lots. Not surprisingly then, less expensive multi-family and cluster type development will be channeled into those neighboring communities without growth controls, further stimulating the call for restrictive legislation in the latter. It may also increase the price of developable lots in the surrounding communities.

In summary, growth controls intend to reduce the burden of new development on a community, and they often achieve this goal. That burden, however, does not disappear; it may simply shift to the new residents and neighboring communities. Many examples of growth control ordinances have been discussed in this section. But for a clear view of how a growth control ordinance is conceived, adopted and implemented, and its internal and external effects, it is best to look to detailed case studies. The next section reviews two of the more publicized growth control ordinances, those adopted in Ramapo, New York and Petaluma, California.

Case Studies of Growth Controls
In Ramapo and Petaluma

THE EFFECT OF RAMAPO'S PHASED DEVELOPMENT ORDINANCE

The origin of Ramapo's growth control ordinance can be traced to 1964 when the township began preparation of its first master plan. This study served to highlight the magnitude of the problem confronting Ramapo: unless more restrictive land use controls were installed, every developable parcel of land within its boundaries would be developed by 1979.[85] Recognizing the overwhelming impact on public services generated by this rate of growth, studies were undertaken by the township to determine the extent to which it would be able to provide the necessary drainage, sewage and recreational facilities to meet this rapidly increasing demand.[86] The results of these investigations were then incorporated into the zoning ordinance by means of newly adopted amendments which slowed growth by linking permission to develop to the availability of public facilities.

Any evaluation of the phased development ordinance's impact on residential construction is, of course, subject to the limitations of attributing causality specifically to the phased development plan. Many other factors, including the amount of developable land and general economic conditions, are in part determinants of the decision to develop. But by comparing new housing starts in Ramapo to those in the remainder of the county, for both the period before and after the ordinance, it is possible to draw some conclusions about the impact of this growth control mechanism.

The Effect on Residential Development   Although a growth control ordinance is aimed at reducing the supply of new housing built in one community, it has little effect on reducing total demand for housing in the region.[87] Unless the community with the growth control ordinance has very special characteristics which set it apart from its neighbors, the housing market, and therefore the price for new units, will be generally consistent throughout the region.

This market phenomenon has produced a rather interesting result. Those developers seeking to build under the ordinance and who incur added expenses because of the delay in qualifying for the special residential permit cannot pass this cost along to the consumer and still be competitive with other developers doing business in neighboring communities not restricted by this type of ordinance. There are two possible responses to this situation: either developers can simply shift their building activity to these other communities, or the owners of land will be forced to absorb the costs associated with the ordinance. Both of these effects will now be detailed.

The Shift to Neighboring Communities   Not surprisingly, residential construction activity in Rockland County has suffered through the housing slump of recent years experienced throughout the nation. The average annual number of new housing units for the six years before the ordinance is 27.5 percent higher than that built since the passage of the ordinance. Of greater interest however is the shift in the number of new units built in Ramapo as a percentage of total units built in the county. (See Exhibit 9.8) From a yearly average of 26.9 percent for the six years preceding adoption of the growth control ordinance, Ramapo has experienced a precipitous

EXHIBIT 9.8

Dwelling Units Built In Rockland County: 1963-1975

	Year	County	Ramapo Township	% of County
	1963	2686	827	30.8
	1964	3372	950	28.2
	1965	3108	943	30.3
	1966	2897	776	26.8
	1967	2232	606	27.2
Pre-Ordinance	1968	2410	443	18.4
Post-Ordinance	1969	1984	289	14.6
	1970	1231	198	16.1
	1971	1661	244	14.7
	1972	2403	234	14.1
	1973	2849	266	9.3
	1974	1975	225	11.4
	1975	1552	205	13.2

Source: Rockland County Planning Department, *Databook 1975.*

drop to an annual average of 13.3 percent of total county housing production during the years since adoption of the ordinance.

Reducing the Price of Land   The second major impact of the growth control ordinance has been to reduce the price of the land not yet qualified for
development under the 15-point system for development. This impact was
noted in an analysis of the Ramapo ordinance conducted for the National
Association of Home Builders.[88] Based on discussions with realtors and appraisers in the area, they found that the price of land not qualified for immediate development was being discounted at 10-12 percent per year. This
discount rate was determined by the holding costs of land which was priced
at about $10,000 per acre for residential use. Interest payments, property
taxes,[89] and opportunity costs resulted in approximately a $1,300 loss to the
landholder. (See Exhibit 9.9) Since this loss probably cannot be passed on to
the consumer, it must be capitalized into the price of land, if it is to be sold.

   In summary, the Ramapo Plan has successfully reduced new residential
construction. The result, however, has been an increase in building activity
in surrounding areas and a reduction in value of those properties not immediately available for development. This effect may be acceptable if the
goal of a better planned community promised by the Ramapo Plan was indeed fulfilled. Seven years after its passage, however, the problems of implementation appear to have overwhelmed this objective.

The Operation of the Plan   A primary objective of the ordinance was to increase the township's authority to relate new residential growth to its ability

EXHIBIT 9.9

CARRYING COST OF LAND IN RAMAPO

	Annual Per Acre Cost
Interest on Mortgage ($10,000 value per acre, 50% mortgage 9.5% interest rate)	$ 425
Property Taxes (6% of value)	600
Opportunity Cost (assumes investor foregoes 5.5% safe return on $5,000 equity)	275
Total Annual Holding Cost	$1,300

$$\text{Percent Cost} = \frac{1,300}{10,000} = 13\%$$

SOURCE: Hammer, Siler, George Associates, May 8th *Memo*, prepared for the National Association of Home Builders, p. 4.

to provide public facilities. A necessary first step in this process is to project the specific capital expenditures that will be undertaken in the years to come. Ramapo attempted to do this for eighteen years through its six year capital budget and its twelve year capital plan. It then geared its point system to the availability of these facilities.

The weak point in this plan has proven to be the fact that the township was projecting the installation of improvements over which it did not have absolute authority. Decisions relating to road improvement are made by the state, county and the township; parks and recreational facilities are heavily dependent upon decisions made by the independent school districts; and drainage and sewage facilities decisions are under the purview of the county. This fragmentation of authority has in part been responsible for the completion of only sixteen of the thirty-seven projects orginally proposed in the capital budget between 1969-74.[90]

The plan also lacks any mechanisms for revisions which would eliminate some of these inefficiencies. For example, Hurricanes Dora and Agnes crashed through the area in 1971 and 1972 causing considerable destruction, and $1.5 million in public funds had to be reallocated for use in cleaning up the damage.[91] While public officials assert this as one reason for their delinquency in undertaking projects, no changes have been made in the capital plans to account for these circumstances.

To overcome this deficiency, if a facility is not in place when it should be according to the capital plan, points are awarded anyway. To the extent that this fail-safe mechanism must be employed, the effectiveness of the growth management system is reduced.

The Ramapo plan has proven neither useful nor accurate as a planning device, and it has also failed to improve the township's municipal fisc. While it is particularly difficult to directly attribute changes in the property tax rate and the level of expenditures to the growth control ordinance, the study conducted for the National Association of Homebuilders does show that compared to the rest of the county, Ramapo's property tax increased at a faster proportional rate after the ordinance than before, despite an overall decline in the relative increase in expenditures.[92] This finding is not surprising in a growth control situation which is often unable to keep pace with the required public facilities, and a backlog of projects develops. Additionally, the growth of the tax base is also slowed to the extent that new development is excluded.[93]

Another operational aspect of the plan which suggests that it was improperly conceived is exhibited by the number of variances granted allowing projects to proceed without their having qualified for fifteen points. In his review of the Ramapo Plan five years after its implementation, Manuel Emanuel points out that, while only seventy-one special permits were granted, 146 variances had been issued with the average point total for this group being only 10.57.[94]

Ramapo Today   There is far less concern now with slowing the rate of growth in Ramapo. To the contrary, hundreds of special permits have been issued but the developers are holding their approvals hoping for an upsurge in the market. In fact, assurance from a developer that he/she has buyers and will proceed immediately with construction will go a long way toward persuading the town board that a permit should be authorized, regardless of the number of points obtained.[95] This turnabout leaves open the question of whether the Ramapo plan was simply a stop-gap approach to slowing growth or was actually a comprehensive plan for guiding the future of the township.

THE EFFECT OF PETALUMA'S RESIDENTIAL BUILDING PERMIT CAP ORDINANCE

Petaluma, California is a suburban city in Sonoma County, some 40 miles north of San Francisco.[96] Once a center of the dairy and poultry industries, Petaluma was destined to change in the early 1960's with the improvement into a modern freeway of Highway 101, the road that leads from Sonoma into San Francisco and other urban Bay Area locations. Currently, it is estimated that from 60 percent to 70 percent of Petaluma's new residents commute to San Francisco or San Rafael, a city just north of San Francisco.[97]

In 1950, Petaluma, still mostly farms, had a population of about 10,000 people. A slow to medium growth trend commenced, as the population increased to 14,000 by 1960. By 1970, the population growth rate had doubled and 24,000 people lived in Petaluma; and 1972 saw a doubling of the growth rate once again, as 5,000 more people had made their home in Petaluma in just two years. By 1972 Petaluma, no longer a sleepy farm village, was a healthy sized bedroom community of almost 30,000.

Petaluma's growth was not unpredicted. In 1962, before any large population increases had occurred, a master plan drawn up by the city had assumed a population of 77,000 by 1985.[98] Despite this prediction, Petaluma's government took little action to control the type or placement of its new development until it had been engulfed by it. The new houses of the 1960's and early 1970's were mostly tract-housing, without the diversity of style and price that usually marks better planned development. Emphasis was clearly placed on the quantity, not quality, of housing. Typically, most new building was centered in the flat, formerly agricultural eastern section of Petaluma, leaving west Petaluma, on the other side of Highway 101, to its older, deteriorating housing stock. Between 1970 and 1973, the 1,300 homes built in eastern Petaluma almost doubled the number of homes previously constructed there.

Beginning in 1970, city officials began to take action to investigate Petaluma's growth and control its development. Studies were made of the sewerage system, the school system, and the supporting tax base. Moratoria on rezoning, annexation and development were instituted. In 1971, a "Statement of Development Policy," a document prepared by a committee of Petaluma citizens and government officials, was adopted by the Planning Commission and City Council. The statement asserted that:

> In order to protect its small town character and surrounding open spaces, it shall be the policy of the City to control its future rate and distribution of growth. . .[99]

This was in part based on data obtained from a questionnaire which was included in the water bill mailed in May, 1971. The response was overwhelmingly in favor of limiting growth:

1. 81% wanted a greenbelt around the city,
2. 80% strongly opposed continuous urbanization of the valley,
3. 62% wanted to preserve Petaluma's small-town atmosphere, and
4. 56% through that growth ought to stop at 40,000.[100]

Meetings and planning conferences followed until August, 1972, when the Residential Development Control System was adopted by city council ordinance, to take effect that fall. The following spring, in an advisory referendum, the citizens of Petaluma approved the plan by a margin of four to one.[101]

"The Petaluma Plan" The Residential Development Control System (RDCS), the major component in the system of growth controls that has

come to be known as the "Petaluma Plan," applied only to large development, i.e., subdivisions of five or more lots, or multiple dwellings on lots of
five or more units. The RDCS encompassed the years 1973-1977 and set a
building limit or quota of 2,500 housing units — or an average of 500 units
per year — for that period. The plan also attempted to correct the east-west
housing maldistribution by allocating the 500 available housing units more
evenly between the less developed western section of Petaluma and
burgeoning east Petaluma. To award the rights to build these housing units,
the city council ordinance called for the establishment of a seventeen member Residential Development Evaluation Board, which would include city
council, planning and school board officials together with nine citizens.[102]

At the core of the Petaluma plan is the competition, judged by the
Board, for the 500 or so housing units awarded each year. Initially, after
receiving the various plans from developers, the Board determines whether
the submitted plans fit into the city's General Plan (of 1962) and Environmental Design Plan[103] (written in 1972 as an outgrowth of Petaluma's
more recent concerns) and discards any that do not. The board then applies
two groups of criteria to the development plans; the first group questions
the development's access to adequate services, the second group questions
the excellence of design, provision for open space, the inclusion of lower-
income housing, etc.[104]

The Petaluma Plan - As Implemented   Towards the end of 1972, the first
Residential Development Evaluation Board recommended to the City
Council the first housing allotment, for 1973-1974. The allocations divided
the units as follows: 125 multi-family and 125 single-family units for the
east side, and 130 multi-family and 120 single-family units for the west side.
Similar allocations, with some changes made to attempt to correct
geographic and multi/single family imbalances were made for subsequent
years.[105]

Several factors, however, affected how many of the allotments were actually awarded. A restraining order issued by Judge Burke in January of
1974 held up the awarding of the building permits until Justice Douglas's
stay of judgement in July of 1974. More importantly, many fewer residential building permits were awarded than allotted. Although partially due to
a general decline in the housing industry, it is nevertheless clear that the
Petaluma Plan was more than successful in meeting its goal of 500 residential units per year; in fact, an average of only 426 permits per year were
issued for 1972-1976. (See Exhibit 9.10) About 10 of these permits were
later rescinded, because the developer decided not to build. Developers apparently had gotten the message: while they had made about 1,000 applications per year for residential building permits in 1970 and 1971, by
1976 Petaluma was receiving less than 500 such applications per year.

EXHIBIT 9.10

RESIDENTIAL BUILDING PERMITS ISSUED FOR PETALUMA AND
SONOMA COUNTY, 1960-1975

	1960-1964 Yearly Average	1965-1969 Yearly Average	1970	1971	1972	1973	1974
Petaluma	151	336	643	880	498	437	490
Sonoma County	2,383	2,291	2,751	4,445	5,309	3,988	3,689
% Petaluma of Sonoma	6.3	14.7	23.4	19.8	9.4	11.0	13.3

SOURCES: Real Estate Research Council of Northern California in City of Peta-
luma, *Housing Element* (July 10, 1972), p. 5 (1960-1971); Personal
Communications with Mr. Leo Rochelle, Planner, Petaluma Planning
Department (August 17, 1976) (Petaluma data for 1972-1975);
California Statistical Abstract - 1975, p. 99 (Sonoma data for 1973-
1974; Security Pacific Bank (Sonoma County data, 1972).

By 1976, the Petaluma Plan began to enter the stage of evaluation and
analysis. An interim plan for 1975-1978 was drawn up so that evaluation of
the previous five years could occur.[106] The Interim Plan was quite similar to
the original plan, but the Planning Department and Commission took over
the role of Residential Development Evaluation Board. Currently, there are
strong indications that some form of the Petaluma Plan will be re-instituted
for the 1978-1979 year.

The Effects of the Petaluma Plan What remains to be considered, of
course, is the specific effects on growth of the Petaluma Plan, two issues are
of pre-eminent importance: the effects of the plan on Petaluma itself, its
population, housing and socio-economic structure; and the costs of the
surrounding area, i.e. Sonoma County, of Petaluma's attempt to control its
growth. The Petaluma plan must be judged not only on its own internal
criteria, to limit population growth, to balance growth between east and
west Petaluma, to provide low-income housing, to provide for open space,
etc. It is equally important to determine whether Petaluma merely isolated
itself from the problems of growth, thereby doing little else but forcing its
problems on neighboring communities.

Based on population trends alone, the Petaluma Plan must be judged as
quite successful. Petaluma's population (See Table 9.11), some 29,000 in
1972, has increased to only 31,200 in 1976; its average annual population
growth rate, which was 7.7% from 1960 to 1972 and 8.5% from 1970 to 1972,

EXHIBIT 9.11
POPULATION, PETALUMA AND SONOMA COUNTY, 1950–1976

	1950	1960	1970	1972	1973	1974	1975	1976
Petaluma	10,320	14,040	24,870	29,070	30,350	31,150	30,500	31,200
% Change Petaluma		36.0	77.1	16.9	4.4	2.6	-2.1	0.3
Average Annual % Change		3.6	7.7	8.5	4.4	2.6	-2.1	0.3
Sonoma County	103,400	147,400	204,885	218,260	227,400	235,100	244,600	250,200
% Change Sonoma County		42.6	39.0	6.9	4.2	3.5	4.0	2.3
Average Annual % Change		4.3	3.9	3.5	4.2	3.5	4.0	2.3
% Petaluma Population of Sonoma County	10.0	9.5	12.1	13.3	13.3	13.2	12.5	12.5

SOURCE: Sonoma County Planning Department; California State Department of Finance Estimates (1972, 1973, 1974, 1975, 1976).

decreased to only 1.8% for 1972 to 1976. Although it is difficult to isolate what other factors may have influenced this decline, there is no doubt that the Petaluma plan played a crucial part. Comparing Petaluma with Sonoma County, the county's average annual growth rate has varied little over the last 25 years, varying only from 3.5 percent to 4.3 percent (excepting only 1976, for which data are not yet finalized.) From this comparison, two conclusions may be drawn: the Petaluma plan has been effective in bringing Petaluma's population growth rate in line with the remainder of Sonoma County (after the comparative boom of 1960-1972); and despite Petaluma's decrease in growth, Sonoma County as a whole has compensated, and continued its steady 4 percent a year growth. Presumably builders seeking to develop in the area have been driven away from Petaluma into other cities and unincorporated areas of Sonoma County (and other Bay Area locations). This last fact is an important one, since it lends support to the major criticism of local growth control schemes like the Petaluma plan; they may solve local problems, but they do so only at the expense of the region.

The number of residential building permits issued by Petaluma and Sonoma County underscores this symbiotic relationship between Petaluma and Sonoma County. In 1960-1964, Petaluma issued few residential building permits, both numerically and as a percentage of the total issued in Sonoma County. Petaluma began a rapid period of growth during 1965-1969, and by 1970-1971 issued about 20 percent of the residential building permits for all of Sonoma County, up from about 6 percent in 1960-1964 and about 15 in 1965-1969. The institution of the Petaluma Plan had a quick effect; in 1971, Petaluma issued only 408 permits, and cut in half its percentage of total Sonoma County results. Sonoma County has continued its level of growth until the present time, while Petaluma continues to slow its growth. Again residential building permit data seem to indicate that many of those builders who might have built in Petaluma have simply shifted to other areas, mostly in Sonoma County.

Besides growth in terms of numbers of houses and people, the Petaluma Plan attempted to affect the style and socio-economic structure of the city. Little success has been attained in this regard. Single-family units still predominate, and there are still many more multi-family houses on the west side than on the east side.[107] The differential between average prices for homes in west and east Petaluma remains — $18,500 (west)/$28,500 (east) in 1971 and $33,250/$44,750 in 1975.[108] Little, if any, progress has been made in rehabilitating older housing stock or in providing lower-income housing. In short, the Petaluma Plan was not effective in meeting many of the needs of the city.[109]

The Petaluma Plan has been demonstrated to be an effective tool for controlling population influxes into one area and for strictly limiting the number of dwelling units that are built in any one locality. It is not an effective way, however, to control geographic maldistribution and the type and placement of the housing that is built.

There is also evidence to indicate that whatever plans Petaluma made were at the expense of surrounding areas. Further, from a legal standpoint, it is questionable whether a Petaluma Plan applied to a larger region or state would be acceptable.[110] In short, Petaluma has accomplished some of its goals by means of isolation. Whether other communities can afford to act similarly is open to many questions: legal, economic, political and ethical.

THE EFFECT OF GROWTH CONTROLS ON HOUSING COSTS

More than in any other area of regulation, the impact of growth controls must be examined in light of their indirect effects in a region's housing market. Closing down development in one area must increase demand elsewhere. The results are cost increases both for the consumer and the receptive communities. The latter in turn will find exclusionary developmental devices more and more alluring. Growth controls have been devised in such a way as to significantly increase control over the type of development allowed in a community. While benefits and even savings are possible by controlling the sequence and timing of future development, all too frequently these positive planning objectives act as a front for excluding moderately priced housing.

NOTES

1. Michael Gleeson, et al., *Urban Management Systems,* Planning Advisory Service, Report No. 309-10, (Chicago, Ill.: American Society of Planning Officials, 1975).
2. Henry Fagin, "Regulating the Timing of Urban Devlopment," *Law and Contemporary Problems,* 20 (Spring, 1955), p. 298.
3. William Reilly (ed.), *The Use of Land,* Task Force on Land Use and Urban Growth, (New York: Thomas Crowell Company, 1973), p. 17.
4. See, for example, *New York Times* five part series on the rise of power in the Sunbelt, Jon Nordheimer, *et al.,* "Sunbelt Region Heads Nation in Growth of Population," (February 8-13, 1976).
5. See the the Case Studies in this chapter.
6. See in general, Marion Clauson, *Suburban Land Conversion in the United States,* Resources for the Future, Inc. (Baltimore: The Johns Hopkins University Press, 1971.)
7. The Sixth Annual Report of the Council on Environmental Quality, *Environmental Quality* (Washington, D.C.: U.S. Government Printing Office, 1975), p. 163.

8. For a summary of each state's program see, Michael Arnold and Anne McDonald (eds.), "A Summary of State Land Use Controls," *Land Use Planning Reports,* Report No. 5, (Washington, D.C., Plus Publications, 1976), p. 18.
9. See for example, Kathryn A. Zeimetz, *et al.,* "Dynamics of Land Use in Fast Growth Areas," Agricultural Economic Report No. 325, (Washington, D.C.: U.S. Dept. of Agriculture, 1976).
10. Telephone interview with Eugene Taylor, Chief of the Crop Reporting Service, New Jersey Dept. of Agriculture, July 1976. This estimate is based both on Census Statistics showing the percentage of non-owner operated farms and the experience of state officials.
11. Sidney O. Dewberry, "Area Building Costs Compared: Higher Figure Seen Due to Rules," *The Washington Post,* March 20, 1976, Col. 1, p. D-17.
12. Robert Freilich, "Editor's Comments," *The Urban Lawyer,* 4, No. 3 (Summer 1972), pp. IX-X.
13. Daniel J. Alesch, "Local Government's Ability to Manage Growth in a Metropolitan Context," The Rand Paper Series, (Santa Monica, California: The Rand Corporation, 1974), p. 21.
14. Gleeson, *Urban Management Systems,* p. 7.
15. *Ibid.,* p. 13.
16. Mary Cranston, et al., A *Handbook for Controlling Local Growth,* Stanford Environmental Law Society, (Stanford, Cal.: 1973), pp. 90-92.
17. Reilly (ed.), *The Use of Land,* pp. 43-44.
18. Gleeson, *Urban Management Systems,* p.v.
19. This relationship has succinctly been described as "supply-activated" as opposed to the traditional "demand-activated" planning by Environmental Analysis Systems, Inc., "Growth Management. . .Practices and Issues," (Sacramento, Cal.: The Assembly Committee on Local Government, 1975), pp. 18-19.
20. Norman Williams, *American Planning Law,* 5 vols. (Chicago: Callaghan Publishing Company, 1975), Vol. III, pp. 355-7.
21. *Ibid.*
22. *Matter of Joseph v. Town Board of Town of Clarkstown,* 24 Misc. 2d 366, 198 NYS 2d 695 (Supreme Court, Rockland Cty, 1960).
23. *Ibid.,* p. 699.
24. San Jose Initiative Ordinance 16764, April 27, 1973.
25. School population in San Jose had tripled in the decade from 1960-70. S.C. Deutsch, "Land Use Growth Controls: A Case Study of San Jose and Livermore, California," *Santa Clara Lawyer,* 15 (1974), pp. 12-14.
26. Cranston, et al., *Handbook for Controlling Local Growth,* p. 107.
27. Deutsch, "Growth Control," p. 13.
28. Cranston, et al., *Handbook for Controlling Local Growth,* p. 90.
29. Deutsch, "Growth Control," pp. 13-14.
30. Livermore Initiative, April 11, 1972.
31. Bureau of National Affairs, "Current Developments," *Housing and Development Reporter* (Washington, D.C.: October 6, 1975), pp. 459-60.
32. Manuel S. Emanuel, "Ramapo's Managed Growth Program," *Planner's Notebook* 4, No. 5 (October 1974), p. 2.
33. §46-13.1 Special Permit Uses; Amended to the township's zoning ordinance in October 1969.
34. *Ibid.* at Section A, "General Considerations."

35. For detailed presentation of the mechanics of the ordinance, see Emanuel Manuel, "Ramapo Five Years After," *Planner's Notebook*, 4, No. 5 (October 1974). Mr. Manuel, working as a consultant to the town, was one of the primary architects of the plan.
36. *Golden v. Planning Board of Town of Ramapo*, Rockland County, Index, No. 525-1970 (NY Sup. Ct., Westchester County), October 26, 1970.
37. *Golden v. Planning Board of Town of Ramapo*, 37 App. Div. 2d 236, 324 NYS 2d 178 (1971).
38. *Golden v. Planning Board of Town of Ramapo*, 30 NY 2d 359, 334 NYS 2d 138, 285 NE 2d 291 (1972), app. dism'd. 409 US 1003 (1972).
39. Williams, *American Planning Law*, Vol. III, p. 367.
40. For example, the Court states:
    There is, then something inherently suspect in a scheme which, apart from its professed purposes, effects a restriction upon the free mobility of a people until sometime in the future when projected facilities are available to meet increased demand. *(Golden v. Planning Board of Town of Ramapo*, 285 NE 2d 291, 1972 at 300).
41. *Ibid.*, p. 301.
42. *Ibid.*
43. See the Case Study of Ramapo's Phased Development Ordinance.
44. Boca Raton, which enacted by initiative a housing unit cap of 40,000 units, was the only one of thirteen communities with growth controls investigated by Gleeson which actually had annual revenues in excess of expenditures. Gleeson, *Urban Management Systems*, p. 5.
45. "St. Petersburg Council Votes to Cut Back Population," *New York Times*, March 26, 1974, p. 24.
46. *Ibid.*
47. See also 26 *Zoning Digest* 4, Number 2 (1974).
48. The population in 1970 was 28,500; 40,000 units would have permitted approximately 105,000 residents. For a description of the circumstances surrounding the adoption of the ordinance, see John Nordheimer, "Rich Boca Resolves to Stop Growth," *New York Times*, February 9, 1973, p. 31.
49. *Arvida Corporation v. City of Boca Raton*, 312 So. 2d 826 (1975).
50. Other measures adopted as part of the plan include establishing an urban extension line beyond which public facilities will not be supplied. For a detailed explanation of the ordinance, see Frank Gray, "The City of Petaluma: Residential Development Control," in Scott Randall (ed.), *Management and Control of Growth*, 3 Vols. (Washington, D.C., The Urban Land Institute: 1975), Vol. II, p. 149.
51. John Hart, "The Petaluma Case," *Cry California*, Spring, 1974, cited in Scott (ed.), *Management and Control of Growth*, 3 Vols: (Washington, D.C., The Urban Land Institute: 1975), Vol. II, p. 127.
52. *Ibid.*, p. 131.
53. *Construction Industry Assoc. of Sonoma County v. City of Petaluma*, 375 F. Supp. 574 (1974).
54. *Ibid.*, p. 581.
55. In the court's "Findings of Fact," *Ibid.* at 577-8.
56. *Construction Industry Association of Sonoma County v. City of Petaluma*, No. 74-2100, August 13, 1975.
57. 422 U.S. 490 (1975).

58. The Construction Industry Association was denied a writ of certiorari by the U.S. Supreme Court, U.S. 96 S. Ct. 1148 (February 23, 1976).
59. See for example, *Rasmussen v. City of Lake Forest,* U.S. Dis. Ct. North Illinois, Nov. 10, 1975. As reported in the Bureau of National Affairs, "Current Develotments," *Housing and Development Reporter,* January 12, 1976, p. 790.
60. *Village of Belle Terre v. Boraas,* 416 U.S. 1 (1973). Anti-groupers ordinance restricts the number of nonrelated individuals who are permitted to share the same residence.
61. Barbara Delativers, "Long Island Draws the Line on Groupers," *New York Times,* August 31, 1975, Sec. 8, p. 1, col. 8.
62. Gleeson, *Urban Management Systems,* p. 24.
63. Burrows, *Growth Controls,* p. III-5-6; Based on Sacramento County, Interdepartmental correspondence, "Explanation of the County's Controlled Growth Policy and the Function of Reserve Areas," March 31, 1975.
64. Letter from Earl Fraser, Planning Director, Sacramento County Planning Department, to Professor Richard O. Brooks, Dept. of Community Planning, University of Rhode Island, (n.d.) explaining the Sacramento program.
65. See, in general, Metropolitan Council, *Development Framework: Policy, Plan, Program,* St. Paul, Minnesota, Sept. 1975.
66. Metropolitan Council, *Development Framework,* p. 19.
67. Lane Council of Governments, "Eugene-Springfield Metropolitan Area 1990 General Plan," Eugene, 1976, p. 11.
68. Rivkin Associates, Inc., "The Sewer Moratorium as a Technique of Growth Control and Environmental Protection," (Washington, D.C.) June, 1973, p. 1.
69. Michael Greenberg, "A Commentary on Sewer Moratorium as a Piecemeal Remedy for Controling Development," in Hughes (ed.), *New Dimensions in Growth Controls,* (New Brunswick: Center for Urban Policy Research, Rutgers University, 1974), p. 189.
70. Rivkin, *Sewer Moratorium,* p. 14.
71. Office of the County Executive, Montgomery County, Maryland, "Memorandum to the County Council on Sewer Authorizations," p. I-1. As cited in Burrows, *Growth Controls,* pp. III-10.
72. *Smoke Rise, Inc. v. Washintton Suburban Sanitary Commission,* U.S. Dist. Court for Maryland, Aug. 18, 1975.
73. For an analysis of *Smoke Rise,* see Bureau of National Affairs, "Current Developments," *Housing and Development Reporter* (October 6, 1975,) p. 458.
74. Rivkin, *Sewer Moratorium,* p. 78.
75. Livingston and Blayney, "Foothills Environmental Design Study: Open Space vs. Development" (prepared for the City of Palo Alto, 1971).
76. *Ibid.,* p. 141.
77. "Had It Not Been for the Courts, . . ."Northern Virginia Builders Association, May 15, 1975, p. 2.
78. Gleeson, *Urban Management Techniques,* p. 7.
79. Deutsch, "Land Use Controls," p. 17-18.
80. Emanuel, *Ramapo Five Years After,* p. 8.
81. William Alonso, "Urban Zero Population Growth," *Daedalus,* (Fall 1973), p. 193.
82. *Ibid.*
83. Metropolitan Council, *Development Framework,* p. 12.

84. *Ibid.*
85. Emanuel, "Ramapo Five Years After," *Planner's Notebook,* p. 2.
86. *Ibid.,* p. 3.
87. The region can be determined by such factors as transportation facilities, job location, and natural boundaries. For the purposes of examining Ramapo, we have selected Rockland County as its region.
88. Memorandum from Hammer, Siler, George Associates, "Economic Analysis of Point System Ordinance in Ramapo, New York,"(Prepared for the National Association of Home Builders, May 8, 1975), p. 3.
89. Some relief may behad by applying for a reduced assessment from the Development Easement Acquisition Commission, but most of the costs remain unaffected.
90. "Report on NAHB Task Force Field Trip to Ramapo, New York," National Association of Homebuilders, n.d.
91. Emanuel, "Ramapo Five Years After," *Planner's Notebook,* p. 8.
92. Hammer, Siler, George Associates, Memorandum to the National Association of Homebuilders, "Ramapo, New York Socio-Economic Profile," March 10, 1975, p. 12-13.
93. For a discussion of a similar result from a growth control ordinance in Cotati, California, see "Town Finds No-Growth Plan Leads to Not Enough Funds," Les Ledbetter, *New York Times,* July 31, 1976, 1, p. 23.
94. Emanuel, "Ramapo Five Years After," p. 7-8.
95. Interview with John Keough, Ramapo Planning Department, June, 1976.
96. Much of the background information for this case study came from Frank B. Gray, (Director of Community Development, Petaluma, California), *Rationale, Operation and Evaluation of Residential Development Control in the City of Petaluma,* California, (1974), pp. 1-14; also of interest were: Frank Schnidman, *Growth Management in Ramapo and Petaluma,* (1974), pp. 8-19; *City of Petaluma, Environmental Design Plans,* (March 27, 1972), pp. 1-22; and William C. McGiven, "Putting a Speed Limit on Growth," *Planning,* (November, 1972).
97. Arata, Misuraca, Clement and Haley (Attorneys to the Construction Industry Association of Sonoma County), Memorandum to the File, April 16, 1973; A Sonoma County Planning Department report indicated that 86.0 percent of that county's commuters traveled Routes 101 or 37 to San Francisco. City of Petaluma, *Petaluma Housing Element—Housing Element Annual Review and Update,* (October 29, 1974) p. 9.
98. City of Petaluma, *Petaluma Area General Plan* - 1962, p. 2.
99. Petaluma Development Policy Conference, "Statement of Development Policy," adopted by Petaluma City Council, June 7, 1971.
100. Peter Barnes, "The California Experience: How to Use Land," *The New Republic,* Sept. 21, 1974, pp. 10-12.
101. Frank B. Gray, Director of Community Development, Petaluma, California, *Rationale, Operation, and Evaluation of Residential Development Control in the City of Petaluma, California,* (1974), p. 5.
102. Gray, *Residential Development Control,* pp. 4-5.
103. City of Petaluma, *Environmental Design Plans,* (March 27, 1972).
104. Gray, *Residential Development Control,* p. 11-12.

105. *Ibid.,* p. 5.
106. City of Petroluma, *Interim Residential Development Control System for the City of Petaluma,* (1976), pp. 1-10.
107. City of Petaluma, *Housing Element Review and Update,* (October 29, 1974), p. 2.
108. *Ibid.,* p. 10.
109. *Ibid.,* p. 15.
110. See generally, Claude Gruen, *The Economics of Petaluma: Unconstitutional Regional Socio-Economic Impacts,* in Scott (ed.), *Management and Control of Growth,* 3 Vols., (Washington, D.C.: Urban Land Institute, 1975), Vol. 2, p. 173.

Chapter Ten: The Effect of Environmental Regulations on Housing Costs

The rise of our nation's environmental consciousness has brought with it a new genre of government regulations which have the potential of significantly increasing the cost of housing. These new controls have as their primary object the prevention of the mistakes of past development, which all too frequently resulted in the destruction of the physical environment. But in addition to protecting the environment, these regulations frequently generate a corollary effect — that of limiting the provision of moderately priced housing.

This conflict between the equally desirable goals of preserving the environment and providing moderately priced housing forms the basis for this chapter.[1] Environmentalists and housing proponents increasingly regard each other as advocates of positions not subject to compromise. And the belief is growing stronger that, particularly in the suburbs, environmental controls are being manipulated to close the door on moderately priced housing.

In an attempt to balance the need for preserving the environment with the need for moderately priced housing, several key, yet not easily answerable, questions must be addressed. First, one must establish exactly the desirable level of environmental protection. In addition one must decide whether or not the proposed level is to be allowed to vary among communities, among the rich and the poor, cities and the suburbs, etc. Another important issue is the cost of preserving the environment. To what extent should those now owning environmentally sensitive properties be forced to shoulder this burden? Finally a regulatory process must be developed which adequately resolves the desired level of protection while fairly allocating any costs.

This chapter attempts to address these issues within the framework of the existing environmental regulations. The first section presents an overview of government's role in preserving the environment. This section also discusses the primary vehicle for that intervention — the environmental impact statement. Attention is then turned to the most significant specific programs of environmental protection. The second section examines the various state land development laws which have spread throughout the country and have been accurately characterized as the "quiet revolution in land use controls."[2] The third section discusses coastal zone protection regulations, which have been the subject of significant federal and state legislation with their attendant regulations.[3] Within each of these sections the existing regulatory mechanism will be briefly outlined, its effectiveness assessed, and its impact on housing costs quantified.

Government's Role in Protecting the Environment

A question which must first be addressed is whether government intervention is even necessary to protect the environment. Put slightly differently, is left to its own devices, would the marketplace, that traditional allocator of resources, be capable of achieving the desired amount of environmental protection? Despite considerable rhetoric describing the benefits of an unencumbered market,[4] past experience, buttressed by considerable economic theory, suggests that the private market will not adequately preserve our environmental resources.[5]

The primary reason why environmental resources are not properly allocated within the free market is that they cannot be considered "private" goods. Only those goods which can be owned and used exclusively by the purchaser can be properly allocated by the marketplace. Environmental resources, such as clean air and water, clearly do not fit within this category of exclusive ownership and use. In the case of other examples of environmental goods, such as aquifers, the coastal zone and flood plains, society has deemed that some aspect of these areas must be made available to everyone and therefore they too cannot be considered private goods.

Historically, the market has failed to adequately assess the costs of environmental degradation. The proliferation of negative externalities, whereby one actor is able to shift costs to another without having to bear this burden, results in the overutilization of these resources not included in that actor's economic calculus.[6] In terms of the environment, production processes and sensitive land will be used regardless of the external costs their use may generate. In sum, the problem of environmental resources not being a "private good" and their use being fraught with externalities provides the mandate for government intervention.

THE SPREAD OF GOVERNMENT REGULATIONS

The recognition of this need for increased government regulation of environmental resources has resulted in the rapid proliferation of laws in this area. In general the federal role has been primarily to provide development money for states to initiate and implement their own programs.[7]

A survey of state environmental programs recently undertaken by the American Institute of Planners for the Department of Housing and Urban Development demonstrates the increased role being played by state governments.[8] (See Exhibit 10.1) All thirty coastal zone states are participating in the federal Coastal Zone Management program, twenty-six states have adopted wetlands programs, twenty states are involved in regulating floodplains, sixteen states require at least a limited environmental impact statement, fourteen states have legislation relating to critical areas control, and seven states regulate developments of regional impact.

While no one common denominator exists within these many different areas of regulation, a number of them do rely on the environmental impact statement (EIS) as their primary regulatory mechanism. Laws regulating critical areas, the coastal zone, and developments of regional impact most frequently use this regulatory mechanism. In addition, several state and many local governments have expanded this requirement to include all private developments regardless of their location. Since the EIS requirement has developed into the primary mechanism to ensure environmental protection, it deserves special attention.

THE ENVIRONMENTAL IMPACT STATEMENT (EIS)

The origins of the EIS requirement can be traced directly to the National Environmental Protection Act of 1969 (NEPA). While this act applies only to major federal actions or legislation significantly affecting the quality of the environment, it has served as the prototype for state and local legislation affecting both public and private actions affecting the environment.

An EIS is usually required for all projects falling within some threshold criteria. This threshold is frequently defined in terms of a minimum development size or it may be based directly on expected environmental impact.

EXHIBIT 10.1

SURVEY OF STATE ENVIRONMENTAL REGULATIONS

	Coastal Zone Management	Wetlands	Floodplains	Critical Areas	State EIS	Developments of Regional Impact
Alabama	X					
Alaska	X	X				
Arkansas			X			
Arizona			X			
California	X	X	X		X	
Colorado				X		X
Connecticut	X	X	X		X	
Delaware	X	X			X	
Florida	X	X	X	X		X
Georgia	X	X				
Hawaii	X	X				
Idaho						
Illinois	X		X			
Iowa			X			
Indiana	X		X	X¹	X	
Kansas						
Kentucky						
Louisiana	X	X				
Maine	X	X		X		X
Massachusetts	X	X			X	X
Maryland	X	X	X¹	X	X	
Michigan	X	X	X		X	
Minnesota	X	X	X	X	X	
Mississippi	X	X				
Missouri		X		X¹		
Montana			X		X	
Nebraska			X			
Nevada			X			
New Jersey	X	X	X		X	
New Mexico						
New York	X	X	X			
New Hampshire	X	X		X		
No. Carolina	X	X	X	X	X	
No. Dakota						
Ohio	X					
Oklahoma						
Oregon	X			X		X
Pennsylvania	X	X	X¹	X	X	
Rhode Island	X	X				
So. Carolina	X					
So. Dakota					X	
Tennessee						
Texas	X	X				
Utah					X	
Vermont		X	X			X
West Virginia				X¹		
Virginia	X	X			X	
Washington	X	X	X	X	X	X
Wisconsin	X	X	X		X	
Wyoming						

SOURCE: American Institute of Planners, *Survey of State Land Use Planning Activity*, prepared for the Department of Housing and Urban Development, January, 1976.

1. Program is currently proposed.

The agency most directly involved with the development, usually an environmental or land use agency, is charged with the responsibility of document preparation. In many cases, however, this task is simply passed on to the developer, with the lead agency assuming responsibility for the review of the draft EIS.

Although the content of an EIS will vary depending on the requirements of each particular jurisdiction, almost all include the basis ingredients outlined in NEPA. Thus the following can be found in almost every EIS:

1. background describing the project and the location;
2. discussion of the primary and secondary environmental impacts resulting from the action;
3. identification of irreversible or unavoidable adverse environmental impacts; and
4. alternatives to the proposed action.[9]

In addition state and local governments when adopting an EIS requirement have often expanded its scope to include an economic analysis of the proposed project's impact.[10]

EVALUATING THE EIS REQUIREMENT

There can be little argument that the goal of an EIS requirement, that of making mandatory the consideration of the environmental impact of a policy or project, is a desirable one. Nor is it possible to attack the EIS mechanism as a highly inefficient way of reaching this goal. But problems do exist in the current EIS process which undermine its effectiveness and unnecessarily escalate the cost of housing.

Few EIS requirements balance environmental considerations against social concerns. An analysis of EIS content undertaken by the Task Force on Land Use and Urban Growth concluded:

In practice, review too often concentrates more on natural values than on human ones — more on fish than on people. In the case of a subsidized housing development, for example, sedimentation of nearby streams may be considered in more detail than improvement in the lives of the residents. We would hope the review process would be used to enhance public awareness of social impact rather than, intentionally or not, to divert attention from it.[11]

While few jurisdictions now require discussion of the social and economic benefits of the proposed project, such a provision would allow for a clearer articulation of the tradeoff between the advantages of growth and its damage to the environment.

The existing EIS process does not invariably produce a reliable environmental analysis of assured quality. Unless the estimated effect of a project on the environment can be accurately forecasted, then decisions based on impact statements would be inadequate and often misguided. Unfortunately the state of the art in estimating environmental impacts is still in its infancy. Particularly at the local level, the EIS appears to be used more as a procedural than substantive requirement, with the very important exception that undesirable projects (for whatever reason) do receive close scrutiny. A recent review of the quality of EIS intent concluded:

> The author's title, the mass of the report, the author's salary, and his dress and bearing often carry more weight with the commission or study board to whom the statement is presented than either his scientific competence or the validity of his scientific investigation.[12]

This problem of forecasting environmental impacts is particularly acute when consideration is paid to the secondary impacts of a project.[13] It is in this area that the environmental damage may be most severe.

As the EIS requirement develops over time, it is reasonable to expect that its ability to accurately forecast environmental impacts will also improve. The next section describes the extent to which the EIS requirement currently affects the housing market.

EIS AND THE RESIDENTIAL CONSTRUCTION INDUSTRY

Because EIS's are increasingly being required by local governments, it is extremely difficult to even approximate the extent of their application. To learn about their use, we asked residential developers the percentage of their projects over the last three years which required that impact statements be filed. The sample was comprised of 400 developers randomly drawn from the respondents to our mail solicitation of the membership lists of the Urban Land Institute and National Association of Home Builders.[14] These 400 developers were interviewed over the telephone by our staff. (See Exhibit 10.2) The results show that 15.4 percent of the developers stated that an EIS had been required for more than 75 percent of their residential projects during the past three years. At the other end of the spectrum, 65.4 percent of those interviewed stated that none of their projects during this time period required an EIS.

A closer look at the data suggests the extent to which EIS's have spread to the local level. By separating those states which require that an EIS be filed for all residential projects above a certain threshold from those states without such a requirement, it is possible to approximate the magnitude of the local EIS requirement. Our results show that 40 percent of developers

EXHIBIT 10.2

RESIDENTIAL PROJECTS REQUIRING AN ENVIRONMENTAL
IMPACT STATEMENT*

Percent of Projects Requiring an EIS be Filed	Developers Operating in States With State Imposed EIS Requirements (N=65)	Developers Operating in States Without State Imposed EIS Requirements (N=319)	Total (N=384)
Never required	35.4%	71.5%	65.4%
1 - 25 percent	15.4	9.1	10.2
26 - 50 percent	9.2	6.0	6.4
51 - 75 percent	6.2	1.8	2.6
76 - 100 percent	33.8	11.6	15.4
Total	100.0	100.0	100.0

*States included in this category were California, Florida, Hawaii, Maine, New Jersey, and Vermont.

SOURCE: Telephone Survey of Home Builders, Center for Urban Policy Research, Summer 1976.

active in EIS states filed on more than 50 percent of their projects. But even in states without a state imposed EIS, 13.4 percent of these developers were required to file an EIS on more than 50 percent of their projects. The latter group's requirement can be attributed primarily to local EIS regulations.

While there is no direct method of evaluating the degree to which EIS requirements have been successful in reducing the environmental destruction caused by residential development, it is possible to determine the extent to which changes in project design to reduce the environmental damage have been made because of this regulation. Our survey asked developers the extent and nature of changes in their development plans because of the EIS requirement. (See Exhibit 10.3) Only 11.3 percent of the developers who have encountered an EIS requirement reported that they made no changes in their construction plans. Meanwhile, 15.8 percent stated that they made changes in their traditional development plans before they were submitted for EIS review, presumably in order to expedite approval. Another 30.8 percent responded that changes had been required in their development plans *after* EIS review. Finally, the largest group (42.1 percent) cited that changes are typically made *both before and after* EIS review.

EXHIBIT 10.3

EIS RELATED CHANGES IN PROJECT PLANS

Action Taken	Number of Developers	Percent
No Changes Made	15	11.3
Changes Made Before EIS Review	21	15.8
Changes Made After EIS Review	41	30.8
Changes Made Both Before and After EIS Review	56	42.1
Total	133	100.0

SOURCE: Telephone Survey of Home Builders, Center for Urban Policy Research, Summer 1976.

Of those developers who changed their plans because of environmental impact review, the most commonly cited alteration (59.4 percent) was a reduction in dwelling unit densities. (See Exhibit 10.4) This was not surprising considering the direct relationship between a project's density and its impact on the physical environment. Over half the developers (54.1 percent) making changes also responded that they were required to relocate the structure relative to the lot in order to minimize the environmental impact. Other changes frequently cited as atrributable to EIS review were the dedication of recreational or open space (47.9 percent) and the provision of additional sewerage handling capacity (31.0 percent).

THE IMPACT OF THE EIS REQUIREMENT

The EIS has now become a firmly established mechanism of regulating the impact of development on the environment. Although the EIS requirement does have its problems — in particular the varying quality of impact assessment and the refusal to examine the non-physical side of the project's impact — there can be little doubt that the design of residential projects is now environmentally less obtrusive.

The Effect of State Land Development Acts on Housing Costs

The past decade has witnessed the awakening of state governments to their responsibility to regulate the use of land.[15] Once satisfied simply to delegate this authority to local governments, states are now beginning to recognize the inadequacies of this fragmented decision-making system.[16] State land development laws, which provide some measure of state input into local land use decisions, are a major step toward remedying this

EXHIBIT 10.4

TYPES OF CHANGES REQUIRED BY EIS REVIEW

Changes	Number of Developers	Percent*
Reduction in Dwelling Unit Densities	44	59.5
Relocation of Structures Relative to Lot	40	54.1
Additional Recreational or Open Space	35	47.9
Additional Sewerage Handling Capacity	22	31.0
Relocation or Termination of Project	3	4.1

*Will not add to 100.0 due to multiplicity of responses.

SOURCE: Telephone Survey of Home Builders, Center for Urban Policy Research, Summer 1976.

situation. Since 1969 when only Hawaii had statewide authority over land use, today nine more states have assumed varying degrees of control over significant land use decisions.[17]

This section examines the effect of these state land use laws on residential construction. The first part provides the background for state action; it explores the problems of purely local control and the potential benefits of state regulation. The second part details the management techniques adopted by various state governments, the regulatory devices used, and examples of their implementation. The final section discusses the cost of compliance with these regulations. Examples of costs in Florida and California will be examined.

THE NEED FOR STATE LAND USE CONTROLS

The recognition that local control over land use decisions may not always be appropriate can be traced at least as far back as the Supreme Court's decision in *Euclid*. In this case, which established the right of local governments to impose zoning restrictions on development, Justice Sutherland noted that this authority is by no means absolute and that situations could arise where:

the general public interest would so far outweigh the interest of the municipality that the municipality would not be allowed to stand in the way.[18]

As the interdependence of society increases, those situations which require a broader than municipal perspective are surfacing with increasing regularity. In particular, local authority has proven inadequate in controlling three types of land use decisions: those which involve environmentally critical areas; those related to large scale development; and those related to developments of regional benefit.

In each of these situations, a broader perspective is crucial. An environmentally sensitive area, such as an acquifer or the coastal area, often is vital to more than just the municipality in which it is located. Large scale developments frequently produce secondary impacts such as increased employment, pollution, etc., which significantly affect an entire region. Finally, developments of regional benefit include such things as landfills and low-income housing, which a region desperately needs, but which each individual community wants to exclude from its own borders.

Lest one think that the state's role will become dominant, it must be recognized that more than 90 percent of land use decisions do not fall within either of these three categories and therefore should be debated at the local level.[19] Nor does state participation in the regulatory process necessarily translate into state domination. The underlying purpose of state intervention is only to extend consideration of land use decisions beyond the parochial considerations of a local government. This does not require that the state directly make these decisions itself. In fact, as we shall soon see, most states have adopted legislation which specifically limits their powers.

THE MECHANISM FOR STATE LAND DEVELOPMENT CONTROLS

Although the actual programs adopted by the states vary considerably, each program must address a basic set of questions which form the framework for state intervention in land use controls. The following questions attempt to isolate the key issues in the development of this type of state control.

What is to be included within the scope of regulated activities? The first issue for a state in drafting its legislation is to determine exactly which development activities are to be subject to the proposed regulation. Establishing a threshold criterion is no easy task. If it is set too low or is too inflexible, inefficiencies will be built into the system. Too much time may be wasted on small projects, while backlogs develop and large projects receive inadequate attention.

No single approach has proven capable of distinguishing between activities which require state review and those which can be properly handled by local governments. As previously discussed, a commonly accepted approach is to regulate both *areas* which are environmentally critical and *activities* which have regional or statewide impact. But even within this framework, it is still necessary to distinguish between those proposals which require examination and those which do not because they will have only minimal environmental impact. The approach used by the state of Vermont emphasizes control over critical areas and large-scale projects. The particular crisis facing this state was the threat of widespread vacation home development generated by the booming ski industry.[20] In an attempt to preserve the natural beauty of the Green Mountains of Vermont, the state included in its definition of an environmentally critical area any land above a 2,500 foot altitude. Any development, regardless of size, proposed at a height in excess of this, was required to apply for a special development permit.[21]

Vermont's Act defines developments of regional impact as any subdivision of more than ten lots, residential development of more than ten units or industrial or commercial property of more than one acre.[22] Any project falling within these categories must also apply for the special development permit required by this act.

In Florida, the administering agency has taken a more specific approach to determining which projects are to be considered within the context of that state's land development act. It has published a list of major facilities, including such developments as airports, power plants, and private facilities, which are deemed to have regional impact. Whether a residential development is considered a development of regional impact depends on both the nature of the area in which it is to be located and the number of units proposed. Included within the review process are projects containing 250 units located in the least populous counties and projects larger than 3,000 units in the most urbanized counties.[23]

What criteria are to be used to evaluate a specific proposal? Once the parameters have been set establishing which projects fall within the scope of the regulatory process, the next step is to specify the criteria and/or standards needed to evaluate the proposal. Such issues as whether the evaluation should consider only the physical impacts, or should be extended to include the social and economic consequences of the proposal must be addressed. Should the magnitude of negative impacts be the only consideration, or should this be balanced against the benefits created by the project? And what is the relative importance of different types of impacts?

In answering these questions, a framework for evaluating applications for development approval evolves. But the state of the art in estimating projected impacts attributable to a proposed development falls far short of a perfect science. The same development will undoubtedly have substantially different impacts depending on the specifics of its location. It becomes essential, therefore, that the criteria used to evaluate proposals remain as flexible as possible.

The Vermont Environmental Control Act (Act 250) specifies 10 criteria of varying importance to be considered by the district commission before granting a permit. It must find that the proposed project:

1. Will not result in undue water or air pollution.
2. Has sufficient water for its reasonably foreseeable needs.
3. Will not cause an unreasonable burden on an existing water supply if one is to be utilized.
4. Will not cause unreasonable soil erosion or reduction in the capacity of the land to hold water.
5. Will not cause unreasonable highway congestion or unsafe conditions.
6. Will not cause an unreasonable burden on the ability of a municipality to provide educational services.
7. Will not place an unreasonable burden on the ability of the local government to provide governmental services.
8. Will not have an undue adverse effect on the scenic or natural beauty of the area, aesthetics, historic sites, or rare and irreplaceable natural areas.
9. Is in conformance with certain statewide plans, which Act 250 required to be prepared.
10. Is in conformance with a duly adopted local or regional plan.[24]

In addition to listing the relevant criteria, the guidelines state who is to provide what information and it also allocates the burden of proof. The applicant for development approval must produce convincing evidence relating to criteria 1 to 4 and 9 and 10. Opponents of the proposal may attack the project based on criteria 5 to 8. But a permit may not be denied solely because it falls short of the requirements of criteria 5, 6, or 7.[25]

To comply with Maine's Site Location Law, an applicant must file a "Record of Intent" form which contains information related to the proposed development. This information is then circulated to affected state agencies for review and comment. The final decision, to be made by the state Board of Environmental Protection, is to be based on four criteria:

1. The financial capacity of the developer to satisfy air and water pollution control standards and to adequately provide for solid waste disposal and the maintenance of adequate water supply.
2. The development includes adequate provisions for traffic flow.
3. The development will fit harmoniously into the existing natural environment.
4. The proposed development is located on soil types suitable to the nature of the undertaking.[26]

How should the regulatory powers be distributed? The most vexing problem in drafting a state land use act, and the one most susceptible to the prevailing political climate, involves determining the suitable distribution of powers. While the mere recognition of the need for a state land use regulation is an acknowledgement that a higher than local authority must in some way participate in the decision-making process, this falls short of pinpointing the exact nature of that authority.

Some states have chosen to simply issue guidelines such as the previously discussed criteria for evaluation, and leave the administration of the program entirely up to local or sometimes regional authorities. For example, Florida's program to regulate developments of regional impact actually involves four government agencies. At the state level, the Florida Cabinet initially promulgated guidelines for the program. These were given the force of law, when adopted by the state legislature. Next, regional planning agencies, based on these guidelines, prepare a "regional impact statement" for use by the local government which has the final say in either accepting or rejecting the proposal.[27]

In other states, ultimate authority has been removed from either regional or local bodies and placed within a state agency. For example, Maine's Site Location of Development Act requires that all developers undertaking projects which fall within the scope of the act must apply directly to the state Board of Environmental Protection for approval.[28]

In summary, several options are available to a state desiring to adopt land use regulations. Which of these is most suitable to a particular state will depend on its particular problems, goals, resources, political climate and existing institutional framework.

A FRAMEWORK FOR ESTIMATING COSTS

In addition to the preparation of the required environmental impact statement, several other factors add to the total cost of complying with state land development regulations. Any delays which can be attributable to the EIS process, the costs of uncertainty involved in dealing with a regulatory agency, and the costs of altering the design of a project once it has been proposed must all be calculated in the costs of compliance with this type of regulation.

EIS Preparation and Review   As the EIS requirement evolved from being used only for public actions to its current status of also involving strictly private development, the responsibility for document preparation has also frequently been shifted to the private developer.

Several approaches have become commonplace. In many jurisdictions, the developer is required to provide the relevant information concerning the proposed project which is then evaluated by the agency staff in terms of its potential environmental impact. Other jurisdictions, lacking the staff capabilities to perform an in-house evaluation, will require that a completed EIS be filed by the developer. In some jurisdictions a specific agency will have review power, but more often the EIS will be circulated to the affected agencies who then make recommendations. Finally, where a large scale development is proposed or a controversy arises, the public agency often hires a consultant (and charges the costs to the developer) to review the EIS prepared by the developer.

While some of the data required for the EIS is essential for the design of the project and is not therefore an added expense, much of the information provided is otherwise extraneous to the development process. This act of accumulating data and projecting impacts would be significantly reduced if a mechanism existed to provide the baseline information common to all impact statements occurring in a specific area.[29] Since the existence of such a databank is more the exception than the rule, developers must start from scratch and often incur significant expense in this first stage of the process.

The actual cost of preparing an EIS can vary significantly, depending on such factors as the size of the project, the environmental complexities encountered, the political pressures brought to bear, and the scope of the review. An analysis of statements filed in California in 1974 showed that they cost from $4,000 to $10,000 or about $17 to $25 per residential unit. In Florida, where reviews are only required for very large projects, costs ranged from $50,000 to $200,000 or approximately $30 per unit.[30]

An additional cost is the expense of EIS review by the government agency. This entails verifying the information and analysis provided by the developer and examining the impact of the project in light of the planning goals of the community and region. Only the largest government agencies have adequate resources to evaluate the EIS themselves. To the extent that filing or permit fees cover these expenses, then the costs are private ones either paid for by the developer or passed on to the consumer. Any expenses not covered by the fees must necessarily be paid from tax revenues and must therefore be considered a public cost.

A review of the California Environmental Quality Act estimated that a total of $19 million was spent on document preparation, review, and administration for private projects. Slightly less than half of this sum, $9 million was calculated as the public cost borne by taxpayers.[31]

Finally, a prerequisite for EIS approval is a definitive plan for the project. Without this information it would be impossible to gauge the projected impacts of the development. While not readily quantifiable as a cost, the resultant inflexibility of a project's design seems to dictate against large scale developments extending over a period of years.

The Costs of Delay   Delay is frequently the most significant factor in the overall cost impact of EIS review. It can and often does develop for several reasons. Inadequate information may be submitted by the developer, the review agency may not have the resources to handle peak loads, and due process requirements may lengthen the review process. Delay may also be used to exclude an unwanted project.

The costs of delay vary considerably, depending on the stage at which the delay occurs. Once land has been purchased, plans drawn, subcontracts signed, financial arrangements finalized and staff hired, a developer's carrying costs soar. Included in the costs of overhead are property taxes, interest paid on loans, opportunity cost of any internally generated funds tied-up in the development and the salaries of staff working on the project. Another consideration must be the rate of inflation affecting the construction industry. If it is in excess of the rate of inflation of per capita income, then it too must be considered as a cost of delay.

An estimate of the cost of delay for private projects in California in 1974 ranged from 3.6 percent to 6.8 percent of the selling price of the unit. Based on a $40,000 home, burdened with an average delay of 3.2 months, the costs were found to range from a low of almost $1,500 to a high of $2,680. The components of this sum are detailed in Exhibit 10.5. The cost of delay is most directly dependent on the stage in the review process at which an EIS is required. If other approvals are being sought at the same time, then the costs of delay will be minimized. Alternatively, if all other approvals have been received and commitments to begin work made, then the costs of delay will be quite significant.

The Costs of Uncertainty While probably not as significant a factor as delay, a developer, once funds are invested in a project, assumes a risk that this undertaking will never reach fruition. Since the vast majority of projects are eventually approved, the risk factor is small. Nonetheless, any developer who has invested in a project which later had to be abandoned must somehow recoup these losses. Such losses are reflected in higher prices for "successful" projects.

The Costs of Mitigation Instead of rejecting a proposal, a more common result is approval with the stipulation that certain specified changes be incorporated into the final plans. Typically a developer is asked by the government agency to dedicate more open space or to reduce the density of the development. These changes may necessitate the added expense of redraf-

EXHIBIT 10.5

THE COSTS OF DELAY

Cost Components	Annual Cost of Delay (low – high range)
Land holding costs	1.2% to 2.2%
Building cost inflation	3.0% to 13.0%
Overhead costs	4.0% to 10.0%
Foregone revenues	1.2% to 1.4%

SOURCE: *CEQA and the Cost of Delay*, Construction Industry Research Board, 1976, p. 5.

ting plans as well as the loss of revenue from the land dedicated and dwelling units not built. In part, these costs may be offset by the increased value of the development attributable to these changes. The ultimate result may be an environmentally inobtrusive but expensive development; one now beyond the means of most families.

Summary of Costs   There has been very little empirical work to date which has estimated the actual costs of the state land use regulations. While complaints about unrighteous time delays and extortionary stipulations are commonplace, the two existing studies suggest that the added costs amount to less than 2 percent of the final selling price of the unit. These case studies shall now be examined.

EIS IN CALIFORNIA AND FLORIDA

The Urban Institute investigated the costs of compliance associated with state land use regulations in California and Florida.[32] They examined the various cost aspects of residential projects seeking EIS approval in 1974-5 in Southeastern Florida and the area surrounding San Diego, California. These two state programs are by no means comparable; they more accurately represent the spectrum of state land use regulations. Florida's law applies only to very large developments, but limits the evaluation to strictly environmental considerations, whereas California's law covers all but the smallest projects, and includes social and economic as well as environmental impacts.

Their findings show that the EIS review process was not that significant a cost element; in California it amounted to $165/housing unit or only .6 percent of the average value of a home built during the study period, while in Florida, the compliance was estimated to cost $386/unit or 1.4 percent of the average value of new homes.[33] (See Exhibit 10.6).

In both cases the most significant costs were attributable to carrying and mitigation costs. Because the Florida EIS evaluation begins before any other development permits may be issued, it was found to add six months to the total building process. In California, the EIS approval process runs concurrent with other local permits and was found to result in only a two month delay. Based on an estimated cost of raw land of $3,750 in California and $2,500 in Florida, and a 12 percent interest rate, the added carrying costs of delay were estimated to be $150 in Florida and $75 in California.

Mitigation costs also varied significantly between states. In Florida, the EIS requirement was used as a device to ensure the fiscal integrity of the community. Land exactions for open space or recreational facilities were required in eleven of the twenty-two projects studied. Approximately one

EXHIBIT 10.6

COSTS OF COMPLIANCE WITH STATE LAND DEVELOPMENT
REQUIREMENTS IN FLORIDA AND CALIFORNIA

Cost Items	(Cost Per Unit)			
	Southeastern Florida	% of Total	San Diego Area	% of Total
Report Preparation[1]	$ 30	7.7%	$ 20	12.1%
Public Sector Review	2	0.5	6	3.6
Delay Costs[2]				
Carrying charges for land	150	38.9	75	45.5
Property taxes[3]	10	2.6	14	8.5
Overhead	N/A	–	N/A	–
Uncertainty	N/A	–	N/A	–
Mitigation	194	50.3	50	30.3
Total	$386	100.0	$165	100.0

NOTES: [1] Florida estimates assume an EIS cost of $150,000 and a housing development of 5,000 units; California estimates are based on an EIS cost of $6,000 for a 300 unit project.
[2] Estimated to be 6 months for Florida and 2 months for California.
[3] Estimates based on an effective property tax rate of 0.8 percent in Broward County, Florida and 2.2 percent in San Diego County.

SOURCE: Muller and James, "Environmental Impact Evaluation and Housing Costs."

acre for every 119 housing units was dedicated at a cost of $168/unit or spread across all the projects — an average of $84/unit. Highways, firehouses and other public facilities were also required by Florida jurisdictions within the context of EIS review. These averaged $110/unit. In San Diego County, far fever stipulations were attached to approvals. On average, such conditions as road paving and underground utilities added only $50 to the price of the unit.

While both the costs of overhead and uncertainty were examined, neither were found to be of significance. Interviews with developers suggested that during periods of delay, staff was either transferred to other projects or cut back. Since very few projects were rejected and not resubmitted in an altered form, the risk factor was determined to be quite small.

Evaluation of the California Environmental Quality Act (CEQA) Similar cost estimates were arrived at in a study prepared for the California Assembly's Committee on Local Government as part of its five year review of CEQA. It found that the most significant sources of costs were related to document preparation and delay, whereas mitigation and risk were only minor factors.[34] Although issuing a warning that any per unit cost is an oversimplification, the study does arrive at a $150/unit cost.[35] This figure was derived from a breakdown of the total costs of the CEQA environmental impact review (EIR) requirement.

Although the sketchy presentation of the dollar estimates of EIR prevents any further evaluation of their findings, their analysis of the EIR process is quite detailed and presents several existing problem areas where costs would be reduced. Their findings highlight the tendency of public agencies to overanalyze environmental impacts without regard to the ultimate utility of this detailed level of scrutiny. As a remedy, the report suggests that the state provide a clearer enunciation of the appropriate level of analysis. A second weakness is the unnecessary and repetitive regeneration of environmental conditions in reports submitted to a specific locality. The report calls for the adoption of a master EIR concept, with much of the information standardized and available from the local or county planning or review agency.

THE IMPACT OF STATE LAND DEVELOPMENT OF CONTROLS ON HOUSING COSTS

State land development laws are surfacing with increasing frequency as the need for a broader than local perspective on land use decisions is becoming more pronounced. This trend can even be expected to speed up with the final adoption of the American Law Institute's Model Land Development Code[36] and the possible passage of a federal land use bill.[37] Both of these measures pay considerable attention to a more active role for states in making land use decisions.

Several different analyses of the cost impact of the state EIS requirement agree that the total expenses are less than 2 percent of the final selling price of a unit. The bulk of these expenses were associated with the costs of delay and mitigation. Little work, however, has been done which examines the extent to which the environment has benefitted from the state EIS requirement. While it is generally presumed that new development has been forced to be more environmentally sensitive, the extent to which this goal has been accomplished remains unknown. For now, based on our existing knowledge, it is only possible to pinpoint the costs of the regulatory process and ways in which those costs can be reduced.

The next section examines a regulation very similar to a state land development law, but which concerns only one specific type of land — the coastal zone.

The Effect of Coastal Zone Management Regulations
on Housing Costs

The passage of the federal Coastal Zone Management Act of 1972 (CZMA) was a major first step toward the preservation of the nation's coastal zone resources. By providing a monetary incentive for states to undertake the planning and control of future development in the coastal zone, the act has provided the funding lacking in past efforts to plan for this environmentally critical area.

In the past, development in the coastal zone was an amalgam of private decisions and local public actions. This resulted in direct conflict between increasing use of this resource, primarily because of its desirable location, and increasing clamor for public recreational use and therefore control. The CZMA attempts to strike a balance between these conflicting interests. It attempts to impose a comprehensive planning and decision-making process on the existing ad hoc control of land use choices in the coastal zone.

This section of the chapter on the environment will look at existing coastal zone programs in California and New Jersey. Emphasis will be placed in each of these case studies on the cost impact on residential construction caused by the coastal zone requirements.

THE CALIFORNIA EXPERIENCE

California became the first state to require a comprehensive plan for resource management in the coastal zone when the Coastal Zone Conservation Act (generally referred to as Proposition 20) was overwhelmingly approved by the voters in 1972.[39]

The coastal zone was defined as the area from the coast extending back to the ridge line of the first mountain range except in the area of Los Angeles where the landward boundary was extended inland for five miles. In the interim, while a comprehensive plan is being prepared, permits are required for all development extending inland for one thousand yards from the mean high tide line throughout the coastal zone.

The regional commission established to review applications must determine that there would be no substantial adverse environmental effect from a development and that it would be consistent with "the maintenance, restoration, and enhancement of the overall quality of the coastal zone environnent, including, but not limited to, its amenities." Developments also have to be consistent with the "continued existence of optimum populations of all species of living organisms" and the avoidance of "irreversible and irretrievable commitments of coastal zone resources."[40]

Permit regulation began on February 1, 1973. An example of the impact of the regulation shows that as of March 1974, the coastal commission in the Los Angeles and Orange counties had approved 2,195 permits with a value of $1.18 billion and had denied 109 permits valued at $188 million. During the following year approval continued at better than a 90 percent rate. This may be somewhat misleading as it fails to take into account those projects modified in anticipation of the review, projects abandoned for fear of not being able to pass muster, and projects approved contingent upon fulfilling conditions imposed by the commission.[41]

An examination of the effect of this act found that, based on assessed value of land, the Coastal Commission's regulations have reduced the value of undevelopable land in the permit zone by roughly fifteen percent. Not surprisingly, owners of developable land in the regulated area have received significant gain from the restrictions on competing land.[42]

A second study of the effect of Proposition 20 seems to support the above findings.[43] Since the creation of the coastal commission in 1972, this study found home building in the cities of the coastal zone fell from 24 percent of the state's total to 17 percent, while apartment construction in this zone dropped from 30 percent to 21 percent of the state's total.[44]

Another effect of Proposition 20 can be seen in the rapid rise of the price of homes in the coastal zone. From a month prior to the passage of the act (January, 1973) to April 1975, existing single-family homes in the permit zone increased an average of 41 percent compared to a 27 percent rise in the cost of similar homes in the coastal counties but outside the planning area.[45]

Proposition 20 also charged the Coastal Commission with the formulation of a comprehensive coastal plan to be submitted to the state legislature in December 1975. Based on the Commission's report, the California legislature passed a sweeping new law on August 23, 1976. Under the new law permits will be required for most development in a zone which extends in most cases approximately 1,000 yards inland along the state's 1,072 mile coast. In addition, the commission is pledged "to policies of preserving natural areas and farmland, concentrating development where it exists already, and maximizing public access to and enjoyment of the shore."[46]

THE NEW JERSEY EXPERIENCE

The New Jersey legislature in 1973 passed into law the Coastal Area Facilities Review Act (CAFRA).[47] The Act gives the State Department of Environmental Protection the final power over proposed developments, both public and private, which may have a significant impact on the coastal zone. This area has been defined to include 1,376 square miles or 15 percent of the state's total land mass.

An analysis of building activity in the coastal zone before and after CAFRA provides insight into its impact on the development process. In 1972, the year preceding the CAFRA regulations, 31 percent of all residential construction in the state occurred in the coastal zone. Specifically, 34 percent of all single-family units and 24 percent of all multi-family units were located in this area.[48]

In 1974, the year following the implementation of the requirement, residential construction approved in the coastal area dropped to 25 percent of the total for the state. Single-family development stayed approximately constant at 35 percent, while multi-family development decreased to 13 percent.[49] The difference between the 1972 and 1974 figures is assumed to be at least partially related to CAFRA requirements. This finding is not at all surprising. The more dense the development, the more likely it will disrupt the natural environment. In fact, a commonly used stipulation for permission to build is the reduction in overall density of a project. It is not surprising therefore that in New Jersey, as in California, multi-family development is hardest hit in the coastal zone.

The Center for Urban Policy Research conducted a study of twenty-one residential developments in Dover Township, New Jersey to determine the cost of the CAFRA permit requirement.[50] The costs were found to be $135.00 for a single-family housing unit and $125.00 per housing unit in multi-family developments. Of this amount, for single-family units, $50.00 was the cost of the permit process and $86.00 the cost of the delay time in applying for the permit. The costs for permit and delay for multi-family units was $33.00 and $92.00, respectively.[51]

This study of the effects on development of the EIS requirement in New Jersey's coastal area indicates that a major determinant of delay is the point of state review in respect to the traditional subdivision and site plan reviews done at the local level. The results of this study indicate that state review of development proposals should coincide with local reviews rather than before or after. (See Exhibits 10.7 and 10.8) When CAFRA was first enacted state review followed the completion of local actions. This procedure caused an unnecessary delay of eleven months for single-family developments and nine months for multi-family projects. The unnecessary delay time was reduced after a change in the review procedure was adopted, providing for CAFRA review during the local process.

Even after the change was instituted, the combined state and local regulatory system forces developers to wait twenty-two months for single-family development approval and twenty-three months for multi-family project approval. Such time periods exceed that experienced under strictly

EXHIBIT 10.7

EFFECT OF STATE INTERVENTION ON SINGLE-FAMILY DEVELOPMENT
IN THE COASTAL ZONE

Time of State Intervention in Relation to the Local Process	Additional Delay Time Attributable to State Intervention (months)	Additional Delay Costs Attributable to State Intervention (per unit)
No State Intervention	-	-
Intervention Following Preliminary Plat Submission	1	$ 86
Intervention Following Preliminary Plat Approval	8	$328
Intervention Following Final Plat Approval	11	$486

SOURCE: Derived from Richardson, *The Cost of Environmental Protection*, pp. 131-137.

EXHIBIT 10.8

EFFECT OF STATE INTERVENTION ON MULTI-FAMILY DEVELOPMENT
IN THE COASTAL ZONE

Time of State Intervention in Relation to the Local Process	Additional Delay Time Attributable to State Intervention (months)	Additional Delay Costs Attributable to State Intervention (per unit)
No State Intervention	-	-
Intervention Following Site Plan Submission	4	$ 92
Intervention Following Site Plan Approval	7	$155
Intervention Following Site Local Approvals	9	$208

SOURCE: Derived from Richardson, *The Cost of Environmental Protection*, pp. 131-137.

local regulations (no CAFRA requirement) by two months for single-family developments and four months for multi-family projects, amounting to estimated cost increases of $86 and $92 per unit, respectively.

THE EFFECT OF COASTAL ZONE MANAGEMENT REGULATIONS ON HOUSING COSTS

Although it is still too early to tell the exact nature and magnitude of the effect on housing costs of efforts to manage the coastal zone, much can be learned from those states with advanced programs. From an examination of programs in New Jersey and California, several tentative conclusions can be drawn. First, by limiting the amount of developable land in the coastal zone, both the price of developable land and of existing houses in this area were increased. A second finding was that the procedural aspects, in particularly delays caused by the permitting process, can add considerably to the costs of the regulation. A third finding was that the coastal zone restrictions act as a greater constraint to the development of multi-family than single-family units. Finally, it is quite clear that we do not know the extent to which coastal zone review is achieving its goal of improving the allocation and management of resources in the coastal zone.

The Costs of Environmental Protection

More so than many other areas of government intervention in the free market system, regulations aimed at protecting the environment are an essential and necessary policy. This chapter has traced the rapid growth of these regulations in two areas — state land development laws and coastal zone management.

Our findings suggest that requiring that the environmental impact of a proposed development be examined can be relatively inexpensive. The entire cost of achieving better environmental design was found to be less than 2 percent of the final cost of a residential unit. In addition, these costs can be further reduced by streamlining the review process and moving it forward towards an earlier stage in development.

The major questions which remain unanswered relate specifically to the effectiveness of the EIS as a regulatory device. The quality of the assessment of the projected environmental impact varies considerably with no generally accepted methodology having yet surfaced. Without this sound footing upon which to base the review process, the effectiveness of the regulation remains in doubt.

Finally, in each of these areas of regulation, the issues of how much environmental protection we want and who should pay for it have not been addressed. This is particularly true in the case of EIS requirements which often examine environmental impacts to the exclusion of economic and social effects.

NOTES

1. For a thorough discussion of this controversy see, Mary E. Brooks, *The Needless Conflict,* (Washington, D.C.: American Institute of Planners, 1976); Richard F. Babcock and David L. Callies, "Ecology and Housing: Virtues in Conflict" in Marion Clawson (ed.), *Modernizing Urban Land Policy,* (Washington, D.C.: Resources for the Future, 1973); and Bruce L. Ackerman, "Impact Statements and Low Cost Housing," *Southern California Law Review,* 46 (1973), p.754.

2. Fred Bosselman and David Callies, *The Quiet Revolution in Land Use Controls* (Washington, D.C.: Council on Environmental Quality, 1971).

3. Sewer moratoria which are certainly related to environmental regulation nonetheless are most often used as a stop-growth measure and therefore are discussed in Chapter 9 under growth controls.

4. See, for example, Bernard H. Siegan, *Other Peoples' Property,* (Lexington, Mass.: Lexington Books, 1976).

5. Much of this explanation is drawn from Robert Dorfman and Nancy S. Dorfman (eds.), *Economics of the Environment,* (New York: W.W. Norton & Company, Inc., 1972).

6. The classic article explaining this theory is Ronald Coase, "The Problem of Social Cost," *The Journal of Law and Economics,* III (October, 1960), pp.1-44.

7. See, for example, provisions of the Federal Coastal Zone Management Act, the Federal Water Pollution Control Act, the Clean Air Act, the National Flood Insurance Act, and the National Environmental Policy Act. The effect on housing costs of both the air and water pollution control measures are at this point only tangential. In particular, provisions of both will affect future land use patterns and therefore the distribution of housing and the price of land. Since these effects have yet to be experienced, no detailed discussion of costs is now possible. For a thorough discussion of future implications, see Fred P. Bosselman et al., "EPA Authority Affecting Land Use" prepared for the U.S. Environmental Protection Agency, (Washington, D.C.: 1974).

8. American Institute of Planners, "Survey of State Land Use Planning Activity" (Washington, D.C.: 1976).

9. National Environmental Policy Act of 1969, 42 U.S.C. 4321-47.

10. See, for example, state EIS requirements in Connecticut, Michigan, Minnesota, Montana and Wisconsin. Council on Environmental Quality, *Environmental Quality, The Fifth Annual Report,* (Washington, D.C.: U.S. Government Printing Office, 1974), p.403.

11. William Reilly (ed.), *The Use of Land: A Citizens' Policy Guide to Urban Growth,* A Report by the Task Force on Land Use and Urban Growth, The Rockefeller Brothers Fund, (New York: Thomas Y. Crowell Company, 1973), p.199.

12. D.W. Schindler, "The Impact Statement Boondoggle," *Science,* 192, Number 4239 (May 7, 1976), p.509.
13. Council on Environmental Quality, *Environmental Quality, The Fifth Annual Report,* pp.409-10.
14. For a discussion of the sample and a copy of the survey, See Appendix B.
15. The first recognition of this state activity was documented in Bosselman and Callies, *The Quiet Revolution in Land Use Controls.* For a more current though less comprehensive analysis of the state of the art, see Robert G. Healy, *Land Use and the States,* Resources for the Future, (Baltimore, Maryland: Johns Hopkins University Press, 1976).
16. For an early view of the problems inherent to a system of local land use controls see, "Problems of Zoning and Land Use Regulation," American Society of Planning Officials, Research Report No. 2, Prepared for the National Commission on Urban Problems, (Washington, D.C.: U.S. Government Printing Office, 1968).
17. These other states are Florida, Nevada, Colorado, Vermont, Maine, California, Wyoming, Wisconsin and Montana.
18. *Village of Euclid v. Ambler Realty Co.,* 272 U.S. 365, (1926), 390.
19. For an analysis of the American Law Institute's Model Land Development Code, see Richard F. Babcock, "Comments on the Model Land Development Code," *Urban Law Annual,* (1972), p.59.
20. For a review of the problems confronting planners in Vermont see, Phyllis Myers, *So Goes Vermont,* (Washington, D.C.: The Conservation Foundation, 1974).
21. For an excellent description of the process leading to the adoption of the Vermont Act, see Healy, *Land Use and the States,* pp.35-63.
22. Vermont Statutes Annotated, (1974), Title 10; §6001 (3).
23. Derived from an official list of the Florida Department of Administration. Cited in Healy, *Land Use and the States, p.11* .
24. *Vermont Statutes Annotated, (1974), Title 38; §6086.*
25. *Ibid.*
26. Maine Revised Statutes Annotated, Vol. 38; §484.
27. Gilbert Funnel, Jr., "Saving Paradise — The Florida Environmental Land and Water Management Act of 1972," *Urban Law Annual,* (1973), p.120.
28. Maine Revised Statutes, Title 38, Chapter 3, §483.
29. A data bank providing information as to soil, topography, climate, etc. as well as all past EIS's filed is now made available to the public in several counties in California. See "The California Environmental Quality Act: A Review," Office of Planning and Research, State of California, (Sacramento, California, 1976), p.30.
30. Tom Muller and Franklin J. James, "Environmental Impact Evaluation and Housing Costs," (Washington, D.C.: The Urban Institute, 1975).
31. Environmental Analysis Systems, Inc., *The California Environmental Quality Act,* 3 vols., prepared for the Assembly Committee on Local Government, (Sacramento, Cal.: 1975), Vol. 1, p.41.
32. Muller and James, "Environmental Impact and Housing Costs."
33. *Ibid.* p.22.
34. Environmental Analysis Systems, Inc. *The California Environmental Quality Act,* Vol. 1, pp.39-41.
35. *Ibid.,* p.42.

36. See in particular section 7 of the Model Land Development Code.

37. For a thorough analysis of the proposed federal action, see Congressional Research Service, *National Land Use Policy Legislation: An Analysis of Legislative Proposals and State Laws,* (Washington, D.C.: U.S. Government Printing Office, 1973).

38. Coastal Zone Management Act of 1972, P.L. 92-583.

39. Cal. Public Resources Code, Vol. 18, Sections 27000 *et seq.*

40. *Ibid.,* Section 27402 and 27302. For an analysis of the operation of Proposition 20, see Melvin B. Mogulof, *Saving the Coast,* (Lexington, Mass.: Lexington Books, 1975).

41. Healy, *Land Use and the States,* p.75.

42. *Ibid.,* p.83.

43. Michael R. Peevey, "The Coastal Plan and Jobs: A Critique," in *The California Coastal Plan: A Critique* (San Francisco: Institute for Contemporary Studies, 1976), p.93.

44. *Ibid.,* p.99.

45. *Ibid.,* p598-99.

46. "California Enacts a Law to Control Development Along 1,000 Mile Coast," *New York Times,* August 25, 1976, sec. 1, p.20; and Bureau of National Affairs, "Current Developments," *Housing and Development Reporter,* Vol. 4, No. 7 (September 6, 1976), pp.303-4.

47. New Jersey Statutes Annotated, 13:19-1 *et seq.* See also *Interim Land Use and Density Guidelines for the Coastal Area of New Jersey,* (Trenton, N.J.: Department of Environmental Protection, 1976).

48. Calculated from *1972 Summary of New Jersey Residential Building Permits,* (Trenton, N.J.: Department of Labor andIndustry, 1972).

49. Calculated from *1974 Summary of New Jersey Residential Building Permits,* (Trenton, N.J.: Department of Labor and Industry, 1974).

50. Dan K. Richardson, *The Cost of Environmental Protection,* (New Brunswick: Center for Urban Policy Research, Rutgers University, 1976).

51. *Ibid.,* p.127.

Chapter Eleven:
The Importance of
Settlement
And Financing
Regulations

Previous chapters have focused on the impact on the cost of housing of building codes, energy codes, and land use ordinances, and environmental regulations. In each of these areas, the costs of regulation affected the initial cost or selling price of the house. This chapter extends the prior analysis to include two additional areas of regulation — settlement and financing — which do not directly influence the initial selling price of a unit, but which do significantly increase housing costs and, therefore, limit housing opportunities. Settlement regulations affect the formal transaction in which ownership of a house passes from seller to buyer[1] and includes title examination, insurance, survey, and recording. Financing regulations, in the context of our discussion, involves obtaining short- and long-term loans for the construction or purchase of residential real estate.[2]

The settlement and financing aspects of purchasing a house evolved from a complex system of laws governing the transfer and purchase of real property.[3] The banks, title insurance companies, appraisers, and other various private and government participants in this process operate in an atmosphere often frustrating and confusing to the housing consumer. Critics attack these procedures as being overly complex and often unnecessary and wasteful.[4] More recently, government regulations aimed at rationalizing this network of controls have come under attack as creating more problems than they solve.[5]

Financing and settlement outlays on single-family homes do result in considerable expense to the housing consumer. Depending on such factors as prevailing state law, type of mortgage (e.g., FHA versus conventional) and location of property (as well as local tradition and the wishes of the buyer and seller, settlement costs usually amount to at least $4,000 per house.[6] While this outlay is somewhat price-elastic, it is not entirely moderated by the cost of a home but rather will reach a certain threshold regardless of whether a more modest or more expensive home is purchased. That is, settlement expenditures might amount to $4,000 for a $50,000 dwelling and $5,500 for an $80,000 unit.

This relationship has a significant practical impact for it means that the purchaser of a lower price dwelling, who often has a lower income, will pay almost as high a settlement transfer fee as the more affluent buyer of an expensive home. The moderate-income homebuyer further suffers because he or she must endure certain expenses, e.g., "points" on FHA/VA mortgages that a more affluent counterpart can avoid. Settlement costs, because they are incurred and must be paid at the time of purchase, are particularly burdensome to the homebuyer. As a front-end expense, settlement costs either delay a homebuyer's entry into the housing market, require that a less expensive home be purchased, or reduce the amount of money available for the downpayment. Finally, unlike most costs discussed in previous chapters, there is no commensurate increase in the structural value of the home.

Financing costs represent potentially the most significant yet the least susceptible area for reform of government regulations. Even the smallest percentage change in the terms of a mortgage can dramatically affect the number of families able to afford new housing. Although a discussion of the federal government's monetary policy, one of the prime determinants of interest rates, falls outside the scope of this work, other government policies and programs specific to mortgage financing will be examined. The magnitude of the impact of mortgage financing terms on the availability of housing is enormous. In today's market, the median-value house is sold for $50,000, with a 20 percent down payment, and is mortgaged at 9 percent interest for thirty years. Under these terms, a family's average mortgage payment could amount to $3,864; using an approximate 1 to 6 ratio of mortgage payment to income, only about 18 percent of families would be financially qualified to purchase this home.[7] If mortgage rates were reduced to 7 percent (not uncommon until the early 1970s), the annual payments would be reduced to $3,197 and the number of families able to afford new housing would increase 29 percent. If instead of a reduction in the interest rate, the payback period were changed from thirty to twenty years, the number of financially qualified families would be reduced from 18 percent to 13 percent.

A consideration of the effects of changes in mortgage terms on changes in rental housing costs further confirms the importance of the former. A one percent increase in interest rates is equivalent to an approximate $5,000 increase in the unit cost of a home, and a 2 percent increase is comparable to a $10,000 cost increase. Conversely, a 1 percent decrease is comparable to a $5,000 unit price reduction while a 2 percent drop would yield a $10,000 effective price reduction. To illustrate, the monthly principal and interest payments on a $50,000 home purchased with a 7 percent mortgage ranges from about $250 to $400 depending on the size of the down payment and the terms of the loan.[8] This same range of payments would be adequate only for a $40,000 home if interest rates increased from 7 to 9 percent. In other words, had there been no price increase in the cost of a single-family home from the late 1960s to 1970s, the effective home-buying power of families would have been reduced about $10,000 because of the approximate 2 percent increase in financing costs during this period.

While these figures suggest that our concern should shift in emphasis from regulations affecting the initial selling price to those influencing mortgage terms, such a shift fails to consider the problems and repercussions of influencing capital markets to reduce mortgage money cost — considerations which are beyond the scope of this book. Nonetheless, through government policies aimed at restructuring the mortgage instrument, it should be possible to reduce the burden to consumers of the existing financing mechanism while limiting social costs.

Before embarking on a more detailed analysis of settlement and financing procedures, it is first necessary to present an overview of the various government regulations involved.

Conceptual Framework of Settlement/Financing Regulations

Settlement processes and regulations are relatively straightforward. They involve the package of activities undertaken when mortgage financing is obtained and title is transferred. This includes such measures as evaluating the credit rating of the potential mortgagor, clearing the title of the mortgaged property, and preparing the necessary mortgage documents.[9]

The financing process is much more complicated. As indicated in Exhibit 1 there is a multitude of pertinent actors and regulations that affects the financing process. The participants, for example, include the Federal Reserve System (FRS), Federal Home Loan Bank Board (FHLBB), Federal National Mortgage Association (FNMA), Federal Housing Administration (FHA), and state banking departments. The list of regulations consists of an alphabet soup of legislation, including Regulation Z (truth in lending),

EXHIBIT 1

SETTLEMENT/FINANCING PROCESS: CONCEPTUAL SCHEME

Step	Settlement	Capital Accumulation	Financing/Loan Disbursement	Loan Repayment
Process:	Ownership of real property passes from seller to buyer.	Lenders accumulate capital to make loans.	Lenders grant short- and long-term loans.	Borrowers repay loans.
Institutional Actors:	Title insurance companies Title search companies Home Inspection companies Credit inspection companies Realtors Attorneys	Primary (Retailers) 1. Savings and Loan Associations: S&Ls are the largest source of residential mortgage loans today. They are thrift institutions which obtain their funds predominantly from the savings of people in their localities. 2. Mutual Savings Banks: Mutual Savings Banks, like S&Ls, are thrift institutions relying on local depositors. 3. Commercial Banks: Both by law and custom commercial banks have invested only a small share of their assets (about 10 percent) in residential mortgages, but they are the largest source of construction loans. 4. Life Insurance Companies: Once second only to S&Ls as a mortgage provider, life insurance companies have slowly reduced their investments in this area and have favored higher yielding competing investments such as corporate bonds. 5. Other Lenders: Mortgage bankers buy blocks of mortgages for others as well as for their own portfolios. They also service loans for a fee.	Primary lenders are the same as in the capital accumulation step. Secondary lenders are not directly involved.	Primary lenders FHA/VA, attorneys.

EXHIBIT 1 (continued)

SETTLEMENT/FINANCING PROCESS: CONCEPTUAL SCHEME

Step	Settlement	Capital Accumulation	Financing/Loan Disbursement	Loan Repayment
		Secondary (Wholesalers)		
		1. Federal National Mortgage Association: Since 1968, FNMA has been a federally chartered but privately owned and managed corporation. FNMA is the nation's largest secondary supplier of mortgage funds.	The regulators are the same as in the capital accumulation step but include the Federal Housing Administration, Veterans Administration, Farmers Home Administration, and state banking commissions.	Same as in capital accumulation step.
		2. Government National Mortgage Association: Founded in 1968, a federally owned and operated agency. One of its major responsibilities is to support mortgage market activities that cannot be carried out by the private sector.		
		3. Federal Home Loan Mortgage Corporation: Created in 1970, FHLMC was formed to buy and sell mortgages. It supplements FNMA's activities.		
		4. Federal Home Loan Bank Board: The FHLBB was created in 1932 to help provide a source of secondary housing credit for S&Ls. It also serves as an important financial institution regulator.		

EXHIBIT 1 (continued)

SETTLEMENT/FINANCING PROCESS: CONCEPTUAL SCHEME

Step	Settlement	Capital Accumulation	Financing/Loan Disbursement	Loan Repayment
Regulators:	HUD State Insurance Commissioners State Bar Associations State Realty Boards	1. Federal Reserve System: The Reserve includes all national banks and those state-chartered institutions which have applied for membership. The Reserve determines general monetary credit and operating policies and imposes detailed regulations such as reserve requirements, and the maximum interest rate that can be paid by members. 2. Federal Home Loan Bank Board: In addition to acting as a secondary credit source, the FHLBB regulates and supervises S&Ls. Its activities include establishing the maximum interest rate that can be paid on savings accounts and approving applications for bank mergers. 3. Office of the Comptroller of the Currency: The Comptroller charters and supervises all national banks and branches. 4. Federal Deposit Insurance Corporation: (FDIC) The FDIC insures deposits of reserve member banks and other financial institutions. It audits insured accounts and sets general underwriting criteria.		

EXHIBIT 1 (continued)

SETTLEMENT/FINANCING PROCESS: CONCEPTUAL SCHEME

Step	Settlement	Capital Accumulation	Financing/Loan Disbursement	Loan Repayment
Major Public Regulations/ Policies Affecting Step:	Real Estate Settlement Practices Act (RESPA) State Property Transfer statutes State Insurance Commission rate regulations Prohibitions on professional (i.e., attorney) advertising Bar Association rate schedules	Regulation Q General monetary/fiscal policy Reserve requirements Branching regulations Financial institution taxation Permitted underwriting criteria	FHA and VA underwriting criteria and Davis Bacon regulations FHA and VA interest rate ceilings FHA and VA environmental clearance procedures State usury laws Equal Credit Opportunity Act Mortgage Disclosure regulations Regulation Z Fair Credit Reporting Act	State foreclosure statutes HUD forbearance regulations FHA/VA repayment requirements, i.e., loans must be fully amortized State Banking Commission regulations concerning allowable mortgage documents and repayment strategies

NOTE: Derived in part from The Federal National Mortgage Association, *A Guide to Fannie Mae* (1975).

ECOA (Equal Credit Opportunity Act), Title VIII of the Civil Rights Act of 1968, and HUD forbearance letters 75:10 (1975) and 76:9 (1976)[10]

Before discussing the specific regulations involved, it would be useful to break down the financing process into its major components: capital accumulation, loan disbursement, and loan repayments (see Exhibit 1). All three stages are intimately affected by government regulations. In order to grant mortgages it is imperative to gather a loanable pool of capital. This necessary aggregation is done by lenders who either accept deposits (e.g., Savings and Loan Institutions), collect premiums (e.g., life insurance companies), or compete on the securities market (e.g., S&Ls selling mortgage-backed securities). "Wholesalers" in the capital accumulation process include a host of public and quasi-public agencies including the FNMA, GNMA, and the FHLMC (see Exhibit 1). There are also numerous regulatory bodies which influence the capital accumulation stage, such as the FRS, FHLBB, the Comptroller of the Currency, and the Federal Deposit Insurance Corporation. These agencies, especially the Federal Reserve (which helps control the money supply), have an extremely significant effect on interest rates. (Some have charged the Reserve's tight money policies in the 1972–1974 period as being the single major cause for the mortgage crunch in those years). The regulatory agencies also impact on mortgage availability and costs by controlling almost every facet of the lending industry. Some examples include:

1. Setting the maximum interest rates that thrift institutions can pay depositors (Regulation Q). This rule affects the competitiveness of the thrifts in attracting capital and is a major influence on the level of disintermediation.
2. Limiting the range of services (e.g., checking accounts) that can be offered by thrift institutions. This rule also affects the competitiveness of these lenders.
3. Establishing reserve requirements for lenders. These ratios influence the amount of funds available for mortgages; the higher the reserves the smaller the available capital pool that can be lent.

In the loan disbursement stage, borrowers receive their loans from lenders. To a large extent the regulators and primary lenders involved in capital accumulation are also found here but there are some crucial additional groups, including the Federal Housing Administration (FHA) and Veterans Administration (VA). The former was established in 1934 to insure long-term mortgages and loans made by private lenders for home construction and sale and to insure lenders against loss on shorter term loans for repairs and improvements. The latter was created in 1944 to guarantee home loans to veterans.

Major facets of the loan disbursement process are governed by public regulations or programs. The risk of making loans is reduced by FHA insurance and VA guarantees. The mortgage interest rate is restricted by state usury laws and by FHA/VA ceilings where FHA/VA programs are used. FHA/VA minimum property standards govern property for which mortgages can be granted, and the wages for workers on governmentally aided parcels is governed by the Davis-Bacon law. The profile of eligible loan recipients is influenced not only by "standard" industry underwriting criteria but also by a spectrum of government regulations, many aimed at protecting minorities (e.g., ECOA and Title VIII of the 1968 Civil Rights Act).

In the loan repayment stage the borrower repays the lender. While there are similar groups involved in loan repayment as in loan disbursement there are far fewer governmental regulations. The roles that do exist pertain primarily to two different issues: how is the loan to be repaid and what happens if the obligation is not met either temporarily (loan delinquency) or permanently (loan foreclosure). A loan can be repaid according to a number of strategies, e.g., fully versus partially amortizing, or at a fixed rate of interest versus a variable interest payment approach. The structuring of a loan hinges not only on negotiations between the mortgages and mortgagor but also on public regulations; e.g., FHA loans must be fully amortized and many states prohibit a VRM instrument. The steps that may be taken by a lender against a delinquent borrower are governed almost entirely by public regulations. States specify the exact procedure that must be followed in the event of a delinquency or foreclosure; even the slightest deviation from the set approach may disqualify the entire action.

It is clear from the above conceptual scheme that the settlement and financing processes are extremely complicated and are governed by a vast array of public controls. A detailed analysis of each of these controls is beyond the scope of this monograph. We will not attempt to go beyond an overview of the capital accumulation stage, despite the critical importance of this step in determining effective housing costs, because of the complexity of the process, the multitude of agencies involved, and the interweaving of issues and motivations that permeate and influence this step (such as what is an acceptable inflation rate and what should the Federal Reserve do to control price increases). Instead this chapter will select three areas of regulation in which costs have the potential to be reduced significantly: *settlement procedures, FHA policies and practices, and mortgage repayment approaches.*

These areas were chosen because in their current state they allegedly add to the cost of housing. On a one-term basis, settlement outlays can be quite high, especially in relation to the entire loan size. FHA policies, which permeate the loan disbursement and repayment steps, can also have an important dollar impact, as can loan repayment strategies. Second, all three areas are viewed as having potential for "opening up the housing market." "Putting a lid on settlement costs," "getting the red tape out of FHA," and allowing innovative mortgages such as VRMs are all being touted to make single-family houses affordable. Third, all three areas are the subject of intense criticism. Many builders, lenders, and housing experts have roundly criticized the current administration of these areas. One builder, for example, stated in a Center for Urban Policy Research interview that "life [was] too short to do business with the FHA. Duplicity, bureaucracy, and inefficiency destroy its effectiveness."[11] A lender described usury restrictions as "expropriation that will eventually destroy the mortgage market."[12] Others have heatedly attacked both settlement procedures and current repayment approaches as archaic and expensive relics.

Settlement Procedures and Costs

Settlement costs result from numerous legal requirements, professional fees, and government-mandated payments which accompany the transfer of title of real property. In general the primary purpose of these procedures is to bring together the prospective buyer and seller and to insure each that the other is dealing in good faith; i.e., that the seller has clear title to the property and that the buyer has adequate financial means to purchase the property.

This section of the chapter describes the most significant costs incurred in the settlement process and then examines each in light of the existing role of government regulations in creating these costs and the potential for reform. Particular attention is focused on recent federal legislation affecting this process, the Real Estate Settlement Procedures Act.

A 1972 study conducted by the Department of Housing and Urban Development concluded that total settlement costs averaged almost $2,000[13] (see Exhibit 2). While certainly many of the costs shown in Exhibit 2 cannot be directly or even indirectly attributed to government regulations, it is still necessary to explore more fully the exact nature and reason for the major cost items constituting settlement costs.[14]

Title Examination. This step is motivated by the need of both the lender and purchaser to be assured that the seller does in fact own what he is conveying. A title examination may be made by an attorney, a professional abstracting company, or by the public registrar where a Torren's title system is available (e.g., Cook County, Illinois). With the exception of the Torren's situation, the examination does not guarantee good title but rather

EXHIBIT 2

ESTIMATED AVERAGE TOTAL (BUYER AND SELLER) COSTS BY TYPE OF COST AND PRICE RANGE
FHA-INSURED AND VA-GUARANTEED CASES, 1972

Item	All Mortgages	Mortgages under $12,000	Mortgages $12,000-$15,999	Mortgages $16,000-$19,999	Mortgages $20,000-$23,999	Mortgages $24,000-$27,999	Mortgages $28,000-or More
Total Settlement Costs	$1,937	$1,349	$1,441	$1,691	$2,067	$2,067	$2,138
Total Closing Costs[1]	558	418	462	511	586	709	835
Credit Report	11	10	10	11	11	12	11
Appraisal Fee	37	35	38	38	38	36	38
Compliance Inspection Fees	18	13	14	17	17	25	24
Survey	43	44	42	42	44	46	50
Title Examination	118	99	105	110	110	142	179
Title Insurance	127	87	107	117	133	165	181
Attorney Fees	106	70	78	104	128	153	150
Origination Fee	190	96	142	177	214	251	309
Preparation of Documents	28	35	26	27	27	25	29
Closing Fees	43	50	41	41	43	37	50
Recording Fees	18	17	17	18	19	19	22
Transfer Taxes	72	69	55	59	70	96	119
Escrow Fees	74	37	51	71	89	93	93
Other Closing Costs	32	30	25	29	38	41	42
Termite Inspection	19	18	17	20	20	21	22
Loan Discount Payment[2]	578	360	450	533	625	707	933

EXHIBIT 2 (continued)

ESTIMATED AVERAGE TOTAL (BUYER AND SELLER) COSTS BY TYPE OF COST AND PRICE RANGE FHA-INSURED AND VA-GUARANTEED CASES, 1972

Item	All Mortgages	Mortgages under $12,000	Mortgages $12,000-$15,999	Mortgages $16,000-$19,999	Mortgages $20,000-$23,999	Mortgages $24,000-$27,999	Mortgages $28,000- or More
Total Prepaid Items[3]	301	216	248	264	315	397	489
Taxes	182	121	139	148	200	256	315
Mortgage Insurance	11	6	9	11	12	14	16
Hazard Insurance	82	66	69	75	84	97	125
Special Assessments	229	156	241	257	230	251	149
Other Prepaid Items	57	32	45	54	61	78	94
Sales Commission[4]	1,019	570	763	922	1,150	1,384	1,780

NOTES: Subtotals do not add to totals because only nonzero costs were used to compute averages.
1. Found in all cases
2. Occuring in 79% of sample.
3. Occuring in 99% of sample.
4. Occuring in 62% of sample.

SOURCE: U.S. Department of Housing and Urban Development and Veterans Administration, *Report on Mortgage Settlement Costs* (Washington, D.C., U.S. Government Printing Office, 1972), p. 73.

is a statement by an attorney or abstractor that after a thorough search there are no irregularities or liens and other encumbrances that may mar marketable titles.

Title Insurance. Given the uncertainties of the above search process, many purchasers as well as mortgagees obtain title insurance. Such coverage indemnifies the insured against poor title. For a one-time premium (which varies according to the amount of coverage) the title insurance company protects the insured against the loss resulting from specified defects in title.

Origination Fee. This is a charge imposed by lenders to cover the processing, inspection, and other costs involved in granting a loan. The origination fee is usually approximately one percent of the loan amount.

Prepaid Expenses. These include real property and special assessment taxes, insurance premiums, and interim loan interest costs.

Loan Discount Payment This includes the "points" (the percentage) of the mortgage usually paid by either the seller of a house purchased with an FHA/VA mortgage or the builder of an FHA/VA approved subdivision where houses will be purchased with FHA/VA loans. Lenders justify this charge by arguing that they will receive less than the face value of the FHA/VA mortgage in selling such "paper" to long-term investors. Because FHA/VA loans have lower than market rate interest rates, the FHA/VA loans are discounted to reflect their noncompetitive return.

Sales Commission. This item is the most expensive of all the settlement components. The sales commission is based on a percentage of the selling price and this share, which is usually governed by the state, varies between 2 and 7 percent.

THE COST OF SETTLEMENT PROCEDURES

It is hard to pin an exact price tag on the settlement process because past surveys have not always included the same items. There is the problem of defining closing versus settlement costs (see Exhibit 2).[15] A 1972 Seattle, Washington analysis, for example, examined only title and selected financing fees in its survey of settlement expenditures.[16] There is also the question of who pays for the different settlement elements; some (e.g., origination expenditures) are paid by the buyer; others (e.g., the realtor's fee) are paid by the seller; still others (e.g., attorneys' fees) are paid by both buyer and seller. (This chapter assumes that seller costs are passed along to the buyer in the form of a higher selling price.) Moreover, there is a range of discretionary and variable settlement costs depending on such factors as whether the buyer wishes a title search and/or title insurance (and the amount of coverage), whether a realtor has been engaged or whether the sale is private, and finally whether the buyer is using an FHA/VA mortgage, which will prompt the payment of points. Although it is difficult to pinpoint an exact total figure it is possible to get some rough idea of the magnitude of settlement expenditures.

In 1966, the U.S. Housing Home Finance Agency (HHFA, predecessor to HUD) completed a short survey of the amounts sellers and homebuyers paid for transaction costs when a house was purchased.[17] Settlement outlays for FHA/VA and conventionally financed purchases were examined in six communities throughout the country. The HHFA found closing costs to be lower for the FHA/VA transactions, although overall settlement outlays were higher for FHA/VA mortgages. The study also found a considerable variation in costs among cities, with Newark being the most expensive community examined (Newark's higher expense was attributed primarily to high attorney fees). But the importance of the HHFA study is not the specification of the dollar amount paid in a particular city at one point in time but rather its having shown that full settlement costs amounted to about 8 to 12 percent of the total cost of the unit.

It is important to realize that although the 8–12 percent ratio is only an approximation it does seem to be supported by other analyses. The most extensive study of settlement expenditures was conducted by HUD and VA in 1972.[18] Over 50,000 FHA/VA transactions were examined (36,000 FHA and 14,000 VA). Total closing outlays ranged from about $400 to over $800, while the entire settlement expenditures were in the $1,500 to $3,000 range—about 10 percent of the total cost of a unit. The survey revealed a considerable range in full settlement expenditures, ranging from a low of 6 percent of the total home cost in Louisiana to a high of almost 15 percent in Maryland. Most states, however, fell in the 8 to 12 percent range. Besides interstate differentials, other significant variations included:

Urbanization. The degree of urbanization, as measured by such factors as location in or out of SMSAs, population density, and percent of population in urban places, was positively related to costs.

Type of Title Proof. The method of title proof predominant in each state also affects costs. Abstracting or personal search with an opinion of title were the least expensive methods of establishing clear title. Title insurance alone, or in combination with personal search, was the most expensive.

Marketable Title Laws. States with marketable title legislation have significantly lower settlement costs.

Type of Mortgage. FHA/VA mortgages having interest rate ceilings have significantly higher loan discount payments and higher overall settlement expenditures.[19]

There has been little updating of the 1972 HUD/VA analysis. The only national study (of homes purchased with either FHA or conventional loans) was being conducted by HUD in the summer of 1976 at the request of the

Senate Housing and Banking Committee.[20] Preliminary results indicated that just some of the closing cost items (loan origination, credit and appraisal reports, mortgage insurance, hazard insurance, advance interest, escrow funds, title charges, and transfer fees) amounted alone to between $600 and $1,200 on $30,000 to $40,000 single-family homes. Given the past cost composition, total settlement expenditure in these units would amount to between approximately $3,000 and $5,000, again in the 8 to 12 percent of unit cost range.

ANALYSIS OF SETTLEMENT COSTS AND GOVERNMENT REGULATIONS

The most significant category in settlement costs consists of expenses for attorneys and realtors. Both are major items (see Exhibit 2) but are currently only indirectly affected by government policies or regulations (e.g., bar association-suggested fee schedules which influence attorneys). Attorney fee schedules have traditionally been accepted as not violating antitrust prohibitions. However, public pressure is increasing to lift such price-fixing by attorneys, and legislative or judicial action in the future is quite possible. A realtor's commission will depend on such factors as local custom, degree of competition, and suggested rates by a public or quasi-public state realtor/real estate board or commission. These practices are also being increasingly scrutinized and criticized, with possible public regulation aimed at faciliting increased consumer awareness likely in the future. A second category of costs includes prepaid items which are not a cost in the same sense as other fees and services paid by the homebuyer or seller but are rather a down payment by the buyer of future legitimate costs; e.g., taxes, insurance, etc., that he will ultimately be required to bear. In addition, prepayment reduces the risk of foreclosure though it is difficult to pinpoint to what extent such risk reduction is justified. For these reasons, prepayment requirements do not appear to be a fertile area for future cost reduction.

"Points" are a third but special category. They are economically motivated and reflect the lesser market value of below-market-interest-rate loans in the secondary mortgage market. From a consumer's perspective, they represent a current payment for future benefits received—the lower interest rate offered through the FHA and VA programs. If the purchaser keeps his lower cost loan for its full term (20 to 30 years) then his point cost is more than recovered.

There are, however, numerous other fees and services constituting about 15 to 20 percent of total settlement outlays, or approximately $800 to $1,000 of the $4,000 to $6,000 total settlement cost for a $50,000 home (8 to 12 percent of the unit price) which are directly influenced by government regulations or the lack of regulation. Of the amount, certain outlays are accepted as justified. To illustrate, recording fees are directly imposed and collected by a public body, often a locality or county. The FHA and VA also collect certain sums for their services—such as a $50 appraisal fee. These assessments have not been criticized as being excessive, however.

What irks most critics is that the *lack* of public action or regulation unnecessarily increases the cost of many of these "other" settlement fees or services, principally, those associated with the searching, insuring, and transfer of title. To give some perspective, these tasks cost the purchaser of the $50,000 home about $500 to $700, and deficiencies in government regulations in these areas are likely increasing these costs by $100 to $300.[21] Previous chapters have concentrated on three different costs of public regulations—direct costs, expenditures resulting from either excessive public requirements or restrictions, and administrative costs. In settlement, another influence is introduced, that of public laxity in taking certain actions that would reduce service costs and would protect the consumer. To illustrate, settlement outlays are higher in states that have not enacted marketable title laws, which give the purchaser "stronger" title in a real estate transaction. In such states, search and related costs are less. It is partially for this reason that midwestern states, which generally have adopted marketable title statutes, have considerably lower closing costs than do their northeastern and western counterparts. Not adopting a marketable title statute therefore directly costs the consumer. Critics also claim that the rates charged by title insurance companies are not sufficiently scrutinized by state insurance commissioners to assess the costs versus the actual risk of coverage, especially in cases where prior work (e.g., an existing title search) is merely being updated.

More important is public laxity in curbing questionable practices in the settlement industry. Title research companies, abstractors, etc. have been accused of allowing and engaging in a system of kickbacks, "fee-splitting," and overcharges that inflate the ultimate cost of settlement to the consumer.

> Competitive forces in the conveyancing industry manifest themselves in an elaborate system of referral fees, kickbacks, rebates, commissions and the like as inducements to those firms and individuals who direct the placement of business. These practices are widely employed, rarely insure to the benefit of the homebuyer, and generally increase total settlement costs.[22]

In 1970, in order to curb abuses Congress gave HUD the power to establish ceilings on settlement-related costs on FHA and VA mortgages (Section 701 of the Emergency Home Finance Act of 1970). In 1972, HUD proposed to establish ceilings in six areas of the country but opposition by the settlement industry led the Department to drop this effort. Instead attention turned to eliminating abuses such as kickback and referral systems.

This effort resulted in adoption of the 1975 Real Estate Settlement and Practices Act (RESPA). This Act is described in detail in Exhibit 3 and is summarized below.

RESPA covers all "federally related mortgage loans." Because of the widespread activities of the "sisters" (i.e., FNMA, GNMA, FHLMC), the term "federally related" in effect includes all mortgages on one- to four-family units. The Act requires that certain forms be used at closing and that information booklets be distributed in order that the consumer (homebuyer and seller) have an idea of the settlement process in general and be told of the exact charges of the transfer. Specifically, the HUD Uniform Settlement Statement (USS), which itemizes expenditures, must be used and the HUD Settlement Costs Information Booklet must be given by lenders to all mortgage applicants.

Other requirements enacted as part of RESPA call for advance disclosure by the lender to the buyer and seller of all costs that would be incurred by these two parties, and such disclosure must be made at least twelve days prior to the actual settlement. Kickbacks are prohibited, as are other questionable practices such as the lender requiring the buyer to purchase title insurance from a specific company. Sellers were required to disclose their original property purchase price if they lived in the parcel for less than two years. Finally, total allowable escrow charges are limited. Other provisions are shown in Exhibit 3.

Criticism of RESPA

While settlement industry representatives originally supported a Settlement Procedure Act as a superior alternative to more stringent regulations, they soon viewed RESPA with horror. The following are some comments by different major lenders on the RESPA-mandated settlement procedures:

Absolute chaos for home mortgage lenders and the customers we serve.

Why the consumer and industry must suffer through such outlandish red tape is not only a mystery to me but to all the people involved.

I have never known of any requirement that has caused so much confusion, misunderstanding, and un-American comments from the general public.[23]

The CUPR survey of lenders revealed widespread dissatisfaction with the original RESPA requirements.[24] Of the eighty savings and loan institutions, mutual savings banks, and mortgage bankers that were interviewed, seventy-five responded that the settlement regulations had caused significant administrative problems and frustrations. One mortgage

EXHIBIT 3

REAL ESTATE SETTLEMENT PROCEDURES ACT
(RESPA) AS AMENDED: MAJOR PROVISIONS

A. Coverage (RESPA Sec. 3, HUD Reg. X, Sec. 3500.5 [d]): RESPA covers all first mortgages which are secured by 1-4 family residential property (including units in condominiums and cooperatives), and which are made by a federally regulated or insured lender. Loans which are intended for sale to one of the federally chartered secondary mortgage market corporations also are covered.

B. Information Booklet (RESPA Sec.5; HUD Reg. X, Sec. 3500.6): The lender must deliver or place in the mail a copy of "Settlement Costs, a HUD Guide" to each loan applicant not later than three business days after, and not including, the day the loan application is received.

C. Good Faith Estimates (RESPA Sec. 5; HUD Reg. X, Sec. 3500.7): Lenders must provide, within three business days after the application is received, a good faith estimate of settlement costs which the buyer is likely to incur at settlement. Such charges include loan origination fees, points, appraisal fees, advance interest, the mortgage insurance premium, title charges, survey costs, pest inspection fees, and government recording and transfer costs . . . .

D. One Day Advance Inspection of Settlement Statement (RESPA Sec. 4: HUD Reg. X, Sec. 3500.10): RESPA requires the person conducting settlement to itemize the exact costs the borrower and seller must pay for each service on HUD Form I, Uniform Settlement Statement Form. The completed form sets forth the items which are known to the person conducting the settlement at the time of inspection. Upon request of the borrower, the person conducting the settlement must permit the borrower to inspect the form during the business day immediately preceding the settlement.

E. Use of Uniform Settlement Statement Form (RESPA Sec. 4, HUD Reg. X, Secs. 3500.8, 3500.9): The HUD Form I, Uniform Settlement Statement, must be used for all mortgages covered by RESPA except transactions where the buyer is not required to pay any settlement costs.

F. Fee (RESPA Sec. 12; HUD Reg. X, Sec. 3500.12): No lender or person conducting the settlement may charge the borrower or seller a fee for preparation of HUD Form I.

G. Escrow Limitations (RESPA Sec. 10): The lender is permitted, at the time of settlement, to require escrow of funds of an amount sufficient to cover insurance and tax payments due since the last date on which the seller paid them through the date of the first mortgage installment, plus 1/6 of the amount due per year.

EXHIBIT 3 (continued)

REAL ESTATE SETTLEMENT PROCEDURES ACT
(RESPA) AS AMENDED: MAJOR PROVISIONS

H. Kickbacks (Amendments, RESPA Sec. 8; HUD Reg. X, Sec. 3500.14 and Appendix B): RESPA prohibits (a) payment or receipt of a "fee, kickback or thing of value" pursuant to an understanding that "business incident to or a part of a real estate settlement service involving a federally related mortgage loan shall be referred to 'any person' and (b) payment or receipt of any portion, split, or percentage of any charge made or received for the rendering of a real estate service—other than for services actually performed." RESPA provides criminal penalties and treble damages.

The 1975 amendments exempted "payments pursuant to cooperative brokerage and referral arrangements or agreements between real estate agents and brokers and such other payments as specified by HUD after consultation with other federal agencies."

I. Prohibition against Seller Selection of Title Company (RESPA Sec. 9): "No seller of property that will be purchased with the assistance" of a loan covered by RESPA may require directly or indirectly as a condition to selling the property, that title insurance covering the property be purchased from any particular company.

J. Relation to State Laws (RESPA Sec. 18; HUD Reg. X, Sec. 3500.13): RESPA specifies that where a state law provides more consumer protection regarding settlement than the federal law, the state law shall take precedence.

SOURCE: Bureau of National Affairs, *Housing and Development Reporter*, Reference File, vol. 3, pp. 130:0911-130:0914, September 6, 1975.

---

banker commented: "RESPA had to be designed by someone who wants to put residential lending to rest for good. It costs at least $100 [per loan] in lost time, not counting the aggravation that reduces general efficiency."[25]

Criticism was voiced universally, not only by the lending-settlement industry fraternity, but also by consumer advocates. Senator William Proxmire, for example, stated that because of the "delays and red tape [created] for lenders and consumers alike, RESPA can only be declared regulatory overkill."[26] These negative comments were prompted by a number of RESPA deficiencies:[27]

1. *Uncertainties.* There were numerous questions concerning when RESPA would be required. While the Act was enacted to cover residential real property transfers, "residential" was not adequately defined. Critical determinants for triggering certain RESPA actions such as a "loan application" and "loan commitment" were also not precisely defined in the administrative regulations. There were also uncertainties concerning the obligation of different parties—such as exactly who had to prepare the uniform settlement statement.

2. *Advance Disclosure of Costs.* Regulations required that the lender had to disclose each closing cost item to the buyer and seller at least twelve days prior to the final settlement. This provision proved very troublesome for it was often difficult to obtain an accurate and exact expenditure breakdown from all the parties involved of all the settlement outlays within the required time period.

3. *Uniform Disclosure Settlement Statement.* This form was criticized as being cumbersome and difficult to complete. One lender responding to the CUPR survey commented that, since RESPA, he had never been to a closing "which went smoothly. Everything is fine until we review the [settlement] statement, where the numbers never seem to add and no one it sure where everything should go."[28]

These and other difficulties increased mortgage processing time and costs. A national survey of 657 savings and loan associations revealed that a year after RESPA had been enacted:

1. Formal loan processing time increased by an average of 11.5 days.
2. The average direct time for processing a loan increased from 4.1 to 6.5 man hours.
3. Processing costs increased by an average of $35 per application.[29]

The reporting S&Ls charged that these changes were largely due to the new RESPA requirements. They found the prescribed twelve-day waiting period to be very bothersome and also encountered difficulties in using the uniform settlement statement.[30]

The adverse public reaction to the original 1975 RESPA regulations led to its revision in 1975–76. There were a number of important amendments. Definitions were tightened to reduce ambiguity. The requirement for advance itemized disclosure of exact costs was repealed; instead lenders were asked to provide a good faith estimate of settlement expenditures. The provision that sellers reveal their original price was dropped. There were also some changes in the uniform settlement statement.

There is little question that these amendments have alleviated many of the more severe RESPA compliance problems. The more important question is whether RESPA, which is the most extensive public regulatory response to the defects in settlement practice, has been successful in addressing these deficiencies. In this regard it is a good first start but is far from complete. As previously discussed, some of the major settlement problems are questionable business practices among the participants. RESPA prohibits some of the more flagrant abuses but tolerates some "grey" area activities that consumer groups have charged work to the disadvantage of the homebuyer and seller. To illustrate, the original RESPA provisions prohibited all kickbacks. Later amendments, however, allowed "payments pursuant to cooperative brokerage and referral arrangements or agreements between real estate agents and brokers as specified by HUD."[31] This change is viewed as possibly continuing excessive settlement costs.

Other drawbacks are not addressed by RESPA, such as the states not adopting a marketable title law causes an increase in costs. What RESPA has done is prohibit some flagrant kickback and similar practices and require that consumers be better informed of the costs they will be bearing. No real effort has been made to investigate why some settlement costs are as high as they are. Possible cost-reducing strategies include:

1. Allowing greater competition among purveyors of settlement services, such as attorneys. This change, which is already being pressed by the Justice Department, may reduce professional fees or will at least give the consumer a better opportunity to shop for settlement services.
2. Enacting marketable title laws. Empirical evidence has clearly shown that settlement outlays are lower in states with such statutes.
3. Computerizing title-recording records. At present much time is lost because records have to be manually traced. A computerized system with different indices, e.g., by tract as well as by grantor and grantee, should be established. The creation of such a file will facilitate not only record searches but other community development activities such as searching for negligent property owners with multiple code violations.
4. Prohibiting questionable practices such as unwarranted commissions and fee-splitting. RESPA has curtailed some such practices but the statute's amendments have weakened the purview of the Act. In addition, professional legal, realtor, and insurance associations must increase their self-policing of settlement activities.
5. Closer monitoring of title insurance rates by state insurance commissioners, especially for recertification (e.g., updating a recent title search).

Federal Housing Administration

The FHA was established in 1934 by the National Housing Act.[32] The agency was originally independent but in 1965 it was incorporated into the then newly created Department of Housing and Urban Development. FHA was formed to be used as a vehicle to improve the housing stock as well as the residential financing system. To achieve these goals, it established insurance programs for single- and multifamily mortgages issued by private lenders. A long list of insurance programs was offered, including the Title I property improvement program, Section 203 (single-family), and Section 207 (multifamily) plans.

In the over thirty-year history of the FHA it has insured $24 billion Title I loans, $138 billion single-family mortgages, and $30 billion multifamily loans.[33] But these numbers do not reveal the full impact of the agency. Prior to FHA it was difficult to obtain residential financing and the loans that could be secured had a short term, a low loan-to-value ratio, and often were not amortizing loans but rather balloon mortgages that had to be refinanced at short intervals. These features made it more difficult to purchase a home because a high down payment was required and monthly payments could be onerous because of the short term. Homeowners also suffered from the possibility that lenders would not continually extend their obligations, in which case owners would lose their properties. The FHA drastically changed the mortgage scene. Because of its insurance programs, lenders agreed to extend the term of the mortgage and also to reduce the required down payment. The Agency also required amortizing loans, which worked to the advantage of both borrower and lender.

Because of its influence on financing, FHA has played a major role in the residential construction and delivery process. It has established minimum property standards (MPS) for the single- and multifamily construction it covers. Its underwriting criteria and manuals have often been adopted almost verbatim by the rest of the industry. It influences wage scales; the Davis-Bacon law requires that workers on insured or subsidized projects be paid at prevailing wage rates. Its environmental review procedures have been adopted by other public bodies.

CRITICISM OF FHA

No one denies that FHA has made notable inroads in modernizing residential financing and in bringing housing to many who without its efforts would not have been able to purchase a home. But the agency has also been accused of increasing housing costs through imposing mandatory requirements and by operating inefficiently. Growing dissatisfaction under FHA is reflected in its declining loan volume. In the early 1970s it insured about 830,000 units annually; by the mid-1970s the figure plummeted to about 650,000 units. Where FHA-backed housing traditionally accounted for 15 percent of new housing stock, by the mid-1970s this share had declined to about 8 percent.[34] FHA found itself competing with private mortgage insurance (PMI) companies which have proven themselves capable of more efficiently performing many of the roles previously served by the FHA.

Representatives of the construction and lender industries have voiced dissatisfaction with a number of FHA requirements and procedures. To illustrate, the 1931 Davis-Bacon Act requires that workers on assisted projects be paid at prevailing wage rates. Critics have charged that the basic thrust of the law increases labor construction costs and that this inflation is aggravated by the way Davis-Bacon has been applied.[35] The statute calls for prevailing but not specifically union-scale wages, yet in most instances the higher cost union scale has been used. And even when nominally prevailing wages are paid they are often higher than the going local construction pay scale. The General Accounting Office concluded in five studies that inappropriately high minimum wages had been found in a variety of federally financed and federally assisted projects.[36]

The FHA minimum property standards (MPS) are another point of contention. There are two major guides for single-family and multifamily properties, with both covering such areas as site specifications, building materials, and construction techniques. The MPS are extremely detailed, going beyond most building codes; the single-family MPS, for example, require certified carpets, certified kitchen cabinets, two towel racks in the bathroom with a soap dish on the wall, etc. Critics charge that the MPS have gone beyond "minimums" and have unnecessarily increased the cost of FHA housing units.[37] They contend that local building and subdivision codes set adequate health and safety standards and safeguards and that the MPS are excessive in their requirements.

Most criticism has focused on FHA "red tape." The administrative operations and regulations of the agency are seen as causing severe time delays which substantially increase housing costs to the consumer. Charges of inefficiency are leveled at many large bureaucratic organizations, but a particularly frustrating aspect of the FHA is the decline in its once superlative performance. In the 1960s the FHA almost always completed single-family appraisals and property approvals in five days or less; by 1971 this level of performance was reached only about half the time.[38]

The drop in efficiency made FHA a weak competitor with the mortgage services offered by private lenders and PMIs. This was strikingly illustrated in a study by Booz-Allen, whose analysis showed that HUD's initiation time (i.e., evaluating and rendering a decision on a loan application) of about eighteen hours per single-family loan was fourteen hours longer than the record for private and public insurors. The FHA compared even less favorably for multifamily loans. The agency expended about 330 hours for initiation of each application compared to four to eighty hours for PMIs.[39]

The CUPR lender survey also revealed a considerably longer processing period for FHA as compared to PMI. When asked how long it took to complete an FHA mortgage package, almost three-quarters of the lenders and mortgage bankers interviewed replied that about three weeks or longer were needed. The PMI processing period was much faster, as is indicated in Exhibit 4. There was an even greater contrast in the respective response times for FHA versus PMI in terms of approving or disapproving a loan insurance request. About three-quarters of the lenders said that PMIs gave an answer in one to two days; at worst a one-week period would elapse. FHA's reaction times were far slower; at best three or four days would elapse and considerably longer periods were not uncommon (see Exhibit 4).

EVALUATION OF CRITICISM OF FHA

There is little doubt that various FHA requirements and procedures increase loan-associated administrative costs. This situation has led to the growing dominance of PMIs, especially with respect to single-family development. But these criticisms must be viewed in perspective. The minimum property standards go beyond establishing minimum construction standards needed to protect life and limb because they are not formulated as a basic building code, but rather are an attempt by an insurer to maintain the long-term value and saleability of its security—the insured mortgaged property. The decline in FHA performance is also a relatively recent phenomenon which occurred in the late 1960s and early 1970s when an administrative reorganization was being effected at HUD and when the FHA was called upon to achieve the difficult goal of expanding housing availability for the urban poor. The fact that FHA is currently a weak competitor against the PMIs may be more a reflection of its shifting focus from the suburban middle class to the urban poor than its internal decline. The questions that must be asked now, and are being considered by HUD and Congress, are:

1. Should the "old" FHA be reinvented or should suburban, middle-income mortgage insurance be left to the private market PMIs?
2. What is the role of the "new" FHA? Should it focus only on those areas abandoned by private lenders and should it act to foster innovative mortgage devices; for example, variable rate loans?
3. How should the "new" FHA be monitored? Old yardsticks such as losses versus permiums may have little meaning.
4. How should the FHA be structured; how can it retain its efficiency by being a quasi-independent agency while still remaining within the larger HUD administrative fold?

EXHIBIT 4

FHA VERSUS PMI SINGLE-FAMILY ADMINISTRATIVE PERFORMANCE

Time to Complete Mortgage Package (in days)	Percentage distribution of lender responses (n = 80)	
	FHA Insured Loans	PMI Loans
1-2	0.0	4.7
3-4	0.0	1.6
5-6	0.0	9.4
7-8	4.5	17.2
9-10	7.5	14.1
11-15	11.9	18.8
16-20	6.0	3.1
21+	70.1	31.1
Total	100.0	100.0

Time for Insuror to Approve or Disapprove Mortgage Package (in days)		
1-2	0.0	73.7
3-4	19.4	16.4
5-6	14.5	3.3
7-8	22.6	6.6
9-10	8.1	0.0
11-15	8.1	0.0
16-20	4.8	0.0
21+	22.5	0.0
Total	100.0	100.0

SOURCE: Center for Urban Policy Research, Rutgers University, Financial Institution Survey, Summer 1976.

Loan Repayment Strategies

The third area that will be examined in this chapter is mortgage repayment strategies and how they affect the ability of families to afford and maintain a single-family home. Government regulations directly affect how loans are repaid. State laws influence the cost of borrowing money by establishing ceilings on interest rates. States and the federal financial supervisory agencies, e.g., the FHLBB and the Federal Reserve, also affect the *method and schedule of repayment* by regulating mortgage documents and repayment strategies, e.g, determining whether VRMs are allowed and if so under what guise.

This area has been the subject of considerable discussion in recent years. There have been many proposals to the effect that if interest rate restrictions could be eliminated or modified and if the basic mortgage instrument could be made more flexible then the "housing market could be opened." Such an argument suggests that current public regulations affecting mortgage repayment either directly or indirectly raise the cost of housing and limit its availability by being archaic and overly restrictive. This section examines this thesis by examining the impact of two principal governmental influences on loan repayment, usury laws and regulations governing innovative mortgages.

USURY RESTRICTIONS

Interest prohibitions and usury restrictions date from Biblical and Babylonian times, and were particularly severe until the Renaissance and the Lutheran reforms. Such restrictions were further relaxed in the eighteenth century and many were repealed in the nineteenth century. Great Britain, for example, repealed its usury laws in 1854.[40]

The United States has not followed suit. The colonies, influenced by England, generally adopted usury statutes. The states have with some exceptions largely retained such laws though there is growing advocacy for more flexible statutes. Usury law advocates argue their cause on numerous grounds.[41] Protection of the borrower who frequently is less knowledgeable and has less financial clout than the lender is a popular justification. Such reasoning was especially important before the development of a free-flowing capital market when, without usury laws, borrowers were at the mercy of local lenders. Lingering ethical and religious sentiments regarding lending and the taking of interest are another element contributing to the continued retention of usury restriction. Many argue that interest restraints are archaic and have adverse effects:

> 1. Usury laws are historical antiques. One reason for usury laws, to protect borrowers from local lenders where there is no established free-flowing

capital market, is no longer applicable. There is now a national capital marketplace (e.g., GNMA trading), although mortgage trading is not as developed as is securities exchange.

2. Usury laws are unrealistic. Interest rates are established by the supply and demand of capital, and interest restrictions cause economic and social distortions (i.e., capital from usury law states will flow to unregulated areas).

3. Usury laws are counterproductive. Rather than helping the small, comparatively high-risk borrower they hinder his chances of obtaining a loan because the limited capital in usury states will flow to well-established, low-risk borrowers.

4. Usury laws are often inequitably modified. California, for example, exempts S&Ls and commercial banks from its interest rate restrictions while Indiana exempts insurance companies other than life insurance corporations.

5. Usury laws have proved to be a legal morass. They frequently are avoided illegally or through questionable means. To illustrate, loans have sometimes been granted by third parties at the legal rate, after which the real lender then purchases the loan at a discount.

Usury laws are allegedly especially onerous and inequitable in limited-supply, high-cost capital periods. Potential homeowners and other borrowers in restrictive-interest states suffer because lenders having capital that can be freely transferred (e.g., insurance companies) will naturally prefer to grant any mortgages in high-interest, non-usury states. Usury statutes may also aggravate the withdrawal of funds from S&Ls in tight capital supply periods. In such years, the interest rates offered on deposits by competitors (e.g., the U.S. Treasury) will often soar above the interest rates offered by S&Ls and mutual banks. To compete, the thrift institutions should increase the interest rate paid to their depositors. They often cannot in usury states because the return they can offer is limited by the non-market, low return on the mortgages they grant. This scenario will lead to disintermediation; depositors will understandably withdraw their funds from the comparatively low-yielding thrift institutions, with a detrimental effect to the latter's economic soundness and ability to grant new mortgages.

THE IMPACT OF USURY REFORM

Usury law critics have made a strong case that such statutes can impede an adequate free flow of mortgage funds, and numerous states have heeded the call for reform. Massachusetts has not had an interest restriction law for many years. Its neighboring state, New Hampshire, voted a repeal of interest restrictions in 1921. In more recent years other states have followed suit; in 1972 Virginia repealed its usury ceiling, which had been in effect since 1796, and Michigan has suspended its interest rate restriction until 1977.

Other states have kept usury laws but have raised the maximum permissible interest rate to more realistic levels. In 1974, both Mississippi and Illinois raised their maximum permissible interest rate ceilings, from 8 percent to 10 percent. Maryland has revised its usury rate from 8 percent to 10 percent; New Jersey raised the interest ceiling from 7.5 percent to 8.5 percent. Virginia and North Carolina have made similar moves.

What has been the impact of usury rate reform? In many instances the outcome has not been gratifying. In most cases the increase has been inadequate and has been aimed at addressing past inadequacies rather than facilitating the future flow of capital; a state might increase the usury rate ceiling from 7 percent to 8 percent just at the time when rates may have jumped from 8 percent to 9 percent. This temporary reaction characterizes the actions taken by many states in the 1973–74 mortgage crunch when they allowed interest rates to float to 8 to 9 percent when the open market price that state financing agencies had to pay for long-term capital (i.e., in the form of certificates) was at or surpassed the rate they were allowed to charge for mortgages. A survey by the National Association of Realtors of eight states which had increased their interest rate ceilings revealed that such action has been little more than a stopgap measure preventing the mortgage market from becoming worse.[42] The realtors argued that tight money policies by the Federal Reserve Board and floating rate notes which offered higher interest rates than thrift institutions were among the reasons the usury increases failed to stem the mortgage crunch.

This "catch-up" deficiency could be avoided by eliminating rather than raising usury rate ceilings. Such a strategy subscribes to an unencumbered market mortgage philosophy that the cost of mortgages should reflect the market price of long-term loans (VRMS are justified on similar grounds). But this approach has serious pragmatic constraints. Admittedly, doing away with usury restrictions may encourage S&Ls and other primary lenders to reenter the market, especially the local primary market, with greater vigor and may induce others such as life insurance companies to again grant mortgages. At the same time, eliminating usury laws and thereby allowing for possibly higher interest rates on mortgages may very well price out even more families from single-family homes. In tight money times, usury ceilings have in effect subsidized the cost of borrowing by reducing the effective interest rate, albeit with a long-term tradeoff of capital flowing to investments other than mortgages. But by eliminating usury restrictions, investments in mortgages would become more competitive with other capital investments and therefore attract more funds. If the market equilibrium point (the mortgage rate) settles at a point higher than that which consumers can afford, then some direct subsidy would be a more effective means of subsidizing the industry than are usury restrictions.

Usury reform illustrates the dilemma of the mortgage repayment strategy to make single-family homes more affordable. By making the mortgage system more cost sensitive and flexible by eliminating interest rate ceilings and allowing flexible mortgages, short-term consumer costs very often increase. The question then is one of short-term economy versus long-term efficiency. Eliminating interest rate ceilings would likely achieve the latter at the expense of the former.

Innovative Mortgage Instruments

In recent years critics have charged that the standard fixed rate mortgage (FRM), with its level and amortized repayment, is keeping many families from purchasing a single-family house.[43] The critics believe that innovative mortgage approaches would, in contrast, increase housing opportunities for consumers. Several flexible and innovative loan strategies are described below.

GRADUATED PAYMENT MORTGAGE (GPM)

The GPM is a plan which sets a fixed interest rate and maturity on a loan but which offers a lower initial monthly payment by deferring amortization. The GPM is designed to enable those with rising incomes, e.g., young professionals, to acquire a home immediately with reduced capital while repaying the greater part of the principal later.

CONTINGENT APPRECIATION MORTGAGE (CAM)

The CAM has a fixed interest rate and term but differs from the FRM by allowing the lending institution to share in the increased value of a property it has financed in the event the property is resold, refinanced, or prepaid. The lender's share would be determined, in advance, by a formula which increases return proportionally with the principal of the loan and inversely with the offered interest rate. CAM advocates believe that such an instrument would encourage greater lending at a lower-than-market-interest-rate since lenders would make part of their profit from their share of the parcel's appreciation.

REVERSE ANNUITY MORTGAGE (RAM)

The RAM is a variation of the CAM. It allows the mortgagee, at a point in the future, to purchase the mortgagor's property by making periodic payments to the mortgagor of a set amount over a set period of time. The

RAM would allow the mortgagee to share in the profit of a unit appreciating and hopefully would make him more amenable to extending more loans at a lower interest rate.

NON-AMORTIZED MORTGAGE (NAM)

The NAM would require only periodic interest payments without any repayment of principal. The loan would theoretically be due at the time of the mortgage's expiration, though it is hoped that the lender would simply extend the loan for another given period. NAMs would have a shorter term than FRMs and it is envisioned that the former would have a higher interest rate than the latter. The consumers' benefits with the NAM would be a lower monthly payment since only interest is being repaid.

This mortgage instrument is very similar to the "balloon" mortgages which were commonly used in the 1920s and which were severely criticized at that time as being unfair to consumers who were confronted with either a large, lump-sum payment at the end of the non-amortized mortgage term or with the option of finding a source of refinancing. Its advantage in today's economic conditions is that families, because of increasing earnings, are typically least able to afford large initial payments, but have increasing financial resources to draw upon later in life. This mortgage format is also extremely attractive for those buying their first house with the intention of trading up after a few years.

VARIABLE RATE MORTGAGE (VRM)

A VRM is a conventional mortgage loan contract which carries an effective cost that changes periodically with the market cost of money. The effective rate could vary by holding the payment constant while the maturity of the loan is lengthened or reduced in response to a selected index. Alternatively, a VRM could be structured so that the term is held constant but the periodic payment is adjusted.

The VRM has been the most touted flexible instrument,[44] and its advocates claim that the variable mortgage offers a number of significant advantages:

1. VRMs will in the future alleviate the problem of thrift institutions borrowing short and lending long. S&Ls and mutual savings banks will still be lending long but, unlike with FRMs, they will avoid the situation of being locked into long-term, comparatively low-yielding mortgages because the VRM's interest rate or return would increase as the cost of capital rises. As the thrift institutions' income matches the current cost of money they could offer competitive interest rates and deter disintermediation.

2. VRMs might encourage new money into the mortgage market from buyers who might be interested in purchasing the new notes as hedges against inflation. This stands in contrast to the current situation of an FRM being a very poor investment in inflationary periods.

3. VRMs would abet adequate mortgage flow in periods of rising interest rates because mortgagors would then be encouraged to accelerate payment of their outstanding commitments in order to forestall rising interest costs. (The reverse is true with FRMs.) These prepayments would enable thrift institutions to grant additional mortgages.

3. VRMs will eliminate the inequities found with FRMs of homebuyers who pay high interest rates in tight market years subsidizing outstanding low-cost mortgages granted in periods when interest rates were lower.

The above discussion is meant only as a very brief overview of suggested innovative mortgage repayment strategies. There are also other possible approaches available: flexible payment mortgages (FPM—a variation of the GAM), purchase assistance mortgages (PAM—a variation of the GAM), Canadian roll-over mortgages (CROM—a VRM variation), and price level adjusted mortgage (PLAM).[45]

Government Regulations and Innovative Mortgage Instruments

There is a maze of government regulations that have influenced the availability of innovative mortgage instruments. Federally chartered thrift institutions are currently not permitted to issue VRMs, for example. Until recently the FHA also was not allowed to insure GPMs. The inability to obtain FHA coverage was a major problem because lenders would not experiment with a new mortgage approach without federal insurance coverage. In addition to federal controls there are also state controls. CUPR contacted approximately one-half of the state banking departments and asked whether they allowed different innovative mortgages. Their replies are shown in Exhibit 5. A most interesting finding was the uncertainty on the part of many state banking departments as to whether certain types of mortgages were allowed.

It should be mentioned that there has recently been a lifting of some of the regulatory restraints. Section 245 of the 1974 Housing and Community Development Act permitted FHA to issue GPMs as long as these mortgages do not exceed 1 percent of the lender's portfolio. FHA has recently released regulations which detail a total of five different GPM plans which will be available in the industry in the fall of 1976. (The Bank of Hawaii was the first lender to participate in the FHA-insured GPM program.) The FHLBB has supported research into the innovative instruments, has established an Advisory Alternative Mortgage Instrument Committee, and has in general advocated mortgage reform. Congress has often shown a lukewarm attitude

EXHIBIT 5

SURVEY OF STATE POLICY WITH REFERENCE TO DIFFERENT INNOVATIVE MORTGAGE INSTRUMENTS

State	Innovative Mortgage Instrument				Comments[2]
	VRM	GPM	RAM	CAM	
Alabama	A[1]	N[1]	N	N	Potential usury law conflicts.
California	A	N	N	N	No existing demand for VRMs evident.
Colorado	A	A	A	N	Very few VRMs existing.
Connecticut	A	A	N	A	RAMS are not likely to be accepted.
Delaware	A	N	A	N	Only a limited number of banks offer VRMs.
Florida	A	P[1]	N	P	Little demand for VRMs.
Georgia	A	P	P	P	
Illinois	P	A	N	P	No proposed legislation for VRMs.
Indiana	A	P	A	P	Limited commercial institution use of VRMs.
Kansas	A	A	P	P	VRMs in effect at S&Ls.
Louisiana	A	A	A	A	Potential enabling legislative amendments for new instruments.
Maryland	P	N	N	N	Allowed only if institution qualifies under regulations.
Massachusetts	A	N	P	A	
Minnesota	P	P	P	P	
Missouri	P	A	A	P	Bank reaction unfavorable to VRMs; usury ceiling a problem.
New Jersey	A	N	N	N	Usury laws prohibit use of VRMs.
New York	P	N	N	N	No demand evident for VRMs.
North Carolina	P	P	P	P	
Ohio	A	P	P	A	VRMs are allowed but are not used; public reaction is negative.
Oregon	A	A	A	P	VRMs are not used; GPM not allowed in S&Ls but allowed in
Pennsylvania	P	N	N	P	commercial banks.

EXHIBIT 5 (continued)

SURVEY OF STATE POLICY WITH REFERENCE TO DIFFERENT INNOVATIVE MORTGAGE INSTRUMENTS

State	Innovative Mortgage Instrument				Comments[2]
	VRM	GPM	RAM	CAM	
Rhode Island	A	A	A	A	Usury law & disclosure regulations impeded use of VRMs.
Texas	A	N	N	N	Banks reluctant to use VRMs; GPM is a new development.
Vermont	A	N	N	N	Recently introduced (last legislative session).
Virginia	A	N	N	N	Very limited utilization of VRM & GPM.
Washington	A	N	N	N	Public reaction favorable to GPM.
Wisconsin	A	A	A	A	Statute passed limiting rate charge period and maximum charge. Banks avoid VRMs - prefer balloon.

NOTES: 1. A = allows; P = prohibits; N = not sure/don't know.
2. Comments of individuals interviewed at indicated state department of banking.

SOURCE: Center for Urban Policy Research Rutgers University, Survey of State Departments of Banking, Summer 1976.

toward allowing new loan formats, though this is believed to be softening. State banking commissions appear now to be more receptive towards mortgage change.

THE COSTS OF INFLEXIBILITY

While greater flexibility is in the offing, many innovative loan payment plans are still currently not permitted. This prohibition is said by critics to cost the housing consumer by denying him the fullest opportunity to purchase a house. Young families are not benefiting from the GPM's nonamortized mortgage, which would allow them to buy a single-family home because their principal and interest payments would be lower at least for the first few years of the loan than with the FRM counterpart. And because VRMs and CAMs are restricted, potential permanent lenders have fled the mortgage market with its current FRM rigidities. This flight contracts the pool of available mortgage capital, thus making it more difficult to purchase a home.

While there is some validity to the above charges, they are overstated. There is a very real question whether restrictive regulations are the main restraint to the use of the innovative mortgages. Even were these prohibitions removed, there is doubt whether the new type loans would proliferate. First there are technical problems in designing the new loans. To illustrate, with VRMs it is difficult to formulate an appropriate cost/capital index.

> Ideally, the variable interest rate should be linked to a reference rate that is beyond the control of the lender, moves with market interest rates, and can be explained in clear and simple terms to borrowers. The use of an index based on the cost of funds would enable a given savings institution to maintain its earnings margin and to compete for savings. But such information is not readily available to the borrower and is not completely beyond the influence of the lender.[46]

VRMs could also encounter problems with state usury laws. No mortgage could be written which would exceed a state's usury ceiling, even if a VRM were permitted. Where the market rate in a state is close to the legally imposed interest maximum, a VRM would not be feasible and a modified VRM with a usury rate ceiling would lose some of its desirability to lenders. The other innovative mortgage instruments pose their own problems.

Further, even assuming that these technical issues could be solved, there is the very real problem of industry acceptance. There is not just the matter of hesitation in using something new, for there are several doubts concerning the assumptions of the proposed mortgage alternatives. As an example, underlying the GPM approach is the belief that rising family income would support increases in principal and interest payments. In fact inflation-adjusted family income has risen very slowly in the past few years, and in addition, this increase has been partially absorbed by higher home energy costs. Lenders are apprehensive that the added income necessary to pay the increasing GPM costs may simply not be forthcoming. Nonamortized mortgage advocates assume that mortgagors will continue to repay their loans despite little or no reduction of the outstanding balance. This assumption is also questionable. The logic of CAMs is that it is reasonable for lenders to forego present profits from their loan portfolio by charging a lower interest rate in order to share in the appreciation of the mortgaged property. This inflation bail-out philosophy has often proved faulty in the past, as is evidenced by the collapse of the Real Estate Investment Trusts (REITs).

That lenders have not wholeheartedly endorsed the innovative mortgage strategies is indicated in the CUPR survey of the industry. When asked to evaluate VRMs, GPMs, and CAMs, VRMs received the strongest vote of approval but even with this mortgage instrument only about half of those interviewed suggested its use. While many felt that the VRM's flexibility was a major asset, there were recurring comments to the effect that an unencumbered VRM (i.e., with no ceiling in the possible rise in interest rate) would never be adopted and a politically acceptable VRM would lose many of its advantages. GPM/CAMs received even less support and both were viewed as being highly questionable (see Exhibit 6).

EXHIBIT 6

LENDERS' EVALUATION OF INNOVATIVE MORTGAGE INSTRUMENTS
(n=80)

| | Innovative Mortgage Instrument | | |
	VRM	GPM	CAM
Strongly approve	25%	10%	5%
Approve	20	13	25
Disapprove	35	30	25
Strongly disapprove	20	47	45
Total	100%	100%	100%

SOURCE: Center for Urban Policy Research, Rutgers University, Financial Institution Survey, Summer 1976.

Lender hesitation over the flexible mortgage instruments does not mean that the new approaches cannot be successful. In California there was initial trepidation over employing VRMs, but the track record, at least as reported by some early reports, appears good. In 1970 alone five major lenders controlling 45 percent of the assets of state chartered savings and loan institutions began offering VRMs. But lender misgiving cannot be ignored and means that the limited availability of innovative strategies cannot be blamed entirely on restrictive public controls. This is graphically demonstrated at the state level where many states allow state-chartered institutions to issue VRMs and comparable loans (see Exhibit 5). Yet there is a very limited offering of the innovative mortgages even in these states.

A last consideration concerns the effective costs of the new loan strategies. While some (e.g., GPM) will reduce initial dollar demands and therefore will help expand potential homeownership, others (e.g., VRM) may very well limit the potential by possibly increasing costs. In a period of rising interest rates, lenders may be more willing to grant VRMs and hence the pool of available mortgage money will rise, but the cost of these loans will be higher (as compared to FRMs) and therefore more families may be priced out of the housing market. As in the case of usury reform, there is a dilemma that policies that remove interest rate restrictions and allow for more flexible loans may indeed induce more lenders to grant mortgages, but at the same time these strategies may also increase consumer costs.

Conclusion

As is evident from the discussion in this chapter, settlement/financing regulations are costly and/or have significant cost considerations. Government regulations add to these expenses, although it is extremely difficult to assign an exact dollar figure. Settlement expenditures amount to between $4,000 and $6,000 on a $50,000 single-family home. Of this total, government regulations affecting searching, insuring and transferring title—activities which cost about $500 to $700 per loan—have been discussed as inadequate, but the cost of these inadequate rules to the housing consumer is not likely to be more than $100 to $300. RESPA paper work adds between $50 and $100 to the mortgagee's expenditures (part of which is likely to be passed along to the consumer) but this outlay is likely to have been reduced by the amendments to this statute and is surely in part offset by the savings resulting from RESPA's prohibition of questionable settlement procedures.

This discussion assumes that attorney and realtor fees are legitimate costs of professional business services. If we question this (and attempts are being made to make these services more competitive through such means as disallowing price schedules and allowing advertising), then current restrictions would be increasing settlement outlays by more than the $100 to $300 figure cited above.

Certain FHA policies, such as its MPS rules and Davis-Bacon requirements, surely add to costs. These are aggravated by its much slower processing schedule. But the FHA's focus, role, and even its administrative structure has changed in recent years. To compare the FHA to PMI illustrates the latter's markedly superior performance but the question remains whether the two are continuing to compete for the same market. The question that must be asked is the appropriate future role for FHA; should it continue as the traditional insuror of suburban homes or should it act as an insuror of last resort for urban areas and as a catalyst for mortgage change.

Loan repayment strategies do have important cost and capital availability implications to the housing consumer. As the unit cost of housing has soared there have been frantic efforts to tinker with new repayment approaches. These experiments are in their infancy and are deserving of further research. One thing that is clear is the potential conflict between the price of loans and the availability of mortgage credit posed by the new mortgage instruments.

The reader should be aware that we have only touched upon a handful of the settlement and financing-related regulations. The importance of the analysis in this chapter is to sensitize the reader to the plethora of settlement and financing rules and to indicate how some increase housing expenditures. Attention must be directed not only at the front-end regulations that influence the cost of a housing unit but also at the subsequent rules that impact on how housing is to be transfered and paid for.

Notes

1. See U.S., Department of Housing and Urban Development, and Veterans Administration, *Report on Mortgage Settlement Costs* (Washington, D.C.: U.S. Government Printing Office, 1972), hereafter cited as *Mortgage Settlement Report.*
2. See Roger Starr, *Housing and the Money Market* (New York: Basic Books, 1975).
3. See Allen Axelrod et al., *Land Transfer and Finance* (Boston: Little Brown & Company, 1972).
4. See note 9 below.
5. This is especially true of the Real Estate Settlement Procedures Act. See note 9 below.
6. *Mortgage Settlement Report,* p. 73.
7. This calculation assumes that housing costs should amount to no more than one-quarter of total annual income. See Market Research Department, McGraw-Hill Inc., ''A Study of Comparative Time and Cost for Building Five

Selected Types of Low-Cost Housing" in the President's Committee on Urban Housing, *Technical Studies*, vol. II. (Washington, D.C.: U.S. Government Printing Office, 1969).
8. These are the monthly payments on a $50,000 home purchased with a loan with a 7 percent rate, loan-to-value ratio ranging from 70 to 90 percent, and terms ranging from 25 to 40 years.
9. For discussion on closing and settlement costs and procedures, see *Mortgage Settlement Report*; Robert E. Duffy Jr., "RESPA Refined and Revisited," *Real Estate Review 6* (Winter 1977):82; William J. McAuliffe Jr., "Revised RESPA Law Requires New Form of Compliance," *The Mortgage Banker* (August 1976):8; Conrad M. Mulvaney, "Real Estate Settlement Procedures Act of 1974," *Illinois Bar Journal* (September 1975):18; William J. McAuliffe, Jr., "New Settlement Law Demands Compliance, Threatens Harder Measures," *The Mortgage Banker* (August, 1975):13; "The Sticky Lessons of Settlement Standard," *Savings and Loan News* (August 1976):40; Fred Feinstein and Michael J. Baker, "How to Live With RESPA and Regulation X," *Chicago Bar Record* (May-June 1975):346; William E. Cumberland, "Federal Law to Monitor Settlement Procedures," *Mortgage Banker* (February 1975):25; Robert E. Duffy, Jr., "The Real Estate Settlement Procedure Act of 1974," *Real Estate Review* (Winter 1976):85; Edward S. Hirschler, "Federal Regulation of Home Closings—The Real Estate Settlement Procedure Act of 1974," *University of Richmond Law Review* 10 (1975):63.
10. See Starr, *Housing and the Money Market*; Henry E. Hoagland and Leo D. Stone, *Real Estate Finance* (Homewood, Ill.: Richard D. Irwin, Inc., 1969); Harold Barger, *Money Banking and Public Policy* (Chicago: Rand McNally, 1970); Ernest M. Fisher and Robert M. Fisher, *Urban Real Estate* (New York: Henry Holt and Co., 1964); U.S. Department of Housing and Urban Development, *Housing and the Seventies* (Washington, D.C.: U.S. Government Printing Office, 1974).
11. In the summer of 1976 CUPR called a random sample of lenders including savings and loan associations, mutual savings banks, commercial banks, and mortgage bankers. One hundred lenders were contacted and eighty agreed to participate in the survey of the impact of government regulations on financing procedures and costs.
12. Ibid.
13. Mortgage Settlement Report, p. 73.
14. Ibid., ch. 3. This section is derived from *Mortgage Settlement Report,* ch. 3. See also Jerome G. Rose, *The Legal Advisor on Home Ownership* (Boston: Little Brown and Company, 1964) and Axelrod et al., *Land Transfer and Finance.*
15. "What's Ahead for Settlement Costs," *Hud Challenge* (May 1972) p.4.
16. Florence T. Hall and Evelyn Freeman, "Survey of Home Buyers' and Sellers' Closing Costs in the Seattle, Washington Area," *Journal of Home Economics* 64 (January 1972):20.
17. "When You Buy a House: How Much for Closing Costs," *Changing Times* (July, 1969), p. 30.
18. *Mortgage Settlement Report.*
19. Ibid. pp. 112–113.
20. Bureau of National Affairs, *Housing and Development Reporter—Current Developments 1975,* p. 701.
21. The $100 to $300 figure was suggested in the Financial Institution survey. See note 11.

22. *Mortgage Settlement Report,* p. 5.
23. "The Sticky Lessons of Settlement Standards," *Savings & Loan News,* p. 40. See also "Complaints Mount Over Law on Closing," *New York Times,* October 26, 1975.
24. See discussion at note 11.
25. Ibid.
26. Ibid.
27. Robert E. Duffy, Jr., "RESPA Refined and Revisited."
28. CUPR Lender Survey; see note 11.
29. See "The Sticky Lessons of Settlement Standards," *Savings and Loan News,* p. 44.
30. Ibid.
31. See Exhibit 3.
32. For discussion of FHA see Horace B. Bazan, *The Fragmentation of FHA* (Washington, D.C.: Mortgage Bankers Association, 1974); Lata Chatterjee et al., *FHA Policies and the Baltimore City Housing Market* (Baltimore, Center for Metropolitan Planning and Research, Johns Hopkins University, April 1974); U.S. Department of Housing and Urban Development, *Housing in the Seventies;* Booz-Allen Public Administration Services, Inc., *Comparative Analysis of Federal and Non-Federal Government Housing Program Procedural and Managerial Implementation* (National Technical Information Services, July 1973); Federal Home Loan Bank Board Office of Economic Research, *Comparative Study of Yields on Conventional and FHA-Insured Home Loans,* Invited Working Paper No. 7, (April 1973); Federal Home Loan Bank Board, Office of Economic Research, *The Future Role of FHA,* Working Paper No. 37, (September 1972); Jack Rubinson, "FHA Revisited," *Savings Bank Journal,* (April 1975): 48–54; Richard F. Janssen, "Increased Federal Aid in Home Mortgage Field Near Takeover Point," *Wall Street Journal,* January 9, 1971, p. 1; Starr, *Housing and the Money Market;* Richard Shafer, "The Once Proud FHA is Beset by Scandals and LOts of Red Tape," *Wall Street Journal,* March 19, 1974, p. 1.
33. See Housing and Development Reporter, Reference File, vol. 1, "HUD/FHA Single Family Mortgage Insurance," pp. 10:0011–10:0016.
34. Horace Bazan, *Fragmentation of FHA.*
35. Edward Cohen, *The Economics of Davis-Bacon* (Washington, D.C.: American Enterprise Institute, 1972).
36. Ibid.
37. Ibid.
38. Horace Bazan, *Fragmentation of FHA,* p. 30.
39. Booz-Allen Public Administration Services, Inc., *Comparative Analysis of Federal and Non-Federal Government Housing Program.*
40. For a discussion of usury laws see Robert Moore Fisher, "Monetary Policy and Its Relation to Mortgage Lending and Land Economics," *Land Economics,* (November 1963):410.; Philip R. Robins, "The Effects of State Usury Ceilings on Single-Family Homebuilders," *The Journal of Finance* (November, 1970):227; Kenneth L. Avio, "An Economic Rationale for Statutory Interest Rate Ceilings," *Quarterly Review of Economics and Business* (1972):61.; Norman Bowsher, "Usury Laws: Harmful When Effective," *Federal Reserve Bank of St. Louis* (August 1974):16; Mendes Hershman, "Usury and the Tight Mortgage Market," *The Business Lawyer* (January 1967):333; Richard Mc-

Manus, "Variable Mortgage Note: Route to Increased Housing," *American Bar Association Journal* (June 1969):557.

41. Ibid.
42. Ibid.
43. See D.L. Smith, "Reforming the Mortgage Instruments," Federal Home Loan Bank Board, Working Paper No. 11, April 1976, pp. 2-10,; S.R. Stansell and J.P. Millar, "How Variable Rate Mortgages Would Affect Lenders," *Real Estate Review* (Winter 1976):115.; G.G. Kaufman, "The Questionable Benefit of Variable-Rate Mortgages," *Quarterly Review of Economics and Business* (Fall 1973):43; W.J. Breuggeman and J.B. Baesel, "The Mechanics of Variable Rate Mortgages and Implications for Home Ownership as an Inflation Hedge," *The Appraisal Journal* (April 1976):236.; U.S. Federal Home Loan Bank Board, "Board Proposes Variable Rate Mortgages for Federal S&L's", *FHLBB Journal* (March 1975):38.; R.J. Werner, "Usury and the Variable-Rate Mortgage," *Real Estate Law Journal* (1976):155.; Richard Marcis, "Variable-Rate Mortgages: Their Use and Impact in the Mortgage and Capital Markets," *American Real Estate and Urban Economics Association Journal* (Spring 1974):21. See also Federal Reserve Board, *Ways to Moderate Fluctuations in Housing Construction* (Washington, D.C.:U.S. Government Printing Office, 1972); "Variable Rate Savings: Too Big a Jump for Associations," *Savings and Loan News,* June 1976, p. 50.; Hunt Commission Report, *An Examination of the Restructuring of the Savings and Loan Industry* (Washington, D.C.: U.S. Government Printing Office, 1971); Raymond J. Weiner, "Usury and the Variable Rate Mortgage," *Real Estate Law Journal* (Fall 1976):155,; David L. Cohn and R. Donald Lessard, "Experience with Variable Rate Mortgages: The Case of the United Kingdom" in Federal Reserve Bank of Boston, *New Mortgage Designs for An Inflationary Environment*, Federal Reserve Bank of Boston (January, 1975), p. 187; Mark J. Riedy, "Variable Rate Mortgages: Thus Far, the Prognosis in California is Good," *California Savings and Loan Journal* (May 1976):11,; Mary Alice Hines, "Promising Future Seen for Non-standard Mortgages," *Mortgage Banker* (July 1976):23.
44. See note 43 and Wray O. Candilis, "Mortgage Rate Variability of the Housing Market," *Construction Review* (May 1973):4.; Stanley G. Quackenbush, "Why Not the Variable Rate Mortgage. But What About the Index," *Savings Bank Journal* 53 (October 1972):27; George M. Von Furstenberg, "The Economics of Variable Interest Rate Mortgages," *Federal Home Loan Bank Board Journal* (June 1972):8.; John Wetmore, "Variable Rate Mortgages," *The Mortgage Banker* (March 1971):16.
45. See note 43.
46. Erdevig, p. 7.

Section III:
Conclusions,
Afterword, and
Appendixes

Our analysis of government's role in regulating the housing industry suggests that the primary issue which must be addressed is not whether we need more or less regulation; instead we are confronted with the need to rethink and redirect existing regulatory policies. This chapter summarizes the key cost-increasing aspects of existing government regulations and posits recommendations aimed at reducing this cost burden.

Chapter Twelve: Summaries, Conclusions, and Recommendations

This book is an effort at objective inquiry into the relationship between government regulations and the costs of housing. The book's structure is that of the distanced study; the emphasis is on fact-finding. Yet the structure and tone of this kind of book may lull the reader into forgetting one paramount observation. It is easy to forget that these regulations, the industry regulated, and the money which supports these enterprises are all the result of human actions. People make regulations, people build the houses, and both of these activities are undertaken so that ultimately people will have houses in which to live. But none of these events happens in a vacuum; the regulations have as their intention the insurance that a dwelling will be safe and adequate, while the housing industry wishes to make and sell houses. Certainly these interests are occasionally in conflict, but they are also as certainly not diametrically opposed.

Yet at some moments, in the flush of self-interest, the potential conflict forces the parties to lose sight of their intentions. The people in one camp begin to think of the people in the other camp as enemies who thwart their best interests. And all the auguring trends indicate that the conflict is overwhelming the virtue of these parties' interests and that the cost of housing will continue to outstrip the incomes of the people. It is not true that government regulations are the sole cause of that trend. In the final analysis, the principal problems of the industry, and the cost increases imposed by many government regulations, seem to arise when those who promulgate such

303

rules lose sight of why they are doing what they do and the human environment in which they do them.

Cicero once wrote in his essay on law that: "The good of the people is the chief law." Those who are pursuing the good of the people must think of them in individual terms. To the extent that government regulations militate against the good of the people, those regulations are violating the chief law. To the extent that builders lose sight of the value of their product, they violate that same chief law. What each of these arms of the housing industry can do is to abet the best purposes of the other.

This book has tried to point to the areas in which the government must intervene, and perhaps intervene more forcefully than it does at present, in the housing industry. It has also tried to point out those areas where government regulations are counter-productive to the common good of the people at large. When such regulations drive up the cost of housing, they do more than a disservice to the housing industry. They unnecessarily deprive Americans reasonable access to a reasonable home.

This book began with an observation by Thomas Hobbes. Hobbes' solution to the human condition was to recommend a strong, authoritarian government which would impose control on the greed of the individual. Yet only a century after Hobbes wrote *The Leviathan*, the American Revolution began, founded on a premise, and a solution, diametrically opposed to that of Hobbes. While Hobbes may have been right that an unregulated society makes individual lives "nasty, brutish and short," it is not an autocratic, authoritative government—removed from the lives and needs of the people—which can better those lives. The genuine good of the people must must be the focus of those who serve the people, either as civil servants who make housing policy, or as merchants who provide a necessary, fundamental product for human life.

In each area of housing regulation which we have examined, government intervention was responsible for increasing costs. In some cases it was clear that the magnitude of these cost increases was relatively small, while in other cases it was apparent that a significant increase was created. Although some circumstance or necessity justified the passage of such government regulations, it was the inefficiencies of the administrative processes and sometimes the misuse of this power for illegitimate ends which was responsible for inflating costs.

This chapter provides a summary of the major findings in each of the seven areas of regulations. It also suggests recommendations for reform of the existing regulatory programs, both in terms of increasing their efficiency and reducing their costs.

Many excellent recommendations concerning reform of government regulations been proposed in the past, but have gone unheeded. Ignoring recommendations aimed at making government more efficient was an easy thing to do when the economy was healthy and housing was affordable; but now, when only the well-to-do can afford new housing, we must confront the very real problem of reducing the costs of government regulations.

Building Codes

Several aspects of the building code system were found to be responsible for increasing costs. The administration of the code was found to be un-coordinated and open to the discretion of local building officials. The code itself was found to increase costs by requiring safety and quality features which are in excess of what can reasonably be defended as minimum requirements. Finally, the standard setting process was found to represent inadequately the interest of consumers.

SUMMARY AND RECOMMENDATIONS

The building code administrative process was found to be overly cum-bersome—too many building officials are called upon to make decisions of-ten beyond their technical capabilities. Mandatory training and licensing of building officials is recommended. As state governments increase their con-trol over the contents of codes, they must also assume a stronger role in the personnel practices of local building departments. A statewide program to train public officials and provide periodic refresher courses can most ef-fectively accomplish this goal. More knowledgeable building officials would also facilitate a reduction in the number of different building department members involved in any one project. Finally, by requiring periodic retraining the status quo orientation of building officials would be minimized.

Under the existing system local officials have too much discretion in ac-cepting or rejecting a specific building proposal. We recommend that states establish a review procedure for the appeal of local officials' rulings. As reliance on performance codes increases, local officials will be called on to make a greater number of technical decisions. Builders must be able to im-mediately appeal these judgments to a higher authority, which would also serve as a watchdog over local policies and ensure that decisions were similar across jurisdictions. This state office would also serve as a clearinghouse for recent decisions, technologies, performances, etc.

The existing code change and product approval processes are often based on inadequate technical information and fail to represent properly the housing consumer's interests. We recommend a more active role for the federal government in supporting and conducting the basic research necessary to promulgate standards upon which code requirements are to be based. Both the National Institute of Building Sciences and the National Bureau of Standards should be fully utilized to perform these functions. Code decisions are too often based on information supplied by vested interests, without adequate checks or balances. A centralized approval process must be established with continuous monitoring by a federal agency.

Recent code changes have tended to mandate use of safety items which should remain optional. The need exists for a more conscious articulation of the trade-off between the cost of a code requirement and the safety or permanence it adds to the structure. The word "safety" seems to grant automatically ratification as a code requirement when urged by asserprotected. There is no realistically probable measure to determine the balance between the disaster to be prevented and the cost of the steps required. We do not, however, recommend the requirement of an economic impact statement before a code change could be approved. This would add an unnecessary layer and expense to an already burdensome process. Instead the same goal could be achieved by opening up the code change process and allowing greater involvement by consumer and citizen groups. This would only be effective, however, if government sponsored research provided *unbiased documentation* of the impact of code changes and if code changes were centralized either at the state or model code level.

There is no reason for the existence of thousands of diverse local codes. Unlike most land use controls, which to some extent must be controlled at the local level because of the diversity of conditions, building codes seek only to set a minimum level of safety and quality which should be similar throughout the country, varying only because of climate and geological conditions. While a national code would accomplish this objective, it is neither necessary nor desirable. Instead, the existing system of several model codes offers a superior private sector substitute. The existence of several codes provides options for state and municipal governments. This competition among the model codes ensures that they maintain their currency and provide the services necessary for the code system to operate effectively. But model codes should be adopted by state governments and made mandatory at the local level.

Energy Conservation Regulations

The trend of higher home heating fuel bills and the goal of "energy independence" has mandated the policy of energy conservation. The federal government has recently passed legislation providing significant levels of funding for state and local governments which adopt measures aimed at reducing the fuel consumption of residential units. Most of these programs operate by requiring the installation of energy saving devices at the time of initial construction. These costs must be balanced against the savings from lower fuel bills. While most of the programs are still in their formative stages, several points are clear.

SUMMARY AND RECOMMENDATIONS

More research is required before a nationally accepted energy conservation standard can be adopted. The existing standards promulgated mainly by private trade groups may not serve to optimize the relationship between initial installation costs and fuel savings. Additional research is required which takes into account not only the changes in fuel consumption, but also the changes in consumer income over the life of his or her ownership. In addition, any standard must be flexible enough to respond to widely varying prices in fuel and insulation and to changes in technology.

If we are to achieve the goal of reduced energy consumption by residential units, some form of financial incentive to housing consumers will be necessary. Several important factors undermine consumer acceptance of higher initial costs for energy-saving devices. Mortgage qualification criteria based on the relationship of current income to selling price favors the unit with the lowest selling price. The income of those who purchase homes usually increases during their tenure in that unit so they are better able to afford higher occupancy costs. For these reasons, from the standpoint of the consumer, a less expensive, though less energy-efficient unit may be the most rational choice. To overcome this logic, it is necessary for government to offer some financial incentive to tilt the balance in favor of energy conservation. While federal programs aimed at this objective have been funded, it is important that they filter down to the state and local level. The possibility of providing the incentive directly to the home builder rather than to the consumer should also be investigated.

Subdivision Controls

Subdivision regulations represent the area in which, over the past decade, costs have most increased. Not coincidentally, it is also the area which is most highly regulated by government policies. The primary reasons for the creation of unnecessary costs are the lack of standards upon which to base subdivision requirements, the complexity of the regulation maze encountered before development can begin, and the tendency to burden the developer with providing facilities that had in the past always been the responsibility of the municipality. Above all, the length and therefore the costs of the subdivision process were found to have increased markedly.

SUMMARY AND RECOMMENDATIONS

The subdivision approval process has increased considerably in its complexity: the number of applications demanded, the number of agencies involved, and the number of approvals required have all rapidly expanded. We recommend a streamlined approval process. One local office should be responsible for coordinating public review and approval of the application. The existing system in which a developer's plans are passed from office to office for comment results in considerable duplication and delay. All too frequently a change required at the end of the process necessitates that the developer begin all over again with the revised plans. The existing system is too inflexible given the length of the process and the changing nature of the housing market. Developers should be permitted minor changes in initial plans without having to seek a host of new approvals. The burden should be shifted to the municipality to show that the new plans differ substantively from those agreed on.

The use of negotiated agreements as to subdivision requirements has been used as a device to extort excessive improvements from the developer. We recommend the use of negotiation only for those categories for which accepted standards exist. The current situation is such that a developer is forced to accept whatever is demanded because the alternative—a legal challenge—has little chance of success unless the courts have an accepted standard upon which to base their decision. Moreover, the costs involved in a legal challenge are minimal to the municipality, but quite significant (often more than the costs of the improvements) to the developer. Legislation permitting the use of negotiation should be drawn in such a manner as to encompass the applicable standards and to state reasons for allowing any departure from them.

Subdivision improvement requirements are determined primarily by local officials and bear very little relationship to minimum health and safety safeguards, and therefore unnecessarily drive up the cost of housing. As suggested in the previous recommendation, the need for standards upon which land improvement requirements can be evaluated are an essential ingredient to minimize cost-inflating practices of local governments and to allow the use of more flexible control mechanisms. Properly drawn standards would also allow for greater innovation in design, without the now prevalent fear that such a proposal will be unfavorably reviewed by the public body. Most important, a greater reliance on standards would act as a safeguard against excessive requirements by local officials.

Subdivision requirements are increasingly being used as a device to shift what once were considered public costs to the shoulders of the developer. There is a pressing need to identify an equitable manner for allocating the costs of new development between the municipality and the new resident. In cases where requirements are in excess of those facilities and services needed specifically by the new residents the answer is clearly that such a requirement is illegal. But the ability to measure use, to predict future demand, and to allocate these costs is currently very limited. Underlying any scheme to allocate costs is the very real issue of balancing both the costs and revenues to a community of new development. Should cost-revenue analysis be permitted as a reason to deny permission to develop? In particular, the spread of land and school dedication requirements should be carefully scrutinized to determine if they are exceeding the bounds of permissable subdivision regulations.

Zoning Regulations

Zoning regulations, which originally were used to separate incompatible uses, have since expanded to include control of specifications of the dwelling unit and even the character of the community. While the most blatant of exclusionary zoning practices have come under assault in the courts, many less obvious techniques are being employed with increasing frequency by local governments seeking to maintain the fiscal and social well-being of their communities. All too frequently the target of these policies is the exclusion of moderately priced housing.

SUMMARY AND RECOMMENDATIONS

Zoning regulations frequently include provisions which severely limit the construction of moderately priced housing. By working within such restrictions as undermapping for high density and multifamily dwelling units and by following ordinances which require excessive frontage, lot size, and house size, a developer is left with no alternative but to build housing for upper income families. There is no set standard for evaluating whether a community's requirements are excessive. To a certain extent large lots, wide frontage, and the other restrictions can be justified. But when a community makes little or no allowance for the construction of moderately priced units, the acceptability of that ordinance must be questioned.

In particular, the exclusion of mobile homes has severly limited the affordable housing options of consumers. The most widely used exclusionary practice is either the outright prohibition or severe limitations on the use of mobile homes. This type of dwelling is shunned for many reasons: it allegedly pays less than its fair share of taxes, attracts an undesirable element to the community, and is aesthetically obtrusive. Yet the banning of mobile homes is clearly an unacceptable solution to the problems they create. The taxing structure could be altered and site design improved. As the gap between conventional housing and mobile homes increases, the latter will increasingly become a very real option for low- and middle-income families.

Zoning variances are increasingly being used by municipalities as a bargaining device aimed at increasing their control over the character of new development. Municipalities frequently zone an inordinate amount of land as a "holding zone" and thereby require anyone seeking to develop that parcel to obtain a variance. In return for approval of the variance, conditions and delays often significantly increase the costs of the development. In a similar fashion, the new flexible zoning techniques also use the negotiation process to increase the cost of housing,, particularly planned unit developments. With an improved master plan and allied zoning ordinance, the need for variances should be reduced.

Zoning ordinances are frequently administered by elected officials who are more attuned to political than planning objectives. While the initial adoption of a zoning ordinance belongs in the political arena, administering a zoning ordinance is a task for a competent professional staff removed from the pressures of the political process. This office would provide for greater continuity between different administrations and generally depoliticize the planning process.

Growth Controls

Our analysis of growth controls has shown that instead of achieving positive planning goals many of these devices are being used to limit new development, particularly the construction of moderately priced housing. In fact, in practice many of these ordinances had a negative effect on development patterns, often contributing to suburban sprawl. Most are adopted with the limited notion of restricting growth without consideration for possible corollary effects. The impact of these ordinances was experienced both in the community itself, where development was restricted, and in surrounding areas which were forced to assume the additional development pressure.

SUMMARY AND RECOMMENDATIONS

The use of growth control techniques should be limited to those situations in which positive planning objectives are being sought or a particular crisis must be confronted. Ordinances such as population and building permit limitations are used specifically to restrict development frequently without any justification other than the desires of the public officials or residents. Other techniques such as adequate public facilities ordinances link population growth to the ability of the municipality to provide the necessary services and therefore do perform a useful function. A third technique, urban service areas, acts to redirect growth without limiting it in any way. The adoption of a particular type of ordinance will depend on the specific circumstances involved, but what must be emphasized is that only in those situations where a particular crisis exists (inadequate sewerage facilities, schools, etc.) should a *growth restriction* ordinance be acceptable and only if positive steps are being taken to remedy the existing problem.

Growth control ordinances, by limiting the amount of developable land, drives up the price of those lots on which construction is permitted. Regardless of the specific type of growth control ordinance, all share in common a restriction on the amount of developable land. This necessarily places a premium on those remaining parcels which are developable, and higher land costs will ultimately result in a more expensive structure and the exclusion of moderately priced dwelling units. A properly drafted growth control ordinance should, where possible, include provisions for allowing a greater supply of developable land than current demand would require. This would prevent land value from becoming artifically inflated.

The cost impact of growth controls is felt more by the surrounding communities than by the municipality adopting the control measure. Growth controls, often adopted in the face of strong development pressures, have the effect of shifting this demand to the surrounding region. While it is an effective method for one municipality to avoid the consequences of growth, it can do this only at the expense of neighboring towns, who then must face overburdened facilities and highly inflated land values. Thus any evaluation of a growth control ordinance must include not only its effect on one community, but also its attendant regional consequences.

Growth controls have given local officials a potent weapon to negotiate and extort changes in development plans which most often increase the cost of housing. By adding a special permit requirement to the existing zoning and subdivision regulations, local officials have significantly increased their control over the make-up and costs of what gets built in their community. By requiring that a developer provide services which traditionally have been supplied by the municipality, the costs to the community are reduced, while at the same time the costs to the housing consumer are increased. In addition, the nonpublic facilities considerations (aesthetic design, etc.) often incorporated into development approval criteria are subject to considerable abuse by officials. Limits must be placed on what is a valid consideration within the scope of protecting a community's health, safety, and welfare.

Environmental Regulations

Of all government regulation, environmental controls have created the most conflict, and the intensity of this debate can be expected to increase in the future. Few would argue that development should be undertaken in such a way as to wantonly destroy the physical environment. But all too often, particularly at the local level, environmental concerns are being used as a guise for excluding undesired growth. The primary mechanism used to ensure the consideration of the effect of development on the environment is the environmental impact statement (EIS). Much of our analysis examined both its current uses and abuses.

SUMMARY AND RECOMMENDATIONS

Environmental impact review has frequently been amended to the regulatory approval process in such a way as to significantly delay construction and increase costs. We recommend restructuring the review process so that environmental approval is considered coterminously with other land use approvals. The existing system, whereby an environmental impact statement is filed only after other approvals have been obtained, necessarily prolongs the final signal to develop and is particularly troublesome when environmentally sensitive changes are required. By approaching both planning and environmental review bodies at the same time, an agreement can more readily be reached as to the final development plans acceptable to all parties.

The environmental impact statement is in many ways ineffective and, above all, without any general planning content. Much is lost by considering only the impact of one project on an area without thought to the surrounding area's development potential. An environmental baseline identifying the physical resources and land uses of an area is essential to all environmental impact statements. Going one step further, only if an assessment is reviewed within the context of a broader land use/environmental plan can a decision be meaningful. Thus we recommend that the review agency perform two additional functions aimed at making the regulatory system more effective. It should provide the baseline data for each analysis and also should evaluate the proposal in terms of a comprehensive plan.

Environmental impact statements are often quite expensive and very lengthy, yet tell very little about the effect of the proposed development. We recommend two basic reforms in the content of an environmental impact statement. First, the ability to forecast the actual impact must be improved. To date the state of the art has advanced very little. Much of what is contained in an EIS is fantasy rather than fact. It is time for increased scientific examination of the question. Second, impact statements must not be limited only to the projected environmental degradation attributable to the project. If we are to protect the environment in the absolute sense, little would ever be built. It is important that the magnitude of the projected damage be weighed against the benefits of the project and that both be placed in the context of the local and regional setting.

Environmental review is currently used as a means to require changes in plan design which often result in excluding moderately priced housing. Because the review process is such an inexact science, local governments are increasingly citing environmental factors as the reason for denying approval to develop. Or they require such changes in the original plans as a reduction in density or increased land dedicating, which has the effect of driving up the cost of what is finally built. Assessment of these requirements should not be done on an individual project-by-project basis, but rather within the context of a plan for the entire region. Moreover, only those requirements directly related to environmental impact should be permitted in order to obtain permission to develop.

Settlement and Financing Regulations

These two categories of regulation are potentially significant cost-reducing areas for reform of government policies. Settlement costs, now often exceeding $4,000 per unit, must be paid at the time of purchase, a time when additional funds are least available to those entering the single-family housing market. In addition, the procedures involved in this initial stage of purchasing a home take place in an atmosphere of confusion and frustration to the housebuyer, who having found a desirable and affordable house, is is now confronted with one last, often unexpected, financial obstacle.

Regulations affecting the financing of a home purchase are the most important determinants of monthly housing costs and therefore significantly affect the number of families able to afford housing. While to a considerable extent, a mortgage's interest rate is determined by policies beyond the scope of this report, e.g., the money supply, rate of inflation, etc., there does exist a significant number of regulations specifically affecting the terms of the mortgage instrument which are potential areas for cost-saving reform. Usury restrictions, FHA processing requirements, and increased flexibility in repaying mortgages were discussed in detail as areas in which changes in existing regulations could result in increased housing opportunities.

SUMMARY AND RECOMMENDATIONS

The settlement process should be streamlined and its legal complexities reduced. Competition should be increased among the title insurance companies, realtors, and lawyers to eliminate excessive fees and questionable practices. The settlement process as it now exists in many states is an historical relic. Laws regulating title have resisted modernization for centuries. A computerized title system, or alternatively a system less burdened by antiquated common law notions of title, would facilitate a speedier and less costly transfer of ownership. A second area of needed reform involves the often excessively high fees charged by the professional groups (realtors, lawyers, title insurance companies, etc.) who are active participants in the settlement process. Government regulation, in particular a workable variant of the Real Estate Settlement Procedures Act is essential to protect consumers from the monopolistic tendencies of these groups.

The future role of the Federal Housing Administration (FHA) must be reconsidered especially in terms of the groups it should serve. The FHA performed an extraordinary service to the public in the 1930s through its insurance, which facilitated a major reform of the mortgage instrument. But its role has now substantially been taken over by private mortgage insurance companies. Has the time now come for the FHA to set out in new directions and once again provide the impetus for satisfying the housing needs of the country? FHA programs to spur development in "grey" areas or to facilitate the acceptance of flexible mortgage instruments are just two such possibilities for future FHA development.

Usury restrictions disrupt the operations of the free market flow of capital for mortgages and by artificially placing a ceiling on interest rates, they severely restrict the supply of mortgage money. The trend toward relaxing and eliminating usury restrictions should be encouraged. Usury restrictions have been ineffective in reducing the interest rate charged on loans and numerous methods to circumvent these restriction are commonplace. But these restrictions place mortgages at a competitive disadvantage to other forms of investment. If lower than market mortgage interest rates are the primary goal of government action, then a direct subsidy rather than a restriction on the market would be a more effective and ultimately less costly policy. *The fixed rate program which is the predominant mortgage instrument, limits the number of families able to purchase homes, while also being an unattractive investment vehicle for lenders.* By altering the loan repayment schedule, or by allowing lenders to share in an appreciation of the property, it may be possible for more consumers to enter the housing market and to make mortgages a more attractive form of investment. What should be emphasized here is the need for increased flexibility in the mortgage instrument. Consumers' current and future financial resources will vary, as will the portfolio objectives of lenders. It is crucial for the mortgage instrument to be capable of adapting to these needs and therefore remain competitive with alternative investments.

Afterword — A Guide to Cost Conversion*

Kristina Ford

Introduction

Americans are finding it increasingly difficult to afford a single-family home. The most recent testimony to this difficulty was the report that the median price for new single-family residences is now $50,000, a price that only a small part of the nation's families can afford. Clearly, inflation is one principal source of the increase in costs. Had the median priced house of $23,000 in 1970 suffered an annual 6 percent inflation rate since then, it would now be priced at nearly $35,000. The interesting issue is the source of the unexplained increase of $15,000 above the inflated price. The study reported in this book has documented and analyzed the full range of government regulations affecting housing production and has detailed the adverse and beneficial effects of the various statutes and rules. This Afterword will consider the relationship of these controls to the construction and occupancy of a residence and will also specify the cost to the housing consumer of governmental over-regulation. A strict definition of over-regulation is employed here: *those forms or variations of governmentally imposed controls which exceed minimum health, safety, and welfare considerations in the provision of housing.*

---

*It should be noted in reading this Afterword that the author of this volume did not participate in its preparation and that the presentation is solely the work of Professor Ford.

317

The information which follows is organized according to costs imposed by governmental regulation during the sequence of development, construction, and occupancy of a house. The controls pertaining to each stage are shown in Exhibit 1. For each stipulation of these controls, excess regulation is defined and the resulting excess cost is calculated for a hypothetical single-family home

In addition, a cost conversion guide is provided (Exhibit 15) which gives an overview of the entire process and enables the calculation procedure to be extended to other sizes and configurations of single-family dwellings. Thus, this Afterword will provide the reader with a definition of over-regulation in a specific area, a gauge of the excess costs included in the price of a single-family home built in a hypothetical municipality with one set of regulations, and a way to calculate excess costs for houses built in municipalities using different assortments of controls.

Two points should be emphasized. The first is that the definition used for excessive costs is a severe one that admits as necessary only minimal standards for health and safety. The second is that a particular development may not be affected simultaneously by as many development controls as are shown affecting the property used as an example here. Both of these factors contribute to a total cost associated with excessive governmental regulation which may be overstated. Therefore, the reader must keep in mind the severity of the test being applied to determine excessive costs, and the effect that this severe test has on the apparent size of these costs.

EXHIBIT 1

GOVERNMENT REGULATIONS THAT AFFECT HOUSING COST

Development Stage	Construction Stage	Occupancy Stage
Zoning Ordinances (restrictions on use of land; minimum lot size/frontage)	Zoning Ordinances (minimum building size)	Financing and Settlement Regulations
Environmental Controls	Energy Conservation Requirements	
Growth Controls	Building Codes	
Subdivision Requirements		

Basic Assumptions

The statistical information presented in this summary is derived entirely from the tables and discussions in the main body of this report. The cost of land is assumed to be $16,000 per acre; mortgages for both land and structures are self-amortizing, featuring 20 percent down payment, thirty-year term, and 9 percent interest. Property tax and insurance costs are assumed to be 2.5 and 0.4 percent of market value, respectively. When opportunity costs are employed, they are computed at a conservative rate of 5.5 percent return on equity for alternative investments. Each of these figures represents approximate national averages at the time of the study.

To make the cost conversion guide more versatile, elementary arithmetic operations have been used to standardize figures offered in the test to three lot sizes and three structure sizes. These represent the array of choices available to the typical house buyer (one-quarter, one-half, and one acre lots; two-, three-, and four-bedroom houses). When necessary, costs of over-regulation derived from empirical studies have been inflated to 1977 according to annual rates specified by the Consumer Price Index. The single-family home that will be used as an example to demonstrate the excess cost computation procedure is a detached three-bedroom unit on a one-half acre lot, with a market value of $50,000.

Development Stage

The controls affecting housing cost during the *development stage* are:

1. *Zoning ordinances* which govern the type and intensity of development.
2. *Environmental controls* which protect natural areas from detrimental development
3. *Growth controls* which govern the pace and mix of development
4. *Subdivision regulations* which determine the level of public infrastructure which must accompany development

The following sections detail the costs to the housing consumer as a result of government over-regulation in these provinces of control.

In employing the cost conversion guide for development costs, the user chooses from three lot sizes. He begins by circling the lot size of the property for which it is desired to calculate excess costs (in the hypothetical example, the one-half acre column is used), and proceeds through Steps I-IV of the guide. Each step involves an arithmetic operation which tallies the cost due to a particular form of over-regulation. This cost is entered in the excess cost column at the extreme right of the page. (See Exhibit 15 for the format and organization of the guide.)

ZONING REGULATIONS

Zoning ordinances which were originally used to separate incompatible uses now are often used to mandate specifications for individual dwelling units and even to control the character of a community. While the most blatant of exclusionary zoning practices have come under courtroom assault, many less obvious techniques are sometimes employed by a local government to maintain the fiscal and social character of the community. These policies can lead to local unavailability of moderately priced housing.

Zoning regulations affect the development phase, first by specifying the use to which the land may be put, and second by stating the minimum area upon which this use may be developed. Both of these aspects of zoning ordinances can create excessive costs.

It is obvious that outdated specifications for the allowed use of land create costs to the holder of such land when these specifications must be changed, although it is less clear that these costs are unnecessary. For instance, suppose that current zoning does not accurately specify highest order or best use of a hypothetical land parcel. On the one hand, the developer knew the use restrictions when he bought the parcel, and it is arguable that he paid a reduced price for the land because of its assigned lower order use. Using this line of reasoning, it could be concluded that delay caused by changing the existing zoning or by obtaining a variance is *not* excessive, but rather is a necessary cost which will result in higher land value. It could also be argued, however, that if a municipality has not recently reviewed and changed its zoning either in light of increased population and housing demand, or in light of hardship to an individual property owner, then any delay caused by rezoning or a variance is unnecessary.

A compromise position will be employed here. National experience indicates that the average length of time necessary to obtain a rezoning is four months; to obtain a variance, two months. These periods will be considered necessary, while longer time periods will be defined as excessive. The holding costs associated with delay (interest, property tax, and opportunity cost) are shown in Exhibit 2.

To compute the excess cost from rezoning, the user of the cost conversion guide should enter the length of the delay under Step I.A. (Zoning Alterations) and subtract the normal time for either rezoning or variance from the time that the procedure actually consumed. The resulting figure is is multiplied by the monthly carrying cost of the land, and the product is the excessive cost of delay to be carried to the excess cost column.

In the example (a $50,000 three-bedroom home, half-acre lot), it will be assumed that the owner held property which had to be rezoned before development could commence, and that a zoning change was granted nine

EXHIBIT 2

COSTS OF DELAY: LAND HOLDING

	Lot Size		
	1/4 Acre	1/2 Acre	1 Acre
Interest on Mortgage	$26/month	$52/month	$103/month
Property Taxes	8/month	17/month	33/month
Opportunity cost	4/month	8/month	15/month
Total Cost of Delay	$38/month	$77/month	$151/month

months after the initial request. In this case, the excess cost is 9 months minus 4 months × $77, or $385.

In addition to procedural delays, specifications of the zoning ordinance for minimum lot area can also occasion excessive costs. There is considerable argument in the literature whether these specifications for minimum lot sizes by themselves significantly affect local housing costs. Limited empirical evidence suggests the large minimum lot sizes with accompanying minimum frontage requirements, when standardized for location of the parcel, type of community, and value of other properties within the community, do indeed *increase cost,* although not in direct proportion to increases in parcel size. The lack of a direct relationship results from each developable lot, large or small, being nothing more than a place to build *one* structure. Although there is some aesthetic benefit from size of property, large parcels of land zoned for single-family residence offer no more than a single building permission and therefore do not increase in price to the extent they would if more than one structure were to be erected. In addition, the lower price of the small lot may result in increase market demand, further narrowing the price difference between the small and the large lot.

Following empirical evidence reported in Chapter Eight, it will be assumed that if the minimum lot size in a municipality is one-quarter acre or less, there is no part of the lot purchase price which may be assigned to confiscatory lot-size requirements. Lot-size minimums above this, however, create additional costs to the consumer that will be assigned at a rate of 10 percent for a half-acre minimum and 30 percent for a minimum of one acre.

To use the cost conversion guide, Step I.B, the local minimum lot size and the price of the lot is entered in the appropriate column. If the minimum is one acre, 30 percent of the price of the land is defined as unnecessary, and should be entered as an excess cost to the consumer. For example, if the price of land is $16,000 per acre, and one-acre lots are required, $4,800 of the price would be excessive due to what has been defined as over-regulation. If one-half acre lots are required, 10 percent of the price would be assignable as cost due to excessive regulation. The house used as an example was built on a one-half acre lot, which was the minimum lot size required by the municipality. Assuming that the land was $8,000 for a half acre, the excess cost is 10 percent of this, or $800.

GROWTH CONTROLS

Growth controls limit, schedule, or channel new population according to the capacity of necessary public services or according to a desired maximum community size. These regulations are sewer or building moratoria, population caps, capital facilities schedules, etc. The original intent of growth controls was to pace and channel, not to slow, development within a community. However, some commentators have noted that such controls may be enacted solely for the latter purpose. The primary impact of these controls is increased land cost in areas proximate to the municipality with such controls. However, there is also a cost to a developer holding land in a growth-controlled municipality — the cost of owning the land but not being able to improve it. While there is a benefit to controlling both the tempo and sequence of development, any delay or holding time caused by these regulations which exceeds one year — a time period sufficient for a municipality to plan and budget for development in accord with an assessment of its facilities — will be considered excessive.

In order to compute the delay associated with growth controls, the user goes to the cost conversion guide, Step II (Growth Controls) and subtracts one year (12 months) from the total delay due to growth controls encountered by the land holder. The difference in months, multiplied by the cost of delay found in Exhibit 2, is the cost of over-regulation. For the one-half acre, $50,000 single-family home built in a growth-controlled community, growth controls delayed development by eighteen months, and this delay was not concurrent with any other delay. By subtracting the delay not considered excessive, it is determined that the cost of excessive growth control delay is (18 months minus 12 months) × $77 per month, or $462.

ENVIRONMENTAL CONTROLS AND
SUBDIVISION PROCESSING

These controls require environmental impact statements from developers so that the governing body can review the effect of development on the physical environment. However, the review of these statements of impact can be appended to the regulatory approval process in such a way as to significantly delay housing construction, thereby increasing consumer costs. For example, the body reviewing the impact statement may not allow any other regulatory agencies to review a proposal for development until it has approved the request. This can add appreciably to the length of time necessary to get a development started.

Furthermore, environmental impact statements are in many ways ineffective and frequently ignore the most basic planning concepts. For instance, a natural resource inventory to identify the physical resources and land uses of an area is essential to all environmental impact statements, but is infrequently a part of any. In this way, environmental impact statements often fail to reveal the real effects of the proposed development.

Even with the weaknesses just discussed, these controls have sometimes provided a significant benefit by preventing egregious errors. Therefore, the costs of preparing an environmental impact statement and of compliance are considered *necessary* costs. However, unnecessary delays due to uncertain reviewers and inefficient administration cause costs which are herein defined as *excessive*.

Most state coastal zone program administrators are attempting to make their project reviews concurrent with local subdivision processing procedures. If concurrent review can be achieved at this level, certainly it can be achieved by local administrators. Therefore, any addition to the average subdivision processing time of six months (Exhibit 7-IV) is considered unnecessary delay.

For the single-family home being used as an example, the environmental review procedure of the State Coastal Zone Program took six months and was the only environmental review required. Since it started three months after subdivision review, total processing time for the two requirements was nine months. Going to the cost conversion guide at Step III (Environmental Controls and Subdivision Processing), the user lists the total processing time for subdivision and environmental requirements (in the example it was 9 months), subtracts 6 months and multiplies the result by the monthly cost of delay shown under the appropriate lot size (in the example it is $77). The product is the excess cost associated with compliance with environmental controls. For the example considered in this summary, the excess cost is (9 months minus 6 months) × $77, or $231.

SUBDIVISION REQUIREMENTS

Subdivision improvement requirements are determined primarily by local officials and can bear very little relationship to minimum health and safety standards for development. If this is the case, they can unnecessarily drive up the cost of housing.

Among the many demands on a developer made by subdivision ordinances, prohibitions against burning vegetation to clear land is of significance. When burning is not allowed, bulldozing and hauling must be used, at substantial increased cost to local developers. There are air quality impacts of moderate consequence as a result of allowing open burning on a large scale. However, the local air quality in suburban areas is affected more by *ambient* air of more populated or industrialized locations than by pollution caused by local vegetation burning. Therefore, in the interest of providing housing at the lowest possible cost, impacts on air quality due to regulation of burning will be ignored, and the costs attendant to bulldozing and hauling vegetation that exceed the costs incurred by burning will be called excessive. These costs, compiled from a national survey of developers, are shown in Exhibit 3.

EXHIBIT 3

LAND CLEARING COSTS

	1/4 Acre	1/2 Acre	1 Acre
Burning allowed	$110	$ 220	$ 442
Burning prohibited	663	1,325	2,650
Excess Cost	$553	$1,105	$2,208

The single-family home used as an example is assumed to have been developed in a community which had an ordinance prohibiting vegetation burning. Using the cost compilation guide, Step IV.A (Subdivision Controls—Vegetation Burning), the user assigns the net cost of clearing vegetation by means other than burning as excess cost associated with the municipality's controls. For the one-half acre site in the example, the assignable excess costs were $1,105.

Another cause of excess costs due to subdivision regulation is the lot width requirement and the excessive amount of street frontage it necessitates. Excessive frontage causes almost direct linear cost increases in the provision of six municipal improvements: sanitary sewers, storm drainage systems, water distribution pipes, curbs and gutters, sidewalks, and street pavement. It is difficult to define excessive lot widths, and there are few recognized standards. Exhibit 4 shows a single lot width and a range of costs associated with each of three lot-size categories. The lot width shown is the breakpoint associated with average frontage requirements for various categories of lot size (see Chapter Seven). It further displays the different improvement costs required by each lot size. Excessive costs are defined as the difference between improvement costs above and below the breakpoint.

EXHIBIT 4

STREET FRONTAGE-RELATED IMPROVEMENTS

	1/4 Acre Lot Width	Cost	1/2 Acre Lot Width	Cost	1 Acre Lot Width	Cost
1. Sanitary Sewers	>80'	$ 697	>90'	$ 848	>125'	$1,375
	≤80'	564	≤90'	685	≤125'	1,047
Excess Cost		$ 133		$ 163		$ 328
2. Storm Drainage	>80'	$ 657	>90'	$ 800	>125'	$1,298
Pipes	≤80'	531	≤90'	646	≤125'	988
Excess Cost		$ 126		$ 154		$ 310
3. Water Distri-	>80'	$ 709	>90'	$ 864	>125'	$1,401
bution System	≤80'	574	≤90'	698	≤125'	1,066
Excess Cost		$ 135		$ 166		$ 335
4. Curbs and	>80'	$ 230	>90'	$ 280	>125'	$ 454
Gutters	≤80'	187	≤90'	226	≤125'	346
Excess Cost		$ 43		$ 54		$ 108
5. Sidewalks	>80'	$ 181	>90'	$ 220	>125'	$ 357
	≤80'	146	≤90'	178	≤125'	272
Excess Cost		$ 35		$ 42		$ 85
6. Pavement (30'	>80'	$1,655	>90'	$2,016	>125'	$3,270
wide)	≤80'	1,340	≤90'	1,629	≤125'	2,489
Excess Cost		$ 315		$ 387		$ 781

NOTE: All numbers extrapolated from Exhibits 7.20 and 7.21 (Chapter 7).

Employing the cost conversion guide, the required lot width is circled under the appropriate lot-size column. If the smaller lot width is circled, there are no excess costs and the user proceeds to Step IV.C. If the larger lot width is circled, the user will have excess costs for each of the six improvements listed in Step IV.B that are required by the local ordinance. For each necessary improvement, the cost shown in the appropriate lot-size column is selected and entered in the excess cost column. For the house in the example, the municipality required a lot width of 100 feet and required that sanitary sewers, a storm drainage system, a water distribution system, curbs and gutters, sidewalks, and pavement on local streets be provided by the developer. Since the frontage requirement of 100 feet is above the break-

point and therefore requires greater improvement costs, the excessive costs
shown on the cost conversion guide pertain. They are:

Sanitary Sewers	$163
Storm Drainage System	154
Water Distribution System	166
Curbs and Gutters	54
Sidewalks	42
Pavement on Local Streets	387
Total	$966

A third cause of excessive costs from subdivision regulations is unnecessary design or dedication requirements. For example, some suburban
muncipalities require utility lines to be underground, a specification arising
solely from aesthetic considerations. As developed in Chapter Seven, excessive costs for this and five other design requirements are defined as
follows:

1. In nonurban areas, all costs of subsurface electric/phone utility services
2. The cost of sewer pipes the diameter of which exceeds the adequate 6-inch
   standard
3. The cost of sidewalks over and above that required for a single side of the
   street
4. All landscaping costs other than those necessary to inhibit run-off
5. The cost of pavement widths in excess of thirty feet, or rights-of-way in excess of fifty feet
6. Expenses related to dedication of acreage or in-lieu fees

Exhibit 5 lists each of these excessive design requirements and the cost each
necessitates.

Step IV.C (Subdivision Requirements) of the cost conversion guide
shows the costs attendant to the above six design specifications. The single-
family home used as an example was developed in a locale which required
underground electric utilities, excessive landscaping (trees), 10-inch sanitary
pipes, sidewalks on both sides of the street, pavement widths of thirty-five
feet (lot size greater than 100 feet), and land dedication at the rate of two
acres for every 250 houses.

The user of the cost conversion guide goes to Step IV.C and selects the
excess cost for each required design improvement for the appropriate lot
size. They are as follows for the hypothetical example:

Underground Utilities	$273
Ten-inch Sanitary Sewer	21
Dual Sidewalks	110
Excess Landscaping	179
Thirty-five-foot Pavement Width	335[a]
Land Dedication	128

Note: a. If both excess pavement width and rights-of-way are required, the user should tabulate excess costs for only the latter. Since the bulk of these costs is land costs and the paved roadway falls within the right-of-way if the same land within each is counted as excess this constitutes a doubling of cost.

Each of these is entered in the excess cost column. A total of $1,046 is thus assignable as excess design costs.

A final source of excessive costs from subdivision regulations is required block length. Short blocks consume more land and require greater road surface, thereby decreasing the amount of land available for the construction of dwelling units and increasing the cost of road building. Among the several sources of standards for design specifications in developing communities, the recurring standard for block length is 1,200 feet for the average suburban subdivision. Block lengths shorter than this dimension

EXHIBIT 5

EXCESSIVE DESIGN REQUIREMENTS

Excessive Requirement	1/4 Acre Excessive Cost		1/2 Acre Excessive Cost		1 Acre Excessive Cost	
1. Underground Utilities	$225		$273		$417	
2. 8″ or 10″ Sanitary Sewer Pipe instead of 6″	$ 18		$ 21		$ 33	
3. Sidewalks on two rather than one side of street	Lot Size ≤80′ >80′	$ 73 $ 91	Lot Size ≤90′ >90′	$ 89 $110	Lot Size ≤125′ >125′	$136 $179
4. Excess Landscaping	$119		$179		$357	
5. Pavement >30′ and/or right-of-way >50′	≤80′ >80′	$ 45 $ 55	≤90′ >90′	$ 54 $ 67	≤125′ >125′	$ 83 $109
	(per additional foot over 30′ and 50′, respectively)					
6. Land dedication or in-lieu fees[1]	$128		$128		$128	

NOTE: 1. 2 acres required per 250 houses.

SOURCE: Extrapolation of Exhibits 7.23 and 4.3.

will be considered as contributing to excessive development costs. Once again, costs vary with lot width. These costs are detailed in Exhibit 6.

EXHIBIT 6

EXCESSIVE COSTS RELATED TO BLOCK LENGTH

Block Length	1/4 Acre		1/2 Acre		1 Acre	
	Lot Width	Excessive Cost	Lot Width	Excessive Cost	Lot Width	Excessive Cost
1,200'		$ 0		$ 0		$ 0
1,000'	≤80'	$ 87	≤90'	$ 92	≤125'	$120
	>80'	$109	>90'	$120	>125'	$172
800'	≤80'	$181	≤90'	$181	≤125'	$248
	>80'	$220	>90'	$248	>125'	$398
700'	≤80'	$278	≤90'	$309	≤125'	$397
	>80'	$347	>90'	$397	>125'	$617
600'	≤80'	$315	≤90'	$354	≤125'	$472
	>80'	$404	>90'	$472	>125'	$708

SOURCE: Exhibit 7.16. In that exhibit, figures were given for 60' x 125' lots. The figures in this exhibit were determined by apportioning excess costs to the lot widths used throughout the summary.

The community in which the house used as an example was constructed required blocks to be 1,000 feet long. Going to the cost conversion guide, Step IV.D, the user finds an excess cost of $120 for a one-half acre lot with a frontage of 100 feet. This is the excessive cost of short blocks.

EXCESSIVE COSTS RELATED TO
THE DEVELOPMENT STAGE

Exhibit 7 details the excess costs associated with over-regulation during the development phase of homebuilding. The extra costs for the hypothetical problem are more than $5,000 or 50 percent of the expenditures on housing during the development phase — assuming development costs constitute 20 percent of total housing costs (.20 × $50,000 = $10,000; $5,000/$10,000 = 50%. Clearly, the main culprits in this example are the several subdivision requirements which together represent nearly 65 percent of the excess costs associated with development. Within subdivision

EXHIBIT 7

EXCESS COSTS RELATED TO THE DEVELOPMENT STAGE

(for the example home)

I.	Zoning: Total	$1,185	
	A. Rezoning		$ 385
	B. Minimum Lot Size		800
II.	Growth Controls	462	
III.	Environmental Review/ Subdivision Processing	231	
IV.	Subdivision Requirements: Total	3,237	
	A. Vegetation Prohibition		$1,105
	B. Lot Width/Frontage		966
	C. Design and Dedication		1,046
	D. Block Length		120
	TOTAL	$5,115	

regulations, the largest contributors are bulldozing/hauling to replace vegetation burning ($1,105), and design and dedication requirements ($1,046).

Having discussed the costs of over-regulation associated with the development phase, a similar approach will be used for construction costs.

Construction Stage

Government controls which affect the price of housing during the *construction* phase are:

1. *Building codes* which specify minimum standards for various materials used in erecting a house
2. *Energy conservation regulations* which require improvements to reduce the amount of fuel and electricity necessary to occupy the house
3. *Zoning ordinances* which require minimum floor areas or building size

The following sections delineate the costs that result from the unnecessary aspects of these controls. In the cost conversion guide for the construction stage, the number of bedrooms is a surrogate for alternative house sizes and all tables are presented using this dimension. (In the previous section on development costs, tables were present using acreage as a gauge of size variation.) Information pertaining to the hypothetical single-family home will be found under the three-bedroom column.

Building Codes

Several aspects of the building code system are responsible for increasing local housing costs. In many cases the administration of the code is uncoordinated and enforcement is at the discretion of local building officials. The code itself may require safety and quality features which are in excess of what can reasonably be defended as minimum requirements.

There is a large body of literature which lists excessive requirements associated with construction of the structural frame and provision of interior systems (i.e., electrical or plumbing) for a residential structure. Exhibit 8 summarizes the improvements which have recurringly been deemed as "nice but not necessary" by researchers, a designation confirmed by national safety organizations. If these improvements are found in local regulations, they will be considered to cause excessive costs. The types of improvements which fall into this category are smoke detectors, copper wiring, iron pipe, stud-grade framing lumber, ground fault interruptors, etc. While these provide qualitative assets to the housing shell, they are unnecessary when the sole consideration is minimum safety standards and base price of shelter.

To use the cost conversion guide, the user goes to Step V (Building Codes), and for any item which is required by the local building code, enters the cost shown for the appropriate house size in the excess cost column. For the house used as an example, the municipality required ground-fault interruptors ($104), smoke détectors ($72), fire rating wall between garage and living area ($53), burner and oven controls placed at the rear of stoves ($32), copper wiring ($159), reinforcing wire mesh in supporting slab ($148), underground cast iron and copper pipe ($297), framing material of stud-grade quality ($42), and one-half inch plyscore siding ($42). The total excessive cost of these building code requirements is $949.

Energy Conservation Regulations

The Carter Administration is currently seeking approval of legislation which would increase funding for state and local governments to encourage adoption of local ordinances that would reduce the fuel consumption of residential units. These ordinances often require a developer to install energy-saving devices. While energy regulations increase the cost of a house, the initial increase in purchase price is soon balanced by the reduction in heating bills that the energy-saving devices allows. Again, however, the stringent definition of excessive costs is employed. Although these conservation regulations protect limited natural resources and necessitate costs

EXHIBIT 8
BUILDING CODE EXCESS COSTS

	2-bedroom house	3-bedroom house	4-bedroom house
Unnecessary Code Provisions[a]			
1. Ground-fault interruptors	$ 64	$104	$143
2. Smoke detectors	37	72	106
3. Fire rating wall between garage and living area	53	53	53
4. Placement of controls at rear of stove	32	32	32
5. Copper wiring	106	159	212
6. Reinforcing wire mesh in supporting slab	111	148[b]	186[b]
7. Underground cast iron and copper pipe (no plastic)	223	297[b]	371[b]
8. Framing material quality	32	42[b]	53[b]
9. 1/2" plyscore siding	32	42[b]	53[b]

NOTES: [a]From Exhibits 5.10 and 4.4.

[b]Extrapolation: Assumes 2-bedroom house uses 60 percent what 4-bedroom house does; 3-bedroom house uses 80 percent what 4-bedroom does.

that result in lower utility bills, they also increase the market price of shelter, thereby limiting the number of families that can afford a house. Therefore, any costs for improvements required by energy conservation regulations will be defined as excess. Exhibit 9 shows the excessive costs of energy conservation regulations for the three modular house sizes.

EXHIBIT 9

EXCESSIVE COSTS CAUSED BY
ENERGY CONSERVATION REGULATIONS

Conservation Regulations	2-bedroom house	3-bedroom house	4-bedroom house
ASHRAE Code	$235[a]	$300[a]	$360[a]

NOTE: [a] These figures were extrapolated from the excess cost given in Exhibit 6.6, which is for a 1,500 sq.-ft. house. This figure was computed, using minimum square footages recommended for 2, 3, and 4-bedroom houses (see Exhibit 11).

SOURCES: Exhibit 6.6.

If the municipality has an ASHRAE or similar code, the user of the cost compilation guide goes to Step VI (Energy Regulations), finds the cost for the specified house size, and transfers this cost to the excess cost column. For the house used as an example, the municipality had an ASHRAE code in effect, and the excess cost is $300.

ORDINANCE: MINIMUM BUILDING
SIZE REQUIREMENTS

As discussed in Chapter 8, the average size of a single-family dwelling has increased significantly over past years, a consequence primarily of consumer preference. Zoning ordinances in many communities have canonized this trend in consumer preference, making large structures the minimum standard. Zoning ordinances which specify a minimum square footage exceeding the standards initiated by the Department of Housing and Urban Development (shown in Exhibit 10) are excessive since they mandate a larger structure than is necessary for the health and comfort of the occupants.

EXHIBIT 10

FLOOR AREA STANDARDS

	2-bedroom house	3-bedroom house	4-bedroom house
Square-foot floor area	815	1,040	1,245

SOURCE: Exhibit 8.11.

To use the cost conversion guide, the user goes to Step VII (Zoning Ordinance — Minimum Building Size), enters the minimum floor area required by the municipality for the appropriate house size, subtracts the HUD recommended floor area, and multiplies the excess square footage by the price of construction (assumed to be $18 per square foot). The product is entered in the excess cost column.

For the single-family home being studied here as an example, the required 1,200 square feet of floor area for a three-bedroom detached dwelling unit. This caused an excessive cost of construction equal to (1,200 sq. ft. = 1,040 sq. ft.) × $18, or $2,880.

EXCESSIVE COSTS RELATED TO THE CONSTRUCTION STAGE

The user of the cost compilation guide at this step will have finished ascribing excess costs to regulations affecting the construction phase of housing development. By summing the figures entered in the excess cost column for Steps V, VI, and VII, the total excess cost attributable to construction controls can be determined. Exhibit 11 shows the excessive costs incurred during construction of the house used as an example.

EXHIBIT 11

EXCESS COSTS RELATED
TO CONSTRUCTION STAGE

V.	Building Codes	$ 949
VI.	Energy Conservation Regulations	300
VII.	Zoning Ordinance (minimum building size requirements)	2,880
	TOTAL	$4,129

It is obvious from the figures presented above that governmental regulations have a greater effect on the development stage than on the construction stage of housing production. Excess costs incurred during the construction phase are 81 percent of the excess costs during the development stage, and only 10 percent of the total outlays required to produce a house assuming construction costs constitute 80 percent of total housing costs [.80 × $50,000 = $40,000; $4,129 ÷ $40,000 = 10%RB. The most significant source of excess costs during construction is the minimum building size requirement which contributes 70 percent of the total excess in the example.

Occupancy Stage

SETTLEMENT COSTS

Settlement fees are the costs to the purchaser for assuming ownership of a house. Regulations which have formalized these procedures do not directly affect the cost to *produce* a house but add significantly to the cost to *purchase* one. Thus, their impact is to limit the number of people who can afford to buy a house.

The settlement phase of purchasing a house has evolved from a complex system of laws governing the transfer and purchase of real property. It includes *title examination* to ensure both lender and purchaser that the seller owns what is being conveyed; *title insurance* which guarantees that the title examination is done properly; *origination fee* to compensate lenders for expenses incurred in making a loan; *prepaid expenses* such as real estate taxes, hazard insurance premiums and special assessments to reduce the chance of early delinquency and foreclosure; *loan discount payments* to cover processing costs of below-market-interest-rate loans; and finally, *brokerage fees* associated with advertising the property and bringing together an acceptable buyer and seller. The banks, title insurance companies, appraisers, realtors, and other various private and government participants in the process operate in an atmosphere increasingly frustrating and confusing to the housing consumer.

Settlement fees have recently received attention because of their relatively high cost. These fees usually approximate 8 to 12 percent of the purchase price of a house, although the most expensive houses do not have proportional costs. Through marketable title laws, lower attorney fees, lower title insurance enabled by extensive analysis of risk, and better regulation of title research companies, savings of approximately one-sixth of the settlement costs could be gained. Exhibit 12 shows hypothetical settlement costs attendant to three different house configurations and the fraction of these costs which could be saved and are therefore considered excessive.

EXHIBIT 12

EXCESS SETTLEMENT COSTS

Costs	$40,000 house	$60,000 house	$80,000 house
Settlement Costs	$ 3,200	$ 4,000	$ 5,000
Excess Costs (1/6 of settlement costs)	$ 500	$ 675	$ 800

The user enters the cost conversion guide at Step VIII (Settlement Costs) and records the settlement cost paid for the house he bought. One-sixth of these costs are excessive and should be entered in the excess cost column. For the $50,000 house used as an example, settlement costs were $3600. This figure was determined by taking the midpoint between the settlement costs for a $40,000 house and a $60,000 house as shown in Exhibit 12. The excess cost was one-sixth of this, or $600.

Summary - The Excess Costs of Governmental Regulation

The previous sections of this summary have detailed potential excess costs of governmental regulation. For the $50,000 single-family home used as an example, excess costs summed to $9,844 as follows:

Development Stage	$5,115
Construction Stage	4,129
Occupancy Stage	600

In this instance, 19.7 percent of the purchase price of a house may be related to government regulatory excesses of one form or another. Exhibit 13 presents examples of the effect on four houses of the regulations described in this summary. The first example is the one that has been used in the preceding text to demonstrate the use of the cost conversion guide. Every regulation discussed in this summary was in effect for that example. The second example is of another $50,000 house with three bedrooms, but in this instance the lot size is one-quarter acre, and the municipality is assumed to have no minimum acreage requirement. The third and fourth examples are of a $40,000 house with two bedrooms on a quarter acre lot, and an $80,000 house with four bedrooms on a one acre lot. In the fourth example, the minimum lot size is one-half acre. In all the examples, land is assumed to cost $16,000 per acre; it is assumed that the larger lot width is required, and that minimum floor areas are 900 square feet for two-bedroom houses, 1,200 square feet for three-bedroom houses, and 1,500 square feet for four-bedroom houses. All other regulations for examples 2,

EXHIBIT 13

EXAMPLES OF EXCESSIVE COSTS
IMPOSED BY GOVERNMENT REGULATIONS

Cost Conversion Guide Step	Example 1 $50,000, 3 br., 1/2 Acre Min. lot = 1/2 acre Min. lot width = 100'	Example 2 $50,000, 3 br., 1/4 Acre No minimum lot Min. lot width = 100'	Example 3 $40,000, 2 br., 1/4 Acre No minimum lot Min. lot width = 100'	Example 4 $80,000, 4 br., 1 Acre Min. lot = 1/2 acre Min. lot width = 150'
I. A.	$ 385	$ 190	$ 190	$ 755
B.	800	0	0	1,600
II.	462	228	228	906
III.	231	114	114	453
IV. A.	1,105	553	553	2,208
B. 1.	163	133	133	328
2.	154	126	126	310
3.	166	135	135	335
4.	54	43	43	108
5.	42	35	35	85
6.	387	315	315	781

EXHIBIT 13 (continued)

EXAMPLES OF EXCESSIVE COSTS
IMPOSED BY GOVERNMENT REGULATIONS

Cost Conversion Guide Step	Example 1 $50,000, 3 br., 1/2 Acre Min. lot = 1/2 acre Min. lot width = 100'	Example 2 $50,000, 3 br., 1/4 Acre No minimum lot Min. lot width = 100'	Example 3 $40,000, 2 br., 1/4 Acre No minimum lot Min. lot width = 100'	Example 4 $80,000, 4 br., 1 Acre Min. lot = 1/2 acre Min. lot width = 150'
C. 1.	273	225	225	417
2.	21	18	18	33
3.	110	91	91	179
4.	179	119	119	357
5.	335	275	275	545
6.	128	128	128	128
D.	120	109	109	172
Subtotal (Excess costs due to development regulations)	$5,115	$2,837	$2,837	$9,700
V. A.	$ 104	$ 104	$ 64	$ 143
B.	72	72	37	106
C.	53	53	53	53
D.	32	32	32	32
E.	159	159	106	212

EXHIBIT 13 (continued)

EXAMPLES OF EXCESSIVE COSTS
IMPOSED BY GOVERNMENT REGULATIONS

Cost Conversion Guide Step	Example 1 $50,000, 3 br., 1/2 Acre Min. lot = 1/2 acre Min. lot width = 100'	Example 2 $50,000, 3 br., 1/4 Acre No minimum lot Min. lot width = 100'	Example 3 $40,000, 2 br., 1/4 Acre No minimum lot Min. lot width = 100'	Example 4 $80,000, 4 br., 1 Acre Min. lot = 1/2 acre Min. lot width = 150'
F.	148	148	111	186
G.	297	297	223	371
H.	42	42	32	53
I.	42	42	32	53
VI.	300	300	235	360
VII.	2,880	2,880	1,530	4,590
Subtotal (Excess costs due to construction regulations)	$4,129	$4,129	$2,455	$6,159

EXHIBIT 13 (continued)

EXAMPLES OF EXCESSIVE COSTS
IMPOSED BY GOVERNMENT REGULATIONS

Cost Conversion Guide Step	Example 1 $50,000, 3 br., 1/2 Acre Min. lot = 1/2 acre Min. lot width = 100'	Example 2 $50,000, 3 br., 1/4 Acre No minimum lot Min. lot width = 100'	Example 3 $40,000, 2 br., 1/4 Acre No minimum lot Min. lot width = 100'	Example 4 $80,000, 4 br., 1 Acre Min. lot = 1/2 acre Min. lot width = 150'
VIII.	$ 600	$ 600	$ 500	$ 800
Subtotal (Excess costs due to occupancy regulations)	$ 600	$ 600	$ 500	$ 800
Total (Excess costs due to government regulations)	$9,844	$7,566	$5,792	$16,659
Excess Cost as % of market price:	19.7%	15.1%	14.5%	20.8%

3, and 4 are as described for example 1. The specifications for each of these four examples are for municipalities that have *all* of the excessive regulations in effect, and therefore represent the *maximum cost attributable to governmental controls for each house.*

Using the first example — which has been used throughout this summary — the impact of the excessive cost on the housing consumer can be approximated by using several housing market rules-of-thumb. One such rule is that 1 percent of the purchase price of a house is an approximate indication of its monthly operating costs (mortgage, taxes, insurance, operating and maintenance). Using this rule for a $50,000 home, approximately $500 would be spent monthly to operate it. If this house had been built without excessive regulations, it would have cost approximately $40,000 and monthly operating costs would be reduced by $100. The decrease in the purchase price of almost $10,000 could be taken as a saving by the homebuyer, thus reducing the monthly share of income allocated to housing by a considerable amount. (Exhibit 14 demonstrates this saving using a more detailed calculation.) On the other hand, the consumer could choose to buy a larger or otherwise more expensive house (up to $50,000) than he would be able to buy under existing governmental regulations.

Another rule-of-thumb asserts that family income must total approximately half of the purchase price of the house for a family to be judged financially capable of maintaining the house. Using this rule for a house selling for $50,000, a family can afford the house if its combined income is approximately $25,000. If, however, the price of the house is reduced to $40,000, family income required to stand the expense of the house need only be $20,000. Even at this relatively high purchase price and the correspondingly high required income, such a reduction in price expands the market to 8 percent more families in the United States.

These approximate cost calculations must be used with care. Ultimately, the exact interest rate and term of the mortgage, annual taxes and insurance, and operating and maintenance costs peculiar to a type of structure in a particular location determine monthly operating costs. Similarly, lenders use cash assets, credit ratings, etc. and not just income-to-value ratios to determine who qualifies for a mortgage.

It must be repeated that the definition of excessive cost is in every instance a stringent one. Few benefits were permitted to offset costs because the intention was to eliminate all requirements that were not absolutely necessary for the health and safety of occupants. However, many of the requirements defined as excessive are so only in the short run. For example, as energy supplies continue to be depleted, heating fuel may become so expensive that the costs of meeting the ASHRAE code will appear as necessary rather than excessive. Furthermore, some requirements called ex-

EXHIBIT 14

EFFECTS ON MONTHLY OCCUPANCY COSTS RESULTING FROM
ELIMINATING THE COST OF EXCESSIVE GOVERNMENT REGULATIONS
(example house)

Monthly Operating Costs	I. With Excessive Regulations Price: $50,000 Assume: 20% downpayment 9% mortgage for a 30 yr. term	II. Without Excessive Regulations Price: $40,156 Assume: 20% downpayment 9% mortgage for a 30 yr. term
Debt Service	$ 322 (on $40,000)	$ 259 (on $32,125)
Heating & Utilities[a]	65[b]	72
Maintenance & Repairs	34	34
Real Estate Taxes	104	84
Insurance	17	13
Total	$ 542	$ 462
Savings		$ 80

NOTES: [a]Extrapolation from Exhibit 6.1.

[b]Assumed that the ASHRAE-required improvements resulted in a 10 percent savings on heating bills.

cessive may not be so in particular areas. The prohibition of vegetation burning may be excessive in the plains of Nebraska where the prevailing breezes quickly dissipate limited pollution, but may be absolutely necessary in the San Bernardino Valley where smog levels are already perilous. These examples of circumstantial variation are intended to suggest that excessive costs must be compiled with a sensitivity to the context in which a house is erected. Obviously, local conditions dictate the severity of the excess cost test.

Even more problematical to the definition of excessive costs is the elusive relationship between consumer preference and governmental regulation. For example, evidence indicates that increased floor area is primarily a function of consumer demand. In those municipalities that have hardened this changeable demand into inflexible minimum standards, it is very uncertain that eliminating the minimum area requirements would result in smaller houses. The same argument can be convincingly made for most of the other requirements that have been called excessive. Seen in this lights, the costs that have been called excessive due to government regulation might better be termed excessive due to buyer preference. Recent evidence shows that the idea of a "no-frills" house — a house built with few amenities resulting in a lower price — has failed to find a market. This would add credence to the argument that the requirements called excessive are what the consumers *want*, and are not artifically imposed by municipalities.

Finally, the examples used here are of the *worst case*, a municipality that has every one of the excessive requirements in effect. Actual circumstances of housing production are unlikely to be so severely regulated.

Perhaps the most valuable result of the study is its usefulness as a guide to the potential cost impact of governmental regulations on savings that could be realized if specific reform suggestions were undertaken.

EXHIBIT 15

COST CONVERSION GUIDE

(Excess costs shown in these last two columns are from the example used throughout this summary)

Circle the lot size of the house the excess cost of which is being computed. All costs for development will be in that column.

Regulation	Lot Size			Excess Cost
	1/4 Acre	1/2 Acre	1 Acre	

DEVELOPMENT STAGE

Step I. Zoning Controls

A. Did the zoning have to be changed or was a variance granted? If so, how long did it take?

	1/4 Acre	1/2 Acre	1 Acre
subtract either:	____ months	_9_ months	____ months
	-4 months	-4 months	-4 months
		if it was a zoning change	
or:	-2 months	-2 months	-2 months
		if it was a zoning variance	
Excess delay	____ months	_5_ months	____ months

EXHIBIT 15 (continued)

COST CONVERSION GUIDE

Regulation	Lot Size			Excess Cost
	1/4 Acre	1/2 Acre	1 Acre	
Monthly cost of delay	x $38	x $77	x $151	
Excess Cost	$	$ 385	$	$ 385
B. Lot Size Minimum. Enter the price of the lot in the appropriate column. If there is a minimum lot size in the zoning ordinance, use the following table to determine excess cost:	$ ____	$ 8,000	$ ____	

minimum   excess

1/4 acre	0
1/2 acre	10% price
1 acre	30% price

	1/4 Acre	1/2 Acre	1 Acre	Excess Cost
Excess Cost	x 0% $	x 10% $ 800	x % $	$ 800

EXHIBIT 15 (continued)

COST CONVERSION GUIDE

Regulation	Lot Size			Excess Cost
	1/4 Acre	1/2 Acre	1 Acre	
Step II. Growth Controls				
How long did growth controls delay construction?	___ months	18 months	___ months	
Subtract:	-12 months	-12 months	-12 months	
Excess delay:	___ months	6 months	___ months	
Monthly Cost of delay	x $38	x $77	x $151	
Excess Cost	$	$ 462	$	$ 462
Step III. Environmental Regulations and Subdivision Processing				
Total processing time for environmental review and subdivision requirements:	___ months	9 months	___ months	
Subtract:	-6 months	-6 months	-6 months	

EXHIBIT 15 (continued)

COST CONVERSION GUIDE

Regulation	Lot Size				Excess Cost
	1/4 Acre	1/2 Acre	1 Acre		
Excess delay:	___ months	3 months	___ months		
Monthly cost of delay:	x $38	x $ 77	x $151		
Excess Cost	$	$ 231	$		$ 231

Step IV. Subdivision Controls

A. Is there a vegetation burning prohibition for land clearance? If so, these are the excess costs:

$ 553 $1,105 $2,208 $1,105

B. Is there a minimum lot width required? If so, circle the required width in the appropriate lot size column. If not, circle the *smaller* lot width, and go to Step IV.C. If the larger lot is circled,

⩽80' width   ⩽90' width   ⩽125' width
(If one of the above is circled, go to Step IV.C)

EXHIBIT 15 (continued)

COST CONVERSION GUIDE

Regulation	Lot Size			Excess Cost
	1/4 Acre	1/2 Acre	1 Acre	
	>80' width	>90' width	>125' width	
and the following items are required by the subdivision ordinance, there is an excess cost. If any of the six items is not required, there is no excess cost for that item.				
1. Sanitary Sewers	$ 133	$ 163	$ 328	$ 163
2. Storm Drainage System	126	154	310	154
3. Water Distribution	135	166	335	166
4. Curbs and Gutters	43	54	108	54
5. Sidewalks	35	42	85	42
6. Pavements on Streets	315	387	781	387

EXHIBIT 15 (continued)

COST CONVERSION GUIDE

Regulation	Lot Size			Excess Cost
	1/4 Acre	1/2 Acre	1 Acre	
C. If the subdivision regulation required any of the following 6 items, the cost to the buyer is excess. Note that for items 3 and 5 the lot width specified in Step IV.B above must be used.				
1. Underground utilities	$ 225	$ 273	$ 417	$ 273
2. 8" or 10" sanitary sewer	18	21	33	21
3. Sidewalks on both sides	≤80' lot: $73	≤90' lot: $89	≤125' lot: $136	$
	>80' lot: $91	>90' lot: $110	>125' lot: $179	$ 110
4. Excess landscaping	$ 119	$ 179	$ 357	$ 179

EXHIBIT 15 (continued)

COST CONVERSION GUIDE

Regulation	Lot Size			Excess Cost
	1/4 Acre	1/2 Acre	1 Acre	
5. Enter required right-of-way width	___ Ft.	___ Ft.	___ Ft.	
or				
pavement width	___ Ft.	35 Ft.	___ Ft.	
Subtract either:	-30 Ft.	-30 Ft.	-30 Ft.	
	If you entered a pavement width			
	or			
	-50 Ft.	-50 Ft.	-50 Ft.	
	If you entered a right-of-way width			
Excess width	___ Ft.	5 Ft.	___ Ft.	
Multiply by Cost per additional foot of width:	≤80' lot: $45 >80' lot: $55	≤90' lot: $54 >90' lot: $67	≤125' lot: $ 83 >125' lot: $109	
Excess Cost	$	$ 335	$	$ 335
6. Land dedication for parks, schools, etc.	$ 128	$ 128	$ 128	$ 128

EXHIBIT 15 (continued)

COST CONVERSION GUIDE

Regulation	1/4 Acre	Lot Size 1/2 Acre	1 Acre	Excess Cost
D. Block length required. Circle the block length that is required; then using the same lot width specified in Step IV.B above, find the excess cost.				
Block Length:				
1,200'	Lot Size 0	Lot Size 0	Lot Size 0	
1,000'	≤80' $87 >80' $109	≤90' $ 92 >90' $120	≤125' $120 >125' $172	$ __ $ 120
800'	≤80' $181 >80' $220	≤90' $181 >90' $248	≤125' $248 >125' $398	$ __ $ __
700'	≤80' $278 >80' $347	≤90' $309 >90' $397	≤125' $397 >125' $617	$ __ $ __
600'	≤80' $315 >80' $404	≤90' $354 >90' $472	≤125' $472 >125' $708	$ __

Steps I-IV: Excess Cost Attributable to Development Regulations: $5,115

EXHIBIT 15 (continued)

COST CONVERSION GUIDE

Regulation	House Size			
	2 bedrooms	3 bedrooms	4 bedrooms	Excess Cost
CONSTRUCTION STAGE	(Circle the size of the house the excess cost of which is being computed. All costs for construction will be in that column.)			
Step V. Building Code				
If the building code includes the following standards, the excess cost is shown.				
A. Ground-fault interruptors	$ 64	$104	$143	$104
B. Smoke detectors	37	72	106	$ 72
C. Fire rating wall between garage and living area	53	53	53	$ 53
D. Controls placed at rear of stove	32	32	32	$ 32
E. Copper wiring	106	159	212	$159

EXHIBIT 15 (continued)

COST CONVERSION GUIDE

Regulation	House Size			Excess Cost
	2 bedrooms	3 bedrooms	4 bedrooms	
F. Reinforcing wire mesh in supporting slab	111	148	186	$148
G. Underground cast iron and copper pipe	223	297	371	$297
H. Framing material quality	32	42	53	$ 42
I. 1/2" plyscore siding	32	42	53	$ 42
Step VI. Energy Conservation				
If the municipality has ASHRAE Code, excess cost is:	$235	$300	$360	$300
Step VII. Zoning Ordinances— Minimum Building Size				
Enter in the appropriate column (by no. of bedrooms) the minimum floor area required:	____ Sq. Ft.	1,200 Sq. Ft.	____ Sq. Ft.	

EXHIBIT 15 (continued)

COST CONVERSION GUIDE

Regulation	House Size			Excess Cost
	2 bedrooms	3 bedrooms	4 bedrooms	
Standard:	-815 Sq. Ft.	-1,040 Sq. Ft.	-1,245 Sq. Ft.	
Excess Footage:	_____ Sq. Ft.	160 Sq. Ft.	_____ Sq. Ft.	
Multiply by cost of construction per sq. ft.				
Excess Cost	x $ 18	x $ 18	x $ 18	
	$ _____	$ 2,880	$ _____	$2,880
				$4,129

Steps V-VII: Excess Cost Attributable to Construction Regulations: $4,129

EXHIBIT 15 (continued)

COST CONVERSION GUIDE

Regulation	House Value			Excess Cost
	$40,000	$60,000	$80,000	

OCCUPANCY STAGE   (Circle the house value of the house whose excess cost is being computed. All costs for occupancy will be in that column.)

Step VIII. Settlement Fees

	$40,000	$60,000	$80,000	Excess Cost
Enter settlement fees paid for the house	$ _____	$ 3,600*	$ _____	
Multiply by 1/6 to determine excess	x 1/6	x 1/6	x 1/6	
Excess Cost	$	$ 600	$	$ 600

*Extrapolation

Step VIII. Excess Cost Attributable to Occupancy Regulations: $ 600

Steps I–VIII: Total Cost Attributable to Excess Government Regulations: $9,844

Appendix A: Survey of the Home Builder Industry

This survey was administered through the mails to the 27,000 builder members of the National Association of Home Builders. For an analysis of the distribution of the respondents and the results see Chapter Three.

SURVEY OF THE HOME BUILDER INDUSTRY

I. Firm's Production Characteristics

1. Name of Respondent: _____

   Name of Firm: _____

   Address: _____

   _____

   Telephone: _____

2. Do you build in one county or throughout a state, region, or nation?

   ( ) a county
   ( ) a single state
   ( ) a region (several states)
   ( ) nationwide

355

3. Using an average over the last five years, how many of each of the following units did you build?

Single family   _____ Units
Garden Apartments   _____ Units
High-rise Apartments   _____ Units
Mobile Homes   _____ Units
Rehab   _____ Units
_____   _____ Units

4. Do your firm's operations primarily involve

( ) land development
( ) residential construction (using finished lots)
( ) both land development and construction
( ) other _____
                (specify)

II. Government Regulations

5. Using the following list as a guide, what do you consider to be your most significant problems in doing business in 1975? (Please number the entire list starting with the *most* difficult problem as number 1.)

( ) lack of suitable land
( ) material shortages/costs
( ) labor shortages/costs
( ) inavailability of financing
( ) government imposed regulations
( ) other _____
                (specify)

---

6. To what extent do you consider possible government interference in making your decision as to where to develop?

( ) not a consideration
( ) considered somewhat
( ) an important consideration

7. What aspects of the overall government regulation picture do you find most burdensome? (Again, please number the entire list starting with the *most* burdensome aspect as number 1.)

( ) local administrative discretion
( ) unnecessary delays
( ) costs of paperwork, filing permits, etc.
( ) limitation on what can be built
( ) lack of coordination among government regulatory agencies
( ) other _____
(specify)

8. For a typical residential project, what changes have occurred from 1970 to 1975 in the time period beginning with the decision to develop and lasting to the day when a building permit is issued?

	Months Required	
Time Interval	*(in 1970)*	*(in 1975)*
0-3 months	( )	( )
4-6 months	( )	( )
7-12 months	( )	( )
13-18 months	( )	( )
19-24 months	( )	( )
25-36 months	( )	( )
37-48 months	( )	( )
49 months or more	( )	( )

9. What effect on the final selling price of a unit would you attribute to the unnecessary* costs associated with each of the following government regulations?

(*Our definition of necessary is that which is essential to health, safety, and public welfare.)

UNNECESSARY COSTS OF REGULATION

Regulations	*No Increase*	*Less than 1% Increase*	*1-3% Increase*	*4-5% Increase*	*6-10% Increase*	*More than 10% Increase*
Building Codes						
Coastal Zone Regulations						
Energy Codes						
Environmental Requirements & Impact Reviews						
Floodplain Restrictions						
Mortgage Financing Requirements						
State Land Development Laws						
Subdivision Requirements (sewer, streets, site review, etc.)						
Settlement & Closing Costs						
Zoning						
Total						

Comments: _____

_____

_____

_____

_____

Appendix B: Telephone Survey of Home Builders

In order to facilitate a more detailed analysis of the problems and costs encountered by home builders in complying with specific government regulations, a detailed questionnaire was administered over the telephone to a random sample of 400 respondents to our NAHB and ULI mail solicitation. That questionnaire is included below. The results are discussed where applicable, throughout this book.

TELEPHONE SURVEY OF HOME BUILDERS

I. Firm's Production Characteristics

Name of Respondent: _____

Name of Firm: _____

Address: _____

_____

Telephone number: _____

1. Do your firm's primary activities involve...
   (last 5 years)   (5)

   (1) land development
   (2) residential construction
   (3) both land development and residential construction
   (4) other _____
   (8) Don't know
   (9) Not applicable

2. Do you build in one county solely or throughout the state
   or nation?   (6)

   (1) county
   (2) a single state
   (3) region
   (4) nationwide
   (8) Don't know
   (9) Not applicable

   Comment: _____

   _____

3. Over the last 5 years, how many of each of the following types of
   residential units did you complete per year, on an average?

   (1) Condos.   __ __ __ __ Units   (7-10)
   (2) Rehab units   __ __ __ __ Units   (11-14)
   (3) Mobile home   __ __ __ __ Units   (15-18)
   (4) High-rise apartments   __ __ __ __ Units   (19-22)
   (5) Garden apartments   __ __ __ __ Units   (23-26)
   (6) Fully pre-fab single family __ __ __ __ Units   (27-30)
   (7) All other conventional
       single-family attached
       and detached   __ __ __ __ Units   (31-34)

   Comment: _____

   _____

4. What income group was this construction generally targeted
   for: (41)

   (1) Mostly upper income ($25,000+)
   (2) Split between upper and middle income ($15-$25,000)
   (3) Split between middle income and low income ($10-$15,000)
   (4) Mostly lower income (under $10,000)
   (5) Other
   (8) Don't know
   (9) Not applicable

   Comment: _____

   _____

   _____

II. Government Regulations

5. Using the following list as a guide, what do you consider to be your
   three most significant problems in doing business in 1975?

   (1) Government imposed regulations
   (2) Lack of market demand
   (3) High interest rates
   (4) Vandalism
   (5) Lack of suitable land
   (6) Material shortages/costs
   (7) Labor shortages/costs
   (8) Inavailability of financing
   (9) NA/DK

   Other Comments: _____

   _____

   _____

   A. First _____ (42)

   B. Second _____ (43)

   C. Third _____ (44)

6. What three aspects of the overall government regulation picture do you find most burdensome?

   (1) Local administrative discretion
   (2) Unnecessary delays
   (3) Costs of paperwork, filing permits, etc.
   (4) Limitations on what can be built
   (5) Lack of coordination among government regulatory agencies
   (6) Unnecessary requirements (materials or specifications)
   (7) Other (Specify) _____
   (8) Don't know
   (9) Not applicable

   A. First _____ (45)

   B. Second _____ (46)

   C. Third _____ (47)

7. To what extent do you consider possible government interference in making your decision as to where to develop?   (48)

   (1) Not a consideration
   (2) Considered somewhat
   (3) An important consideration
   (8) Don't know
   (9) Not applicable

8. Have you recently begun a specific residential construction or land development project and later had to terminate plans for development because of government regulations or restrictions?   (51)

   (1) Yes   (2) No
   (8) Don't know   (9) Not applicable

   What was the nature of this regulation?

   _____

   _____

   _____

   _____

9. For a typical (residential project) land development project, how much time was necessary to obtain all approvals to develop (build) in 1970 and 1975?

Months Required
1970   1975
(Col 52) (Col 53)   *Time Interval*

(1)	(1)	0-3 months
(2)	(2)	4-6 months
(3)	(3)	7-12 months
(4)	(4)	13-18 months
(5)	(5)	19-24 months
(6)	(6)	25-36 months
(7)	(7)	37-48 months
(8)	(8)	Over 48 months
(9)	(9)	Don't know/Not applicable (52, 53)

10. Which of the following subdivision improvements are typically required by the municipality in which you are now developing?

	Required				Excessive			
	Yes	No	DK	NA	Yes	No	DK	NA
Interior Streets	(1)	(2)	(8)	(9)	(1)	(2)	(8)	(9) (54, 55)
If excessive, please specify								
Pavement Width					(1)	(2)	(8)	(9) (56)
Right of Way					(1)	(2)	(8)	(9) (57)
Pavement thickness, Materials					(1)	(2)	(8)	(9) (58)
Lack of Flexibility in Design					(1)	(2)	(8)	(9) (59)
Pavement Width	__ __ __							(60-62)
Right of Way	__ __ __							(63-65)
Curbs	(1)	(2)	(8)	(9)	(1)	(2)	(8)	(9) (68-69)
If excessive, please specify								
Design Standards					(1)	(2)	(8)	(9) (70)
Not Always Needed					(1)	(2)	(8)	(9) (71)

	Required				Excessive				
	Yes	No	DK	NA	Yes	No	DK	NA	
Gutters	(1)	(2)	(8)	(9)	(1)	(2)	(8)	(9)	(72-73)
If excessive, please specify									
Other techniques					(1)	(2)	(8)	(9)	(74)
Not Always Needed					(1)	(2)	(8)	(9)	(75)

CARD #2

	Required				Excessive				
	Yes	No	DK	NA	Yes	No	DK	NA	
Sidewalks	(1)	(2)	(8)	(9)	(1)	(2)	(8)	(9)	(4-5)
If excessive, please specify									
Width					(1)	(2)	(8)	(9)	(6)
Thickness					(1)	(2)	(8)	(9)	(7)
Not Always Needed					(1)	(2)	(8)	(9)	(8)
Sidewalk Width									(9-10)
Watermain	(1)	(2)	(8)	(9)	(1)	(2)	(8)	(9)	(12-13)
If excessive, please specify									
Pipe Diameter					(1)	(2)	(8)	(9)	(14)
Materials					(1)	(2)	(8)	(9)	(15)
Depth Underground					(1)	(2)	(8)	(9)	(16)
Hook-up Fees					(1)	(2)	(8)	(9)	(17)
Sanitary Sewers	(1)	(2)	(8)	(9)	(1)	(2)	(8)	(9)	(18-19)
If excessive, please specify									
Pipe Diameter					(1)	(2)	(8)	(9)	(20)
Materials					(1)	(2)	(8)	(9)	(21)
Depth Underground					(1)	(2)	(8)	(9)	(22)
Hook-up Fees					(1)	(2)	(8)	(9)	(23)
Lay-out Design					(1)	(2)	(8)	(9)	(24)
Storm Sewers	(1)	(2)	(8)	(9)	(1)	(2)	(8)	(9)	(26-27)
If excessive, please specify									
Pipe Diameter					(1)	(2)	(8)	(9)	(28)
Materials					(1)	(2)	(8)	(9)	(29)
Underground Piping					(1)	(2)	(8)	(9)	(30)
Hook-up Fee					(1)	(2)	(8)	(9)	(31)

	Required				Excessive				
	Yes	No	DK	NA	Yes	No	DK	NA	
Landscaping	(1)	(2)	(8)	(9)	(1)	(2)	(8)	(9)	(37-38)
Street Trees	(1)	(2)	(8)	(9)	(1)	(2)	(8)	(9)	(39-40)
Street Lighting	(1)	(2)	(8)	(9)	(1)	(2)	(8)	(9)	(41-42)
Underground Utility Lines	(1)	(2)	(8)	(9)	(1)	(2)	(8)	(9)	(43-44)
Telephone	(1)	(2)	(8)	(9)	(1)	(2)	(8)	(9)	(45)
Electric	(1)	(2)	(8)	(9)	(1)	(2)	(8)	(9)	(46)
Land Dedication									
Recreation	(1)	(2)	(8)	(9)	(1)	(2)	(8)	(9)	(47-48)
Schools	(1)	(2)	(8)	(9)	(1)	(2)	(8)	(9)	(49-50)
Fee in lieu of: (As an Option)	(1)	(2)	(8)	(9)	(1)	(2)	(8)	(9)	(51-52)
Specify _____									

Percentage of Total Land Dedicated to

Recreation ___ ___   88 Don't know   (53-54)

Schools ___ ___   99 Not Applicable   (55-56)

11. To what extent are the specifications of subdivision requirements written into law or negotiated with the municipality? (57)

    (1) primarily written into law
    (2) roughly half negotiated, half specified by law
    (3) mostly negotiated
    (8) Don't know
    (9) Not applicable

12. In the past 2 years, based on your own experiences, how often have zoning changes been necessary before construction has been permitted: (58)

    (1) Almost never
    (2) 5-10% of the time
    (3) 11-25%
    (4) 26-50%
    (5) 51-75%
    (6) 76% and above
    (8) Don't know
    (9) Not applicable

13. Have zoning regulations affected or changed your development in any
    of the following ways?   (59-62)

	Yes	No	DK	NA
Build more expensive structures	(1)	(2)	(8)	(9)
Build less dense developments	(1)	(2)	(8)	(9)
Build in less populated areas	(1)	(2)	(8)	(9)

Other (specify) _____

_____

Comments: _____

_____

_____

_____

14. Have you been confronted in your development plans by any of the
    growth control restrictions such as:

	Yes	No	DK	NA	
Interim zoning restrictions	(1)	(2)	(8)	(9)	(63)
Sewer moratorium	(1)	(2)	(8)	(9)	(64)
Phased development controls	(1)	(2)	(8)	(9)	(65)
Limitation on the total annual number of building permits issued	(1)	(2)	(8)	(9)	(66)
Other _____	(1)	(2)	(8)	(9)	(67)

_____

_____

15. During the last three years, for what percent of your residential
    development have you had to file an EIS: (69-71)

    ___ ___ ___   888 Don't know

    ___ ___ ___   999 Not applicable

16. Have you made any design changes in the project, either before submitting an EIS, or as a result of conditions placed on the project after the agency has reviewed the EIS? (72)

   (1) before EIS reviewed
   (2) after EIS reviewed
   (3) both
   (4) no changes made
   (8) Don't know
   (9) Not applicable

   Comments: _____

   _____

   _____

   If design changed, what types of changes were they? (73-79)

	Yes	No	DK	NA
Additional open space and recreational facilities	(1)	(2)	(8)	(9)
Additional sewage handling capacity	(1)	(2)	(8)	(9)
Change of location of structure in relation to lot	(1)	(2)	(8)	(9)
Change in design of residential structure	(1)	(2)	(8)	(9)

   Specify: _____

   _____

Reduction in dwelling unit densities	(1)	(2)	(8)	(9)

   Specify: _____

   _____

Relocation of entire project	(1)	(2)	(8)	(9)
Other	(1)	(2)	(8)	(9)

Comments: _____ _____

_____

CARD #3

17. What is your current most important source of mortgage financing arrangements for the consumer? (NA for Land Developer)   (1-3)

(1) FHA/VA
(2) Savings and loan associations
(3) Commercial banks
(4) Savings banks
(5) Mortgage brokers
(6) REITS
(7) Internal sources
(8) Don't know
(9) Not applicable

Comments: _____

_____

18. What impact do FHA/VA mortgage regulations have on the final cost of buying one of your homes? (NA for Land Developer)   (5-11)

	Yes	No	DK	NA
Decrease costs	(1)	(2)	(8)	(9)
Have no impact	(1)	(2)	(8)	(9)
Increase costs – red tape	(1)	(2)	(8)	(9)
Increase costs – minimum property standards	(1)	(2)	(8)	(9)
Increase costs – appraisals	(1)	(2)	(8)	(9)
Other	(1)	(2)	(8)	(9)

Specify: _____

_____

_____

18a. If you have indicated that minimum property standards add to the cost of construction, which of the following present the greatest expense, in conforming to regulations? (14-17)

	Yes	No	DK	NA
a) Site design	(1)	(2)	(8)	(9)
b) Building design	(1)	(2)	(8)	(9)
c) Materials	(1)	(2)	(8)	(9)
d) Construction technique	(1)	(2)	(8)	(9)

19. What impact do conventional mortgage regulations have on the final cost of buying one of your homes? (NA for Land Developer) (20-26)

	Yes	No	DK	NA
Decrease costs	(1)	(2)	(8)	(9)
Have no impact	(1)	(2)	(8)	(9)
Increase costs — red tape	(1)	(2)	(8)	(9)
Increase costs — appraisals too low	(1)	(2)	(8)	(9)
Increase costs — usury laws	(1)	(2)	(8)	(9)
Increase costs — restrictive underwriting	(1)	(2)	(8)	(9)
Other	(1)	(2)	(8)	(9)

Specify _____

_____

_____

20. *Unnecessary** aspects of the following regulations increase the final selling price of a unit by what percent?

(*Our definition of necessary is that which is essential to health, safety, and public welfare.)

20. (cont.)

	No Increase	Less than 1% Increase	1–3% Increase	4–5% Increase	6–10% Increase	11–20% Increase	More than 20% Increase	Don't Know	Not Applicable	
Subdivision Requirements	(1)	(2)	(3)	(4)	(5)	(6)	(7)	(8)	(9)	(30)
Zoning	(1)	(2)	(3)	(4)	(5)	(6)	(7)	(8)	(9)	(31)
State Land Development Laws	(1)	(2)	(3)	(4)	(5)	(6)	(7)	(8)	(9)	(32)
Coastal Zone Regulations	(1)	(2)	(3)	(4)	(5)	(6)	(7)	(8)	(9)	(33)
Floodplain Restrictions	(1)	(2)	(3)	(4)	(5)	(6)	(7)	(8)	(9)	(34)
Building Codes (NA for L.D.)	(1)	(2)	(3)	(4)	(5)	(6)	(7)	(8)	(9)	(35)
Energy Codes (NA for L.D.)	(1)	(2)	(3)	(4)	(5)	(6)	(7)	(8)	(9)	(36)
Mortgage Financing Requirements (NA for L.D.)	(1)	(2)	(3)	(4)	(5)	(6)	(7)	(8)	(9)	(38)

GENERAL COMMENTS: _____

_____

_____

_____

_____

_____

_____

                                                    CARD 3   (80)

Appendix C: Legal Limitations on the Subdivision Control Power

A primary limitation on the scope of permissible subdivision requirements has evolved, based on judicial interpretation of what can be justified under the police power. In discussing the legal limitations on the subdivision control power, this section will attempt to describe first the legal principles and tests based primarily on the Constitutional limitations which the courts and legislatures have developed. These principles are then applied to the various requirements that are encountered in most subdivision ordinances.

The Legal Principles

That subdivision regulation is a Constitutional land use control mechanism was established in the landmark case of *Mansfield & Swett, Inc. v. Town of West Orange.*[1] The justification for municipal imposition of subdivision exactions is rooted in the police power — the right of political entities to regulate for the health, safety and general welfare.[2] Although the police power is a highly elastic concept, there are limits to its use as a rationale for municipal imposition of subdivision regulations. These limits are:

1. the necessity for proper state enabling legislation,
2. federal and state constitutional provisions, and
3. a broad standard of reasonableness.[3]

STATE ENABLING LEGISLATION

The states are charged with the responsibility of delegating subdivision control powers to municipalities. In the absence of this delegation of power, local regulations may be held invalid.[4]

Model enabling acts have achieved limited success in standardizing state legislation. The clear trend, however, has been towards greater specificity and an expansion of local subdivision powers. This trend can be illustrated by a comparison of the Standard City Planning Enabling Act of 1928, and a more recent effort by the American Law Institute.[5] The 1928 code limited the parameters to:

> the proper arrangement of streets in relation to other existing or planned streets and to the master plan for adequate and convenient open spaces, for traffic, utilities, access of firefighting apparatus, recreation, light and air, and for the avoidance of congestion of population.[6]

By contrast, the ALI's Model Land Development Code emphasizes, in addition, control over the sequence of development and the "exact location and nature of development."[7]

CONSTITUTIONAL LIMITATIONS: THE "TAKING" CLAUSE

The prohibition against "taking" of property without just compensation has been the principal constitutional yardstick for assessing the validity of subdivision exactions.[8] The issue of taking arises where subdivision ordinances require dedication of land within a subdivision for streets, sidewalks, recreational facilities or schools. When the power to regulate has been exceeded, a municipality must resort to its powers of eminent domain to acquire land for public purposes. Such a taking requires "just compensation" to the owner. Developers challenging dedication requirements claim that they cannot be forced to dedicate land without receiving in return its fair market value.

FURTHER LIMITS ON THE POLICE POWER:
THE REASONABLENESS TEST

Subdivision regulations which do not involve land dedication, and are thus not subject to scrutiny under the "taking" rubric, must nonetheless pass the test of "reasonableness." One approach to the issue of reasonableness distinguishes between regulations which eliminate a nuisance and those which provide a positive benefit to the community at large.[9] The limiting factor is that a subdivision resident should bear only the cost of the nuisances his/her occupancy has created. This reasoning is the legal counterpart to an economic approach based on externalities. The theme that subdivision residents should bear only the costs which they generate runs throughout judicial opinions on the validity of subdivision exactions.

Application of the Legal Principles to Particular Requirements

MUNICIPAL FEES

The litany of municipal fees and permits required to obtain subdivision review and approval is a substantial component of development costs. Fees include charges for filing, review, inspections and permits for various procedures. The validity of municipal imposition of fees for subdivision plat review is well established, provided such fees are not overly large,[10] and are not used as a revenue-producing tax measure.[11] Thus, the primary question raised in examination of municipal fee schedules is whether the fees accurately reflect the administrative costs involved in the review process.

ON-SITE IMPROVEMENTS

Construction of streets,[12] sidewalks,[13] sewers,[14] water mains,[15] and curbs and gutters,[16] have all been upheld as valid subjects of regulations under the police power. The public benefit in terms of access, community health and sound planning are seen to far outweigh the extra cost that subdivision residents must bear.[17] The subdivision residents also directly benefit from these improvements and the increased property values which they create.

The law is equally clear, however, that subdivision residents should not be required to pay for improvements which have no particular connection to their subdivision,[18] or which are not necessitated by extra needs generated by that subdivision.[19]

OFF-SITE IMPROVEMENTS

A more difficult question arises, however, with respect to the installation of off-site improvements. In *Lake Intervale Home, Inc. v. Township of Parsippany - Troy Hills,*[20] a requirement that the developer extend water lines outside the subdivision boundaries were invalidated on the ground that other property owners would benefit from the improvement.[21] A further question which has yet to be resolved is the extent to which a developer can be required to provide an enlarged system of improvements to account for future development. The leading case of *Ayres v. City Coun-*

cil of Los Angeles[22] suggested that future as well as present needs and population may be considered in determining exactions. But where dedication is required for street widening to occur in the indefinite future, a court has recently held such land-banking impermissible under the guise of regulating subdivisions.[23]

DEDICATION OF LAND AND FEES IN LIEU OF DEDICATION

A municipality's power to require dedication of land for streets providing access to and within a subdivision is firmly established.[24] The provision of safe and adequate streets is seen to be directly related to the public health, safety and general welfare, particularly in an automobile-dominated age. Viewed in the light of the benefit conferred on the subdivision,[25] such requirements easily pass muster. Most subdividers would prefer to transfer title to the municipality to avoid the expenses of maintenance and repair. The subdivision residents likewise benefit by the increased access and enhanced property values created by public roads.

The courts have been divided as to the validity of local land dedication and in-lieu fee requirements for parks and schools. The trend, however, has been toward upholding these requirements, provided the proper state enabling legislation is present.

Earlier cases often struck down the local dedication and in-lieu fee provisions, on the basis that the exactions were not authorized by the state enabling statute.[26] However, where enabling legislation is present, some courts have merely trotted out the traditional deference to legislative judgment as a rationale for upholding local ordinances, thus avoiding the tougher consititutional questions.[27]

The leading case of *Pioneer Trust and Savings Bank v. Village of Mount Prospect*[28] addressed the "taking" issue directly in invalidating an Illinois enabling statute on the ground that the exactions authorized — school and park land dedication — were not related to the costs generated by the subdivision. The court held that the needs to be fulfilled by an exaction must be "specifically and uniquely attributable" to the subdivision bearing the cost.[29] The more recent California case of *Associated Home Builders, Inc. v. City of Walnut Creek,* however, took the broader view that land dedication and fee requirements are not improper merely because the whole city will benefit thereby.[30] The urgent public need for rapidly diminishing open spaces was cited as the public policy justification for this exercise of power. The case is significant for its recognition of a municipality's right to internalize, through exactions, the congestion costs created by subdivisions.[31]

While dedicated parkland within a subdivision may be assumed to directly serve subdivision residents, the question of fees in lieu of dedication has been more problematic. Where the fees are to be applied to a general fund for educational and/or recreational purposes, the relationship between the use to which the exaction is put and the needs of the residents is more tenuous.[32] However, a liberal interpretation is "uniquely attributable" was used in *Jordan v. Menomonee Falls*[33] to uphold in-lieu fees. That court held that such fees are valid where the evidence resonably shows that the municipality would be required to provide more land for school and parks as a result of the new subdivision.[34] This approach, if refined, could lead to a cost-accounting technique in which each subdivision would be assessed the exact amount of the costs it generates.[35] However, the exclusionary effects of such a cost-accounting system, particularly with regard to schools, may bring the validity of the technique into question.

Some courts have struck down as arbitrary dedication ordinances whose terms were not closely keyed to the extra burden created by the subdivision residents. *Frank Ansuini, Inc. v. City of Cranston*[36] invalidated a regulation requiring subdividers to dedicate seven percent of gross land area for recreation purposes. The Court reasoned that a fixed percentage did not take into account the unique needs created by each subdivision, and was thus arbitrary in its terms and inequitable in its effect.[37]

PERFORMANCE GUARANTEES

Many municipalities require that the developer post a performance bond, or other guarantee that improvements will be made, as a prerequisite to plan approval. This relieves the developer of the necessity of installing all improvements before the final plan application is approved. The validity of such requirements to ensure performance is well established.[38] When a developer fails to make the improvements as per the bond agreement, the city may recover on the bond, but most courts hold that only the stipulated amount, not the cost of completion, may be recovered.[39] For this reason it is important that careful estimates of improvement costs are made by the municipality.

THE LEGAL CONSTRAINTS: A SUMMARY

The predominant tendency of the Courts has been to enlarge the scope of municipal power to impose subdivision exactions on developers. Where state enabling legislation is drawn with the proper specificity, and even in a few cases where it is not,[40] local ordinances will generally be upheld, subject to a showing that the regulation is reasonably related to the public facility needs generated by the subdivision. This may include:

1. proper flexibility in the regulations to account for variations among subdivisions;[41]
2. reasonable levels of exactions and fees which do not unduly burden subdivision residents;[42] and
3. in the case of in-lieu fees, a showing that the fees will be used to benefit the subdivision in question.[43]

NOTES

1. 198 A. 235 (1938). "The baneful consequences of haphazard development are everywhere apparent. . .To challenge the power to give proper direction to community growth and development in the particulars mentioned is to deny the vitality of a principle that has brought men together in organized society for their mutual advantage." at 229.
2. Earlier cases dealing with the validity of various subdivision requirements used the concepts of "voluntariness" and "privilige" to justify the exactions: the decision to subdivide was a "voluntary" one (*Ridgefield Land Co. v. Detroit,* 217 N.W. 58[1929]), and recordation and plan approval were "privileges" which municipalities granted to deserving subdividers. (*Ross v. Goodfellow,* App. D.C. 1 (Ct. App. 1895)). The weakness of these rationales became apparent as subdivision restrictions multiplied and questions of constitutionality became unavoidable.
3. The overlap between the constitutional constraint and the criterion of reasonableness is considerable. The constitutional issue of "taking," for example, hinges largely upon what constitutes a "reasonable" regulation of property.
4. Earlier cases strictly applied the principle that a local planning body's powers are derived from the state enabling act, and any conditions for plan approval must be authorized by the state legislation. *State ex rel. Strother v. Chase,* 42 Mo. App. 343 (1890). However, the modern trend is to tie local subdivision controls to the local police power, thus obviating the need for specifically-drawn authorization. *Ayres v. City Council of Los Angeles,* 207 P. 2d 1 (1949).
5. American Law Institute, *Model Land Development Code,* Proposed Official Draft (1974).
6. Standard Planning Enabling Act, Title II, Section 14, U.S. Department of Commerce.
7. Robert H. Freilich and Peter S. Levi, *Model Subdivision Regulations,* (Chicago: American Society of Planning Officials, 1975), p. 105.
8. The equal protection clause (Amendment 14, Section 1) has also been invoked in attempts to eliminate the wide discrepancies in the treatment of various sections of the community. Charges of denial of equal protection have been made with respect to: discrimination against subdivision residents in favor of older residents, dissimilar treatment of residents of different subdivisions, and discrimination in favor of apartment dwellers. However, as in most economic regulation cases, the courts have generally not applied a very stringent equal protection test. Thus the clause has not been a significant barrier to local controls.

9. Alison Dunham, "A Legal and Economic Basis for City Planning," *Columbia Law Review,* Volume 58 (1958), p. 650.
10. *Prudential Coop. Realty Co. v. Youngstown,* 160 N.E. 2d 695 (1928).
11. *Kesselring v. Makefield Realty Co.,* 227 S.W. 2d 416 (Ky. Court of Appeals, 1950).
12. *Ayres v. City Council of Los Angeles,* 207 P. 2d 1 (1949).
13. *Allen v. Stockwell,* 178 N.W. 27 (1920). But see contra, *Magnolia Development Co. v. Coles,* 89 A. 2d 664 (1952).
14. *Medford v. City of Tulare,* 228 P. 2d 847 (1951).
15. *Rounds v. Board of Water and Sewer Commissioners.* 196 N.E. 2d 209 (1964).
16. *Petterson v. Naperville,* 137 N.E. 2d 371 (1956).
17. Most writers on the subject assume that the developer passes all increased subdivision costs on to the purchasers of the subdivision homes. This "broker" theory of the developer has been challenged by some authors. See Richard P. Adelstein and Noel M. Edelson, *Subdivision Exactions and Congestion Externalities: An Efficiency Analysis,* Philadelphia: Fels Center of Government, (1974), p. 17, who posit that the costs may be shifted to the owner of the raw land to reflect the decreased economic value of land to which subdivision improvement costs are attached. Sagalyn and Sternlieb, in *Zoning and Housing Costs,* (Rutgers University Center for Urban Policy Research, 1972), have suggested the possibility of this backward cost shift, but have also proposed that they resulted in an inflation in the cost of land with lower requirements, p. 39.
18. *Longridge Builders, Inc. v. Princeton Planning Board,* 245 A. 2d 336 (1968). *181 Incorporated v. Salem County Planning Board,* 336 A. 2d 501 (1975).
19. *People's Exchange National Bank v. City of Lake Forest,* 239 N.E. 2d 819 (1968).
20. 147 A. 2d 28 (1958).
21. The facts in this case were extreme in that the developer owned scattered sites in an undeveloped subdivision tract, and installation costs would have been prohibitive. The courts in recent years, however, have been developing more refined methods for judging cost apportionment. *Divan Builders, Inc. v. Planning Board of the Township of Wayne,* 334 A. 2d 30 (1975) which found certain requirements for providing off-site drainage facilities to be excessive, provides a discussion of cost apportioning.
22. 207 P. 2d 1 (1949).
23. *181 Incorporated v. Salem County Planning Board,* 336 A. 2d 501 (1975).
24. *Ayres v. City Council of Los Angeles,* 207 P. 2d 1 (1949); *Brous v. Smith,* 106 N.E. 2d 503 (1952).
25. This so-called "correlative benefit" test was employed in the early case of *Plymouth Coal Company v. Pennsylvania,* 232 U.S. 531 (1914).
26. *Kelber v. City of Upland,* 318 P. 2d 561 (1957). See *Haugen v. Gleason,* 359 P. 2d 108 (1961).
27. *Billings Properties, Inc. v. Yellowstone County,* 394 P. 2d 182 (1964.
28. 176 N.E. 2d 799 (1961).
29. *Ibid.,* at 801 (1961). Similar reasoning was used in *Rosen v. Village of Downers Grove,* 167 N.E. 2d 230 (1960), to invalidate a fee for "educational purposes" in lieu of dedication.
30. 484 P. 2d 606 (1971).
31. The court reasoned in the following manner: "It seems reasonable to employ the fee [in lieu of dedication] to purchase land in another area of the city for

park purposes to maintain the proper balance between the number of persons in the community and the amount of park land available" at 612 Fn. 6. See also Adelstein and Edelson, "Subdivision Exactions and Congestion Externalities: An Efficiency Analysis" for an excellent discussion of the externalities problem.

32. See *Haugen v. Gleason,* 359 P. 2d 108 (1961) which struck down a fee which was applied to a general county fund. See also *Aunt Hack Ridge Estates, Inc. v. Planning Commission of Danbury,* 230 A. 2d 45 (1967).

33. 137 N.W. 2d 442 (1965).

34. See also *Jenad v. Village of Scarsdale,* 258 N.Y.S. 2d 777 (1965), which upheld fees in lieu of dedication.

35. This technique has been advocated by some commentators as an alternative test of constitutionality of subdivision exactions. Ira Heyman and Thomas Gilhool, "The Constitutionality of Imposing Increased Community Costs on New Suburban Residents Through Subdivisions Exactions," *Yale Law Journal,* 73, (1964), p. 1141.

36. 264 A. 2d 919 (1970).

37. See also *Admiral Development Corp. v. City of Maitland,* 267 So. 2d 860 (1972), which invalidated a five percent dedication requirement.

38. *Pennyton Homes, Inc. v. Planning Board,* 197 A. 2d 870 (1964). A contrary case, *Magnolia Development Co. v. Coles,* 89 A. 2d 664 (1952) was decided on the narrow ground that the municipality did not rely on the proper enabling statute.

39. *County of Los Angeles v. Margolis,* 44 P. 2d 608 (1935).

40. See for example, *Jordan v. Menomonee Falls,* 137 N.W. 2d 442 (1965).

41. See, for example, *Frank Ansuini, Inc. v. City of Cranston,* 264 A. 2d 910 (1970).

42. *Prudential Coop. Realty Co. v. Youngstown,* 160 N.E. 695 (1928).

43. *See Aunt Hack Ridge Estates, Inc. v. Planning Commission of Danbury, 200 A. 2d 45 (1967) and Jordan v. Menomonee Falls, 137 N.W. 2d 442 (1965) for the narrow and broad views, respectively.*

Appendix D:
Legal Limitations on the Use of Zoning Regulations

For a variety of reasons judicial response to exclusionary elements in zoning ordinances has been slow. Besides the traditional resistance to change exhibited by real property law, challengers of exclusionary zoning have had to contend with courts reluctance to inquire into the motives of public officials and the lack of guidance from the U.S. Supreme Court, which until recently had imposed an almost fifty-year moratorium on review of zoning questions.

In addition, inadequacy of hard data on the actual cost impact of zoning, as well as the excessive cost of providing these proofs for litigation purposes, have contributed to this delay. Without knowledge of the absolute level of the exclusionary effects of various provisions, courts tend to be willing to invalidate only the most egregious examples of exclusionary zoning. More facts relating zoning to housing costs are essential in order to provide a rational basis for judicial opinions, as well as to aid legislative solutions to the problem of exclusionary zoning.

As a further barrier to judicial effectiveness, court cases which do strike down exclusionary provisions are not characterized by clarity of analysis. This may be partially explained by the fact that exclusionary zoning issues are in most cases questions of degree, not of principle,[1] so that decisions are not susceptible to armchair analysis. The issue is generally reducible to the factual question: is a zoning provision so exclusionary to low and moderate-income families as to outweigh any legitimate police power purposes which may be operating?

The pages that follow will discuss the principles which have been used as a basis to challenge exclusionary zoning. This will be followed by an examination of the legal parameters of each of the major aspects of zoning ordinances which increase housing costs. A final section will discuss: 1) related federal cases dealing with the issues of referenda requirements and other procedural obstacles to providing low-income housing, and 2) recent U.S. Supreme Court cases which begin to flesh out the high court's attitude towards the exclusion of low- and moderate-income families from the nation's suburbs.

Principles Used to Challenge Exclusionary Zoning

THE "TAKING" PRINCIPLE: RIGHTS OF THE PROPERTY OWNER

Early challenges to zoning regulations generally achieved success by employing the constitutional doctrine of "taking" to argue that the landowner — in most cases, the developer — had been deprived of the rightful use of his/her property.[2] Where a regulation results in the destruction of the economic use of property, that legal action may be adjudged a "taking," in which case compensation must be given. The distinction between regulations for which no compensation is necessary and "takings" for which "just compensation" must be awarded to victims has caused an all-or-nothing step — a function with respect to compensation which many feel has caused great inequities.

Judicial reception of the claim that property values must be protected against the intrusion of lower-quality residential developments has been mixed. While the protection of property values has been cited in numerous cases as one of the purposes of zoning, there is no agreement as to whether it will stand as the only, or primary, motive for excluding undesired land uses. The Wisconsin case of *State ex rel. Saveland Park Holding Corp. v. Wieland,* held that property values in themselves are sufficient reason for such regulations.[3]

Other cases make clear their position that property values alone are an insufficient motive for restrictive ordinances.[4] At the far end of the spectrum are some cases which question whether the "property value" rationale has any legitimacy at all.[5]

The deficiency of the emphasis on property rights was that it failed to take into account the rights of prospective homebuyers who were excluded from any municipalities by the excessive cost of suburban homeownership.

To redress the grievances of excluded homebuyers, legal arguments based on the equal protection clause of the 14th Amendment began to emerge. Based on the fact that a disproportionate number of lower-income families are minorities, racial discrimination claims have been made against highly restrictive communities. An equal protection argument based on economic, or wealth, discrimination has also been widely used, but with less success.[6]

THE REASONABLENESS TEST: LIMITS OF THE POLICE POWER

A third handle for legal challenge to zoning is the broad test of reasonableness applicable to all government regulations. Where municipalities are held to exceed the powers granted to them by enabling legislation, and they otherwise fail to heed the traditional trinity of health, safety and general welfare, a zoning ordinance may be invalidated. The nebulous character of any reasonableness test may account for the murkiness of the zoning law based on this principle. Great difficulties lie in the task of establishing the fine line between the legitimate goals under the police power and illegitimate, or legally insufficient, motives such as racial discrimination, protection of property values or fiscal zoning.[7] Some recent cases, however, have chosen to define "the general welfare" as the welfare of the region rather than that of the residents of each of the thousands of municipalities which exercise zoning powers. This test has formed the basis of recent courts' invalidation of exclusionary provisions.[8]

The next section examines the judicial responses to various restrictive zoning devices, in light of the different theories advanced on both sides of the debate.

Judicial Responses to Zoning Restrictions

RESTRICTIONS AGAINST MULTI-FAMILY HOMES

In a number of recent cases ordinances have been invalidated which totally exclude multi-family uses.[9] *Baker v. City of Algomac*[10] ruled that multi-family uses were not incompatible with single-family use. Recognizing that a municipality can easily subvert judicial attempts to remove land use barriers to low-income people, the court in *Twp. of Willistown v. Chesterdale Farms, Inc.*[11] held that a municipality's attempt, through various cost-increasing requirements, to permit only high-cost multi-family dwellings is invalid. The recent case of *Bereson v. Town of New Castle*[12] mandated the town to zone for a "balanced and integrated community."[13] Bedroom restrictions were held invalid by the New Jersey Superior Court in *Molino v. Borough of Glassboro.*[14]

PROHIBITION OF MOBILE HOMES

The 1962 New Jersey case of *Vickers v. Twp. Committee of Gloucester Twp.*, which contains Justice Hall's famous dissent, upheld a prohibition on mobile homes on the ground that they "would strike a discordant note and be detrimental to property values, present and prospective, and retard the progress of the township."[15] The majority adopted the attitude that the prohibition was within the township's zoning power and therefore carried a heavy presumption of validity. Justice Hall's dissent pointed out the need for more active judicial review to inquire into the reasonableness of the zoning and its actual social amd economic effects on the community. The dissent discounted the aesthetic argument and came squarely to grips with the exclusionary nature and intent of the mobile home prohibition.

The reasoning in Hall's dissent was later to be used in cases striking down such provisions. The recent case of *Bristow v. City of Woodhaven,*[16] for example, held invalid an ordinance which permitted trailers only in the business district.[17]

MINIMUM LOT SIZE

Many early cases failed to deal seriously with the exclusionary issues involved in large minimum lot size requirements.[18]

Although consistently recognizing the legitimacy of low density zoning, many early cases did issue warnings about potential abuses of this device. The court in *Simon v. Town of Needham,* for example, asserted that a zoning law could not be adopted:

> For the purpose of setting up a barrier against the influx of thrifty and respectable citizens who desire to live there and who are able and willing to erect homes on lots upon which fair and reasonable restrictions have been imposed, nor for the purpose of protecting the large estates that are already located in the district. The strictly local interests of the town must yield if it appears that they are plainly in conflict with the general interests of the public at large. . .[19]

Ths precedent-setting Pennsylvania case of *National Land and Investment Company v. Kohn*[20] held a four-acre minimum lot size requirement to be unrelated to the public interest. In declaring fiscal zoning to be invalid when it is the primary purpose of an ordinance, the court addressed the issue of a municipality's obligation to the larger society:

> The township's brief raises. . .the interesting issue of the township's responsibility to those who do not yet live in the township but who are part, or may become part, of the population expansion of the suburbs. Four acre zoning represents Easttown's position that it does not desire to accommodate those who are pressing for admittance to the township unless such admittance will not create any additional burdens upon governmental functions and services. The question posed is whether the township can stand in the way of the natural forces which send our growing population into hitherto undeveloped areas in search of a comfortable place to live. We have concluded not.[21]

The court in *In re Appeal of Kit-Mar Builders, Inc.*[22] invalidated on similar grounds a Philadelphia suburb's two- and three-acre minimum lot requirements which allowed the township to do "precisely what we have never permitted — keep out people, rather than make community improvements."[23]

Large lot zoning has also been challenged successfully where the zoning is inconsistent with the character of the surrounding land.[24] Where the minimum lot sizes are much larger than the lots on the surrounding areas, the court will view the restrictions more harshly.[25]

Particularly to be considered when deciding whether large minimum lot size requirements are exclusionary, is the extent of mapping for large lots. Norman Williams makes this point in *American Land Planning Law:* "The central point is not the existence of a multi-acre zone, or the precise acreage requirement in that zone — but rather the amount of available vacant land in the town zoned for much higher density, so that low and moderate – income housing may be possible."[26]

The courts have not been consistent when dealing with the problem of substantial economic loss that may be suffered as a result of zoning for large lots.[27] The loss would be determined by proven market demand for housing on various sized lots and the difference in rates of return under proposed or existing zoning. In *Senior v. Zoning Commission of New Canaan,*[28] substantial economic loss was permitted. However, the argument that economic loss should be given greater consideration was successful in *Aronson v. Town of Sharon*[29] and *Grant v. Washington Twp.*[30]

MINIMUM LOT WIDTH

Since lot size and width are usually correlated to a great extent and lot size is the more obviously exclusionary technique, lot width restrictions *per se* have received little attention in the units. Where minimum lot widths have been the challenged device, they have received a mixed reception in the courts. While the court in *Korby v. Redford*[31] upheld a minimum width requirement, in *Hitchman v. Twp. of Oakland*[32] a similar requirement was invalidated as a "taking" of the affected property owner's land.

MINIMUM HOUSE SIZE OR FLOOR AREA REQUIREMENTS

Minimum house size restrictions, or the more common minimum livable floor area restrictions, are a means of ensuring high assessed value in new homes. This not only provides a greater tax base, but also establishes a quality "character" within a neighborhood, thus protecting residential property values. Minimum floor area requirements, although they accomplish the same result, have not always been equated by the courts with minimum cost provisions.

There is a paucity of case law on minimum cost provisions; however, the cases that exist are unanimous in holding such provisions unconstitutional. *Cassel v. Lexington Twp. Board of Zoning Appeals,*[33] held a minimum cost provision invalid, as did the Court of Quarter Sessions of Washington County, Pennsylvania. The latter court stated:

> We have not found a single case which sustains a regulation that a dwelling house must cost at least a certain sum. This would appear to be rather a means of social exclusion than for the purpose of promoting health, safety, morals or general welfare.[34]

Although minimum floor area provisions may accomplish an identical purpose, courts are more receptive to the various rationales advanced to support a lower limit on house size.

An early case, *Senefsky v. City of Huntington Woods,*[35] invalidated a minimum house size requirement of 1,300 square feet, holding such segregation of housing according to cost to be an "unjust limitation of a reasonable and lawful use of the developer's property."[36] Other courts, most notably in Michigan have struck down minimum floor area provisions.[37]

A strong contrary trend, however, is found in other states, with the leading and most-discussed case, *Lionshead Lake, Inc. vs. Wayne Township,*[38] appearing in New Jersey. In this celebrated case, the New Jsrsey Supreme Court reversed a lower court decision holding minimum livable floor area requirements of 768 square feet (single-floor homes) and 1,000 square feet (two-story homes) invalid. Using the weak standard of review which invalidates an ordinance only when it is "arbitrary and unreasonable'', the court upheld the ordinance on the basis of the public health rationale advanced by the municipality. The court intoned that:

> In the light of the Constitution and of the enabling statutes, the right of a municipality to impose minimum floor area requirements is beyond controversy.[39]

The *Lionshead Lake* opinion has spawned a large body of commentary.[40] One follow-up study of the municipality's development vindicates the views of those who predicted a high degree of economic and racial segregation as a result of the ruling. Williams and Wacks found that in the fifteen years since since the *Lionshead Lake* decision, the black population of Wayne Township increased from fifty-five to sixty-three, while the white population rose from 12,000 to 48,000.[41]

In an article written in the 1950's, Williams stated the case against minimum floor area requirements:

> To regard these merely as ineffectual attempts to regulate overcrowding as, in effect, legislative ineptitude over and above the call of duty is to miss the point. The point is that these requlations were concerned with something else, quite specific and quite recognizable; and the public health argument was merely an illfitting afterthought. . . .
>
> If regulations such as these are widespread and successful, the implications for the future are clear enough. The great mass of lower-income groups will continue to live in the existing slum housing, since there would be practically no place left where any substantial amount of new low-cost housing could be built on vacant land. Moreover, the cost of providing for the education and the health of the next generation would be thrown more upon the already heavily overburdened big cities, which are already increasingly unable to provide adequate services for their inhabitants. One may be permitted to doubt whether, all in all, this is a very effective way to promote public health.[42]

Federal Litigation of Exclusionary Zoning Issues

Litigation of exclusionary zoning issues at the federal level gives insight into the types of obstacles which localities erect against low and moderate income people. Due process and equal protection are the most common legal handles employed by plaintiffs. Where proof of racial discrimination cannot be educed, the argument of economic discrimination is made, but with less success. As the court in *Lindsey v. Normet*[43] stated:

> [The] Constitution does not provide judicial remedies for every social and economic ill. We are unable to perceive in that document any constitutional

guarantee to access to dwellings of a particular quality . . . Absent constitutional mandate, the assurance of adequate housing . . . is a legislative not a
judicial function.[44]

REFERENDA CASES

Attempts to invalidate referenda requirements for rezoning thus far
have been unsuccessful in the Federal Courts.[45] Where the referendum
procedure is authorized by state law, the federal courts have viewed referenda as "the city legislating itself through its voters."[46] In *Ranjel v. City of
Lansing,* the U.S. Court of Appeals upheld a referendum demanded by
citizens of a municipality, who sought to reverse the rezoning of twenty
acres of land to permit low cost townhouses. A similar referendum was
upheld in *Southern Alameda Spanish-Speaking Organization v. City of
Union City.*[47]

ADMINISTRATIVE OBSTACLES TO LOW-COST HOUSING

Attempts to obstruct the construction of low-cost housing by administrative means have been viewed unfavorably by the federal courts. In
Crow v. Brown,[48] county officials refused to issue building permits for two
low-rent public housing projects, even though the land was appropriately
zoned and the projects had been approved by the Atlanta Housing
Authority. The court ordered the issuance of the permits, stating: "It
should be obvious that the county may not restrict the class of Americans to
be housed therein."[49] Similarly, the court in *Kennedy Park Homes
Association, Inc. v. City of Lackawanna, N.Y.*[50] thwarted attempts by
Lackawanna city officials to exclude a proposed church-sponsored low-
income housing project in a predominantly white ward of the city.[51] The
court found purposeful racial discrimination in the city's actions, based on
the weakness of the other rationales, and the inconsistency with which they
were advanced.[52]

The case of *U.S. v. City of Black Jack*[53] stands out as a tribute to the
creative imaginations of those who wish to keep out the poor. The threat of
subsidized housing, to be constructed in an unincorporated area outside of
St. Louis, moved the residents to incorporate into a municipality — the City
of Black Jack, Missouri — which then used its newly-won zoning powers to
rezone for single-family use. The plaintiffs in this case succeeded in
establishing their claims of racial discrimination, and the U.S. Supreme
Court, in denying review of the case, let the lower court's ruling stand.

RECENT U.S. SUPREME COURT CASES

After the seminal zoning cases of *Euclid*[54] and *Nectow,*[55] decided by the Supreme Court in the 1920's, the court was silent for fifty years on zoning issues, leaving development of the law to the state courts. The silence has been broken in recent years by a series of cases which further define the high court's view of the zoning power.

The case of *Village of Belle Terre v. Borass*[56] evinced the court's traditional deference to local land-use strategies in upholding an ordinance limiting the number of unrelated persons who could form a household. Justice Douglas' language, in holding the maintenance of "quiet seclusion" to be a proper goal of zoning, does nothing to set the minds of zoning activists at ease. Similarly, *Warth v. Seldin,*[57] in which the court's narrow reading of the law on standing limited federal zoning review to cases involving regulations which block the development of a specific housing project, has further limited the federal courts' role in striking down exclusionary provisions in zoning ordinances.

The high court in *James v. Valtierra,*[58] established the validity of referenda requirements to obtain voter approval of state-sponsored low-rent housing projects. While minorities may be more harshly affected by the disapproval of low-rent housing projects, the court opined that: "the record here would not support any claim that a law seemingly neutral on its face is in fact aimed at a racial minority."[59] The recently-decided case of *City of Eastlake v. Forest City Enterprises*[60] further establishes the principle that a referendum requirement is valid even though it serves to exclude low-income people from a municipality. The court's interpretation of referenda as an exercise of democratic rights appears to override any *de facto* exclusionary effects of the outcome of such referenda.[61]

In contrary trends, however, the Supreme Court, in *Hills v. Gautreaux,*[62] has recently held that the Chicago Housing Authority and the U.S. Department of Housing and Urban Development may be ordered to take metropolitan-wide remedial steps to counteract years of racially-discriminatory selection of public housing sites. Since the Chicago Housing Authority possesses the authority to build housing in the suburbs, a court order requiring efforts to locate public housing in the suburbs is not impermissible as a matter of law.

In another recent development, the Supreme Court has agreed to review *Metropolitan Housing Development Corp. v. Village of Arlington Heights,*[63] in which Arlington Heights refused to rezone church-owned land from single-family to multi-family use for a Section 236 multi-family housing project. Claims of racial discrimination made by the plaintiffs were accepted in the lower court.

SUMMARY

The pattern of exclusionary zoning cases in recent years has been from essentially a "hands off" attitude on the part of the courts to a more searching judicial review. Many state courts are no longer willing to grant the municipality the strong presumption of validity its zoning ordinance once would have been accorded. Particularly in the area of exclusion of multi-family homes, courts have begun to demand that municipalities zone at least some land for this less expensive form of housing. Zoning for the general welfare of a region, to provide land on which various types of homes may be built to house the region's workforce, has proved to be the most powerful principle on which to base an exclusionary zoning suit.

In the federal courts, and especially in the Supreme Court, exclusionary zoning suits have fared less well. Referendum requirements have been upheld even though the outcome serves to enforce economic barriers to the poor and middle-income groups. The most fruitful approach to challenging a zoning ordinance in the federal courts has been to rely on the equal protection principle. Where racial, rather than economic, discrimination may be proved, plaintiffs have been successful in breaking down the exclusionary barriers.

NOTES

1. Norman Williams, *American Land Planning Law,* (Chicago: Callaghan Publishing Co. 1974), § 62.01, Vol. II, p. 609.
2. See Donald Hagman's discussion of this issue in "Windfalls for Wipeouts," *The Appraisal Journal,* (Jan., 1976), pp. 69-82.
3. 69 N.W. 2d 217 (1955). See also *Fischer v. Bedminster Twp.,* 93 A. 2d 378 (1952) which held that the protection of property values is one of the bases for the exclusion of undesirable land uses, at least in combination with other factors.
4. *Senefsky v. City of Huntington Woods,* 12 N.W. 2d 387 (1943); *Elizabeth Lake Estates v. Twp. of Waterford,* 26 N.W. 2d 788 (1947). See the U.S. Supreme Court holding in *Pennsylvania Coal v. Mahon,*1 260 U.S. 393 (1922) for the general proposition that adjoining property owners have no cause of action merely because a zoning action reduces the value of their property.
5. *Tranfaglia v. Bldg. Com'rs. of Winchester,* 28 N.E. 2d 537 (1940), *In re Spring Valley Development,* 300 A. 2d 736 (1973).
6. The U.S. Supreme Court has been unwilling to treat economic discrimination in the same "suspect" category as discrimination based on racial motives. See, for example, *James v. Valtierra,* 402 U.S. 137 (1971) and *Lindsey v. Normet,* 405 U.S. 56 (1972).
7. A number of recent cases have held fiscal zoning *per se* to be an impermissible goal under the police power. See *In re Appeal of Joseph Girsh,* 263 A. 2d 395 (1970); *Oakwood at Madison v. Twp. of Madison,* 320 A. 2d 223 (1974);

Southern Burlington County NAACP v. Township of Mt. Laurel, 336 A. 2d 713 (1975).

8. See, in particular, *Southern Burlington County NAACP v. Township of Mt. Laurel,* 336 A. 2d 713 (1975) and *Urban League of Greater New Brunswick v. Borough of Carteret,* Chan. Div. No. C-4122-73 (Sup. Ct. May 4, 1976).
9. *Appeal of Girsch,* 263 A. 2d 395 (1970); *Oakwood at Madison, Inc. v. Twp. of Madison,* 283 A. 2d 353 (1971).
10. 198 N.W. 2d 13 (1972).
11. 341 A. 2d 466 (1975).
12. No. 430 (N.Y. Ct. of Appeals, December 2, 1975).
13. *Id.* at 111.
14. 281 A. 2d 401 (1971). The Borough required that "in any given garden apartment complex, at least 70 percent of all units could have no more than one bedroom. No more than 25 percent may have two bedrooms, and no more than 5 percent could have three bedrooms," at 403.
15. 181 A. 2d 129 at 137 (1962).
16. 192 N.W. 2d 322 (1971).
17. For further discussion of mobile home prohibition, see Norman Williams and Thomas Norman, "Exclusionary Land Use Controls: The Case of Northeastern New Jersey," *Syracuse Law Review* 22 (1971) 475.
18. *Simon v. Town of Needham,* 42 N.E. 2d 516 (1952); *Dilliard v. Village of No. Hills,* 94 NYS 2d 715 (2nd Dept. 1950); *Gignoux v. Village of Kings Point,* 99 NYS 2d 280 (Sup. Ct., Nassau County, 1950); *Flora Realty and Inv. Co. v. City of Ladue,* 246 S.W. 2d 771 (1952).
19. 142 N.E. 2d 516 (1942) at 519.
20. 215 A. 2d 597 (1965).
21. *Ibid.* at 612.
22. 268 A. 2d 765 (1970).
23. *Ibid.* at 768 (1970).
24. See, for example, *State v. Kiefaber,* 181 N.E. 2d 905 (1969); *Senior v. Zoning Commission of Town of New Canaan,* 153 A. 2d 415 (1959).
25. See *Homer v. Roos,* 382 Pa. 2d 375 (1963); *Schere v. Twp. of Freehold,* 292 A. 2d 35 (1972).
26. Williams, *American Land Planning Law,* Vol. 11, p. 40.
27. Richard Babcock & Fred Bosselman, *Exclusionary Zoning: Land Use Regulations and Housing in the 1970's* (New York: Praeger Publishers, 1973).
28. 153 A. 2d 415 (1959).
29. 195 N.E. 2d 341 (1964).
30. 203 N.E. 2d 857 (1963).
31. 82 N.W. 2d 441 (1957).
32. 45 N.W. 2d 306 (1951).
33. 127 N.E. 2d 11 (1955). In this case, the Township's refusal to grant building permits for prefab homes costing about $10,000 was held invalid as an arbitrary and capricious exercise of the zoning power.
34. Cited in *Medinger Appeal,* 377 Pa. 217 (1954).
35. 12 N.W. 2d 387 (1943). See also *Frischkorn Construction Co. v. Redford Twp. Building Inspector,* 24 N.W. 2d 209 (1946), which invalidated 800 square feet and 14,000 cubic foot minimums, and *Brookdale Home, Inc. v. Johnson,* 10 A. 2d 477 (1940) which held invalid a requirement that homes contain at least two stories. "No person under the zoning power can legally be deprived of his right to build a house on his land merely because the cost of that house is less than the cost of his neighbor's house," at 478.

36. 12 N.W. 2d 387 at 389. (1943).
37. See, for example, *Elizabeth Lake Estates vs. Waterford Twp.*, 26 N.W. 2d 788 (1947).
38. 89 A. 2d 693 (1952).
39. *Id.* at 697.
40. See for example, Charles Haar, "Zoning for Minimum Standards: The Wayne Township Case," *Harvard Law Review,* 66 (1953), p. 1051; Nolan & Horack, "How Small a House?" *Harvard Law Review,* 67 (1954), p. 967; Williams & Wacks, "Segregation of Residential Areas Along Economic Lines: Lionshead Lake Revisited," 1969 *Wisconsin Law Review,* 1969 (1969), p. 827.
41. William and Wacks, *Wisconsin Law Review,* 1969 (1969), p. 827.
42. Norman Williams, "Planning Law and Democratic Living," *Law and Contemporary Problems* (1955), pp. 345-46.
43. 405 U.S. 56 (1972).
44. *Id.* at 74.
45. *Ranjel v. City of Lansing,* 417 F. 2d 321 (6th Cir. 1969); *Southern Alameda Spanish-Speaking Organization v. City of Union City,* 424 F. 2d 291 (9th Cir. 1970).
46. Daniel Lauber, "Recent Cases in Exclusionary Zoning," Report No. 292, American Society of Planning Officials (1973), p. 9.
47. 424 F. 2d 291 (10th Cir. 1970).
48. *Crow v. Brown,* 332 f. Supp. 382 (N.D. Georgia 1971).
49. 80 percent of the public housing residents in Fulton County were black; 90 percent of those on the waiting list were black.
50. 318 F. Supp. 669 (W.D. New York 1970), aff'd, 436 F. 2d 108 (2nd Cir. 1970), cert. denied, 401 U.S. 1010 (1971).
51. The city officials tried every device to stop the project from rezoning for recreation and parkland to denial of sewer extension approvals.
52. See *Daily v. Lawton,* 425 F. 2d 1037 (10th Cir. 1970) in which the court placed the burden on the municipal officials of showing that their ordinance blocking a low-cost housing project was not the product of discriminatory motives. See also *Sisters of Providence of St. Mary of the Woods v. City of Evanston,* 335 F. Supp. 396 (N.D. Illinois 1971), which held that a city cannot "use arbitrary land use criteria to refuse to rezone for black projects where under the same circumstances it would have granted a variance to an all-white project," at 404.
53. 508 F. 2d 1170 (8th Circ. 1974) cert. denied, 422 U.S. 1042 (1976).
54. 272 U.S. 365 (1926).
55. 277 U.S. 183 (1928).
56. 416 U.S. 1 (1974).
57. 422 U.S. 490 (1975).
58. 402 U.S. 137 (1971).
59. *Id.* at 141.
60. 96 Sup. Ct. 2358 (1976).
61. The court in *City of Eastlake* disregarded the lower court's objections to the absence of standards given to the electroate by maintaining that a referendum is not a delegation of legislative power. The court reasoned that since all power derives from the people who can delegate it to representative instruments, a referendum is a reservation of power which might otherwise be assigned to the legislature.
62. 96 Sup. Ct. 1538 (1976).
63. 517 F. 2d 409 (7th Cir. 1974), cert. granted 423 U.S. 1030 (1975).

Appendix E: Survey of Municipalities' Building Departments

The following questionnaire was administered to the building officials of 100 municipalities. The sample was drawn randomly from a listing of municipalities of population of 10,000 or more based on the 1970 Census. The findings are reported in Chapter 9 on building codes.

BUILDING CODES SURVEY

I.D.# __ __ __
BUILDING CODES

A. Population

1. 10-24,999
2. 25-49,999
3. 50-74,999
4. 75-99,999
5. 100,000-499,999
6. 500,000+

B. Region

1. Northeast
2. South
3. North Central
4. West

1. What is the technical basis for your current building code covering
    residential construction?

    ( ) state recommended code

    specify: _____

    ( ) state mandated code

    specify: _____

    ( ) model code

    specify: _____

    ( ) locally promulgated code

    specify: _____

1a. Types of Codes

    1. Uniform B.C
    2. Basic B.C.
    3. Southern Building Congress
    4. National B.C.
    5. Local code
    6. State Code
    7. 1 & 2 Family code

2. If a model or state recommended building code is used, what changes
    were made upon adoption?

	Yes	No
Administrative Changes	( )	( )

    Specify: _____

    _____

    | Technical Changes | ( ) | ( ) |

    Specify: _____

    _____

3. What year was this building code first adopted?

    1. ( ) 1975
    2. ( ) 1971–74
    3. ( ) 1966–70
    4. ( ) 1960–65
    5. ( ) 1950–59
    6. ( ) Before 1950

4. What type of code did it replace?

( ) a state code
( ) a different model code
( ) a local code
( ) only have had one code

5. When were amendments last made that pertained to 1 and 2 family homes?

1. ( ) 1975
2. ( ) 1974-73
3. ( ) 1971-72
4. ( ) 1969-70
5. ( ) 1967-68
6. ( ) 1965-66
7. ( ) Before 1965

6. How often are amendments usually made?

1. ( ) annually
2. ( ) every two years
3. ( ) every three to four years
4. ( ) every five to six years
5. ( ) no pattern (e.g., when thought necessary)
6. ( ) infrequently/rarely

7. How are amendments proposed?

	Yes	No
Recommended by model code associations	( )	( )
Recommended by state building department	( )	( )
Recommended by in-house staff	( )	( )
Recommended by local builders	( )	( )
Recommended by suppliers, trade associations, manufacturers	( )	( )
Recommended by testing agencies	( )	( )
Recommended by state government	( )	( )
Recommended by federal government	( )	( )

8. Are building officials required to be licensed within your state?

( ) Yes
( ) No

9. What are the qualifications for becoming a building official in your department?

   1. ( ) no specific qualifications
   2. ( ) building trades
   3. ( ) general contractor
   4. ( ) architecture
   5. ( ) engineering
   6. ( ) other

      specify: _____

      _____

   7. ( ) 2 and 3, 4, or 5.
   9.   NA/DK

10. Have any of your officials participated in training programs for instructing building officials?

   ( ) state mandatory program
   ( ) model code mandatory sessions
   ( ) state optional
   ( ) model code optional
   ( ) none

11. Which of the following building related officials or departments usually participate in the approval and inspection process before a certificate of occupancy is granted for 1 and 2 family homes?

	Yes	No
Plan inspector, if different from building inspector	( )	( )
Fire inspector	( )	( )
Health inspector	( )	( )
Zoning inspector	( )	( )
County officials	( )	( )
Electrical inspector	( )	( )
Other	( )	( )

Specify: _____

_____

State officials	( )	( )

Specify: _____

| Mechanical inspector | ( ) | ( ) |

12. How many full time professional staff are included in your department?
   - ( ) 1 part time
   - ( ) 1 full time
   - ( ) 2-5 people
   - ( ) 6-50 people
   - ( ) 51-100 people
   - ( ) 101+ people

13. Which of the following building materials or practices are currently included in your code?

	Yes	No	Year Permitted
1. Requirement of smoke detectors	( )	( )	( )
2. Security requirements for doors and windows	( )	( )	( )
3. Prohibit use of automatic plumbing vents in buildings	( )	( )	( )
4. Use of ABS or PVG plastic pipes in drain waste and vent plumbing	( )	( )	( )
5. Require 30 lb. felt on roofing installation	( )	( )	( )
6. Require ground fault interrupter	( )	( )	( )
7. Require fire rating wall and door between garage and living area	( )	( )	( )
8. Prohibit aluminum wiring	( )	( )	( )
9. Other code requirements that are unnecessary and significantly add to costs	( )	( )	( )

14. What is the fee schedule used by your department for 1 or 2 family homes?
   1. Flat Rate
   2. Valuation
   3. Dollars per sq. foot

15. What percentage of the operating expenses of your department is covered by fees?
   1. ( ) 100% (Self supporting)
   2. ( ) more than 75%
   3. ( ) between 50-74%
   4. ( ) less than 50%

16. Has your department recently added energy conservation provisions
     to its building code?

     1. ( ) Yes
     2. ( ) No
     3. ( ) Under consideration

     What was the nature of these provisions?

     1. insulation
     2. windows and doors
     3. both 1 and 2
     4. solar heat potential
     5. ASHRAE 90-75/performance standards

17. If a particular technique or material is not specifically approved or dis-
     approved by a building code on what basis is a decision made as to its
     acceptability?

          ( ) manufacturers specifications and recommendations
          ( ) tests conducted by independent labs (UL/ASTM)
          ( ) tests conducted by trade associations
          ( ) government standards (NBS, MPS)
          ( ) professional judgment of building official
          ( ) recommendation from model code

             specify: _____

18. How much variation is there between your municipality's residential
     building code and those used by the neighboring communities?

     1. ( ) no variation
     2. ( ) only minor variation
     3. ( ) significant variation
     4. ( ) other

             specify: _____

             _____

             _____

19. In what ways, if any, do you believe building codes unnecessarily increase housing costs?

    1. ( ) do not increase costs
    2. ( ) cause time delays
    3. ( ) restrict use of innovative materials
    4. ( ) require excessive safety features
    5. ( ) both 3 and 4
    6. ( ) other

        specify: _____

        _____

20. What percent of the total cost per unit could be saved if unnecessary aspects of the building code were eliminated?

    1. ( ) 0 percent
    2. ( ) 1-2 percent
    3. ( ) 3-5 percent
    4. ( ) 6-10 percent
    5. ( ) 11-15 percent
    6. ( ) 16-20 percent
    7. ( ) more than 20 percent

Appendix F:
Survey of
Municipalities' Zoning
and Subdivision
Practices

In an attempt to better ascertain the exact nature of zoning and sub-division practices throughout the nation, the Center for Urban Policy Research conducted, in the summer of 1976, an extensive analysis of these regulations in eighty municipalities.

The sample was randomly drawn from a listing of municipalities of 10,000 or more in population based on the 1970 Census. Although the initial list included 100 municipalities, several were unable to provide ordinances for various reasons, such as ordinances being out of print or under revision. Non-respondents did not appear to have any special characteristics which would bias our sample. The final sample included seventy-four municipalities with both subdivision and zoning ordinances and six municipalities each with only a subdivision or zoning ordinance.

The inital step in our survey was to secure and analyze the actual ordinances used by these municipalities. For subdivisions, usually found within the ordinance was such information as the number of steps in the ap-proval process, the agencies involved, fees charged, bonding arrangements permitted, etc. With regard to zoning, the zoning map was measured and the amount of land allocated to various uses calculated. To fill in any missing information, to get a better sense of the implementation of the or-dinances, and to obtain any information about possible peculiarities of a specific municipality, an extensive telephone interview with the local of-ficial in charge of administering the ordinances was used as a follow-up to our in-house analysis of the ordinances.

Characteristics of Sample Municipalities

A breakdown of the basic characteristics of the municipalities surveyed shows that they do present a well-distributed cross-section of the nation. The eighty-six municipalities were divided among the four regions used by the Census Bureau, (See Exhibit F-1) with the number of cities sampled in the West and Northeast slightly higher than that in the remaining two regions.

EXHIBIT F-1

REGIONAL DISTRIBUTION OF MUNICIPALITIES SURVEYED

Region	Number of Municipalities	Percent of Total
Northeast	22	26
South	21	24
North Central	19	22
West	24	28
Total	86	100

SOURCE: Survey of Municipalities, Center for Urban Policy Research, Summer 1976.

The population distribution also represents a well-balanced sample with an almost equivalent number of cities under 25,000 as there are over 25,000. (See Exhibit F-2) The cut-off point of 10,000 was initially adopted in an attempt to avoid those smaller municipalities without zoning and subdivision ordinances.

EXHIBIT F-2

POPULATION DISTRIBUTION OF MUNICIPALITIES

Population	Number of Municipalities	Percent of Total
10,000 - 17,999	18	21
18,000 - 24,999	20	23
25,000 - 49,999	27	31
50,000 and more	21	25
Total	86	100

SOURCE: Survey of Municipalities, Center for Urban Policy Research, Summer 1976.

Since a principal hypothesis to be tested by these data was that these ordinances are used as an exclusionary device, e.g., higher income communities have more costly requirements, it was important to examine the
median income of those communities sampled (See Exhibit F-3). Once again
a wide distribution exists. While 14 percent of the municipalities had an annual family median income of under $8,000 in 1970, 11.6 percent had in-
comes of over $15,000. The sample ranged from a low of $4,905 to a high of
$33,886.

EXHIBIT F-3

DISTRIBUTION OF MUNICIPALITIES BY MEDIAN
FAMILY INCOME: 1970

Annual Median Family Income	Number of Municipalities	Percent of Total
Low (less than $8,000)	12	14.0
Moderate ($8,000 to $9,999)	30	34.9
Middle ($10,000 to $14,999)	34	39.5
High ($15,000 or more)	10	11.6
Total	86	100.0

SOURCE: Survey of Municipalities, Center for Urban Policy Research, Summer
1976. Income figures based on 1970 Census Bureau figures in
General, Social and Economic Characteristics.

Included below is the questionnaire used in surveying these
municipalities.

ID#__ __ __

Interviewer #_____

SUBDIVISION AND ZONING ORDINANCES
SURVEY OF MUNICIPALITIES

Name of Respondent _____

Name of Agency _____

Municipality _____

Telephone No. _____

1. What is the approximate population of the municipality?

   — — — — — —

2. Taking an average of the last three years, approximately how many
   subdivisions are granted tentative (or preliminary) plat approval by
   your municipality annually?

   — — — — —

3. Into which one of the following size ranges do the majority of approved
   subdivisions fall?
   ( ) less than 6 dwelling units
   ( ) 6–25 dwelling units
   ( ) 26–50 dwelling units
   ( ) more than 50 dwelling units

Subdivision Regulations

4. *Streets*   (in feet)

   Right-of-way
      Subcollector (secondary)   ___ ___ ___

      Local   ___ ___ ___

   Pavement width
      Subcollector (secondary)   ___ ___ ___

      Local   ___ ___ ___

5. *Streetscape*

	Yes	No	DK	NA
Street signs	(1)	(2)	(8)	(9)
Street lighting	(1)	(2)	(8)	(9)
Shade trees	(1)	(2)	(8)	(9)

6. Is off-street parking required?

   (1) Yes
   (2) No
   (8) DK
   (9) NA

   Comments: _____

   _____

7. Is the developer ever responsible for off-site streets or off-site street improvements?

	Yes	No	DK	NA
Installation of streets or street improvements	(1)	(2)	(8)	(9)

Specify: _____

_____

Fees for developer's share of streets or street improvements	(1)	(2)	(8)	(9)

In approximately what percent of new subdivisions is responsibility for these off-site streets or off-stie street improvements given to the developer?

(1) more than 50%
(2) 26-50%
(3) 10-25%
(4) less than 10%
(8) DK
(9) NA

8. *Curbs & Gutters*

Are curbs & gutters:

(1) mandatory in ordinance
(2) permissive in ordinance
(3) not specified in ordinance

If permissive or not specified, what percent of the time required?

(1) always required
(2) more than 75% of the time
(3) 51-75%
(4) 25-50%
(5) less than 25%
(6) never required
(8) DK
(9) NA

9. *Sidewalks*

   (1) always required on both sides of street
   (2) generally required on both sides
   (3) always required on one side
   (4) generally required on one side
   (5) generally not required
   (6) never required
   (8) DK
   (9) NA

   Sidewalk width _____ ft.

   Block Length

   Minimum length __ __ __ __ft.

   Maximum length __ __ __ __ft.

   Average length required in practice __ __ __ __ ft.

10. *Sanitary Sewerage*

	Yes	No	DK	NA
Are septic tanks permitted?	(1)	(2)	(8)	(9)

    If yes, what is minimum lot size required, if any?

    (1) 1/2 acre-1
    (2) 1–2 acres
    (3) more than 2
    (4) no minimum
    (8) DK
    (9) NA

11. Is there any overdesigning of sewerage system capcity for future use?

    (1) Yes, for reasonably foreseeable population increase only
    (2) Yes, for largest population permitted by zoning ordinance
    (3) No overdesigning
    (8) DK
    (9) NA

    Comments: _____

    _____

    _____

12. In approximately what percent of new subdivisions (in last 3 years) are there pre-existing sewer mains?

    (1) more than 75%
    (2) 51–75%
    (3) 25–50%
    (4) less than 25%
    (8) DK
    (9) NA

13. Are fees required for hook-up (tap-in) to pre-existing sewer mains?

    (1) Yes
    (2) No
    (8) DK
    (9) NA

    Amount of fee __ __ __ __(per dwelling unit)

14. For which of the following sewer improvements is the developer responsible?

    Sewer mains (where necessary)

    (1) Yes
    (2) No
    (8) DK
    (9) NA

    Minimum diameter __ __ inches

    Manholes

    (1) Yes
    (2) No
    (8) DK
    (9) NA

    If yes, average interval:

    (1) less than 200 ft.
    (2) 200–400 ft.
    (3) 401–600 ft.
    (4) over 600 ft.
    (8) DK
    (9) NA

15. Is the developer ever responsible for off-site sewerage facilities?
    (e.g., sewage treatment facilities, sewer main extensions, etc.)

	Yes	No	DK	NA
Installation of improvements?	(1)	(2)	(8)	(9)

    Specify: _____

    _____

Fees for developer's share of improvements?	(1)	(2)	(8)	(9)

    Specify: _____

    _____

16. In approximately what percent of new subdivisions is responsibility for
    off-site sewerage facilities given to the developer?
    (1) more than 50%
    (2) 26-50%
    (3) 10-25%
    (4) less than 10%
    (8) DK
    (9) NA

17. *Drainage and Storm Sewers*

    Is the developer responsible for installing storm drainage facilities?
    (1) Yes
    (2) No
    (8) DK
    (9) NA

    Comment: _____

    _____

    _____

18. Are fees for hook-up to pre-existing storm sewers required?
    (1) Yes
    (2) No
    (8) DK
    (9) NA

    Amount of fee ___ ___ ___ ___ (per dwelling unit)

19. Is the developer ever responsible for off-site storm drainage improvements?

	Yes	No	DK	NA
Installation of improvements	(1)	(2)	(8)	(9)

Specify: _____

Fees for developer's share of improvements	(1)	(2)	(8)	(9)

Specify: _____

20. In approximately what percent of new subdivisions is responsibility for such off-site storm drainage improvements given to the developers?

    (1) more than 50%
    (2) 26-50%
    (3) 10-25%
    (4) less than 10%
    (8) DK
    (9) NA

21. *Water Facilities*

    In approximately what percent of new subdivisions (in the last 3 years) are there pre-existing water mains?

    (1) more than 75%
    (2) 51-75%
    (3) 25-50%
    (4) less than 25%
    (8) DK
    (9) NA

22. Which of the following improvements is the developer required to provide?

    Water mains (where necessary)

    (1) Yes
    (2) No
    (8) DK
    (9) NA

    Minimum pipe diameter __ __ inches

22. (cont.)
    Water laterals

    (1) Yes
    (2) No
    (8) DK
    (9) NA

    Fire hydrants

    (1) Yes
    (2) No
    (8) DK
    (9) NA

    Interval __ __ __ __ __ft.

23. Are hook-up fees to pre-existing water mains required?

    (1) Yes
    (2) No
    (8) DK
    (9) NA

    Amount of fee__ __ __ __ (per dwelling unit)

24. Is the developer ever responsible for off-site water facilities?
    (e.g., water main extensions, water treatment plants, etc.)·

	Yes	No	DK	NA
Installation of improvements	(1)	(2)	(8)	(9)

    Specify: _____

	Yes	No	DK	NA
Fees for developer's share of improvements	(1)	(2)	(8)	(9)

    Specify: _____

25. In what percent of new subdivisions is responsibility for such off-site
    water facilities given to the developer?

    (1) more than 50%
    (2) 26-50%
    (3) 10-25%
    (4) less than 10%
    (8) DK
    (9) NA

26. For public improvements generally, (this applies most particularly to off-site improvements) is there any provision for reimbursement of costs the developer incurs in installing improvements in excess of the needs of his subdivision?

    (1) Yes
    (2) No
    (8) DK
    (9) NA

    Comments: _____

27. *Public Utilities* (electric, telephone, cable television, etc.)

    Is underground installation of public utilities mandatory?

    (1) Yes, always
    (2) about 1/2 the time
    (3) rarely or never
    (8) DK
    (9) NA

Land Dedication for Recreation, Schools, etc.

28. For Open Space, Recreation?

    (1) mandatory in ordinance
    (2) permissive, at discretion of decision-making body
    (3) no requirement
    (8) DK
    (9) NA

29. If permissive, in what percent of cases is dedication required?

    (1) more than 50%
    (2) 26–50%
    (3) 10–25%
    (4) less than 10%
    (5) never
    (8) DK
    (9) NA

30. What is the typical percentage of total land area required to be dedicated for recreational purposes?

    __ __(%)

30. (cont.)

Fees in lieu of dedication used as an alternative?

(1) Yes
(2) No
(8) DK
(9) NA

Average fee ($) __ __ __ __

31. *The Approval Process*

Which of the following steps in subdivision approval process are required by the municipality?

	Yes	No
Sketch plat approval — requires plat map showing topography, adjoining property ownership, and general location of proposed structures.	(1)	(2)
Preliminary plat approval — detailed presentation of proposed development, showing location and type of structures, general plan for public improvements, etc. After approval of this phase, application *must* be approved, provided all terms and conditions are met.	(1)	(2)
Final plat approval — approval of all technical details, approval of bonding arrangements.	(1)	(2)

32. *Fees and Permits*

Which of the following fees are imposed on the developer?

	Amount (per unit)	Yes	No	DK	NA
			Filing Fees		
Sketch plat	_____	(1)	(2)	(8)	(9)
Preliminary plat	_____	(1)	(2)	(8)	(9)
Final plat	_____	(1)	(2)	(8)	(9)

Review and Inspection Fees

	Yes	No
Engineering review fees	(1)	(2)
Water system review fees	(1)	(2)
Sanitary sewer plan review	(1)	(2)
Drainage system inspection	(1)	(2)
Water system inspection	(1)	(2)
Sanitary sewer inspection	(1)	(2)
Drainage system inspection	(1)	(2)
Percolation tests	(1)	(2)
Other fees, specify: _____	(1)	(2)

Permits

	Amount (if any)	Yes	No
Clearing and grading permit		(1)	(2)
Tree removal		(1)	(2)
Well permit		(1)	(2)
Sediment control permit		(1)	(2)
Paving & storm drain permit		(1)	(2)
Other permits, specify: _____		(1)	(2)

33. Do you feel that the fees charged to cover administrative costs adequately cover such costs?

    (1) Yes
    (2) No
    (8) DK
    (9) NA

    Specify: _____

34. If no, approximately what percentage of the administrative costs are being covered by fees?

    (1) 0–25%
    (2) 26–50%
    (3) 51–75%
    (4) 76–100%
    (8) DK
    (9) NA

35. *Improvement Guarantees*

    Which of the following types of performance guarantees are used?

	Yes	No	DK	NA
Surety bonds	(1)	(2)	(8)	(9)
Escrow account (cash or note)	(1)	(2)	(8)	(9)
Property escrow	(1)	(2)	(8)	(9)
Sequential approval of subdivision segments (no bond)	(1)	(2)	(8)	(9)

	Yes	No	DK	NA
Maintenance guarantee	(1)	(2)	(8)	(9)
Other guarantee method	(1)	(2)	(8)	(9)

    Specify: _____

    _____

    | Bonding not permitted – all improvements must be installed before final approval. | (1) | (2) | (8) | (9) |

36. Is there any provision for reduction of the bond amount as certain improvements are completed?

    (1) Yes
    (2) No
    (8) DK
    (9) NA

    If yes, is it used:

    (1) frequently
    (2) sometimes
    (3) never
    (8) DK
    (9) NA

37. What is the average time period between completion of improvements and release of the performance guarantee?
    (1) less than two weeks
    (2) 2-4 weeks
    (3) 5-7 weeks
    (4) more than 7 weeks
    (8) DK
    (9) NA

38. What is the average time period between initial submission of a (typical) subdivision application and tentative (or preliminary) approval?
    (1) less than 2 months
    (2) 2-4 months
    (3) 5-7 months
    (4) 8-10 months
    (5) over 10 months
    (8) DK
    (9) NA

39. When delays do occur, what are usually the problem areas?

	Yes	No
Agency approvals (e.g., environmental commission, health dept., etc.)	(1)	(2)

Specify: _____

Review by the final decision-making body	(1)	(2)
Public hearings	(1)	(2)
County or state review	(1)	(2)
Provision of utilities	(1)	(2)
Inadequate information provided by the developer	(1)	(2)
Change in plans by the developer	(1)	(2)
Others	(1)	(2)

Specify: _____

40. What is the average time period between submission of final plat application and final plat approval?

   (1) less than 1 month
   (2) 1–2 months
   (3) 3–4 months
   (4) more than 4 months
   (8) DK
   (9) NA

41. When delays do occur, what are usually the problem areas?

	Yes	No
Utility negotiations	(1)	(2)
Agency approvals	(1)	(2)

   Specify: _____

Bonding arrangements	(1)	(2)
Inadequate information provided by the developer	(1)	(2)
Change in plans by the developer	(1)	(2)

	Yes	No
Inadequate installation of public improvements	(1)	(2)
Other	(1)	(2)

   Specify: _____

42. Is there any provision for automatic approval of a subdivision application if the municipality fails to act within a certain time period?

   (1) Yes
   (2) No
   (8) DK
   (9) NA

   What is the time period? __ __ __ days

   Any provision for extension of time period?

   (1) Yes
   (2) No
   (8) DK
   (9) NA

43. What agencies besides the final approval body participate in the subdivision review process?

	Yes	No
Environmental commission	(1)	(2)
Health department	(1)	(2)
Shade tree commission	(1)	(2)
Board of fire commissioners	(1)	(2)
Municipal sewerage authority	(1)	(2)
Local school board	(1)	(2)
Community design review board	(1)	(2)
Park authority	(1)	(2)
County planning board	(1)	(2)
County sewerage authority	(1)	(2)
State planning commission	(1)	(2)
State board of health	(1)	(2)
State transportation department	(1)	(2)
Other	(1)	(2)

Specify: _____

---

44. In general, what percent of all requirements are negotiated between the developer and the municipal agencies (or approval body) rather than specified by ordinance or regulation?

   (1) no requirements negotiated
   (2) less than 10%
   (3) 10–25%
   (4) 26–50%
   (5) more than 50%
   (8) DK
   (9) NA

45. Which two aspects of subdivision regulations involve the greatest amount of negotiation between the developer and the municipality?

   (01) streetscape — streets, sidewalks, curbs, gutters, etc.
   (02) sanitary and storm sewers
   (03) water lines and facilities
   (04) public utilities (gas, electric, telephone)
   (05) off-site improvements generally
   (06) land dedication for recreation or schools
   (07) fees in lieu of dedication

45. (cont.)
    (08) performance guarantee arrangements
    (09) other

       specify: _____
    (88) DK
    (99) NA

46. Over the past 5 years, what changes have been made in your munici-
    pality's subdivision requirements, either in the ordinance itself or in
    actual practice?

	Yes	No	DK	NA
New requirements not previously imposed	(1)	(2)	(8)	(9)

Specify: _____

Increased specifications	(1)	(2)	(8)	(9)

Specify: _____

	Yes	No	DK	NA
Decreased specifications	(1)	(2)	(8)	(9)

Specify: _____

More agencies/commissions involved in the approval process	(1)	(2)	(8)	(9)
Lengthier review period	(1)	(2)	(8)	(9)
Other	(1)	(2)	(8)	(9)

Specify: _____

47. Does your municipality have a Planned Unit Development (or PRD, etc.)
    ordinance?

    (1) Yes
    (2) No
    (8) DK
    (9) NA

       If yes, when was it enacted? ___ ___ ___ ___

48. How many developments have been built under this ordinance?

    (1) none
    (2) 1 or 2
    (3) 3-5
    (4) 5-10
    (5) more than 10
    (8) DK
    (9) NA

49. How does the extent of public improvements required of PUD developers compare to improvements required of subdivision developers?

    (1) usually more requirements
    (2) usually fewer requirements
    (3) about the same
    (4) can't generalize
    (8) DK
    (9) NA

    Specify: _____

50. How does the time period required for PUD approval compare with the time period for a subdivision of equal size:

    (1) much shorter
    (2) somewhat shorter
    (3) about the same
    (4) somewhat longer
    (5) much longer
    (6) can't generalize
    (8) DK
    (9) NA

    Specify: _____

51. Which of the following are true of your municipality's PUD ordinance? (check all applicable answers)

	Yes	No	DK	NA
Permits staged platting so that developer need not initially submit the entire area for tentative plat approval.	(1)	(2)	(8)	(9)
Encourages clustering of housing units.	(1)	(2)	(8)	(9)

51. (cont.)

	Yes	No	DK	NA
Permits substantially greater gross density than that generally found elsewhere in the community.	(1)	(2)	(8)	(9)
Permits housing types (e.g., townhouses, duplexes, etc.) not found elsewhere in the community.	(1)	(2)	(8)	(9)

Zoning

52. In which one of the following categories would you classify your municipality?

    (1) rural, undeveloped
    (2) developing
    (3) mostly developed
    (8) DK
    (9) NA

53. What is your municipality's total land area?

    _ _ _ _ _ _   in acres

54. Of the total land area, what percent is zoned for:

    Residential use __.__

    Industrial use __ __

55. What percent of total residentially zoned land area is zoned for each of the following zoning districts?

    1.   __ __
    2.   __ __
    3.   __ __
    4.   __ __
    5.   __ __
    6.   __ __
    7.   __ __

56. In the last three years, in approximately what percent of all requests for residential building permits did the developer apply for relief from the municipal zoning ordinance (by means of variance, rezoning, special exception, etc.).

    (1) less than 5%
    (2) 6-10%
    (3) 11-25%
    (4) 26-50%
    (5) more than 50%
    (8) DK
    (9) NA

57. More particularly in what percent of these cases did the developer apply for:

    Rezoning to *more dense single-family* zoning category

    (1) less than 1%
    (2) 1-5%
    (3) 6-10%
    (4) more than 10%
    (8) DK
    (9) NA

    Rezoning to multi-family (or to more dense multi-family)

    (1) less than 1%
    (2) 1-5%
    (3) 6-10%
    (4) more than 10%
    (8) DK
    (9) NA

    Variance for relief from lot size, frontage, minimum floor area, setback, etc.

    (1) less than 1%
    (2) 1-5%
    (3) 6-10%
    (4) more than 10%
    (8) DK
    (9) NA

57. (cont.)

Special exception or conditional use for a different type of residential structure (e.g., duplex, townhouses, etc.)

(1) less than 1%
(2) 1-5%
(3) 6-10%
(4) more than 10%
(8) DK
(9) NA

58. In what percentage of these cases was the request ultimately granted?

(1) less than 25%
(2) 26-50%
(3) 51-75%
(4) more than 75%
(8) DK
(9) NA

59. What is the average time period required to process requests for:

Rezoning

(1) less than 1 month
(2) 1-2 months
(3) 3-4 months
(4) more than 4 months
(8) DK
(9) NA

Variances, Special Exceptions

(1) less than 1 month
(2) 1-2 months
(3) 3-4 months
(4) more than 4 months
(8) DK
(9) NA

60. In the past 5 years, has your municipality passed any zoning ordinance amendments which affect residential uses?

    (1) Yes
    (2) No
    (8) DK
    (9) NA

    If yes, please specify: _____

	No Change	Increase	Decrease
Rezoning for a different proportion of commercial or industrial use	(1)	(2)	(3)
Minimum lot size	(1)	(2)	(3)
Frontage requirements	(1)	(2)	(3)
Minimum house size requirements	(1)	(2)	(3)
Choice of housing type (e.g., town-houses, duplexes, etc.)	(1)	(2)	(3)
Multi-family zoning	(1)	(2)	(3)
Other	(1)	(2)	(3)

    Specify: _____

    _____

    _____

61. *Growth Controls*

    Have you recently enacted any of the following types of growth control or managed growth ordinances?

	Yes	No	DK	NA
Interim zoning restrictions	(1)	(2)	(8)	(9)
Sewer moratorium	(1)	(2)	(8)	(9)
Adequate public facilities ordinance	(1)	(2)	(8)	(9)
Phased development controls	(1)	(2)	(8)	(9)
Absolute limit on the annual number of permits to be issued	(1)	(2)	(8)	(9)
Impact fee payments	(1)	(2)	(8)	(9)
Other	(1)	(2)	(8)	(9)

    Specify: _____

    _____

62. If you currently have or are considering enactment of a growth control ordinance, what was the *major* concern underlying this action?

   (1) to better control the cost of providing municipal services
   (2) to prevent environmental degradation
   (3) to preserve the "character" of the community; to preserve the existing quality of life
   (4) other

   specify: _____

   _____

   _____

   (8) DK
   (9) NA

Selective Bibliography

This bibliography presents a selected list of publications found to deal most directly with the issue of government regulations and housing costs. After the initial section which presents general reports touching on this subject, six separate sections follow, each dealing with one specific area of regulation.

I. GENERAL REPORTS

Bergman, Edward. *Development Controls and Housing Costs.* 3 Vols. Chapel Hill, North Carolina: The Center for Urban and Regional Studies, August 1974.

Burchell, Robert; Hughes, James W.; and Sternlieb, George. *Housing Costs and Housing Restraints: Newark, New Jersey.* New Brunswick: Center for Urban Policy Research, Rutgers University, 1970.

DeLeeuw, Frank, and Struyk, Raymond J. *The Web of Housing.* Washington, D.C.: The Urban Institute, 1975.

Eaves, Elsie. *How the Many Costs of Housing Fit Together.* Research Report #16, National Commission on Urban Problems. Washington, D.C.: U.S. Government Printing Office, 1969.

Kaiser, Edward, and Weiss, Shirley F. "Public Policy and the Residential Development Process." *Journal of the American Institute of Planners* 36 (January, 1970): 30.

Lozano, Eduardo E. "Technical Report: Housing Costs and Alternative Cost Reducing Policies." *Journal of the American Institute of Planners* 38 (May 1972):173.

Manvel, Allen D. *Local Land and Building Regulations.* Research Report #6, National Commission on Urban Problems. Washington, D.C.: U.S. Government Printing Office, 1968.

Muth, Richard, and Wetzler, Elliot. *Effects of Constraints on Single-Unit Housing Costs.* Springfield, Va.: National Technical Information Services, 1968.

National Commission on Urban Problems. *Building the American City.* Report of the National Commission on Urban Problems. Washington, D.C.: U.S. Government Printing Office, 1968.

Neutze, Max. *The Suburban Apartment Boom.* Resources for the Future, Inc. Baltimore: The Johns Hopkins Press, 1968.

Scott, Randall W. *Management and Control of Growth.* 3 Vols. Washington, D.C.: The Urban Land Institute, 1975.

Sumichrast, Michael, and Frankel, Sara A. *Profile of the Builder and His Industry.* Washington, D.C.: National Association of Home Builders, 1970.

U.S. Congress, Subcommittee on Housing and Urban Affairs. *Housing Goals and Mortgage Credit 1975-80.* 94th Congress, September 1975.

U.S. Congressional Research Service. "Availability of Homes for Middle-Income Families." Joint Economic Committee, April 1975.

U.S. President's Committee on Urban Housing. *A Decent Home.* 3 Vols. Washington D.C.: U.S. Government Printing Office, 1969.

Williams, Norman. *American Land Planning Law.* 5 Vols. Chicago: Callaghan and Company, 1975.

II. BUILDING CODES

American Insurance Association; Building Officials and Code Administrators International, Inc.; International Conference of Building Officials; and Southern Building Code Congress International. *One and Two Family Dwelling Codes.* 2d ed. Danville, Ill.: Interstate Printers and Publishers, 1975.

"The Building Code Dilemma: Pros and Cons of Building Codes." *HUD Challenge,* (November — December 1970):21-24.

"Building Codes and Residential Rehabilitation: Tilting at Windmills." *Columbia Journal of Law and Social Problems,* 5 (1969):88-97.

Center for Auto Safety. *Mobile Homes: The Low-Cost Housing Hoax.* New York: Grossman Publishers, Viking Press, 1975.

Cibula, Evelyn. *Product Approvals for Building: An International Review.* Garston, England: Building Research Establishment, Department of the Environment, 1971.

Clarke, Fredric B., III, and Ottoson, John, "Fire Death Scenarios and Fire Safety Planning." *Fire Journal* (May 1976):20.

Cooke, Patrick W.; Tejuja, Hotchand K.; Dikkers, Robert D.; and Zelenka, Louis P. *State Building Regulatory Programs for Mobile Homes and Manufactured Buildings: A Summary.* Washington, D.C.: U.S. Government Printing Office, 1974.

Demarest, William. *Building Codes: Product Approvals.* New Haven, Connecticut: Ludlow and Bookman, 1964.

Falk, David. "Building Codes in a Nutshell." *Real Estate Review* 5 (1975):82-91.

Field, Charles G., and Ventre, Frances T. "Local Regulation of Building Agencies, Codes and Politics," In *Municipal Yearbook 1971.* Washington, D.C.: International City Management Association, 1971.

Field, Charles G., and Rivkin, Steven R. *The Building Code Burden.* Lexington, Mass.: Lexington Books, 1975.

Finger, Harold B. "Operation Breakthrough's Approach to Building Codes, Zoning and Site Design." *George Washington Law Review* 39 (1971):764-787.

Green, Colin H. *Building Regulation, Liability, Insurance and Consumer Protection.* Urbana: Center for Advanced Study,University of Illinois, 1973. Mimeographed.

Green, Colin H. *Context, Issues and Missions of Building Regulation.* Urbana: Center for Advanced Study, University of Illinois, 1974.

Hemenway, David. *Industrywide Voluntary Product Standards.* Cambridge, Mass.: Ballinger Publishing Co., 1975.

Howe, Warner. "The Growing Bureaucracy of State and National Building Regulations." *Code Administrative Review* (1974):43-51.

McKinny, Patricia, "NAHB Housing Warranty Program." *Urban Land* 33 (1974):9-14.

Muth, Richard F., and Wetzler, Elliot. "The Effects of Constraints on House Costs." *Journal of Urban Economics* 3 (1976):57–67.

"NAHB's Home Warranty Plan: Where and How it Works." *The Building Official and Code Administrator,* May 1975, p. 30.

National Commission on Fire Prevention and Control. *America Burning.* Washington, D.C.: U.S. Government Printing Office, 1973.

Nunnally, S.W. *Reducing Florida's Housing Costs Through Building Code Reform.* 2 Vols. Gainesville, Fla.: Engineering and Industrial Experiment Station, University of Florida, 1973.

O'Hare, M. "Structural Inadequacies in Urban Environmental Management." *Regional and Urban Economics* 3 (1973):63-82.

Rhyne, Charles S. *Survey of the Law of Building Codes.* Washington, D.C.: American Institute of Architects and the National Association of Home Builders, 1960.

Richardson, Ambrose M. "Building Codes: Reducing Diversity and Facilitating the Amending Process." *Harvard Journal of Legislation* 5 (1968):587-611.

Rivkin, Steven. "Courting Change: Using Litigation to Reform Local Building Codes." *Rutgers Law Review* 26 (1973):774-802.

Rowland, Gene A., and Gallagher, Neil E. *Performance Standards: Their Compatibility with the Building Regulatory System.* Washington, D.C.: Center for Building Technology, Institute for Applied Technology, National Bureau of Standards, 1972.

Sanderson, Richard L. *Codes and Code Administration: An Introduction to Building Regulations in the United States.* Chicago: Building Officials Conference of America, 1969.

Schodek, Daniel L. "Fire in Housing: Research on Building Regulations and Technology." Working Paper No. 38. Joint Center for Urban Studies of the Massachusetts Institute of Technology and Harvard University, Cambridge, Mass., 1976.

Sternlieb, George, and Listokin, David. "Building Codes: State of the Art, Strategies for the Future." Paper prepared for Department of Housing and Urban Development Policy Evaluation Committee, June 1973. Mimeographed.

U.S. Advisory Commission on Intergovernmental Relations. *Building Codes: A Program for Intergovernmental Reform.* Washington, D.C.: U.S. Government Printing Office, 1966.

U.S. Congress. House Select Committee on Small Business. Subcommittee on Activities of Regulatory Agencies. *The Effect Upon Small Business of Voluntary Industrial Standards.* Hearings before the Subcommittee on Activities of Regulatory Agencies. Volume 2. 90th Congress. April 2, 1968. Washington, D.C.: U.S. Government Printing Office, 1968.

U.S. Congress, Senate, Committee on the Judiciary, Subcommittee on Antitrust and Monopoly. *Voluntary Industrial Standards — 1976.* Hearings before the Subcommittee on Antitrust and Monopoly. 94th Cong. 2nd Sess. March 22, 1976. Washington, D.C.: U.S. Government Printing Office, 1976.

Ventre, Francis T. "Maintaining Technological Currency in the Local Building Code: Patterns of Communication and Influence." *Urban Data Service* 3 (1971):1-16.

Willis, Sidney L. "The Municipalities' Role Under the New Jersey State Uniform Construction Code Act." *New Jersey Municipalities* (January 1976), p. 12.

III. ENERGY CODES

The American Institute of Architects. *A Nation of Energy Efficient Buildings by 1990.* Washington, D.C.: American Institute of Architects, 1974.

Arthur D. Little Co., *An Impact Assessment of ASHRAE Standard 90-75, Energy Conservation in New Building Design.* Washington, D.C.: December, 1975.

The Council of State Governments. *State Responses to the Energy Crisis.* Lexington, Ky.:1974.

Dunlop, Beth. "Energy Standards: Design Stimulus or Straightjacket?" *AIA Journal,* October, 1975: 41-3.

Energy, Report to the Governor of New Jersey. The Task Force On Energy. (Thomas O'Neill, director). May, 1974.

Fraker, Harrison, and Schacker, Elizabeth. *Energy Husbandry in Housing.* Report No. 5. Princeton: Center for Environmental Studies, 1973.

Harris, Carl M. "Incentives Lacking to Build Energy-Conserving Structures." *The Mortgage Banker* (September 1975): 54-60.

Moyers, John C. *The Value of Thermal Insulation in Residential Construction: Economics and the Conservation of Energy.* Oak Ridge: Oak Ridge National Laboratory Report, 1971.

Pearson, George A. "Life Cycle Costing in an Energy Crisis Era." *Professional Engineer* (July, 1974): 26-9.

Report to the Congress on National Standards Needed for Residential Energy Conservation. By the Comptroller General of the United States. Washington, D.C.: General Accounting Office, 1975.

Socolow, Robert. "Energy Conservation in Housing: Concepts and Opinions." In *Future Land Use.* Edited by Robert W. Burchell and David Listokin. New Brunswick: Center For Urban Policy Research, Rutgers University, 1975.

Stratton, Sandy. "Energy Conservation in Buildings — Making Our Limited Resources Last." *The Building Official and Code Administrator* (April, 1975): 20-31.

U.S. Congress, House, Committee on Banking, Currency, and Housing. *Energy Conservation in Buildings Act of 1975. Hearings* before a sub-

committee on Housing and Community Development, House of
Representatives, on H.R. 8650, H.R. 8540, and H.R. 2650, 94th Cong.,
1st sess., 1975.

U.S. Congress, Senate, Committee on Banking, Housing and Urban Affairs. *Emergency Housing and Housing/Energy. Hearings* before a subcommittee on Housing and Urban Affairs, Senate, on S.594, 94th
Cong., 1st sess., 1975.

U.S. Department of Commerce, National Bureau of Standards. *Building
Energy Authority and Regulations Survey: State Activity,* by Robert M.
Eisenhard. Washington, D.C.: U.S. Government Printing Office, 1976.

U.S. Department of Commerce, National Bureau of Standards, in
cooperation with Federal Energy Administration. *Retro-fitting Existing
Housing for Energy Conservation: An Economic Analysis,* by Stephen
R. Peterson. Washington, D.C.: U.S. Government Printing Office,
1974.

U.S. Department of Housing and Urban Development. *Residential Energy
Conservation,* by Hittman Associates. Report No. HUD-HAI-8.
Washington, D.C.: U.S. Government Printing Office, 1975.

Vollman, June R. "High Energy Costs: How They're Squeezing Housing."
House and Home, (April, 1975), pp. 54-55.

Vollman, June R. "Saving Energy: How Builders Are Doing It. . . and
Selling It." *House and Home,* (April, 1976), pp. 58-64.

Yannacone, Victor John Jr. *The Energy Crisis.* New York: West Publishing
Co., 1974.

IV. SUBDIVISION CONTROLS

Adelstein, Richard P., and Edelson, Noel M. *Subdivision Exactions and
Congestion Externalities: An Efficiency Analysis.* Philadelphia: Fels
Center of Government, 1974.

Area Housing Council. "Development Regulations and Housing Costs."
Draft paper submitted to the Regional Planning Council, Baltimore,
Maryland: September 1975. Mimeographed.

"Birth Control for Premature Subdivision — A Legislative Pill." *Santa
Clara Lawyer* 12 (1972):523.

City of Boulder Planning Department. *A Study of Land Dedication
Requirements.* Prepared by Mary B. Jones. Boulder, Colorado: January
1969.

Brooks, Mary. *Mandatory Dedication of Land or Fees-in-Lieu of Land for
Parks and Schools.* Planning Advisory Service Report No. 266. Chicago:
American Society of Planning Officials, 1971.

Cunningham, R.A. "Interrelationship Between Exclusionary Zoning and Exclusionary Subdivision Control." *University of Michigan Journal of Law* 6 (1973): 290.

Freilich, Robert H., and Levi, Peter S. *Model Subdivision Regulations: Text and Commentary.* Chicago: American Society of Planning Officials, 1975.

Heyman, Ira Michael, and Gilhool, Thomas K. "The Constitutionality of Imposing Increased Community Costs on New Suburban Residents Through Subdivision Exactions." *Yale Law Journal* 73 (1964):1119.

Johnston, John D. Jr. "Constitutionality of Subdivision Control Exactions: The Quest for a Rationale." *Cornell Law Review* 52 (1967):871-924.

Massie, Richard L. *Subdivision Code: An Evaluation of Park and Residential Street Elements.* Little Rock, Ark.: Manes and Associates, 1975.

Newville, Jack. *New Engineering Concepts in Community Development.* Technical Bulletin No. 59. Washington, D.C.: Urban Land Institute, 1967.

"The Municipal Land Use Law." *New Jersey Municipalities* (March 1976), p. 6.

Platt, Rutherford. "Open Space Dedication Requirements: The Externality Fallacy." Paper presented at the American Society of Planning Officials Annual Planning Conference, May 1974, Mimeographed.

Rogal, Brian. "Subdivision Improvement Guarantees." *Planning Advisory Service.* Report No. 298. Chicago, Illinois: American Society of Planning Officials, January 1974.

"Subdivision Land Dedication: Objectives and Objections." *Stanford Law Review,* 27 (January, 1975):419.

Urban Land Institute; American Society of Civil Engineers; and National Association of Home Builders. *Residential Storm Water Management: Objectives, Principles, and Design Considerations.* Washington, D.C.: Urban Land Institute, 1975.

_____. *Residential Streets: Objectives, Principles, and Design Considerations.* Washington, D.C.: Urban Land Institute, 1974.

Wu, Ming-Shyong. *Public Improvement Costs for Residential Land Development: A Comparison of Five Counties in the Baltimore Region.* Baltimore: Regional Planning Council, 1973.

Yearwood, R.M. *Land Subdivision Regulation: Policy and Legal Considerations for Urban Planning.* New York: Praeger Publishers, 1971.

Yokley, E.C. *The Law of Subdivisions.* Charlottesville, Va.: The Michie Co., 1963.

V. ZONING

Babcock, Richard F., and Bosselman, Fred P. *Exclusionary Zoning: Land Use Regulation and Housing in the 1970s.* New York: Praeger Publishers, 1973.

Bailey, Martin J. "Note on the Economics of Residential Zoning and Urban Renewal." *Land Economics* 35 (1959):288-92.

Branfman, Eric J.; Cohen, Benjamin I.; and Trubek, David M. "Measuring the Invisible Wall: Land Use Controls and the Residential Patterns of the Poor." *Yale Law Journal* 82 (1973):483-508.

Bruhn, John A. "Zoning — Its Effect on Property Value." *Appraisal Journal* 37 (October 1969):555-651.

Coke, James G. and Liebman, Charles S. "Political Values and Population Density Control." *Land Economics* 37 (1961):347-61.

Crecine, John P.; Davis, Otto A.; and Jackson, John E. "Urban Property Markets: Some Empirical Results and Their Implications for Municipal Zoning." *Journal of Law and Economics* 10 (1967):79-99.

Franklin, Herbert M.; Falk, David; and Levin, Arthur J. *In-Zoning: A Guide for Policy-Makers on Inclusionary Land Use Programs,* Washington, D.C.: The Potomac Institute, 1974.

Hagman, Donald G. "Windfalls for Wipeouts." *Appraisal Journal* (January 1976):69-82.

James, Franklin J., Jr., and Windsor, Oliver Duane. "Fiscal Zoning, Fiscal Reform, and Exclusionary Land Use Controls." *American Institute of Planners Journal* (April 1976):130-141.

Marcus, N., and Groves, Marilyn W., (eds.) *The New Zoning: Legal, Administrative, and Economic Concepts and Techniques.* New York: Praeger Publishers, 1970.

Mills, Edwin, S., and Oates, Wallace E., (eds.) *Fiscal Zoning and Land Use Controls: The Economic Issues.* Lexington, Mass.: Lexington Books, 1972.

New Jersey, Department of Community Affairs, Division of State and Regional Planning. *Land Use Regulation: The Residential Land Supply.* Trenton: April 1972.

Ohls, James C.; Weisberg, Richard C.; and White, Michelle J. "The Effect of Zoning on Land Value," *Journal of Urban Economics* (October 1974):428-444.

Rochester, Chamber of Commerce, Civic Development Council. *Town Zoning and the Shortage of Moderate and Low Income Housing.* Prepared by Friedrick J. Gasberger. Rochester, N.Y.: Rochester Bureau of Municipal Research, 1967.

Sagalyn, Lynne B., and Sternlieb, George. *Zoning and Housing Costs.* New Brunswick, N.J.: Center for Urban Policy Research, Rutgers University, 1972.

Sager, Lawrence Gene. "Tight Little Islands: Exclusionary Zoning, Equal Protection, and the Indigent." *Stanford Law Review* 21 (1969):767-800.

Schoenbrod, D.S. "Large Lot Zoning." *Yale Law Journal* 50 (1969): 1418-1441.

Siegan, Bernard H. *Land Use Without Zoning.* Lexington, Mass. Lexington Books, 1972.

Stull, William J. "Community Environment, Zoning and the Market Value of Single-Family Homes." *Journal of Law and Economics* 18 (1975):535-57.

Stull, William J. "Land Use and Zoning in an Urban Economy." *American Economic Review* 64 (1974):337-347.

Williams, Norman, Jr.; and Norman, Thomas. "Exclusionary Land Use Controls: The Case of North-Eastern New Jersey." *Syracuse Law Review* 22 (1971):475-507.

Urban Land Institute.. *The Effects of Large Lot Size on Residential Development.* Technical Bulletin No. 32. Washington, D.C.: Urban Land Institute.

Yeates, M.H. "The Effect of Zoning on Land Values in American Cities: A Case Study." In *Essays in Geography,* edited by J.B. Whittow and P.D. Woods. Reading, England: University of Reading, 1965.

VI. Growth Controls

Alesch, Daniel J. "Local Government's Ability to Manage Growth In a Metropolitan Context." The Rand Paper Series. Santa Monica, California: Rand Corporation, 1974.

Alonso, William. "Urban Zero Population Growth." *Daedalus* (Fall 1973):191.

Barnes, Peter. "The California Experience: How to Use Land." *The New Republic,* 21 (September 1974):10-12.

Bascon, S.E.; Cooper, K.G.; Howell, M.P.; Makrides, A.C.; and Robe, F.T. *Secondary Impacts of Transportation and Wastewater.* 2 Vols. Socioeconomic Environmental Studies. Washington, D.C.: Office of Research and Development, U.S. Environmental Protection Agency, 1975.

Burrows, Lawrence B. *Growth Management: A Planner's Perspective — Issues Techniques and Suggestions.* New Brunswick: Center for Urban Policy Research, Rutgers University, 1977.

Clawson, Marion. *Suburban Land Conversion in the United States: An Economic and Governmental Process.* Baltimore: John Hopkins Press, 1971.

Cranston, Mary; Garth, Bryant; Plattner, Robert; and Varon, Jay. *A Handbook for Controlling Local Growth.* Stanford, California: Stanford Environmental Law Society, Stanford University, 1973.

Deutsch, Stuart L. "Land Use Growth Controls: A Case Study of San Jose and Livermore California." *Santa Clara Lawyer* 15 (1974):1-49.

Emanuel, Manual S. "Ramapo's Managed Growth Program: A Close Look at Ramapo After Five Years Experience." *Planners Notebook* 4 (1974):1-8.

Environmental Analysis Systems, Inc. *Growth Management: Practices and Issues.* San Diego, Calif.: Environmental Analysis Systems, 1974.

Fagin, Henry. "Regulating the Timing of Urban Development." *Law and Contemporary Problems.* 20 (Spring 1955):298.

Finkler, Earl; and Peterson, David L. *Nongrowth Planning Strategies.* New York: Praeger Publishers, 1974.

Franklin, Herbert M. *Controlling Urban Growth: But for Whom?* Washington, D.C.: The Potomac Institute, 1973.

Freilich, Robert H. "Interim Development Controls: Essential Tools for Implementing Flexible Planning and Zoning." *Journal of Urban Law* 49 (1971):65-119.

Gleeson, Michael. "Urban Management Systems." Planning Advisory Service Report No. 309-10. Chicago: American Society of Planning Officals, 1975.

Lamm, Richard D., and Davison, Steven A.G. "The Legal Control of Population Growth and Distribution on a Quality Environment: The Land Use Alternatives." *Denver Law Journal* 49 (1972):1-51.

Real Estate Research Corporation. *The Costs of Sprawl: Environmental and Economic Costs of Alternative Residential Development Patterns at the Urban Fringe.* Washington, D.C.: U.S. Government Printing Office, 1974.

Reilly, William K., (ed.). *The Use of Land: A Citizen's Policy Guide to Urban Growth.* New York: Thomas Y. Crowell Co., 1973.

Research and Executive Staff of the NVBA. "Had It Not Been for the Courts. . ." Testimony Before the Virginia Housing Study Commission, 15 May 1975. Mimeographed.

Rivkin Associates, Inc. *The Sewer Moratorium as a Technique of Growth and Environmental Protection.* Washington, D.C.: Rivkin Associates, 1973.

Rolph, E.S. "Decisionmaking by Residential Developers in Santa Clara County." Santa Monica, Calif.: Rand Corporation, 1973.

Schnidman, Frank. "Growth Management in Ramapo and Petaluma: A Study of the Ordinances and Litigation." *Land Use Planning Reports,* No. 3. Washington, D.C.: Plus Publications, 1974.
Stahl, David E. "Cost Repercussions of the No-Growth Movement." *Urban Land* (December 1973):17–20.
U.S. Congress, Senate, Committee on Interior and Insular Affairs. *National Land Use Policy.* 92nd Congress, 2d Sess, 1972.
Zeimetz, Kathyrn A.; Dillon, Elizabeth; Hardy, Ernest E.; and Otte, Robert C. *Dynamics of Land Use in Fast Growth Areas.* Agricultural Economic Report No. 325. Washington, D.C.: Economic Research Services, United States Department of Agriculture, 1976.

VII. Environmental Regulations

Ackerman, Bruce L. "Impact Statements and Low Cost Housing" *Southern California Law Review,* 46 (1973):754.
Arnold, Michael; and McDonald, Anne. "A Summary of State Land Use Controls." *Land Use Planning Reports,* Report No. 5. Washington, D.C.: Plus Publications, 1976.
Bosselman, Fred; and Callies, David L. "Ecology and Housing: Virtues in Conflict." In *Modernizing Urban Land Policy,* Marion Clawson (ed.) Baltimore: The Johns Hopkins Press, 1973.
Bosselman, Fred, and Callies, David. *The Quiet Revolution.* Washington, D.C.: U.S. Government Printing Office, 1971.
Bosselman, Fred; Callies, David; and Banta, John. *The Taking Issue.* Washington, D.C.: U.S. Government Printing Office, 1973.
Bosselman, Fred P.; Feuer, Duane, A.; and Callies, David L. *EPA Authority Affecting Land Use.* Prepared for the U.S. Environmental Protection Agency. Washington, D.C.: U.S. Government Printing Office, 1974.
Brooks, Mary E. *The Needless Conflict: Housing Equity and Environmental Protection.* Washington, D.C.: American Institute of Planners, 1976.
Burchell, Robert W. and Listokin, David. *The Environmental Impact Handbook.* New Brunswick: Center for Urban Policy Research, Rutgers University, 1975.
Coase, Ronald. "The Problem of Social Cost," *The Journal of Law and Economics,* 3 (October, 1960):1.
Council on Environment Quality. *Annual Report.* Washington, D.C.: U.S. Government Printing Office, 1974.

Daffron, Carolyn. "Using NEPA to Exclude the Poor," *Environmental Affairs,* (Winter 1975):81-122.

Dorfman, Robert; and Dorfman, Nancy S. (eds.) *Economics of the Environment.* New York: W.W. Norton & Company, 1972.

Management. New York: Praeger Publishers, 1973.

Healy, Robert G. *Land Use and the States.* Resources for the Future, Baltimore: The Johns Hopkins University Press, 1976.

Institute for Contemporary Studies. *The California Coastal Plan: A Critique.* San Francisco: The Institute for Contemporary Studies. 1976.

Institute for Contemporary Studies. *No Land is An Island.* San Francisco: The Institute for Contemporary Studies, 1975.

Ketchman, Bostwick H. *The Water's Edge.* Cambridge, Mass: MIT Press, 1972.

Mandelker, Daniel, "Critical Areas of Controls." *AIP Journal* (January 1975):21-31.

Mogulof, Melvin B. *Saving the Coast.* Lexington, Mass: Lexington Books, 1975.

Muller, Tom, and James, Franklin J. "Environmental Impact Evaluation and Housing Costs." Washington, D.C.: The Urban Institute, 1975.

Richardson, Dan K., *The Cost of Environmental Protection.* New Brunswick: Center for Urban Policy Research, Rutgers University, 1976.

Schnidman, Frank, and Kendall, Susan. "CZM: An Overview." *Environmental Comment,* (April 1975):1.

Solomon, Arthur P. "The Effect of Land Use and Environmental Controls on Housing: A Review." Working Paper No. 34. Cambridge, Mass: Joint Center for Urban Studies, 1975.